The Book of John Mandeville

with Related Texts

The Book of
John Mandeville

with Related Texts

Edited and Translated,
with an Introduction, by
IAIN MACLEOD HIGGINS

Hackett Publishing Company, Inc.
Indianapolis/Cambridge

Printed in the United States of America

15 14 13 12 11   1 2 3 4 5 6 7

For further information, please address
Hackett Publishing Company, Inc.
P.O. Box 44937
Indianapolis, Indiana 46244-0937

www.hackettpublishing.com

Cover design by Abigail Coyle
Text design by Mary Vasquez
Composition by William Hartman
Printed at Sheridan Books, Inc.

Library of Congress Cataloging-in-Publication Data
Mandeville, John, Sir.
    [Itinerarium. English]
    The book of John Mandeville with related texts / edited and
translated, with an Introduction, by Iain Macleod Higgins.
        p. cm.
    Includes bibliographical references and index.
    ISBN 978-0-87220-935-0 (pbk.) -- ISBN 978-0-87220-936-7 (cloth)
    1. Geography, Medieval. 2. Travel, Medieval. 3. Mandeville,
John, Sir. Itinerarium. 4. Travelers' writings, English--History and
criticism. I. Higgins, Iain Macleod. II. Title.
G370.M2M3613 2011
915.04'2--dc22

                                                              2010042269

CONTENTS

ACKNOWLEDGMENTS

This is the first English translation of *The Book of John Mandeville* from its original French since about 1400, and some of the texts in Appendices A and B are the first-ever English renderings. My work owes much to scholarship since the nineteenth century, in particular the editorial labors of Christiane Deluz and M. C. Seymour and the source studies of Deluz and George F. Warner. My thanks to colleagues who rescued me when oddities of medieval French, German, or Latin stumped me: Hélène Cazes, Cedric Littlewood, Elena Pnevmonidou, Mark Vessey. My thanks too to colleagues and friends who have offered their encouragement over the years: Nicola Bessell, Shamma Boyarin, Adrienne Williams Boyarin, Mary B. Campbell, Monique Dull, Fraser Easton, Tony Edwards, Kathryn Kerby-Fulton, Tom Hahn, Catherine Harding, Geraldine Heng, Erik Kwakkel, Eric Miller, Marcus Milwright, Allan Mitchell, David Staines, John Tucker, Scott Westrem. Suzanne Conklin Akbari read an earlier draft for the publisher and provided generous and astute guidance. Susan Wilson ably helped prepare the index. Editor Rick Todhunter patiently provided good advice as I underestimated almost everything about this project, and Mary Vasquez expertly solved questions of design. All errors are my responsibility. This book is for Ewa, Stefan, and Nicholas.

INTRODUCTION

Variously brilliant, entertaining, unpredictable, disturbing, even baffling and boring in places, *The Book of John Mandeville* (*TBJM*) is one of the most fascinating medieval works, not excluding masterpieces like the *Canterbury Tales* or the *Divine Comedy*. It initially presents itself, a bit vaguely, as a guidebook for Jerusalem pilgrims with an account of places farther east, and claims, not at all vaguely, to have been composed from memory in the mid-1350s by an English knight who had spent the previous three and a half decades traveling beyond the Mediterranean. This initial self-description is only partly accurate, however: the whole work does unfold more or less as promised, yet *TBJM* is anything but a memoir of one man's experiences. Not only has no trace of a Sir John Mandeville, or even an acceptable substitute, ever been found, but the only travels recorded in the book belong to others: the author may have traveled everywhere he says he did, or nowhere, or somewhere in between, but "what [he] can remember" about the eastern world is drawn almost entirely from others' works.

Forging East, Critically, Creatively, Vicariously, Popularly

Insofar as it claims to be something it is not, *The Book of John Mandeville* is a forgery—and the deceit is not redeemed by calling the work a "romance of travel,"[1] since it presents itself as historical. The sometimes-contested distinction between history and fiction was even less clear-cut in the fourteenth century than nowadays, but it was not altogether absent, and it is hard to imagine anyone then reading *TBJM*'s truth claims as equivalent to those of, say, *Sir Gawain and the Green Knight*. Unlike the imaginary realms of romance (even when they contain real forests, castles, or people), *TBJM*'s alternative worlds are depicted as real, as many of them in fact were. Indeed, one might argue that the *Mandeville* author's original deception was not a simple trick for its own sake, but rather that it allowed him the freedom to speak his mind in a society that did not encourage such expression: to critique the moral state of his fellow Christians through an unusually open-minded presentation of the sectarian Christian and non-Christian world beyond Latin Christendom,[2] an open-mindedness extended to nearly every

---

1. Bennett 1954, 39–53. "Mendacious romance" (Hodgen 1964, 103) is hardly better, though.

2. The regions under the authority of the Roman Catholic Church, as distinguished from those under another hegemonic religious institution, whether the Greek or Eastern Orthodox Church or any other (e.g., Georgian, Ethiopian) or

group except the Jews and some nomads like the Bedouins. If so, the
deception can be considered akin to the sort of literary device used
by his near contemporary, William Langland, who, to obtain similar
critical freedom, couched his impassioned critique of Christendom in
an allegorical dream vision called *Piers Plowman* (five of whose some
fifty surviving copies are bound with *TBJM,* suggesting that they have
concerns in common).[3] Still, even if the deception is a literary device
and thus was well-meaning rather than malicious, there is no evidence
that the work was originally read as fiction, and to read it only or primarily as such—rather than as an accomplished forgery mostly based on
accepted pictures of real worlds—is to limit its medieval typicality and
its Mandevillean singularity.[4]

The result of creativity and research (or "theft"), of speculation,
inference, and imagination as well as fact-gathering, this self-styled
guidebook-and-memoir stands distinctly apart from its sources even as
it resembles them. It is distinguished by being an unprecedented fusion
and personal interpretation of both learned and popular traditions of
writing that had only ever, and rarely, been brought together in manuscript miscellanies.[5] To make this singular work, the author drew on
two sets of Latin Christian writing: those devoted to the biblical East,
especially as seen by pilgrims since the fourth century and crusaders
since 1096; and the more varied traditions of writing about the farther, marvelous East, especially as seen by missionaries and merchants
since the mid-thirteenth century, but also as in accounts of the wonders
of India first recorded in Greco-Roman Antiquity. As if writing about
TBJM, Montaigne complains in *"Des cannibales"* (1580) about "topogra-
phers" who should make "detailed narratives of the places where they
have been, but" who, "because they have the advantage . . . of having
seen Palestine, . . . want to enjoy the privilege of telling us new things
about all the rest of the world."[6]

Although scholars have sometimes anachronistically called this patchwork plagiarized,[7] it is innovative in a typically medieval way: it transforms existing works into something new through active recombination.

Islam. *TBJM*'s world is not based on the opposition "European" / "Non-European,"
even where (as in Ch. 24) a modern reader might think so, but on "Latin Christian"
/ "other religion" and "over here" / "over there."

3. Benson 2004, 113–56, considers the affinities between *Piers, TBJM,* and *The
Book of Margery Kempe.*

4. For excellent literary readings, see Zacher (1976, 130–57), Howard (1971; 1980,
53–76), Campbell (1988, 122–61), and Heng (2003, 239–305).

5. Higgins 1997, 51. Miscellanies: composite books (in the physical sense); custom-
made mini-libraries.

6. Montaigne 1967, 99.

7. Campbell 1988 (9, 126, n. 8, etc.); Greenblatt 1991 (24, 31). See Higgins 1997,
12–13.

In our e-jargon, one might call it a "mash-up." Whatever we call it, though—mash-up, patchwork, or compilation—the new thing that emerged from the author's recombination of sources is a coherent yet digressive work of description, narration, explanation, and exhortation characterized by a shifting mix of genres.

Achieving its coherence from a distinctive mix of the impersonal and the personal in its address to the reader, the work also has a kind of minimal formal unity that results both from its being arranged as an itinerary and from being shaped as a single book. *The Book of Margery Kempe,* an otherwise very different memoir of travel by an early fifteenth-century English visionary, is similarly held together by its being formally a "book." In many respects, though, the work's closest formal analogue is a map, or rather a series of maps organized in sequential panels like chapters: namely, the unprecedented *Catalan Atlas* (c. 1375), an almost contemporary visual patchwork that fuses the modern-looking navigator's chart of the Mediterranean region (*portolan*) with the circular world map (*mappamundi*), although unlike *TBJM* it starts rather than ends in the Far East.[8]

Such a hybrid, I believe, is not accurately represented by the title by which it has been commonly known since the sixteenth century (*The Travels of Sir John Mandeville* or *Mandeville's Travels*), not least because such a title sets up misleading expectations. True, an overall itinerary drawn from two genuine travel memoirs structures the book, as the excerpts in Appendix B show, but in contrast to its sources (and Margery Kempe's *Book*), this underlying quasinarrative path is *not* followed by the author: the itinerary is given to an everyman-pilgrim/traveler who might one day retrace it, and the work sometimes even recounts more than one route to a given destination. This structuring, impersonal, vicarious journey, moreover, is often obscured by the copious digressions justified at the beginning of Chapter 4: "Although these things have nothing to do with showing the way [to Jerusalem], they are nevertheless relevant to what I promised to explain." What Laurence Sterne's Tristram Shandy said of his own "memoir" applies here: "Digressions, incontestably, are the sunshine;—they are the life, the soul of reading;—take them out of this book for instance,—you might as well take the book along with them;—."[9] Whether or not the author himself ever went anywhere, his work is not a personal record of travels, nor does it resemble formally the records left by later European voyagers and explorers: using the modern title thus shoehorns a *sui generis* book into a later genre that fits it only partly, if at all. Surviving copies reveal that, like many medieval works,

---

8. Deluz 2007, 13, considers *TBJM* the first medieval work devoted to the earth alone, and in this respect too it differs from the *Catalan Atlas,* whose first two panels are devoted to cosmology. For images of the *Atlas's* six panels, see: http://expositions.bnf.fr/ciel/catalan/index.htm. For more on medieval maps, see Appendix C.1.

9. Sterne 1967, 95.

this book circulated under various names, including *Itinerary, Book of Marvels,* and *The Book of John Mandeville,* which I use because it leaves open the question of what kind of book this might be.[10] Organized geographically as a vicarious tour of the East from Constantinople to the Earthly Paradise, *TBJM* often resembles "a kind of non-alphabetical encyclopaedia in the vernacular, in which everything gets mentioned somewhere,"[11] but its anecdotes and *"choses estranges"* (things variously foreign or strange) make for livelier reading than one usually gets from encyclopedic works. In what other medieval book, for instance, can one find such a remarkably diverse, even contradictory collection of ideas, facts, lore, history, legends, and tall tales as the following? Empirical and biblical proofs that the earth is a sphere that can be circumnavigated and that Jerusalem is situated in the middle; theological and botanical explanations of how and why Christ's Cross was made out of four kinds of wood; copious description of the Great Khan of Cathay's wealthy realm, including his magical mealtime entertainments; an account of how "the Jews" of Gog and Magog, long shut away in the Caucasus by Alexander the Great and indirectly guarded by the Amazons, will in Antichrist's time perfidiously bring about the world's end; and the claims that people everywhere, so long as they have reason, believe in God and share at least some Latin Christian beliefs or practices, and that no one knows whom God loves or hates.

Clearly, more than almost any other medieval book, *TBJM* offered something to everybody. For over two hundred years courtiers, priests, and ordinary people as well as explorers, mapmakers, artists, and writers took an interest in the book. They include Columbus, Sir Walter Raleigh, Gerardus Mercator, Leonardo da Vinci, Christine de Pizan, the English *Pearl* poet, and an Italian miller called Menocchio. In 1402, for instance, in her *Chemin de Long Estude* (*Way of Long Study*), Christine follows the Mandevillean itinerary and vicariously tours the world, while in 1595 Raleigh suggests that what he and others had found on the Orinoco River (in present-day Venezuela) corresponds to some wonders mentioned in *Mandeville,* and in 1599 Menocchio was burnt to death for heresy, having used the book (borrowed from his parish priest) to work out his own radically independent religious ideas.[12]

From its initial publication in the late 1350s until about 1600, *TBJM* was one of the most widely circulated medieval books. Including fragments and excerpts, it survives in some three hundred manuscripts (some expensively made and lavishly illustrated) and in more than ten

---

10. Marco Polo's *Travels* (c. 1299; originally *Devisament dou monde,* or *Description of the World*) is similarly misrepresented by its modern editorial title.

11. Pearsall 1992, 80, on Jean de Meun's late thirteenth-century continuation of the *Roman de la Rose.*

12. On Christine de Pizan, see Toynbee 1892. For Raleigh, see Chapter 22, n. 423. On Menocchio, see Ginzburg 1980.

languages: the original French as well as Czech, Danish, Dutch, English, German, Irish, Italian, Latin, Spanish, and Welsh, plus an unfinished text-free pictorial version.[13] Marco Polo's *Description of the World*, by contrast, survives in about half as many copies and several fewer languages, while a masterpiece like Dante's *Commedia* (a cosmic rather than earthbound traveler's memoir) was for a long time only regionally popular (though astonishingly so) and far less frequently translated or widely circulated internationally.[14] To find works that reached as many far-flung corners of Latin Christendom, one has to turn to saints' lives (in particular, the mid-thirteenth-century *Legenda Aurea*, or *Golden Legend*), or to the still more international legends of Alexander the Great, both of which provided the author with some of his material. By about 1500, moreover, printed editions of *TBJM*, often with woodcut illustrations, had been issued in all its medieval languages except Danish, Irish, and Welsh, and were reissued in some regions into the seventeenth century.[15] If any medieval book can be called an international best seller, *TBJM* can, and if any medieval book can tell us something about the common and diverse interests of Latin Christian readers from the later fourteenth to the early seventeenth centuries, this one can.

How, What, When, Where, and Who

Of the basic circumstantial questions about *The Book of John Mandeville*, only some have been answered with certainty. How was it made? In which language? What is it? These questions have received the clearest answers, even if the answers to the third have been contradictory, because of the work's nature as a creative recombination. The question, where was it made? however, has produced only two vague answers, and still more uncertain is the answer to the question, who was the author?

The most certain fact is also the most important: that *TBJM* was written out of other books, in particular out of two genuine, early fourteenth-century travel books spliced together, one after the other, to make a geographical spine and basic body. While thus splicing them together, the *Mandeville* author transformed their individual first-person, past-tense presentations ("I went") into a generic third-person tour in the perpetual present ("one goes") that—although aimed at a Latin

---

13. Manuscripts are listed in Seymour 1993, 38–49. On the interrelations of the different versions, see Higgins 1997, 21–23. Spanish: Castilian, Aragonese (a Catalan version has not survived: Riquer 1988). On the newly discovered sixteenth-century Welsh version, see Tzanaki 2003, 16. On the early reception, see Higgins 1997 and Tzanaki 2003.

14. Polo: Larner 1999, 106. More than eight hundred manuscripts of the *Commedia* in its original Italian survive, but the work was not translated for about a hundred years (Friederich 1949, 45).

15. Listed in Seymour 1993, 50–56.

Christian audience—can be taken by anyone at any time. The text is
not a narrative, then, although scholars often call it one, confusing constituent elements with overall construction: the underlying itinerary is
at most a *potential* narrative, full of smaller and larger inset narratives
that considerably enliven it. These inset narratives include two framing
quasi-legal testimonials ("I John Mandeville, knight"), and occasional
interruptions in which Sir John's ostensible deeds are recounted: his
military service under the Sultan and the Great Khan, for example.[16]
These unpredictable and typically lively "personal" interventions are
designed to authenticate the work, since they often show the English
knight receiving or declining favors or inquiring after local knowledge,
but for readers nowadays they raise questions about the author's identity
and experiences. He could well have served under the Sultan, but not
under the Khan: at least not as claimed, since the mentioned battles
occurred in the thirteenth century! The authorship question will be
considered below, but anyone unfamiliar with the work might find it
useful to read the framing passages now—the Prologue's last few paragraphs, and the second-to-last paragraph of Chapter 34—since they
bear on the rest of this discussion.

Enlivening the impersonal itinerary even more than the "authorial"
appearances is much material rewritten from some three dozen other
books, including encyclopedias, histories, romances, and a scientific
treatise, most of them from the thirteenth and fourteenth centuries.
As a glance at the sources listed in Appendix B reveals, the *Mandeville*
author typically drew on well-known, well-regarded works, putting into
circulation his own "take" on material that was often widely accepted as
true. The work's claim on the attention of readers both medieval and
modern, but especially the latter, thus lies not in its imparting of things
previously unknown (like the thirteenth-century reports on the Mongol
Empire by John of Plano Carpini, William Rubruck, and Marco Polo),
but in the author's distinctive use of received knowledge.

The two works providing the structural itinerary are introduced in
Appendix B, but can be briefly presented here: William of Boldensele's
Liber de quibusdam ultramarinis partibus (*Book of Certain Regions beyond the
Mediterranean*) and Odoric of Pordenone's *Relatio* (*Account*). William
was a Dominican who in 1332 made a pilgrimage to the Holy Land
and nearby regions, and then in 1337 in Avignon set down in Latin
a first-person record, while Odoric was a Franciscan who in the early
1320s made a missionary journey to India and China and in 1330 in
Padua dictated a first-person Latin account of his adventures. Two
more different texts could hardly be imagined, even though both were
the work of friars and near contemporaries. William's is the orderly,
informative memoir of an intelligent, sometimes skeptical traveler who

---

16. The term "knight" appears only in the Prologue's testimonial, not in the closing statement (Ch. 34). See also Chapters 6 and 23.

thinks well of himself, whereas Odoric's is a more miscellaneous and less well organized relation of a pious missionary almost overawed by foreign marvels. Something of the spirit of each can be found in *TBJM*, although both have undergone Mandevillean modifications, Odoric's record more than William's. In addition, the *Mandeville* author did not work primarily from the Latin originals, but rather, as the excerpts in Appendix B show, from somewhat altered French translations made in 1351.

This next well-established fact, that *TBJM* was composed in French, has implications for its origins and authorship, but it is necessary first to clear up a still-lingering misunderstanding. In the English-speaking world there has been confusion, even recently, about the work's original language: the result of reading as authorial the closing passage in the Prologue in a Middle English translation known as the Cotton Version. According to this passage, which creatively reworks its French source (see Appendix A.3), the author composed his work in Latin and then translated it himself into French and from French into English. Cotton survives in only one copy and seems to have had no influence before the sixteenth century, when a simplified version of its claim was repeated by John Bale and Richard Hakluyt. The claim was given wider circulation with the publication in 1725 of Cotton in the first (more or less) scholarly edition, whose text, being often reprinted, effectively represented the work for more than two centuries thereafter.[17] Some readers in the eighteenth century, however, already knew that *TBJM* had been composed in French and by 1869, when a German scholar drew attention to translation errors in Cotton,[18] there could be no possible doubt about the matter.

The question is, which French? There are, as explained in Appendix A, three distinct French versions named after their likeliest place of origin: Insular, Continental, and Interpolated Continental (also known as Liège or Ogier). The third of these, with its interpolations giving Ogier the Dane (a legendary peer of Charlemagne) credit for spreading Christianity by the sword throughout the East, is clearly not authorial, since it obviously reworks Continental, but the other two potentially are. Because the author claims in the Prologue to have been "born and raised in England in the town of St Albans," one might expect the Anglo-Norman Insular Version to contain his text, but the author never says *where* he made his book, only that he did so after he "came to rest" ("*[je] suy venuz a repos*"; Ch. 34). These words do not necessarily imply that the

---

17. John Bale: "he wrote in three languages, English, French, and Latin," in Hakluyt's *Principall Navigations* (1589, 22–23), a (more or less) scholarly edition (see Appendix A.5). See Higgins 2004 for more details. Cotton and two other English prose versions contain a closing passage in which the pope approves the book (see Appendix A.3): this too has mistakenly been read as authorial.

18. See Appendix A.3.

author "return[ed] home to England," as some claim,[19] although they could. Unfortunately, since only Insular has been published in a critical edition, it is impossible to compare it thoroughly with Continental, and the available evidence, external as well as textual, is insufficient to confirm which textual tradition is prior and (presumably) authorial.[20] A further complication is the possibility that, given the likely date of composition, the original dialect need not correspond to the place of composition. An exact date cannot be established, but the claim in the French copies that the text was composed in 1356 or 1357 fits well enough with external evidence: the work could not have been put together before 1351, when Long John of Ypres translated William's and Odoric's itineraries, or after 1371, when the earliest dated manuscript was copied in Paris.[21] Since the 1371 text is faulty, the date of composition might well be closer to 1360 than to 1370. If so, if *TBJM* was composed, as claimed, in the later 1350s, then it was made in a period of much traffic of people and books between England and France during the Hundred Years' War: a struggle perhaps alluded to in the Prologue's disparaging mention of Christian lords who want to disinherit one another rather than reclaim the Holy Land.[22] In such circumstances, an English knight, or an English cleric claiming to be a knight, could have composed an Anglo-Norman book on the Continent, while conversely a French knight or cleric claiming to be an English knight could have composed the work in Continental French in England. Given that the work is an imposture, there is no way to decide which, if any, is the least implausible of other possible impostures. Lacking decisive evidence, we can only say that *TBJM*'s "Frenchness" links England to the Continent as the text heads east.

There are, however, other international dimensions to this "Frenchness" that the text itself raises at the end of the Prologue: "Know that I should have put this writing into Latin so as to explain things more briefly, but because more [people] understand French better than Latin, I have put it into French so that everyone can understand it, and the knights and the lords and the other noble men who know no Latin,

---

19. E.g., Kohanski 2007, 6.

20. Bennett (1954, 146) and DLMM (33) consider Insular authorial, while de Poerck (1955, 155) and Seymour (1993, 5; 2002, xi) prefer Continental. (See Abbreviations for a key to those used in the notes here and throughout the text.)

21. Bibliothèque Nationale MS nouv. acq. fr. 4515, made at the court of Charles V by Raoulet d'Orléans for the king's physician, Gervais Chrétien; edited in LMT 2.229–413.

22. Bennett 2006 (esp. 276–77) summarizes the Anglo-French contacts of the period in trying to make the case for an Anglo-French origin (his case, contra Seymour, merits consideration but is conjectural). Only the Vulgate Latin (made from Liège) openly refers to the War (see Ch. 50 in Appendix A.5), but since it was probably made in the 1390s the reference must be an authenticating fabrication.

or a little, and who have been beyond the sea know and understand whether I speak the truth or not." The first thing to note is that this vernacular book claims to be worthy of Latin, the international language of scripture, theology, and learning, while the second thing is that although it defines its "French" audience broadly, it singles out the courtly estate. Since the text has just described itself as a guide "especially for those who have the . . . desire to visit . . . Jerusalem and the holy places that are around it," and since many of *TBJM*'s sources began life in Latin, this claim is true enough.[23] Like the appeal to other noble travelers, it authenticates the work. The announced choice of French over Latin, however, is important for still another reason: it signals that the author is bringing together the concerns of the international clerical world with those of the international courtly world, but on the latter's territory. His work thus belongs to the broader medieval trend of making Latin learning more widely available, especially through courtly intermediaries: a trend that began in the later thirteenth century, in French first, then in other vernaculars, and lasted well into the fifteenth century.[24] The author's claim to be composing for "everyone," then, is more than simple self-promotion, as is the claim that his material is worthy of Latin.

Indeed, there is evidence that, despite the vernacular's growing importance, some of *TBJM*'s readers agreed with the Prologue's claim that the author "should have put this writing into Latin." Vernacular texts were sometimes translated into Latin for a narrower circle of readers, but *TBJM* is unusual in that no fewer than *five* separate Latin versions were made from the French. Four of these were more or less faithfully made from Insular and survive in about a dozen copies, suggesting a small demand in the British Isles, where French and English versions dominated. The rendering made on the Continent from the Liège Version, however, survives in more than forty copies, revealing that there the Latin *Mandeville* was as popular as the French and German.[25] Known as the Vulgate Latin because of its wide circulation, this redaction pulls a kind of Mandevillean trick on its readers, silently changing the work's attitudes and even some of its claims, as the excerpts in Appendix A.5 reveal.

It does not, however, substantially change the Liège source's unexpected concluding claim about *TBJM*'s origins: that the English knight composed his work in Liège at the behest of a physician, "Master John

23. Pilgrims' guides were almost solely in Latin until the latter part of the fourteenth century (Richard 1981, 44). The same is true of the more miscellaneous accounts of the farther East.

24. One of the earliest such works, Brunetto Latini's *Livres dou Tresor,* a popular encyclopedia written about a century before *TBJM,* was also one of the *Mandeville* author's sources. See also the Prologue, n. 15.

25. For very basic details and a list of manuscripts, see Seymour 1993, 43, 46–47.

of Bourgogne, called 'with the beard,'" who happened to have been in Cairo at the Sultan's court at the same time as the pilgrim soldier. This account is of interest in itself, in that it shows one of *TBJM*'s intermediaries practicing the same sort of creative, authenticating deception as the *Mandeville* author himself: perhaps taking his cue from the claim that the author had "come to rest despite [him]self because of arthritic gouts, which constrain [him]" (Ch. 34). But the claim also raises the last of the circumstantial questions: who made *TBJM*? Diligent archival work, especially by Josephine Waters Bennett, has turned up a few Englishmen with the right name, but none remotely fits the authorial bill, not even the recently discovered John Mandeville who in 1357 found himself indirectly involved in some high-level Anglo-French contacts following the 1356 Battle of Poitiers.[26] This lack of evidence by itself does not necessarily mean that there was no John Mandeville—only that he has not been found—but it is undoubtedly made more troubling by the fact that *TBJM* is a forgery.

Accordingly, since modern readers prefer a named author to "Anon.," scholars have found substitutes for Sir John Mandeville. The earliest were associated with the Liège textual tradition, because it named local names that proved to have been real: the street and the inn where the knight stayed while receiving treatment for his gout. The first surrogate was John of Bourgogne, whose name was associated with a lapidary and a plague treatise and therefore with sufficient learning to be responsible for the Mandevillean compilation. The tenuous evidence for his authorship, however, mostly comes from the unreliable John of Outremeuse (1338–1400), an inventive Liège historian, who became the next substitute. Chronology and *TBJM*'s textual history make both of these Continental Johns (the learned and the liar) highly unlikely proxies, although the latter may well have been responsible for the Interpolated Continental Version.[27] More recently, and more plausibly in both chronology and textual history, still another John has been proposed: the Benedictine translator Long John of Ypres. The principal difficulty with this proposal, apart from the fact that *TBJM*'s attitudes are quite different from those of its sources, is that the textual evidence suggests that the *Mandeville* author used French sources in preference to Latin, presumably because his Latin was not especially good, whereas Long John translated it extensively.[28] Besides "Anon.," then, the main candi-

26. Bennett 1954, 181–216; for the latest John Mandeville, see Bennett 2006.

27. On the Liège traditions and attributions, see Bennett 1954, 89–134, and Lejeune 1964.

28. Seymour 1993, 23–34, and 2007. Seymour does not raise these objections, nor does he note that John sometimes makes his French translation more negative than his Latin source (cf. Ch. 22 [French] with Ch. 23 [Latin]). Larner, "Plucking Hairs from the Great Cham's Beard" (in Akbari and Iannucci 2008, 133–55) adds nothing to Seymour's case.

dates for *TBJM*'s authorship have been an English knight, a Burgundian physician, a Liège liar, and a Flemish monk.

Faced with such an unsatisfactory choice, one can see why the work's most recent editor still prefers a version of Bennett's view that the author was more or less who he says he was: an English knight, whether a young noble educated in the Arts, or an apostate cleric with a chivalric background (like William of Boldensele).[29] The latter, more recent hypothesis shows Deluz moving towards Seymour's insistence that the author must have been a cleric. There is something to be said for this view, given the *Mandeville* author's habit of citing scripture in Latin without translating it: in contrast to the translator Long John, who follows Latin citations with the words "in [our] French this means . . ." Indeed, in more than fifty citations the *Mandeville* author quotes, if not always entirely accurately, from some twenty biblical books, especially the Psalms and the Gospels; and he shows a wide knowledge of the Bible. Moreover, three other passages indicate his familiarity with the canonical hours of monastic prayer.[30] If he was not a cleric, he likely had some clerical training and access to clerical circles, but was more open to religious difference (except where the Jews were concerned) than clerics usually were. At the same time, however, his obvious interest in the courtly world, evident throughout the work, might mean that he (also) came from or partly moved in a courtly milieu.

Clearly, the *Mandeville* author is so deeply encrypted in his work that he can only be known by inference. Whether any of his circumstantial claims—that he was an English knight from St Albans called John Mandeville who spent some thirty-five years traveling beyond the Mediterranean—are true, the claim he composed from memory is demonstrably false. What we know for sure boils down to this: sometime between 1351 and 1371, probably in the later 1350s, almost certainly in the territories on either side of the English Channel then contested in the Hundred Years' War, someone of French or English origin with both courtly and clerical interests had extensive access to a good library, either ecclesiastical or courtly, and there consulted many books in Latin and French (preferring the latter), reworking them into his own French, which he handles with native fluency. Moreover, and no less important, we also know that the *Mandeville* author's clerical-cum-courtly interests were so widely shared that his "memoir" of the eastern world was soon translated into some ten other languages (sometimes more than once, and sometimes indirectly) and was widely popular for over two centuries.

---

29. DLMM 14 (apostate cleric); Deluz 1988, 71 (young noble). Part of the evidence for the latter is the author's use of Sacrobosco's *De Sphera*, a basic university textbook (see Ch. 20, n. 382).

30. See Index of Scriptural and Related Citations in Latin; some of my attributions differ from Deluz's. Canonical hours: see Chapter 16, n. 323; Chapter 18, n. 351; Chapter 33, n. 569.

The World According to Sir John

Although the author presents himself as an English knight writing in French, he addresses himself from the start to fellow Latin Christians, distinguishing them from the "cruel Jews" and the "miscreants [Muslims]," and the vital distinctions in his work remain religious. Indeed, even before the socially and nationally defined Sir John appears,[31] the work establishes his orthodoxy with high-flown praise of the Holy Land, Jesus Christ, and the Virgin Mary, plus a call for Christian political unity to enable the reconquest of "the inheritance our Father left to us." This loudly professed desire to see the Promised Land "reclaim[ed]" reechoes quietly throughout the whole work, moreover, in prophecies of Latin Christian triumph (in Chs. 15 and 28), if only the faithful will reform themselves. The last Latin Christian holding in the Holy Land, Acre, had fallen to Muslim forces some sixty years earlier, in 1291, but in Sir John's world, the crusades are not over, just as they were not over for most of his audience. Pro-crusading sentiment remained strong into the fifteenth century, such that Columbus in the Caribbean could write of seeking gold to finance the reconquest of the Holy Sepulcher.[32] Surprisingly, however, given its showy opening, *TBJM*'s crusading rhetoric all but disappears when the Prologue ends and the guidebook begins, and despite its underlying Christian triumphalism, its accounts of religious difference, whether Christian or non-Christian, tend to be quite neutral.

Indeed, difference as such is rarely denigrated, being part of *TBJM*'s advertised appeal alongside the celebration of the One, True Faith. The Prologue promises information about "many different peoples with diverse laws and diverse customs," and at the start of Chapter 4 Sir John defends his practice of retailing such material by invoking the pleasure it gives: "many people enjoy . . . hearing foreign things spoken about." The Prologue's theological declarations apart, though, questions of belief interest the knight less than pious practice, however "diverse [the] customs." The main exceptions are Greek Christianity (Ch. 3) and (partly) Islam (Ch. 15), the Greek differences being presented more negatively than the Islamic, where points of contact are emphasized. Indeed, the same author who calls Muslims "miscreants" in the Prologue can say in closing that "amongst all these diverse peoples . . . and the diverse laws and the diverse beliefs they have, there is no people . . . who do not have some articles of our faith and some good points of our belief, and who do not believe in God who made the world, whom they call God of

---

31. We know nothing about how the *Mandeville* author might resemble his textual persona, Sir John.

32. In his log for December 26, 1492 (Columbus 1492–1493, 290–92). Cf. the great Muslim traveler Ibn Battuta's *Rihla* (composed 1356–1358), which shows no interest in the Crusades.

Nature." And he can make an even more radical claim in Chapter 32: "although there are many diverse laws throughout the world, I believe that God always loves those who love him and serve humbly in virtue and loyalty and who do not value the vainglory of this world." What distinguishes *TBJM*'s world from that of its sources, then, is its syncretism: its tendency to try at least to amalgamate the world's difference, diversity, and divergence, to make its seemingly endless variety fit inside Latin Christian categories, broadly interpreted. Thus, as the closing remark quoted above reveals, not only are other religious practices and beliefs presented as entertaining to hear about; they are sometimes also depicted as analogous to Christian ones (Ch. 19), or as quasi- or proto-Christian (Chs. 32 and 34), even in the Islamic case (Ch. 15).[33] In two places (Chs. 18 and 34), moreover, the *Mandeville* author looks something like a scholar of comparative religion, distinguishing "simulacra" (likenesses) from idols so as to defend some forms of the veneration of images. This sometimes-assimilating openness to otherness extends to customs and manners, which are usually described neutrally and, if explained, are represented as rational. Accordingly, one might call the author's attitude *anthropological* (recognizing that, even here, Western anthropology is complexly linked to Christian European expansion and that its apparently disinterested mode of observation can disguise appropriative interests). This is not to say, however, that Sir John the anthropologist simply approves of everything. Like most who take for granted a city-based human order (civilization), he has no time for nomads (Ch. 9), a view that might also influence his hatred of the Jews, since the Ten Lost Tribes are said "not [to] have their own land [anywhere] in the whole world except . . . between the mountains" where Alexander the Great confined them (Ch. 29). Nor apparently does Sir John approve of belief in reincarnation (Ch. 22) or political assassination (Ch. 30), and he condemns cannibalism outright, if seemingly reserving judgment on nakedness and economic and sexual communism (Ch. 20). Still, there is more to these passages than moral approval or disapproval: the account of reincarnation, for instance, raises questions about poverty and charity. Clearly, whatever the *Mandeville* author actually believed, his surrogate Sir John's mostly open-minded presentation of the world is, despite its appropriating Christian embrace of almost everything, meant to provoke critical thought, self-reflection, and speculation as well as pleasure.

Such provocative syncretism extends even to physical geography: the earth not only has a central Jerusalem (Prologue, Chs. 10 and 20) and an unreachable eastern Paradise (Chs. 2 and 33), but it is also spherical, circumnavigable, and inhabited everywhere (Chs. 20 and 34). Biblical,

33. Again, the glaring exception is Judaism, whose practices and beliefs receive no attention, while the Jews themselves are demonized (see Braude 1995 and 1997).

theoretical, and empirical proofs reinforce these views, and through them Sir John reveals himself as a kind of amateur practical scientist and theorist.[34] Nor are his amalgamating scientific interests limited to the earth; they extend to its elements, including balm (Ch. 7), pepper (Ch. 18), and diamonds (Ch. 17). In keeping with medieval practice, his natural philosophy (which we would call science) at times shades into moral philosophy, and his spherical earth is thus shown to be symmetrical as well as various (Chs. 20 and 29), linking as well as dividing peoples through the relation between perception and place: "For in whatever part of the earth one dwells, either above or below, it always seems to those living there that they walk more upright than any other people" (Ch. 20). Everyone everywhere is ethnocentric.

In addition to the religious, ethnographic, and scientific domains just mentioned, Sir John pays attention to the political sphere, another interest announced in the Prologue. Conquerors who rule well-ordered societies particularly interest him, and military order sometimes stands in for social order more generally. The Sultan of Egypt (Chs. 6 and 15), the Amazons (Ch. 17), the Great Khan of Cathay (Chs. 23–26), Prester John (Chs. 30 and 32), Alexander the Great (Ch. 32), and the Old Man of the Mountain (Ch. 30) receive the most attention, especially the Khan. Sir John explains how each of these figures actually rules (or ruled), but what most attracts his attention is the sumptuous organization of the courts of the Sultan, the Khan, and Prester John.

Details of courtly splendor often feature prominently in romance, and here *TBJM*'s political interests shade into those of romance, which rarely hesitated to blur the fuzzy boundary between history and fiction. In fact, as noted, *TBJM* has been read as a romance of travel, and it certainly has romance elements: the tales of Hippocrates' daughter (Ch. 4), the watching of the sparrowhawk (Ch. 16), and Sir John's harrowing journey through a diabolical valley (Ch. 31). No less romance-like are the natural, cultural, and other wonders, from the Danube and the apple-dropping statue of Justinian in Chapter 1 to the odd funeral, dietary, and grooming customs in Chapter 34. Yet such wonders are also found in medieval encyclopedias and on the encyclopedic world maps produced in the thirteenth century: maps that in overtly placing earthly diversity under the sign of Christian history might be thought of as visual analogues to *TBJM* in its open-armed, yet appropriating embrace of the world's "*choses estranges.*"[35] To the extent that the work is a romance, then, it is so by virtue of having absorbed romance modes and materials, and Sir John only rarely presents himself as a romance

---

34. The elements of this account of the earth are in all the great medieval encyclopedias, but their placement in a vernacular text not meant for specialists, in the context of theoretical reflection, in literary form, is new (Ridder 1996, 237, 243). On *TBJM*'s geography, see Deluz 1988.

35. For more on these maps, see Appendix C.1.

hero (e.g., in Chs. 6, 18, and 23), admitting that he failed to live up to Alexander the Great's example (Ch. 32). Clearly, neither Sir John himself nor *TBJM*'s material belongs to any one medieval genre. He can appear as a romance hero, anthropologist, scientist, historian, cultural critic, or bigot, and his world is as various as medieval worlds come, even its finitude: I have not told you everything, he says in Chapter 34, since "someone else who took the trouble . . . to go into those far places . . . would have nothing new to say in which the listeners could take pleasure." The knight's primary role, however, remains that of tour guide, and his world is organized as an itinerary on which each place, as a container of information, is a node in a network of fascinating historical, cultural, religious, or other associations. No wonder the work has never lacked readers.

A Note on the Translation

This is the first English translation of *The Book of John Mandeville* from its original French in some six hundred years.[36] It tries to steer between the poles represented by the Middle English Cotton and Egerton versions, its two fullest predecessors: fidelity to the source and readability (while resisting the urge to tidy up the original prose, as E does). By fidelity, though, I do not mean word-for-word conformity like that of sometime slavish C translator, but rather respect for the text's historical idiosyncrasies. The Middle French word *loi* ("law"), for instance, could be rendered as "religion," but that would obscure the medieval understanding of religion as a system of binding obligations and constraints.[37] A more prominent historical idiosyncrasy is the prose, which like much early vernacular prose is loose-jointed. A simple example (from Ch. 22) shows how it works at the sentence level, as two relative clauses refer to separate antecedents (signaled here by single or double underlining). Many translators would recast this syntactically, but unless the result is incomprehensible, I have preferred to render the looser syntax as is, punctuating for clarity (C and E are given for comparison):[38]

Insular. *De celle cité vait homme par eawe solaciant et joiant jusques a une abbeye des moignes qe est assez près qe sont bien religious solonc leur loi.*

Present Translation. From this city one goes by water, merrily and delightedly, to an abbey of monks that is quite near who are very pious according to their law.

---

36. The most widely available modern English text (Moseley 1983; 2005 with new editorial material) translates a Middle English version: see Appendix A.3.
37. See Prologue, n. 3.
38. Insular: DLMM 362 (emphasis added). C: HMT 1.137 (emphasis added). E: WBJM 102 (emphasis added).

<table>
<tr><td>

C. From that cytee men gon
be watre solacynge &
disportinge [t]hem[selves] till
thei come to an Abbeye of
monkes that is faste by that
ben gode religious men after
here [their] *feyth & lawe*.

</td><td>

E. Fra this citee *may* [can]
men *ride in schippe or in bate*
[boat] by that *river* till [to]
ane abbay of mounkes a
lytill fra the citee; *and thai*
er wonder [amazingly]
religious after thaire lawe.

</td></tr>
</table>

Similarly, I have not always altered mid-sentence changes in syntax or rationalized the pronouns when they shift between singular and plural. Such "ungrammatical" sentences should not be difficult for anyone who is willing to accept prose that behaves like casual speech, as in these examples from Chapters 5 and 34: "And whoever puts any metal into this pit in the middle of the sand, this metal is changed into glass" ("*Et qe mectroit ascun metal en ceo fosse entremy l'aregne ceo metal se converteroit en voirre*"); "And the priests throw pieces of the flesh [*des pieces*] to them, and they carry it [*la portent*] not far away and eat it [*la mangent*]."[39]

To tidy up such sometimes stumbling prose, to tighten or recast its sentences and channel their sometimes headlong rush into more neatly articulated steps, would be to falsify the experience that the text originally created for its readers and hearers: that of a fact-crammed memory unburdening itself at length and only occasionally pausing for breath. Thus beyond ensuring that the word order makes sense in modern English, adding clarifying punctuation, and dividing the text into paragraphs to help mark its overall shape, I have not recast the original syntax and style. The most notable stylistic change I have made is to reduce the number of sentences connected by "and" or "the which," since present-day readers find such run-on prose tiresome. My hope is that after a few pages, readers will find themselves easily adjusting to the work's idiosyncratic medieval rhythms, which are one of its strange pleasures.

As noted, the *Mandeville* author sometimes studs his prose with Latin quotations, leaving them untranslated (as Langland did in *Piers Plowman*). These quotations, almost all scriptural, would have given the text an air of authority and orthodoxy. *TBJM*'s medieval translators typically kept the Latin, but also translated it. I have likewise left the Latin, translating it in footnotes and not correcting it where (for whatever reason) it does not coincide exactly with the source; divergent citations are marked "cf." (e.g., "cf. John 19:21"); where "cf." is not used, the Latin coincides with the accepted text. All biblical passages have been translated with reference to the Douay-Rheims translation of the Vulgate Latin as revised by Bishop Richard Challoner.

---

39. DLMM 127 and 474, respectively.

Proper Names. The spelling of proper names varies considerably (Margery Kempe's scribe requested indulgence for misspelled names: "he that wrote them had never seen them, and therefore have him excused").[40] For well-known and easily identifiable names (Jerusalem, Herod), the customary modern English form is usually given; but for lesser-known or garbled names or when the medieval spelling matters, the medieval form is given, typically with the known (or likely) modern English equivalent in parentheses (some names remain obscure), because medieval authors and readers sometimes made inferences from them that would otherwise be inexplicable: see "Bersabee" (Beersheba) in Chapter 9 and the Great *Chan*'s relation to *Cham* (Noah's son) in Chapter 24. Important place and personal names are usually glossed on their first appearance.

Annotations. This translation emphasizes *TBJM*'s sources and its variants and versions. Only especially significant or obscure passages have been annotated in detail. For more information, consult Deluz 2000; Hamelius 1919–1923, vol. 2; Kohanski 2001; Kohanski and Benson 2007; Seymour 1967; Seymour 2002; and Warner 1889.

Further Reading. Studies of *TBJM* and its contexts are available in French, German, and Spanish as well as English; scholars and advanced students know how to find them. Those new to medieval travel and its writing, especially undergraduates and nonacademic readers, can orient themselves with Howard (1971 and 1980), Olschki (1943), Phillips (1988), and Sumption (1975), recognizing that some of their claims have since been challenged or corrected. Dunn (1986), retracing the travels of the *Mandeville* author's contemporary, Ibn Battuta, offers a historical overview of many of the places in *TBJM* as seen through Muslim eyes. Battuta's book is informative in its own right, as are other medieval travel texts (Marco Polo's, William of Rubruck's, those published by the Palestine Pilgrims' Text Society).

Illustrations. *TBJM* was frequently illustrated, both in manuscript and print, and these images have influenced its reception. Increasingly, such illustrations are available online. The British Library's Catalogue of Illuminated Manuscripts is particularly rich: search for "Mandeville" (www.bl.uk/catalogues/illuminatedmanuscripts/welcome.htm). The French Bibliothèque Nationale has partly digitized the sumptuous *Livre des merveilles:* search for "Français 2810" in its catalogue Mandragore (mandragore.bnf.fr/jsp/rechercheExperte.jsp). E-codices, the Virtual Manuscript Library of Switzerland, has a richly illustrated copy of Otto von Diemeringen's German: search for "Mandeville" (www.e-codices.unifr.ch/en). Other copies can be found through the

40. Kempe 1996, 217 (spelling modernized here).

Digital Scriptorium: search for "Mandeville" (scriptorium.columbia. edu). Early English Books Online (EEBO), usually accessible through a research library, contains early printings illustrated with woodcuts: search for "Mandeville."

ABBREVIATIONS

App	Appendix
C	Cotton Version (Middle English)
D	Defective Version (Middle English)
DLMM	Deluz 2000
E	Egerton Version (Middle English)
HMT	Hamelius 1919–1923
L	Liège (or Interpolated Continental) Version (French)
LMT	Letts 1953
LPJ	*Letter of Prester John*
OP	Odoric of Pordenone
TBJM	*The Book of John Mandeville*
WoB	William of Boldensele
WBJM	Warner 1889

The Book of John Mandeville

This schematic medieval diagram of the world characteristically Christianizes its inherited Roman geography. Known as a Noachid T-O map (see Appendix C.1), it is oriented to the east and depicts the three then-known continents as having been peopled by Noah's sons: Asia by Shem, Africa by Ham, Europe by Japheth (but cf. *TBJM*, Ch. 24). The continents themselves are surrounded by the Ocean Sea and divided here by the Great Sea (the Mediterranean). From Isidore of Seville, *Etymologiae* (Augsburg: G. Zainer, 1472). By permission of the Library of Congress, Washington, D.C.

[Prologue]¹

Since it is so that the land beyond the sea—that is, the Holy Land, which is called the Promised Land²—is beyond all other lands the most excellent and the most worthy and lady and sovereign of all other lands, and was blessed and sanctified and consecrated by the precious body and blood of Our Lord Jesus Christ—

in which land it pleased Him to be conceived in the Virgin Mary, and to take human flesh and food, and to walk and go all around the said land on His blessed feet;

and where He would perform many miracles, and preach and teach the faith and the law³ of us Christians as to His children;

and where He would endure much blame and much mockery and suffer for us;

and of this land in particular He wished to be called king, He who is king of Heaven, of earth, of air, of sea, and of all things contained in them;

and He Himself is called king of this land especially, saying *"Rex sum Judeorum,"*⁴ for at that time this land belonged to the Jews;

and He chose this land for Himself amongst all other lands as the best and the most virtuous and the most worthy in the world, for it is the heart and the middle of all the land of the world, and just as the philosopher says, *"Virtus rerum in medio consistit"*;⁵

in this very worthy land the heavenly king wished to lead His life and be harmed by the cruel Jews and suffer passion and death for the love of us, to redeem us and free us from the pains of Hell and the terrible perpetual death that was prepared for us for the sin of our first father

---

1. The Prologue differs notably in style from the rest of the work and has been laid out for ease of reading.

2. "beyond the sea": the Mediterranean. The idea of a Promised Land comes from Gen. 12:1–12, where God calls Abraham and promises him land (Canaan in Gen. 15:18), a promise reaffirmed to his descendants and renewed in Moses' time (Exod. 6:5–8). Paul uses the idea symbolically (Heb. 11:8–16), reframing it in Christian terms and associating it with pilgrimage. Since in Judaic and Christian tradition the Lord alone is truly holy, the places where He manifested Himself are also holy. By the fourth century the Christian practice of Holy Land pilgrimage had emerged, especially to the places linked to Jesus, and Christians came to see the Holy Land as the Promised Land. Holy sites linked to local saints also emerged in Christendom, but there was only one true Holy Land, as this Prologue makes clear.

3. What we call religion, medieval writers called "law" (*loi* in *TBJM*), emphasizing the *obligations* of the faithful.

4. "I am king of the Jews." Cf. John 19:21.

5. "The virtue/power/excellence of things is found in the middle." Cf. Aristotle, *Nicomachean Ethics* 2.6.

Adam, and for our own sins as well; for on His own account He deserved
no evil, for He never thought evil nor did evil;

and well did the king of glory in this place more than in any other
land wish to suffer death and passion;

for whoever wants to make something public so that everyone might
know it has it cried out and announced in the middle of the town, so
that the matter might be known and spread about everywhere;

therefore the creator of the whole world wished to suffer death for
us in Jerusalem, which is in the middle of the world,[6] so that the matter
was made public and known to all parts of the world: how dearly He paid
for man whom He made in His image, and how dearly He redeemed us
because of the great love He has for us without our having deserved it,
for He could offer no higher price nor greater ransom for us than His
holy body, His precious blood, and His blessed life, which He wholly
offered and gave up for us—He who never had in Himself any taint of
sin wanted through great love to give His body for sinners.

Ah God, what love He had for His subjects when He who was guiltless
wished to suffer death for the guilty.[7] Indeed man should love, honor,
fear, and serve such a lord, and honor and prize this holy land that
bore such fruit by which each person is saved, unless it be by his own
failure.

Well ought the land to be delightful and fruitful that was watered
and softened by the precious blood of Jesus Christ, which is the land
that Our Lord promised us as an inheritance.

And in the said land He wished to die so as to leave it as a possession
to His children—which is why every good Christian who has the power
and the means ought to take pains and do great work to conquer our
above-mentioned and right inheritance and take it from the hands of
the miscreants and appropriate it to us, for we are called Christians
after Christ, who is our Father; and if we are true sons of God, we ought
to reclaim the inheritance our Father left to us and wrest it from the
hands of the foreigners.[8]

But today pride, greed, and envy have so enflamed the hearts of the
lords that they seek more to disinherit others than they do to reclaim and
conquer their own and lawful inheritance mentioned above. And those
commoners who with goodwill have given their bodies and possessions

---

6. The idea of a central Jerusalem goes back to a fourth-century Christian reading
of Ezek. 5:5, but few pre-twelfth-century *geographical* writings mention it, and (with
one exception) Jerusalem was not placed at the center of pre-thirteenth-century
world maps. The *Mandeville* author makes more of this idea than most (see Chs.
10 and 20 and Appendix C.1; see also Deluz 1995 and Higgins 1997b).

7. "guiltless . . . guilty": *sanz coulpes* and *les coulpables* can also mean "faultless/
perfect" and "the faulty/imperfect."

8. After the loss of Acre in 1291, Latin Christians had no Palestinian territory, but
retaking the Holy Land remained an active ideal, inspiring much pro-crusading
rhetoric: cf. William of Boldensele's prologue (Appendix B.1).

to conquer our above-mentioned inheritance can do nothing without the sovereign lords. For a gathering of the commons without a chief lord is like a flock of sheep without a shepherd: it spreads out and does not know where it should go or what it should do. But if it pleased our holy apostolic father[9]—for it would please God well—that the landed princes were reconciled and with each of their commons would undertake the holy voyage overseas, I believe it to be certain that in a short time the Promised Land would be restored[10] and placed in the hands of its rightful heirs, the sons of Jesus Christ.

And because it has been a long time since there was a general passage[11] over the sea and many people delight in hearing the said Holy Land spoken about and take pleasure in it, I John Mandeville, knight—

although I am not worthy, born and raised in England in the town of St Albans,

who from there have crossed the sea in the year 1322 on Michaelmas Day[12] and who have since been beyond the sea for a long time, and have seen and gone around many countries and many different provinces and many different regions and different islands and have passed through Turkey, Lesser and Greater Armenia, Tartary, Persia, Syria, Arabia, Upper and Lower Egypt, Libya, Chaldea, a great part of Ethiopia, Amazonia, Lesser and Middle and a part of Greater India, and many different islands around India where there dwell many different peoples with diverse laws and diverse customs—

of which lands and islands I will speak more fully and describe some part of the things that are there when there is room to speak of them according to what I can remember,

especially for those who have the will and desire to visit the noble city of Jerusalem and the holy places that are around it;

and I will describe for them what way they might take;

for I have passed along many of them [the ways] and ridden with good company, thank God.

Know that I should have put this writing into Latin so as to explain things more briefly,[13] but because more [people] understand French

---

9. The pope.

10. "restored": *reconsilie* can also mean "[a church] purified [after pollution]" or "[a spouse] restored."

11. Cf. Latin *passagium generale* (a large-scale crusade, like the First Crusade) and *passagium particulare* (a smaller crusade with limited goals, like those of the fourteenth century).

12. September 29. Copying errors were common, due to the use of Roman numerals: several manuscripts (and E) have 1332, one has 1312, and another 1342 (DLMM 92, textual note n; WBJM 3). A correct date would be important if, as some believe, a real John Mandeville went from England to the Holy Land.

13. See Introduction (pp. xvi–xvii) for a discussion of this important claim.

better than Latin, I have put it into French so that everyone can understand it, and the knights and the lords and the other noble men[14] who
know no Latin, or a little, and who have been beyond the sea know and
understand whether I speak the truth or not. And if I err in describing
through not remembering or otherwise, they can amend and correct
it,[15] for things long since passed out of view get forgotten and human
memory cannot retain or contain everything.

---

14. "Lords, knights, and ladies" in Michel Velser's German (Morrall 1974, 4).
TBJM had female readers, including Christine de Pizan and Valentina Visconti,
the Duke of Milan's daughter; her 1388 French copy is related to Velser's source
(Morrall 1968, 185).
15. A conventional request, appealing to readers' goodwill, repeated in
Chapter 14.

[Chapter 1][1]

About the Way from England to Constantinople[2]

Now in the name of glorious God, whoever wants to go beyond the sea along many routes can go by sea and by land according to the regions he sets out from, many of which reach the same goal. Do not expect me to list all the places—cities, towns, castles—that have to be passed through, for my account would be too long, but only some countries and principal places through which one must pass to go the right way.

First, whoever sets out from the regions of the West—as from England, Ireland, Wales, Scotland, or Norway[3]—can, if he wants, go through Germany and the kingdom of Hungary, which borders on the lands of Poland, Pannonia, and Silesia. The king of Hungary is a very powerful and very worthy lord and firmly holds much land; for he holds Hungary and Slavonia and a large part of Comania and Bulgaria, which is called the land of the Bulgars, and a large part of the kingdom of Russia (of which he was made duke), which extends to the land of Niflan [Livonia?][4] and borders on Prussia. And one passes through this lord's land through the city of Cipron [Sopron] and the castle of Neiseburgh [Newburgh] and Male Ville, which is situated towards the end of Hungary, and there one crosses the Danube River.

This Danube River is a very large river. It originates in Germany beneath the mountains towards Lombardy and receives forty other rivers into itself; and it flows through Hungary and Greece and Thrace, and enters the sea to the east—and so forcefully does it pour into the sea that the water keeps its freshness twenty leagues into the sea without mixing with the seawater.

---

1. Chapter numbers are not found in medieval copies, which divide the text up differently in different manuscript traditions and whose chapter headings vary considerably (E contains no chapter divisions or headings and the related C some thirty-five).

2. William of Boldensele (hereafter referred to as WoB), the main source from here to Chapter 14, begins by recording himself sailing to Constantinople from near Genoa, but the *Mandeville* author starts by tracing an *impersonal* overland route borrowed from Albert of Aachen's *History* of the First Crusade. See Appendix B.1.

3. These "western" regions are at the *bottom* of circular medieval world maps oriented to the east, opposite the Earthly Paradise; Chapter 20 mentions travelers *climbing* towards Jerusalem before descending again, imagining the mapped territory as spherical. Readers familiar with more recent European writings might take this passage to be setting up an "Orientalist" framework, but *TBJM*'s contrasts are more various: "over here" / "over there" (see Ch. 4, n. 32); Latin Christian / other Christian; Christian / non-Christian.

4. See "Proper Names" at the end of the Introduction (p. xxv). The work's basic structure emerges here: an impersonal itinerary with information linked to places. Its "digressions" vary greatly in size and nature.

7

Then one comes to Belgrade and enters the land of the Bulgars. There one crosses a stone bridge on the River Marroe [Marrok], and passes through the land of Pincemarcz and comes to Greece at the city of Ny [Nis], and then to Ffinepape [Philippopolis] and then to the city of Adrianople and then to Constantinople, which used to be called Besanzon [Byzantium]. The emperor of Greece usually dwells there.[5] The most beautiful and most noble church in the world is there, the Church of Saint Sophia.[6] In front of this church is the statue of the Emperor Justinian covered with gold, and he is on a horse, crowned; and he used to hold in his hand a round gilded apple, but it has long since fallen out. They say that this signifies that the emperor has lost a great part of his land and his lordship. For he used to be emperor of Romany and Greece and all of Asia Minor, of the land of Syria, the land of Judea, where the city of Jerusalem is, and the land of Egypt, Persia, and Arabia. But he has lost everything except Greece and the country that he alone possesses. And many times some have thought to put the apple back in the hand. But it does not want to stay. This apple signifies the lordship that he had over the world, which is round. And the other hand he holds raised against the East as a sign threatening the wrongdoers. This image stands on a marble pillar.

[Chapter 2]

About the Cross and the Crown of Our Lord

In Constantinople is Our Lord Jesus Christ's cross and His seamless robe, and the sponge and the reed with which He was given gall and vinegar to drink on the cross, and there is also one of the nails with which

---

5. Constantinople, inaugurated by the Roman ruler Constantine as his capital in 330, became the center of eastern Christianity and chief rival to Rome after the seventh-century expansion of Islam when the other early Christian patriarchates (Antioch, Alexandria, Jerusalem) ceased to be in Christian territory. These "Greeks" are the "Byzantines" (who called themselves Romans). Theirs is a Greek (Orthodox or Byzantine) rather than a Latin (Roman Catholic) world, and it is here, where Christian divisions first shape political geography, that the *Mandeville* author begins his account of the world's diversity.

6. Saint Sophia mistranslates "Hagia Sophia," the church's original name (Aya Sophia nowadays), Greek for "Holy Wisdom," meaning Christ, not a female saint, as the Vulgate Latin redactor knew (see Ch. 3 in Appendix A.5). Built in the 530s, this massive church has an enormous dome that seems to float on light, but as Chapter 2 shows, the *Mandeville* author is more interested in its contents than its structure. This architectural wonder became a mosque after the Ottoman Turkish conquest in 1453 and a museum in 1935, soon after the Ottoman Empire collapsed.

He was fixed to the cross.[7] Some people suppose that half of Our Lord's cross is on Cyprus in an abbey of monks that is called the mountain of the Holy Cross of Cyprus, but it is not so. For that cross on Cyprus is the one on which Dismas the good thief was hung.[8] But not everyone knows this and that is harmful; for to profit from the offerings, the monks have it honored and let it be understood that it is Our Lord's cross.

Know that Our Lord's cross was [made] of four kinds of wood, as this verse explains: *In cruce sunt palma cedrus cipressus oliva.*[9] The piece that went straight from the ground to His head was of cypress; and the one that went across to which His hands were nailed was of palm; and the block beneath that was fixed in the rock (in which there was a mortise to hold the foot of the cross) was of cedar; and the tablet that was above His head (which was a foot and a half long, on which the title was written in Hebrew, Greek, and Latin) was of olive.

The Jews made the cross out of these four kinds of wood indeed, for they thought that Our Lord should remain hanging there for as long as His body[10] might last. Therefore they made the foot out of cedar, for cedar does not rot in soil or in water, and they wanted it to last a long time. Then they thought that Our Lord's body would rot and stink, and they therefore made the shaft of the cross out of cypress, which is fragrant, so that the stench of His body might not annoy passersby. The crosspiece was made out of palm, because in the Old Testament when someone won victory he was crowned with palm; and because they thought to have conquered Jesus Christ they made it out of this wood. The tablet with the inscription they made out of olive, because olive signifies peace—as the story of Noah testifies, when the dove brought the olive branch[11] that signaled peace to be made between God and man—and so the Jews thought that they would henceforth have peace after Our Lord's death, for they said that He had caused dissension amongst them.

---

7. See John 19:23. Relics (bodily remains of biblical figures and saints, or objects that had touched their bodies) were important in medieval Christianity, especially the Passion relics. Their importance grew in the later Middle Ages as Latin Christian devotion increasingly emphasized Jesus' suffering. His last hours are recounted in all four Gospels, but the author also draws on extrabiblical sources. Note that this early chapter about Constantinople leaps ahead to the two most important Christian sites, Jerusalem and Paradise, and also mentions Paris, England, and Germany, linking past and present, east and west.

8. See Luke 23:32–43. Dismas is a traditional, not a biblical, name.

9. "In the cross are palm, cedar, cypress, olive." Most of this extrabiblical lore comes from "The Finding of the Holy Cross" in Jacobus de Voragine's mid-thirteenth-century *Legenda Aurea* (*Golden Legend*).

10. "The cross" in some copies, perhaps due to the closeness of *corps* to *croiz.*

11. Gen. 8:11.

Know that Our Lord was fixed to the cross lying on the ground and then was raised with the cross, and thus in its raising He suffered more pain.[12]

Also, the Greeks and likewise the Christians who live overseas say that the tree of the cross that we call cypress was the apple tree whose fruit Adam tasted; and they have it thus in writing. This writing says that when Adam was ill, he told his son Seth to go to Paradise[13] and beseech the angel guarding Paradise to send him some oil from the tree of mercy to anoint his limbs and restore his health. The said Seth went there, but the angel would not let him enter. He also told him that he could not have any oil of mercy, and gave him three seeds from the same apple tree and told him to place them in his father's mouth, and when the tree grew and bore fruit then his father would be healed. When Seth returned he found his father near death, and he put the seeds in his [father's] mouth that grew and became three large trees from which the cross was made that bore the good fruit Jesus Christ—by which fruit Adam and those descended from him are healed and freed from perpetual death, if it were not for our sins.

This holy cross was hidden by the Jews in the ground under the rock of Mount Calvary, and there it remained for two hundred years and more until it was found by Saint Helen, the mother of Constantine, the emperor of Rome. This Helen was daughter of Coel, king of England (which was then called Great Britain), and the Emperor Constans took her as a wife because of her beauty when he was in those regions.[14]

You can know that Our Lord's cross was eight cubits long and the crosspiece was three and half cubits long.[15]

One part of the crown with which He was crowned on the cross and one of the nails and the spearhead and many other relics are in France in the king's chapel. The crown lies in a very ornate crystal vessel, for a king once bought these holy relics from the Genoese, to whom the emperor had given them as collateral because of his great need for money.[16]

---

12. This sadistic mode of crucifixion is not mentioned in the Gospels, but it is depicted in some mystery plays popular in the fourteenth century, such as the English N-Town play 32 or the York Crucifixion play.

13. As Chapter 33 shows, Paradise was considered a real place. It appears more often on medieval world maps than does a central Jerusalem. See Appendix C.1.

14. Helen's discovery (retold with a different emphasis in Ch. 10) is undoubtedly as legendary as her English origins, but the English connection fits with the work's claim that the author was English (his source, the *Golden Legend*, mentions Helen's English roots, but only as one of several unsubstantiated claims).

15. A cubit is an ancient measure of length (about 18 inches) based on the forearm.

16. Baldwin II, King of Jerusalem (r. 1118–1131), bought the relics from the Venetians, not the Genoese. Louis IX (r. 1226–1270) reimbursed the Venetians, obtained the relics, and built the Sainte-Chapelle in Paris as a reliquary, a

Although people say that this crown is of thorns, know that it is of white sea reeds that prick like thorns, for I have seen it and many times have looked most carefully at the one in Paris and the one in Constantinople. For it was all one crown woven of reeds, but someone has split it in two, one part of which is in Paris and the other in Constantinople. And also I have one of the precious thorns that resembles a hawthorn, and it was given to me as a great favor; for there are many broken and fallen off in the vessel where the crown lies, since the thorns break off when the vessel is moved to be shown to great lords.[17]

Know that when Our Lord was taken at night,[18] He was first led into a garden and very harshly questioned; and there the worthless Jews scorned Him and made Him a crown from the branches of the hawthorn that grew in the garden, and they placed the thorns on His head and pressed so hard that the blood ran in many places down His face, His neck, and His shoulders. Therefore the hawthorn has many virtues, for whoever carries a branch with him need not fear lightning, thunder, or storms; and no evil spirit can approach the house he is in or the place where the branch is.

In this garden Saint Peter three times denied Him [Our Lord].[19] Then Our Lord was led before the bishops and the masters of the law in a garden that belonged to Annas; and there He was again questioned and then scorned and harmed and again crowned with a white thorn called barberry that grew in the garden. It has many virtues, and thus a good ointment is made from the leaves of this thorn. Then He was led into Caiaphas' garden and there was crowned with a briar rose. Then He was led into Pilate's chamber (which was strewn with sea rushes) for questioning, and there He was crowned with a crown of sea rushes, and there the Jews sat Him on a chair and dressed Him in a robe and made Him a crown of his [Pilate's] rushes, and knelt before Him scorning Him and saying "*Ave rex Judeorum*."[20] This is the crown—one round half of which is in Paris and the other half is in Constantinople—with which Our Lord was placed on the cross and suffered death for us.

---

glittering jewel of Gothic architecture, consecrated in 1248. The crown of thorns (Matt. 27:29; John 19:2) is first mentioned as a relic in the fifth century. On the spearhead, see n. 21 in this chapter.

17. These statements (two of several such "personal" claims) might be true, but there is no evidence to decide the question. Here as elsewhere, their *rhetorical* function is authenticating.

18. The events described in this and the next paragraph are loosely based on the Gospels (Matt. 26, 27; Mark 14–15; Luke 22–23; John 18–19).

19. See Matt. 26:69–75, for example.

20. "Hail, king of the Jews" (Matt. 27:29).

The emperor of Germany has the spearshaft, but the head is in Paris.[21] Nevertheless the emperor of Constantinople says that he has the spearhead. I have seen it, and it is quite a bit larger than that which is in Paris.

[Chapter 3]
About the City of Constantinople and the Faith of the Greeks

In Constantinople lies Saint Anne, Our Lady's mother, whom Saint Helen had brought from Jerusalem. The body of Saint John Chrysostom, who was archbishop of Constantinople, also lies there; and Saint Luke the Evangelist lies there as well, for his bones were brought there from Betanie [Bithynia], where he had been buried; and many other relics are there.[22] There too is the stone vessel—the marblelike stone is called *enydros*—that always drip water and fill up by themselves every year until they overflow without anything being put into them.[23]

Constantinople is a very beautiful city and very noble and well walled; and the city is triangular, and there is an arm of the sea there called the Hellespont, and others call it the Mouth of Constantinople and others Saint George's Arm; this arm surrounds the two sides of the city. Higher up towards the top of this arm of the sea, towards the Great Sea, used to be the city of Troy on the shore on a very beautiful plain, but the city is scarcely visible there because it was destroyed so long ago.

Around Greece there are many islands, such as Calistres [Thera], Calcas [Colcos], Critige [Critigo], Tesbria [Lesbos], Mineafflaxon [Paros and Naxos], Melo [Milo], Carpate [Scarpanthos], and Lempne [Lemnos]. On this island is Mount Athos, which reaches above the

---

21. The Holy Spear or Lance is mentioned only in John 19:31–37. The one originally venerated in Constantinople was supposedly rediscovered in the fourth century with the Holy Cross. Another spear, also thought to be the biblical one, was discovered in 1098 during the siege of Antioch on the First Crusade; due to political infighting on that expedition, Latin Christians soon doubted its authenticity, but many Eastern Christians took it to be a nail from the Cross. It is possible that this is the spear in question here, since the one discovered earlier was taken by the Turks during the 1453 conquest of Constantinople and given to the papacy in 1492.

22. Much of *TBJM* is structured as a kind of list, like this paragraph, whose syntactic uniformity cannot quite be reproduced in modern English. Besides "and," a common connective is *item* (Latin "also"), typically used in inventories; its frequent use shows the text's kinship with such documents.

23. Many sentences thus change grammatical horses in midstream. The *enydros* goes back to Pliny's *Natural History* (first century CE), but the *Mandeville* author gets it from WoB's mention of columns in the Church of the Holy Sepulcher said to weep for Jesus' death (Ch. 7, not included in Appendix B). Its appearance here shows the author to have been a conscious rewriter of others' texts.

clouds. There are also many languages there, and many countries that all obey the emperor—the Turcople, the Pincenard [Pecheneg], the Comain [Cuman], and many other peoples—and the country of Thrace and Macedonia, of which Alexander was king. Aristotle was born in that country in a city called Strageres [Stagira], quite close to the city of Thrace. Aristotle lies in Stagira, and there is an altar on his tomb, and every year a great holiday is celebrated as if he were a saint; and they come to hold their grand councils together on his altar, and it seems to them that through divine inspiration the best counsel comes to them there beforehand.

In this country there are many high mountains. Towards the end of Macedonia there is a mountain that is called Olympus that separates Macedonia and Thrace and is so high that it reaches above the clouds. And there is another that has the name Athos that is so high that its shadow reaches Lempne [Lemnos], which is an island seventy-seven miles from the mountain. On the summit of these mountains the air is so pure that no wind or breeze blows, and therefore no bird or beast can live there, because the air is too dry.[24] And people in those regions say that philosophers once climbed these mountains and held against their nostrils a sponge softened with water to have moist air, or else they would not have been able to breathe, but would have died for lack of breath because the air is too dry. High up on these mountains they wrote letters in the dust with their fingers, and at the end of a year they climbed back up and found all the letters just as they were written without anything missing, whereby it is clear that the mountains reach right to pure air.

In Constantinople is the very beautiful and well-arranged palace of the emperor; and beside it there is a beautiful area for jousting and games that is all in tiers, and there are steps all around so that everyone can see without blocking anyone else's view; and under these steps are arched stables for the emperor's horses and all the pillars in them are of marble.

An emperor once wanted to have one of his dead relatives placed in the Church of Saint Sophia, and when they dug the hole they found another body in the earth, and on this body [they found] a large plate made of fine gold, on which letters had been written in Hebrew, Greek, and Latin that say this: "Jesus Christ will be born of the Virgin Mary and I believe in Him."[25] The date showed that it was buried one thousand

---

24. High-mountain air is thin because of diminished gravity; it therefore holds less water. In medieval cosmology, however, the four elements (earth, water, air, fire) find their proper place according to their relative weight: at a great height one would find only "pure air." See Chapter 33, n. 574.

25. Unusually for *TBJM*, the inscription is given in French only. This was a very widely circulated legend. Cf. a similar pre-Christian prophecy of Christ in Chapter 32, at the other end of the text.

years before Our Lord was born, and the plate of gold is still in the church treasury, and they say that it was Hermes the Wise.[26]

Although the Greeks are Christians, nevertheless they vary greatly from our right belief,[27] for they say that the Holy Spirit does not proceed from the Son, but only from God the Father, and they do not obey the Church of Rome or the Pope, and they say that their Patriarch has as much power over there as the Pope does over here. Therefore Pope John XXII wrote letters to them saying how Christendom should be entirely united and that they ought to obey a pope who is God's true vicar and to whom God gave full power to bind and loose, for which reasons they ought to obey him. But they sent a very different answer and said this amongst other things: "*Potenciam tuam summam circa tuos subjectos firmiter credimus. Superbiam tuam summam tollerare non possumus. Avariciam tuam summam satiare non intendimus. Dominus tecum quia Dominus nobiscum est.*"[28] And the Pope could get no other answer from them.

They also make the sacrament of the altar out of leavened bread and say that we are mistaken in making it from unleavened bread, for Our Lord used leavened bread at the Last Supper. On Holy Thursday they make their leavened bread in memory of the Last Supper, and they dry it in the sun and keep it all year and give it to the sick instead of the *Corpus Domini*.[29] They perform only one anointing in baptism and do not give unction to the sick. And they say too that there is no Purgatory and that souls have no joy or pain until Judgment Day.

They say that fornication is not a mortal sin but rather is something natural; and that men and women ought to marry only once, and that the children of those who marry more often are illegitimate and engendered in sin. Thus they undo marriages with little reason. And their priests are all married as well. They say that usury is not a mortal sin, and they sell the benefices of holy churches, and others now do the same elsewhere, which is harmful and a great scandal; for nowadays Simon is the crowned king in Holy Church.[30] May God amend it, for insofar as Holy Church staggers and limps, the people cannot be in a good state.

---

26. Hermes Trismegistus ("thrice-greatest"), believed in the Middle Ages to be the author of Neoplatonist and mystical texts in Greek, Latin, and Coptic (the so-called Hermetic books).

27. The following typical mix of the true, the false, and the fantastic comes mostly from Jacques de Vitry's well-known *Historia Orientalis* (Eastern History, early thirteenth century). The Greek response has no known source.

28. "We firmly believe in your supreme power over your subjects. We cannot tolerate your supreme pride. We do not intend to satisfy your supreme avarice. My God be with you because God is with us." Note that the pope is addressed with the singular Latin *tu*.

29. The "Lord's body," meaning the Eucharist (here called the sacrament of the altar).

30. *Simony* (named for Simon Magus; see Acts 8:18–24) is the buying or selling of spiritual things.

The Greeks say that in Lent mass ought not to be sung except on Saturdays and Sundays. And they do not fast on Saturdays at any time of the year except on Christmas Eve or Easter Eve. And they do not let Latin Christians sing at their altars, and if by any chance the Latins do sing there, they wash the altar with holy water. And they say that only one mass a day ought to be sung at the altar. They say that Our Lord never ate, but only gave the appearance of eating. And they say that we sin mortally in shaving our beards, for a beard is the sign of manhood and Our Lord's gift, and those who have it shaved do so to be more pleasing to others and to women. They say that we sin in eating those animals that were forbidden in the Old Testament, such as pigs, hares, and other animals that do not chew their cud. And they say that we sin in eating meat on the three days before Lent, and in eating meat on Wednesdays and eggs and cheese on Fridays. And they excommunicate all those who abstain from eating meat on Saturdays.

In addition, the emperor of Constantinople appoints the patriarch, the archbishops, and the bishops, and bestows the honors and benefices and withdraws them and takes them away when he finds any reason [to do so]. Thus he is lord of the temporal and the spiritual in his country.

If you want to know their alphabet and which letters it has, you can see them here along with the names that they call them:[31]

Alpha Betha Gama Delta Ebrevis Elonge Epilmon Zetha Hetha Iota Kapda Lapda Or Ni Exi Obrevis Pi Cophe Ro Summa Thau Vi Fy Chi Psi Othomega Diacosin.

[Chapter 4]

About Saint John the Evangelist and Hippocrates' Daughter Changed into the Shape of a Dragon

Although these things have nothing to do with showing the way [to Jerusalem], they are nevertheless relevant to what I promised to explain: a part of the customs, manners, and diversities of some countries. And because this is the first country varying from and disagreeing with our country over here in faith and in writing, I have therefore included it so that you might know the diversity that exists between our belief and theirs, for many people enjoy and take pleasure in hearing foreign things spoken about.[32]

---

31. On the alphabets, see Appendix C.3. This long ethnographic "digression" is justified at the start of Chapter 4.

32. This paragraph expresses *TBJM*'s *raison d'être:* to please with *choses estranges* (foreign/strange things). Contrasting "over here" (*deçà*) with "over there" (*delà*) is central to its world (DLMM 24–27).

Now I will return to explaining my route. From Constantinople whoever wants to go by land to Turkey should go towards the city of Nike
[Nicea]; and one passes by the port of Chievetout [Civetot] and all the
time sees Civetot mountain ahead, which is very high. It is a league and
a half from Nicea, where anyone who wants to go by water goes by way of
Saint George's Arm and by sea towards the place where Saint Nicholas
lies and towards many other places. First one goes to the island of Silo
[Chios]. On this island mastic grows on little shrubs and comes out like
the gum of plum or cherry trees.

Then one goes by the island of Patmos, where Saint John the
Evangelist wrote the Apocalypse. And you can know that when Our Lord
suffered His Passion, Saint John was just thirty-two years old, and after
the Passion he lived sixty-seven years and died in his one-hundredth
year. From Patmos one goes to Ephesus, a beautiful city near the sea.
Saint John died there, and was buried behind the altar in a tomb. There
is a very beautiful church there, for Christians used to hold that place;
but there is only manna in Saint John's tomb, for his body was translated
to Paradise. And now the Turks hold the city and the church and all
of Asia Minor, and that is why Asia Minor is called Turkey. Know that
Saint John had his grave dug in his lifetime and then lay in it completely
alive. That is why some say that he did not die, but that he is resting until
Judgment Day. And truly there is a great wonder there, for the earth
of his tomb is often seen visibly crumbling and moving on top, and the
dust as well, as though there were a living man stirring underneath, and
everyone who sees it marvels greatly, and with good reason.

Then from Ephesus one goes by many islands of the sea to the city of
Pateran, where Saint Nicholas was born, and then to the city of Marrea
[Myrrha], where he was elected bishop through God's grace. They make
very good and very strong wines there that are called Myrrhan wine.
From there one goes to the island of Crete, which the emperor gave to
the Genoese.[33]

Then one passes by the island of Cohos [Cos] and the island of
Langho [Lango], of both of which Ypocras [Hippocrates] was lord. They
say that Hippocrates' daughter is still on that island of Lango in the
form of a large dragon that is a good one hundred fathoms long—as
they say, for I have not seen it.[34] And the islanders call her the Lady of
the country. She lies in the vaults of an old castle and shows herself two
or three times a year and harms no one if no one harms her. She was
thus changed and transformed from a beautiful young woman into a
dragon by a goddess with the name Diana, and they say that she will

---

33. Crete was held by the Venetians after the Fourth Crusade (1204).

34. No exact source has been found for this legend, which recalls widespread tales
of the daring kiss (*fier baiser*) and (half-)dragon or (half-)serpent ladies (e.g., the
fabled Melusine; see Ch. 16, n. 325); some later travelers (e.g., Felix Fabri) also
mention it. Cf. the story of "a beautiful lady of Fairy" in Chapter 16.

return to her [former] state when they find a knight brave enough to dare go and kiss her on the mouth. But after she is changed back into a woman, she will not live long. Not long ago a knight of the Hospital of Rhodes[35] who was worthy and brave said that he would go and kiss her. And he mounted a courser and went to the castle and entered the cellar and the dragon began to raise its head towards him. And when the horse saw how hideous it was, he fled and carried the knight against his will to a rock and from that rock he jumped into the sea, and thus the knight perished.

Also, a young man who knew nothing about this dragon got out of a ship and went about the island right to the castle and entered the cellar and went so far in that he found a room and saw there a young woman combing her hair and looking into a mirror. She had a great deal of treasure around her, and he thought that she was a loose woman who stayed there to receive her clients. He waited until the young woman saw his shadow in the mirror and turned towards him and asked what he wanted. He answered that he wanted to be her lover, and she asked whether he was a knight, and he said no. "Well then," she said, "you cannot be my lover. But go back to your companions and get yourself knighted, and tomorrow I will come out of here and come to you up above and you are going to kiss me on the mouth—and do not be afraid, for I will do you no harm, and although it seems to you that I am hideous to see, that is caused by a spell, for I am such as you now see me. And if you kiss me, you will have all this treasure and be my husband and lord of this island." At this point he left and went towards his companions in the ship and got himself knighted. Then the next day he went to meet the young woman to kiss her. When he saw her come out of the cellar in such a terrible shape he was so afraid that he fled to the ship and she went after him; and when she saw that he would not return to her she began to cry and roar like a woman in pain[36] and turned back; and right away the knight died, and ever since no knight can see her without dying right away. But when someone so brave comes that he dare kiss her on the mouth, he will not die, but will transform the young woman into her right shape and be lord of the land.

Then one comes to the island of Rhodes, which the Hospitallers hold and govern. They took this island from the emperor in former times; and this island used to be called Collos [Colos] and the Turks

---

35. The Knights Hospitaller: a military religious order, officially recognized by the pope in the early twelfth century, that tended the sick while also defending crusader territories. With the Knights Templar (Ch. 11, n. 168), they were the most dominant such order in the Holy Land. Originally of Jerusalem (Ch. 10, n. 149), they were displaced several times as Latin Christian holdings were lost to Muslim reconquest. In the fourteenth century, when this passage was composed, they were known as the Knights of Rhodes.

36. "like a woman in pain": *come dolente*. C, D, and E are more literal: "as a thing that hadde muche sorwe" (HMT 1.16; cf. Seymour 2002, 16; WBJM 13).

still call it that, and Saint Paul wrote to the islanders there in his letters *ad Collosenses.*[37] This island is a good eight hundred leagues from
Constantinople going by sea.

[Chapter 5]

About the Diversities on Cyprus. About the Way from Cyprus to Jerusalem and about the Miracle of a Pit Full of Sand

From this island of Rhodes one goes to Cyprus, where there are very
strong wines that are red first and after a year they become white;
and the older they are, the whiter they are, and the clearer and more
fragrant.

By way of this route one passes near the gulf of Cathalie [Sathalie],
where there used to be a great land and a beautiful city that had the
name Cathalie, but the city and country were lost through a young man's
folly. For he had a beautiful and well-formed young lady[38] who died
suddenly, and he had her placed in a marble sarcophagus, and because
of the great love that he had for her, he went at night to her tomb and
opened it and lay with her and then left. When he went there at the end
of nine months, a voice came to him and said to him, "Go to the tomb
of that woman and open it and look at what you have begotten on her
and take good care not to avoid doing this, for if you do not go harm will
come to you." He went there and opened the tomb, out of which flew a
greatly disfigured head that was hideous to see. This head gazed at the
city and the country, and right away the city collapsed into the abyss.
The crossing there is most dangerous and bottomless.

From Rhodes to Cyprus it is five hundred leagues and more, and
whoever wishes to could easily go to Cyprus without entering Rhodes,
leaving Rhodes aside. This Cyprus is a very beautiful island and very
large, and there are four main cities, and there is an archbishop in
Nichocie [Nicosia] and three other bishops in the country. In Famagoust
[Famagosta] there is one of the world's main seaports. Christians and
Saracens[39] and peoples of all nations arrive there, and also at Limeceez
[Limassol].

---

37. Epistle to the Colossians (New Testament). Medieval authors often confused
Colossae (a city in Phrygia) with the Colossus of Rhodes (the statue), one of the
ancient world's Seven Wonders.

38. "young lady": *damoisele,* which here could also mean "loose woman." Akin to
the Gorgon/Medusa myth and usually associated with the Gulf of Sathalie, this
legend was well known in various medieval retellings: for example, as the *Laide
Semblance* (hideous form) in a thirteenth-century Merlin story. The version found
here may have come from Gervase of Tilbury's *Otia Imperialia* 2.12.

39. Of uncertain origin, *Saracenus* (Latin) seems originally to have meant a
nomadic Arabic tribe, but by the eighth century Latin authors were using it

On Cyprus is the Mountain of the Holy Cross where there are black monks.[40] And the cross of the good thief Dismas is there, as I told you above.[41] Some believe that it is half of Our Lord's cross, but it is not, and they do harm who let this be understood. On Cyprus lies Saint Zenonime [Sosomen], for whom those of the country celebrate a great festival, and in the castle of Damurs [God-of-Love] lies the body of Saint Hilarius, and they look after it very respectfully. Near Famagosta, Saint Barnaby the Apostle was born.

On Cyprus they hunt with papions[42] that look like tamed leopards that catch the wild animals all too well. They are a little bigger than lions and fiercer, and they catch the wild animals more violently and more fiercely than the dogs do. They also hunt with tamed dogs, but the papions hunt more fiercely.

On Cyprus they have a custom that lords and servants all eat on the ground, for they have pits dug around the halls as deep as the knees and they pave these well; and when they want to eat they jump in and sit down, and then the tablecloth is put on the other side on the paving. For this is the way to be cooler over there, because the country is hotter than it is here. At great festivals and for foreigners, if they come, they set out both benches and tables, just as is done in these regions, but they prefer to sit on the ground.

From Cyprus one goes towards Jerusalem and towards other places that the Saracens hold. And in one day and one night, if the wind is good, one is at the port of Thir [Tyre], which is now called Sur, and it is an entrance to Syria. There used to be a very beautiful Christian city there, but the Saracens destroyed much of it and guard the port very attentively because they are afraid of the Christians and in order to receive the tribute. One could well go straight to this port without going into Cyprus, but one usually goes to Cyprus to rest on land or to get the things necessary for their provisions there. On the seashore many rubies and garnets are found. The fountain of which Holy Scripture speaks is there: "*Fons ortorum et puteus aquarum vivencium.*"[43] In this city of Tyre the

---

of the Muslim invaders of Christendom. From Latin the word entered various European vernaculars and became the generic (often negative) term for any Muslim. "Saracens" has not been translated as "Muslims," however, so as not to substitute modern associations for medieval.

40. Of the Benedictine Order; the monks would actually have been Orthodox (Greek) Christians.

41. In Chapter 2.

42. Papions are large carnivores, probably of the cat family. The name comes from Jacques de Vitry's *Eastern History:* "there are *papions* there that they call wild dogs" (quoted from DLMM 130, n. 7). WoB calls them *domestici leopardi* (Deluz 1972, 210; Grotefend 1855, 242); they also appear as *luppars princiez* ("princely leopards") in Long John's French (Deluz 1972, 302).

43. "A fountain of gardens and a well of living waters" (Song of Sol. 4:15).

woman said to Our Lord, "*Beatus venter qui te portavit et ubera que suxisti.*"[44] Our Lord pardoned the sins of the woman of Canaan there.[45] In front of Tyre used to be the rock on which Our Lord sat and preached, and on this rock was founded the church of Saint Savior.

Eight miles from Tyre to the east, on the sea, is the city of Sarphen or Sarepte of Sidoniens [As-Sarafand, Lebanon]. Elijah the prophet used to dwell there, [and] there he raised Jonas the widow's son from the dead. And five miles from Sarphen is the city of Sidon, where Dido came from, who was Aeneas' wife after the destruction of Troy and who founded the city of Carthage in Africa, and Sidon is now called Saiete. In the city of Tyre Dido's father Agenor reigned.[46] And sixteen miles from Sidon is Beirut; and from Beirut to Sardenar is three days' travel. And from Sardenar it is five leagues to Damascus.

Whoever wants to go farther by sea and come closer to Jerusalem goes from Cyprus to the port of Jaffa, which is the closest port to the city of Jerusalem; for from that port to Jerusalem is only a day and a half's travel. This city is called Jaffa after one of Noah's sons who had the name Japhet, who founded it, and it is now called Joppa. And know that Jaffa is the oldest city in the world, for it was founded before Noah's flood. And still visible in the rock is the place where the iron chains were attached with which Andromeda, a great giant,[47] was imprisoned before Noah's flood. One of this giant's rib bones is fifty feet long.

Whoever arrives at the first port of Tyre or Sur, about which I have spoken, goes by land, if he wishes, to Jerusalem. And one goes from Sur to the city of Acre in one day. This city used to be called Tholomaida [Ptolemais], and it was once a very beautiful Christian city, but it is utterly ruined, and it is situated by the sea. And from Venice to Acre by sea is two thousand and eighty Lombard leagues.[48] And from Calabria

---

44. "Blessed is the womb that bore you and the breasts that you suckled" (Luke 11:27–28).

45. Matt. 15:21–28; Mark 7:24–30.

46. Elijah and the widow's son (unnamed in the Bible): 1 Kings 17:17–24. Dido, legendary queen of Carthage (cf. Virgil, *Aeneid* 1 and 4), was Aeneas' wife only in a Christian sense (through consummation). Her father was called Belus. This is one of the text's few literary references.

47. Andromeda was not a giant but the king of Ethiopia's daughter and a sea monster's captive. After taking the Gorgon Medusa's head, Perseus rescued her from the rocks where she was chained. "Maiden" became "monster" by a misreading of a brief reference in a popular encyclopedia compiled in the third century CE (Solinus, *Collectanea,* Ch. 34).

48. A *league* is a locally variable measure (about 2.5 to 4.5 miles, or 4 to 7.5 kilometers). Like the mile, it also had a longer nautical length. C and E misleadingly translate "league" as "mile." WJBM (162, nn. 11 and 13) takes a league to be two miles; DLMM (131, n. 15) takes it to be a nautical mile, claiming that for the maritime distances here it gives accurate measures. The *Mandeville* author equates Lombard *miles* with English *miles* in Chapter 13, where he discusses varying local

or Sicily to Acre is one thousand three hundred Lombard leagues. The island of Crete is exactly halfway. And near this city of Acre one hundred and twenty stades[49] towards the sea, southwards on the right-hand side, is Mount Carmel, where Elijah the prophet dwelt. The Carmelite Order of Friars was first founded there. This mountain is neither large nor high, and at the foot of this mountain there used to be a beautiful and good Christian city that was called Caiaphas [Haifa] because Caiaphas founded it, but it is all quite ruined. And to the left of Mount Carmel there is a town with the name Saffran [Shefaram] situated on another mountain. Saint James and Saint John were born there and in the place of their birth is a beautiful church. From Tholomaida, which now has the name Acoun [Acre], to the great mountain that is called the Ladder of Tyre is one hundred stades.

Past this city of Acre runs a small river with the name Beleoon [Belus], and close by is the Fosse of Mennon, which is a round pit that is a good one hundred cubits in size. It is all full of bright sand from which they make beautiful and clear glass. People come to seek that sand by sea in ships and by land in carts, and when they have entirely emptied that pit of this sand, the next day it is again as full as before, and this is a great wonder. There is always a great wind in this pit that always disturbs the sand and makes it whirl about marvelously. And whoever puts any metal into this pit in the middle of the sand, this metal is changed into glass. And the glass too that is made of this sand, if one puts it back into that pit, it becomes sand as before. Some say that this pit is a vent of the Sandy Sea.[50]

Also, from the above-mentioned Acre one goes in four days to the city of Palestine, which belonged to the Philistines and is now called Gaza, which is to say "rich city"; and it is very beautiful and well peopled and situated a bit above the sea. From this city Samson the Strong brought the gates on to a high knoll when he was captured in this city, and in the palace he killed the king and himself and many of the best of the Philistines who had blinded him and sheared his hair and then imprisoned him, for they mocked him. And that is why he brought the house

---

measures of distance. The Vulgate Latin offers a clearer definition (Hakuyt 1589, 26), while Michel Velser recounts his own search for a definition (Morrall 1974, 27 and 21 n. to line 14). One sees here the difficulties created by the absence of an internationally standardized system of measurement.

49. Stade: an ancient Greek measure, 600 Greek feet long (about 175–200 meters). At its next mention, three French copies offer a definition: "note that one stade is counted as 120 steps, each step as 10 feet." On the cubit, mentioned below, see Chapter 2, n. 15.

50. This legend goes back to Josephus' first-century *Jewish War* 2.10.2 and Pliny's *Natural History* 36.65, but the *Mandeville* author probably took it from Thietmar's Latin memoir of his 1217 pilgrimage (Régnier-Bohler 1997, 941). The "Sandy Sea" is described in the account of Prester John's Land below (Ch. 30).

down on them.[51] From there one goes to the city of Caesarea and then to the Castle of Pilgrims and to Ascalonge [Ascalon] and then to Jaffa and to Jerusalem, if one wants to.

Whoever wants to go first by land to Babylon[52] where the Sultan usually dwells—to request from him the favor of going more safely through the country, or to go to Mount Sinai before one goes to Jerusalem and then to return through Jerusalem—then one goes[53] there from Gaza to the Castle Daire [Darum], and then one comes out of Syria and enters the desert, where the routes are very sandy, and this desert extends for a good eight days' travel. But inns are always found along the way, a days' travel apart, where all the necessities of life are found. This desert is called Alhilet, and when one comes out of this desert one enters Egypt, and Egypt is called Canopat, and according to another language it is called Mersin. One finds first a good town that has the name Balbez and it is at the end of the kingdom of Halappe [Aleppo], and from there one goes to Babylon and to Cairo.

[Chapter 6]

About the Many Names of the Sultans and About Their Way of Life and About the Tower of Babylon

In Babylon[54] there is a beautiful church of Our Lady where she dwelt for seven years when she fled the land of Judea for fear of King Herod. And there lies the body of Saint Barbara the virgin, and there Joseph dwelt after he had been sold by his brothers. And there Nabugodonosor [Nebuchadnezzar] had the three children put in the fire because they

---

51. Samson's last days: Judg. 16. Misreading WoB, the *Mandeville* author goes on to muddle the geography; north to south the real route is Acre, Castle of Pilgrims, Caesarea, Jaffa, Ascalon, Gaza.

52. Near Cairo. On Babylon/Cairo, see n. 54 below.

53. Another sentence that changes grammatical horses in midstream.

54. The ancient (and biblical) city of Babylon in southern Mesopotamia is confused here with the Egyptian city, one of three contiguous settlements that became Cairo. Egyptian Babylon was a military center developed by the Romans in the first century CE from a Persian city on the Nile's east bank. It next belonged to the Byzantines, whom the expanding Muslim Arabs expelled in 641; the latter's siege camp became al-Fustat, Egypt's Muslim capital under the Umayyads and Abbasids. The Shi'ite Fatimids captured al-Fustat in 969 and founded a new political center beside it that they soon called al-Qahira (the Victorious). It was burned down in 1168 to prevent its capture by the crusaders. Saladin, founder of the Sunni Ayyubids, rebuilt it soon after, incorporating it into Cairo (it is now known as Masr al-Atiqah, or Old Cairo). Between al-Fustat and al-Qahira, Saladin built the Citadel, el-Kalah ("Calahelit" in the text), which became the center of power; enclosed within walls, this tripartite site soon became one of the world's great cities.

were of good faith who in Hebrew were called *Ananie, Azarie,* and *Misaël,* just as the psalm *Benedicite* names them; but Nebuchadnezzar called them something else: *Sidrac, Misac,* and *Abdenago,* that is to say, glorious God, victorious God, God over all kingdoms. It was by a miracle that he saw the Son of God, just as he said, go with his children through the fire.[55] There the Sultan dwells in his Calahelit, for his seat is normally there in a beautiful and strong and large castle set on a rock. This is in Cairo near Babylon. In this castle, when the Sultan is there, there are always more than six thousand people in residence to serve him and guard the castle; they receive everything they need from the Sultan's court when there is no war or other important matter.

I ought to know this well, for I dwelt with him as a soldier in his wars for quite a while against the Bedouins, and he would have married me very highly to a landed prince's daughter and given me great inheritances if I had wanted to renounce my Creator. But I had no desire to have anything that he could promise me.[56]

Know that the Sultan is lord of five kingdoms, which he conquered and took possession of by force. These are the kingdom of Canopat, which is Egypt; and the kingdom of Jerusalem, of which David and Solomon were kings; and the kingdom of Syria, whose capital city is Damascus; and the kingdom of Halappe [Aleppo] in the land of Matz [Homs?]; and the kingdom of Arabia, which belonged to one of the three kings who went to offer gifts to Our Lord when He was born;[57] and he possesses many other lands. Besides this he is Califfes [Caliph], which is a very great thing. *Sultan* in their language is as much as to say *king.*

There used to be five Sultans, and now there is only the Sultan of Egypt.[58] The first Sultan was Xaracon, who was from Media [in Persia] and was the father of Sahaladin [Saladin], who took the Caliph of Egypt and killed him and became Sultan by force. Then Saladin was Sultan, at which time King Richard of England was there with many others who guarded the passage that Saladin could not go through.[59] After Saladin,

---

55. On Mary and Herod, see Matt. 2:13–15; on Joseph, Gen. 37:26–28; on Nebuchadnezzar, Dan. 3, where the children are named Shadrach, Meshach, and Abednego (Hananiah, Mishael, and Azariah in Hebrew). The *Benedicite* ("Bless [the Lord]"), also known as "The Canticle [Song] of the Three Holy Children," derives from a sixty-eight-verse passage at Dan. 3:23, found only in some textual traditions, including that of Jerome's Vulgate. It was sung at Lauds, an early-morning prayer in the sequence of daily prayers.

56. Christians did indeed serve Muslim rulers, so this unverifiable claim has a whiff of truth in its heady perfume of romance.

57. Cf. Matt. 2:1–12.

58. On this tangled account see Appendix C.4. "Melech" in the Sultan's names comes from the Arabic *Malik,* or king.

59. Richard I (1157–1199, known as Coeur de Lion, or Lionheart): one of the leaders of the partly successful Third Crusade (1187–1192), a response to Muslim re-conquests under Saladin (1137–1193), who in 1187 brought an end to the Latin

his son Boradin reigned, and afterwards his nephew. Then the Comains [Cumans], who were like serfs in Egypt, sensed their great power and chose a sultan from themselves, whom they had named Melechsala. And in his time the king of France Saint Lodowyz [Louis IX] entered the country and fought against him and was captured and imprisoned. He [Melechsala] was killed by his own serfs, who then chose another [Sultan] by the name of Timpieman, and he had Saint Louis freed from prison for a ransom.[60] Then another of the Comains by the name of Cachas reigned, and he killed Timpieman in order to be Sultan, and he was called Melechimees. And then another by the name of Bendochdar who killed Melechemees; and then another man so as to be Sultan, and he was called Melechdar. In his time the good king Edward of England[61] entered Syria and did great harm to the Saracens, and then this Sultan was poisoned in Damascus. His son thought to reign after him as heir, and he had himself called Melechsach. But another man by the name of Elphi drove him out of the country and made himself Sultan. This latter took the city of Tripelle [Tripoli] and massacred many Christians in the year of grace 1289. Then he was imprisoned by another man who wanted to be Sultan. But this latter was soon killed.

Afterwards the son of Elphi was elected Sultan and called himself Mellechassera, and he took the city of Acoun [Acre] and drove out all the Christians. Then he too was imprisoned, and his brother was made Sultan and called Melechnasser. Then someone called Guytoga took him and put him in prison in the castle of Montruial [Montreal] and made himself Sultan by force and called himself Melechadel, and he was a Tartar.[62] But the Comains drove him out of the country and made one of their own Sultan by the name of Lachin, and he had himself called Melechmanser. This same Melechmanser was playing chess one day and his sword was lying beside him such that someone grew angry with him and killed him with his own sword. Afterwards they had much disagreement over the choice of a Sultan and finally they agreed on Melechnasser, whom Guytoga had put in prison in Montruial [Montreal]. He reigned long and governed wisely, such that his eldest son Melechmader was

---

Kingdom of Jerusalem. The likely reference here is to the Battle of Arsur (Arsuf) in September 1191, when Richard's army successfully defended itself against Saladin's attack; a year later the two brilliant military commanders negotiated a truce at Jaffa, effectively ending the crusade.

60. The pious warrior Louis IX (1214–1270) of France led two unsuccessful crusades (1248–1254 and 1270), dying on the latter. The reference here is to events of 1250, when Louis was captured invading Egypt and ransomed a month later; he remained in the East for another four years, working to improve the crusader states' defenses. Canonized in 1297, he thus became Saint Louis.

61. While still Prince, England's Edward I (1239–1307) led a crusade alongside Louis IX's second expedition but stayed on until 1272.

62. That is, a Mongol: see Chapter 23, n. 444. For more on the Mongol invasion of the Islamic world, see Chapter 24.

elected after him. Melechmader's son had him secretly killed in order to have power and had himself called Melechmadabron, and he was Sultan when I left there.[63] Also, the Sultan can easily lead out of Egypt more than twenty thousand armed men. And from Syria and Turkey and the other countries he holds he can draw more than fifty thousand, and they all belong to him, without mentioning the people of his own country, who are countless. Each gets nearly one hundred and twenty florins a year.[64] But on that each has to keep three horses and a camel. Throughout the cities and the towns are admirals who have to govern these people: one has to manage four,[65] another five, another more, another less, and the admiral takes as much [pay] for himself alone as all the other soldiers under him have. Therefore when the Sultan wants to promote any brave soldier, he makes him an admiral. And when times are hard the knights are poor and sell their horses and their gear.

Also, the Sultan has four wives, one Christian and three Saracen, one of whom remains in Jerusalem and the other in Damascus and the other in Ascalon. But they move about to the other cities, and when he wants to he goes to visit them. And he has as many lovers as he wants, for he has the most beautiful and the most noble young women of his country brought before him, and he has them watched over and served most honorably; and when he wants to have one to sleep with her, he has them all brought before him and looks everywhere to see who best pleases him, and to her he sends or throws the ring from his finger, and right away she is led away to be bathed and dressed and adorned nobly, and at night she is led into his bedchamber; and he does this as often as he likes.

No foreigner comes before the Sultan who is not dressed in gold cloth or tars or camlet[66] in the manner in which the Saracens are dressed. As soon as anyone first sees the Sultan, whether at the windows or elsewhere, he is required to kneel and kiss the earth, for that is the manner in which those who would speak with him show their reverence. And while foreign messengers are before him and speaking to him, the Sultan's men are around him with drawn swords and gisarmes[67] and axes, their arms raised to strike them [the foreigners], if they say something that displeases the Sultan. Also, no foreigner comes before

---

63. See Appendix A.1 for an anticrusading letter inserted here in three French and two Latin manuscripts.

64. First minted in Florence (hence the name) in the mid-thirteenth century, the florin was a gold coin that became a standard measure of value in European and Mediterranean trade until the sixteenth century.

65. Towns? Hundred or thousand people?

66. "tars or camlet": luxurious fabrics made in the East, the latter possibly of camel hair.

67. "gisarmes": probably pike-like weapons, each consisting of a long pointed blade on a shaft.

him and makes a request that he does not grant, should it be reasonable and not contrary to his law [religion]. And the other princes over there do likewise, for they say that no one should come before a prince without being better off, and a visitor should be happier on leaving his presence than he was on coming before him.

Know that this Babylon that I have spoken to you about, near where the Sultan dwells, is not the great Babylon where the different languages were made through a miracle of God when the great Tower of Babel had begun to be built where the walls were once made sixty-four stades high; that is in the great desert of Arabia on the way when one is going towards the kingdom of Chaldea. But it has been a long time since anyone has dared go near the tower, for it is completely deserted and there are dragons and large snakes and different poisonous animals round about. Together with the city, this tower was a good twenty-five leagues in circumference around the walls, as the people of that country say and as one can estimate and understand. Although it is called the Tower of Babylon, nevertheless many houses and many grand and large dwellings were laid out there. This tower encompasses a large territory, for the tower alone encompasses ten square leagues. This tower was founded by the King Nembroch [Nimrod], who was king of that country; and he was the first king of the world, and he had an image made in his father's name and forced all his subjects to worship it; and other lords at that time began to do the same, and thus began idols and simulacra.[68] The tower and the city are very well situated and on a fine plain called the plain of Semaar [Shinar]. The walls of the city are two hundred cubits high and fifty cubits thick, and the Euphrates River flows through the middle of the city and the tower as well. But Cyrus the king of the Persians took their river and destroyed the whole city and the tower also, for he divided the river into three hundred and sixty small streams; for he had sworn that he would make the river such that a woman could easily cross it without having to undress, for he had lost many brave men who thought to cross the river by swimming.[69]

From Babylon where the Sultan dwells to go straight between east and north towards this great Babylon is a forty-day journey through the desert. This great Babylon is not in the Sultan's land or in his power. Rather, it is in the power and in the lordship of Persia, but that is held

---

68. Tower of Babel: Gen. 11:1–9; Nimrod: Gen. 10:8–12. Both partly come through Brunetto Latini's *Tresor* 1.24. Nimrod's responsibility for Babel and idolatry is a traditional claim rather than scriptural; the idolatry has been given a peculiarly Mandevillean form: see Chapters 18 (n. 354) and 34 for more on idols and simulacra. On the stade, see Chapter 5, n. 49; on the cubit, mentioned shortly, see Chapter 2, n. 15.

69. This version of the story of the Persian king, Cyrus the Great (sixth century BCE), comes from Martinus Polonus' popular, late thirteenth-century Latin chronicle of popes and emperors; it ultimately goes back to Herodotus (*Histories* 1.189) and may be alluded to in Isa. 44:27 and Jer. 50:23 and 51:29.

by the Great Chan [Khan], who is the great emperor and the most sovereign of all the regions over there, and lord of the island of Cathay and of many other islands and a great part of India; and his land borders on Prester John's Land, and he holds so much land he does not know where it ends, and he is incomparably greater and more powerful than the Sultan is. I will speak more fully about his power and his estate when I speak about the land and the countries of India.

Also, the city of Methon [Mecca] where Machomet lies[70] is likewise in the great deserts of Arabia; there his body lies most honorably in their temple that the Saracens call *Musket* [mosque]. And from lesser Babylon[71] where the Sultan dwells to Mecca mentioned above is a good thirty-two days' travel.

Know that the kingdom of Arabia is a very large country, but there is too much desert there and no one can live in that desert for lack of water, for all the land is sandy and dry; and it is not fertile because there is no moisture and because there is so much desert; for if there were rivers and springs and the land were as it is elsewhere, it would be all populated with people as much as places elsewhere; for there is a great multitude of people where the lands are habitable. Arabia extends from the ends of the kingdom of Chaldea to the far end of Africa and borders on the land of Idumea towards the end of Botron [Basra].

In Chaldea the capital city is Baldak [Baghdad?], and of Africa the capital city is Carthage, which Dido the wife of Aeneas founded. This Aeneas was from Troy and then was king of Italy.[72] Mesopotamia also borders on the deserts of Arabia and is a very large country. In this country is the city of Arrami [Haran], where Abraham's father dwelt and which Abraham left at the angel's command. And Affraim [Ephrem], who was a great scholar and a great teacher, was from this city. And Theophilus, whom Our Lady saved from the enemy, was also from there. Mesopotamia lasts from the Euphrates River to the Tigris, for it lies between these two rivers; and beyond this river of the Tigris is Chaldea, which is a very large kingdom. In this kingdom, in Baldak mentioned above, the caliph used to dwell who used to be like emperor and pope to the Arabs, lord of the temporal and the spiritual. He was successor to Muhammad and his descendants. This city of Baldak used to be called Suthiz [Susa]. Nebuchadnezzar founded it, and there Saint Daniel the prophet dwelt, and there he had many divine visions and there he gave the explanation of dreams.[73] In the past there used to be three caliphs,

---

70. A common Christian pilgrims' error. Muhammad was buried in Medina.

71. Called "lesser," this Babylon is thus distinguished from the great Babylon mentioned above.

72. On Dido and Aeneas, see Chapter 5, n. 46.

73. Abraham: Gen. 12:1–5. Theophilus' pact with the Devil (a precursor of the Faust story) comes from the popular Miracles of the Virgin, as E points out (WBJM 22). "Saint" Daniel and dreams: Dan. 2.

that of the Arabians and the Chaldeans, and they dwelt in the city of Baldak [Baghdad] mentioned above. And in Cairo near Babylon dwelt the Caliph of the Egyptians, and in Morocco on the West Sea dwelt the Caliph of the Barbarians and the Africans. And now there are no more caliphs since the time of Saladin, for at that time the Sultan was called Caliph. Thus did the caliphs lose their name.

Also, know that lesser Babylon where the Sultan dwells and the city of Cairo that is nearby are very great cities and very beautiful, and they are situated near each other. Babylon is situated on the River Gyon [Gihon], otherwise called the Nile, which comes from the Earthly Paradise.[74] This river of the Nile, every year when the sun enters the sign of Cancer, begins to rise, and it rises for as long as the sun is in Cancer and in Leo and rises in such a manner that it is sometimes so large that it is a good twenty cubits or more in depth, and as a result it causes great damage to the goods on the land, for as a result no one can work the land because of the great moisture, and therefore there are hard times in the country. Also, when it barely rises there are hard times in the country for lack of moisture. When the sun enters the sign of the Virgin, then the river begins to grow smaller and smaller, such that when the sun is in the sign of Libra it returns to within its banks. This river comes flowing from Paradise through the deserts of India, and then runs into the ground and flows for a long time and a large country under the earth, and then it comes out under a mountain that people call Aloch [Atlas] that is between India and Ethiopia, five months' travel from the way into Ethiopia. Then it flows around Ethiopia and Morekane [Mauretania] and goes all along the land of Egypt to the city of Alexandria at the end of Egypt, and there it flows into the sea. Around this river are many birds (storks) that they call ibises.

[Chapter 7]

About the Country of Egypt. About the Phoenix of Arabia. About the City of Cairo. About the Knowledge of Balm. And About Joseph's Granaries

Egypt is a long and narrow country, for it cannot be widened towards the desert.[75] Because of a lack of water the whole country is situated along this river of the Nile; for the country extends only as far as this

---

74. Gihon, one of Eden's four rivers (Gen. 2:13; see Ch. 33), often identified with the Nile, which was regularly depicted on medieval world maps. See Appendix C.1.

75. For medieval Latin Christians Egypt evoked not pyramids and mummies but biblical history (the Holy Family fleeing there; the Israelite Exodus), crusading (from the twelfth century on), and the wonders of the wealthy Islamic world.

river can serve by flooding or otherwise, and the country is as wide as
the flood can spread through it. For it never rains or rains only a little
in this country. They have no water except from this river; and because
it never rains in this country, but the air is always pure and clear, there
are therefore good astronomers in this country; for they find no clouds
to hinder them. Also, the city of Cairo is larger than that of Babylon
and is situated above towards the desert of Syria, a little above the just-
mentioned river.

There are two parts in Egypt: the upper, which is towards Ethiopia;
and the lower, which is towards Arabia. The land of Ramses and the land
of Gessen [Goshen] are in Egypt. Egypt is a strong country, for there
are many bad ports there because of the large rocks that are hard to
navigate past. In Egypt towards the east is the Red Sea, which extends
to the city of Coston [Kus]. Towards the west is the land of Libya, which
is a very dry land and not very fertile, for it is too hot, and that land is
called Ffuth [Qush?]. Towards the south is Ethiopia, and towards the
north is the desert, which extends to Syria. Thus the country is strong on
all sides. It is a good fifteen days' travel in length and more than twice
as much through the desert, and it is only three days' travel in breadth.
And between Egypt and Nubia it is a good twelve days' travel through
desert. The Nubians are Christians, but they are black as blackberries[76]
because of the great heat of the sun.

In Egypt there are five provinces: one by the name of Sahitz [Sâ
el-Hagar]; the other Demeser [Damanhûr]; the other Resich [Rosetta],
which is an island in the Nile; the other Alexandria; and the other is the
land of Damietta. This city used to be very strong, but it was twice won by
the Christians; and therefore the Saracens then knocked down the walls
and the fortifications and built another city farther from the sea and
called it New Damietta, so that no one lives in the Old Damietta. One
of the ports of Egypt is there and the other is in Alexandria, which is a
very strong city, but it would have no drinking water, if it did not come
by canal from the Nile to go into their cisterns; and if their water were
cut off they could not last. There are few fortresses in Egypt because the
country is strong in itself.

In the deserts of Egypt a holy worthy hermit encountered a monster[77]
just like a man with two large sharp horns on his forehead, and he had
a man's body to the navel and beneath he had a body like a goat's. The
worthy man asked him who he was, and the monster answered that he

---

76. *More* or *mors* (depending on the copy): either "blackberry" or "Moor"; the
Mandeville author's source, Brunetto Latini's *Tresor* 1.124, reads *meure*, or
"blackberry."

77. A story usually associated with Saint Anthony, as in the *Mandeville* author's
likely source, Gervase of Tilbury's *Otia Imperialia* (1.18, on fauns and satyrs). C
defines "monster" as "a thing difformed agen[st] kynde [nature] bothe of man or
of be[a]st or of anything elles" (HMT 1.30).

was a mortal creature such as God had created him and that he dwelt in that desert seeking his sustenance, and he entreated the hermit to pray for him to God who, to save the human race, descended from Heaven and was born of the Virgin and suffered His Passion and death, as we know, and through whom we live and have our being. The head of this monster with the horns is still in Alexandria as a wonder.

In Egypt is the city of Heliopolis: that is to say, the city of the sun. In this city there is a temple that was built round in the manner of the Temple of Jerusalem. The priests of this temple have in writing the date of the bird that has the name phoenix, of which there is only one in the world; and it comes to burn itself on the altar of the temple after five hundred years, for it lives that long. The priests adorn this altar and place on it thorns and live sulfur and other things that light easily, such that the bird comes to burn itself all to ashes. On the first day afterwards a worm is found in the ashes, and on the second day the bird is found completely intact, and on the third day it flies away, and thus there is always only a single bird of this nature and truly it is a great miracle of God. This bird can easily be compared to God, in that there is only one God and in that Our Lord rose again on the third day.[78] This bird is often seen flying in those parts, and it is hardly bigger than an eagle and has a crest on its head bigger than a peacock's, and its neck is all yellow the color of a brilliant oriole, and its back is indigo, and its wings are a purple color, and the tail [is] striped across in yellow and red, and it is very beautiful to see in the sunlight, for it shines most nobly.

Also, in Egypt there are gardens that bear fruit seven times a year. And very many beautiful emeralds are found lying in the earth, and therefore they are cheap. Also, when it rains once in the summer in the land of Egypt the country fills up completely with mice. Also, in Cairo they commonly sell men and women of other laws [religions], just as beasts are sold here at market. And there is a common house in the city that is all full of small furnaces, and the women of the town bring their eggs (chicken, goose, or duck) there to put them into these furnaces;[79] and those who look after the house shelter them with the heat of horse manure without a hen and without any other bird, and at the end of three weeks or a month the women return and take their chicks and raise them such that the whole country is full of them, and they do this in winter and in summer.

Also, in this country and elsewhere one finds long apples for sale in season and they are called apples of Paradise, and they are sweet and good tasting, and if you slice them across in several places you always find in the middle the figure of the cross of Our Lord. But they go rotten within a week, and therefore this fruit cannot be taken to far

---

78. This Christian allegory goes back to the early Church Fathers.

79. I.e., incubators. E renders the word as "holes, as it ware hen nestes" (WBJM, 25).

countries. A good hundred of them are found in a bunch and they have large leaves a foot and a half long and proportionately wide. One also finds Adam's apple tree that has a bite on one of its sides. There are also fig trees there that have no leaves and bear their figs on their branches, and they are called Pharaoh's figs.[80]

Also, near Cairo outside that city is the field where balm grows.[81] It comes from small shrubs that are no higher than a man's waist, and they resemble the wood of the wild grape. In that field are seven wells, one of which was made by the feet of Our Lord Jesus Christ when He went to play with the other children. The field is not so fully closed off that one cannot go into it, but in the season when the balm is there, such good guards are placed there that no one dares enter. This balm grows nowhere but in this place. And although people carry away cuttings to plant elsewhere, they grow well but bear no fruit. The balm leaves do not wither; and the branches are cut with a sharp stone, or with a sharp bone, when one wants to prune them. For whoever prunes them with iron corrupts its virtue and its nature. The Saracens call the wood *enothblasse,* and the fruit, which is like cubebs,[82] they call *abebissam,* and the sap that flows from the branches they call *quybalse.* The Christians are always made to cultivate this balm, for otherwise it will not bear fruit at all, as the Saracens themselves say, for they have often proved it. It is also said that balm grows in India Major in that desert where Alexander spoke to the Tree of the Sun and the Tree of the Moon.[83] But I have not seen it, for I have not been that far forward, for there are too many dangerous routes to navigate.

Know that whoever does not well understand how to recognize and test it should really keep from buying balm, for one can quite easily be deceived. For some people sell a seed[84] called *terebenttine* [turpentine] and they mix it with a little balm to give it a good scent. And some cook the wood [and] the fruit of the balm in oil, and say that it is balm. And

---

80. The fruits in question are the plantain, some sort of melon, and the sycamore fig.

81. The garden of Matarea (al-Matariyya), important to Christian and Muslim pilgrims, is famous for both "balm" and its association with the Holy Family; it was known by word of mouth but also through the widely circulated apocryphal Gospels, especially the Infancy of Jesus, which goes back to a sixth-century Syriac version. Also called Balm of Gilead or Mecca, the myrrh-like resin of the balsam tree (*Commiphora opobalsamum,* or *gileadensis*) was scarce and expensive, valued for medicinal, alchemical, and ritual purposes. The *Mandeville* author also draws on Vincent of Beauvais, *Speculum Naturale* 13.99.

82. A tropical berry resembling a pepper grain. On the Arabic names, see WBJM 172, n. to 26.

83. An episode in the popular medieval Alexander legends (see also Chs. 29 and 32).

84. *greine:* both C and E have, more correctly, "gomme [gum]," a variant not listed by Deluz.

some distill cloves and spikenard and other good-smelling spices, and they call the liquor that results balm. Thus many great lords and others are deceived and think that they have balm and it is nothing, for the Saracens adulterate it to deceive the Christians, as I have seen many times. Then the merchants and the pharmacists adulterate it another time, and it is even more worthless.

But if you like, I will show you how you can test and check it so that you will not be deceived. You should know that natural balm is very clear and lemon-colored and very aromatic, and if it is cloudy or red or blackish, it is adulterated. Also, if you place a little balm in your palm [and hold it] towards the sun, if it is good and pure, you will not be able to bear holding your hand in the sun's heat. Also, take a little balm with the point of a knife and touch it to flame and if it burns that is a good sign. Then take a drop of balm as well and put it into a bowl or a goblet where there is goat's milk, and if it is real balm the milk will immediately curdle and congeal. Or place a drop in clear water in a silver goblet or in a clean basin and move it vigorously with the clear water, and if the balm is genuine the water will not be cloudy, and if it is adulterated the water will become cloudy. And if the balm is pure it will sink to the bottom of the vessel as if it were quicksilver [mercury], for pure balm is twice as heavy as adulterated balm.

Now I have spoken about balm, and I will speak about something else that is beyond Babylon across the Nile River towards the desert between Africa and Egypt: these are Joseph's Granaries, which he had made to store the wheat for hard times. They are made of well-hewn stone. Two of them are amazingly large and tall and the others are not so big. And each granary has an entrance for going inside a little above the ground, for the land has been ravaged and ruined since the granaries were built. Inside they are completely full of snakes; and outside on these granaries are many writings in different languages. Some say that they are tombs of the great lords of antiquity,[85] but that is not true, for the common word through the whole country near and far is that they are Joseph's Granaries, and they have it written thus in their chronicles. On the other hand, if they were tombs, they would not be empty inside, nor would they have entrances for going inside, nor are tombs ever made of such a large size and such a height—which is why it is not to be believed that they are tombs.

In Egypt there are also different languages and different letters and of another kind than they have elsewhere, and I shall describe them to

---

85. These include the *Mandeville* author's source, WoB (Ch. 3 in Appendix B.1). Joseph: Gen. 37–50; granaries: Gen. 41. The pyramids are called Joseph's granaries as early as Gregory of Tours' later sixth-century *History of the Franks* 1.10, but the idea received support from another medieval mode of explanation, etymology: the Greek *pyramidos*, of uncertain origin, was said to derive either from *pyr*, "fire," or *pyros*, "wheat or grain." The "granaries" appear on the famous thirteenth-century Hereford world map.

you such as they are and the names they are called such that you know the difference between these and the others:

ᚨ	**ᛒ**	*c*	**ᚦ**	*e*	*f*
Athomus	*Bunchi*	*Chirok*	*Duram*	*Em*	*Fui*
ᚷ	**ᚺ**	**ᛁ**	**ᚠ**	**ᚱ**	
Gomor	*Heket*	*Ianni*	*Karacta*	*Lusanin*	

ᛗ	*n*	*o*	*p*	*q*
Mithe	*Narm*	*Oldalch*	*Pilou*	*Qyn*

Yron	*Sichen*	*Tela*	*Urmron*	*Yph*

Zarin		*Touch*

[Chapter 8]

About the Island of Sicily. About the Way from Babylon to Mount Sinai. About the Church of Saint Catherine and the Marvels There

Now I want to return, before I proceed further, to explain to you the other ways that likewise head to Babylon, where the Sultan dwells, which is at the entrance to Egypt, because many people go there first and then to Mount Sinai and then return by Jerusalem, just as I told you before. For they first complete the farthest pilgrimage and then return by way of the nearest, although the nearest is the most worthy, and that is Jerusalem. For no other pilgrimage can compare to it. But to accomplish everything most easily and most confidently one goes farthest rather than nearest.

Therefore, whoever wants to go to Babylon by another and shorter route from those parts of the West that I named above,[86] or from other parts near them, goes through France, Bourgogne, and Lombardy. It is unnecessary to name the cities or towns of that route, for the way is

---

86. In Chapter 1.

common and thus is known and familiar to many nations. There are many ports where one can put to sea. Some put to sea in Genoa, some in Venice, and cross the Adriatic Sea, which is called the Venetian Gulf that divides Italy and Greece on that side. And some go to Naples, others to Rome, and from Rome to Brindisi and put to sea there and in many other places where there are ports. And one goes through Tuscany, Campania, Calabria, Apulia, and by way of the islands of Italy, Corsica, Sardinia, and Sicily, which is a very large and good island.

On this island of Sicily there is a kind of garden in which there are many different fruits, and the garden is green and flourishing in all the seasons of the year, in winter as in summer. This island is a good three hundred and fifty French leagues[87] in circumference. Between Sicily and Italy there is only a small arm of the sea that is called the Strait of Messina, and Sicily is between the Adriatic Sea and the Sea of Lombardy. And from Sicily to Calabria is only eight Lombard leagues. There is in Sicily a kind of snake with which men test whether the[ir] children are illegitimate or from a faithful marriage. For if they are born in a marriage, the snake circles them without harming them, and if they are born of adultery, the snake bites them and poisons them; and many married men thus test whether the children are theirs.[88] Also, on this island on Mount Etna, which is called Mount Gybel,[89] there are vents that are always burning. And there are seven fiery places that spew various flames of various colors, and by the change in these flames the people of the country know when it will be hard times or good times, or cold or hot, or wet or dry, and all the other ways in which the weather behaves. From Italy to these vents is no more than twenty-five leagues. And they are said to be the chimneys of Hell.[90]

Also, whoever goes through Pisa—as some do, where there is an arm of the sea where one goes to other ports in that region—puts to sea and passes the island of Gref [Corfu], which belongs to the Genoese, then reaches Greece at the port of the city of Myroch [Mavrovo], or at the port of Valone [Valona], or at the city of Duras [Durazzo], which belongs to the Duke of Duras, or at other ports along those coasts, and goes all the way to Constantinople, and then goes by water to the island of Crete and to the island of Rhodes and to Cyprus.[91] Thus from Venice to Constantinople taking the most direct way by sea is one thousand

87. See Chapter 5, n. 48 on medieval and Mandevillean measures. The distances given here are not in the author's known sources; as converted by DLMM (170, n. 2), they are reasonably accurate.
88. A version of this story, set in Malta, is told in the *Golden Legend*'s account of Saint Paul the Apostle.
89. From Arabic *jebel*, "mountain."
90. The manuscripts vary here between *cheminées* ("chimneys [of]") and *chemins* ("ways [into]").
91. Ungrammatical in the original, but lightly edited to be readable here.

eight hundred and eighty Lombard miles. Then from Cyprus one goes by sea to Egypt, leaving Jerusalem and all the country to the left, and arrives at the city of Damietta, which used to be very strong and is situated at the entrance to Egypt. And from Damietta one goes to the city of Alexandria, which is also situated on the sea. In this city Saint Catherine was beheaded and Saint Mark the Evangelist was martyred and buried. But the Emperor Leo had the bones taken to Venice.[92] And there is still in Alexandria a beautiful church that is all white without paintings; and the other churches that belonged to the Christians are likewise all white inside, for the pagans and the Saracens have them whitewashed to destroy the images of saints that were painted on the wall.

This city of Alexandria is a good thirty stades in length, but it is only ten in breadth; and it is a very beautiful and very noble city. In this city the Nile River empties into the sea, as I told you before. In this river many precious stones are found and much *lignum aloes:* it is a kind of wood that comes from the Earthly Paradise[93] that is good in many medicines, and it is quite expensive. From Alexandria one goes to Babylon, where the Sultan dwells, that is also situated on this Nile River. This way is the shortest to go straight to Babylon.

Now I will tell you the way that goes from Babylon to Mount Sinai, where Saint Catherine lies. It is necessary to cross the deserts of Arabia through which Moses led and guided the people of Israel. One passes the well that Moses made with his hand in those deserts when the people grumbled[94] because they could find nothing to drink, and one passes by the well of Marath [Mara] whose water was originally bitter. But the children of Israel put a tree therein and right away the water was sweet and good to drink. And so one goes through the desert all the way to the Elim Valley, in which there are twelve wells, and it has seventy-two palm trees that bear the dates that Moses found with the Children of Israel. From this valley it is only a good day's travel to Mount Sinai.

Whoever wants to go another way from Babylon goes by the Red Sea, which is an arm of the Ocean Sea,[95] and there Moses crossed with the Children of Israel completely dry when Pharaoh king of Egypt

---

92. In the *Golden Legend,* Saint Mark, supposed author of the Gospel of Mark, was murdered by angry pagans in Alexandria and his bones smuggled to Venice. On Saint Catherine, see n. 98 below.

93. Stade: see Chapter 5, n. 49. Following Gen. 2:10–14, the four rivers of Paradise were said to feed the world's major rivers (Nile, Euphrates, Tigris, and Ganges in this book: Ch. 33). *Lignum aloes:* likely an aloeswood (*Aquilaria*), a genus of Asian trees that, when diseased, produce an oil used in incense and medicines.

94. The account of Moses here and in the next paragraph is from Exod. 14–15. For the biblical grumbling (*murmuroit;* Exod. 15:24), some scribes wrote "were dying [of thirst]" (*mouroit [de soif]*).

95. In ancient and medieval geography, the *Mare Oceanum* surrounded the *Orbis Terrarum,* or circle of lands, containing the three known continents, Asia, Africa, Europe (see Appendix C.1).

drove them away. It is a good seven leagues across. In this sea Pharaoh
was drowned with all his army that he led. This sea is no redder than
any other sea, but in some places there is red gravel and therefore it
is called the Red Sea. This sea extends right to the bounds of Arabia
and Palestine. Along this sea one goes more than four days' travel and
then one goes through the desert to the Elim Valley and from there to
Mount Sinai.

You can know that no one can go by horse through this desert, for
the horses would not find anything to eat or to drink.[96] Therefore one
crosses this desert on camels, for the camels always find something to
eat in the trees and in the shrubs that they browse on, and they easily go
without drinking for two or three days, and the horses could not do that.
And know that from Babylon to Mount Sinai is a good twelve days' travel.
Some take more time and others hurry and drive themselves and take
less time. And whoever wants to go through this country or another over
there always takes interpreters until they know the language.[97] It is necessary there to have carried through this desert all the essentials of life.

Mount Sinai is called the desert of Sin, which means "burning red,"
because Moses saw Our Lord several times in the form of fire on this
mountain and also in the Burning Bush, and God spoke to him and
that was at the foot of the mountain.[98] There is an abbey of monks there
well sealed off and very well enclosed with iron gates for fear of the wild
animals; and the monks are Arab or Greek. There is a large monastery
there, and [the monks are] like hermits, and they drink no wine except
on the main feast days, and they are most devout and live in poverty and
simplicity on vegetables and dates, and they often practice abstinence
and do much penance.

The Church of Saint Catherine is there in which there are many
lamps burning, for they have enough olive oil for both eating and burning. They have it thus plentifully by the miracle of God; for the ravens
and the crows and the starlings and the other birds of the country flock
together once a year and fly there, as if on pilgrimage, and each carries

---

96. WoB boasts of crossing on horseback (Ch. 4 in Appendix B.1); as in Chapter
7, the author is here opposing his source.

97. Few medieval travelers say much about the challenges of communication. A
rare exception is William of Rubruck, a Franciscan who in 1253, for Louis IX
of France, sought out the Mongol rulers in central Asia; his long letter to Louis
complains about his interpreters' inadequacies on theological matters.

98. Exod. 3:1–6. Mount Sinai was thus an important pilgrimage site since at least
the fourth century. The monastery described here, originally called *tou Batou* (of
the Burning Bush), was built in the sixth century. By the tenth or eleventh century
it was linked with Saint Catherine of Alexandria (an early fourth-century virgin
martyr, one of the most popular late medieval saints), whose body was supposedly
discovered there around 800, brought by angels (see the *Golden Legend*). The
Mandeville author augments WoB's more sober description with borrowed and
invented material.

olive branches in its beak instead of an offering, and they leave them there, from which the monks make the oil by drops, and this is a great miracle.[99] And since the birds, which have neither natural understanding nor reason, go there to seek out that glorious virgin [Saint Catherine], man ought indeed to take the trouble to pray to her and worship her.

Also, behind the altar of this church is the place where Moses saw Our Lord in the Burning Bush. When the monks go into this place, they remove their shoes right away, because Our Lord said to Moses: "put off the shoes from thy feet: for the place whereon thou standest is holy ground."[100] The monks call this place *Dozeleel,* which is to say God's Shadow. And beside the high altar three steps up is the alabaster reliquary where the bones of Saint Catherine lie. The prelate of the monks shows the relics to the pilgrims, and with a silver instrument he rubs the bones and a little oil appears out of them just like a sweat that resembles neither oil nor balm but is more blackish, and he gives a little of it to the pilgrims, for not a large amount comes out. Then he shows Saint Catherine's head and the cloth in which she was wrapped, which is still all bloody. The angels brought her body wrapped in this cloth to Mount Sinai and buried her with it. And they show the bush that burns and is not consumed in which Our Lord spoke to Moses and enough other relics.

Also, when the prelate of the abbey died, I had heard that his lamp would go out, and when they chose another prelate, if he was a good man worthy of being prelate, his lamp would light itself through God's grace without anyone having touched it; for each one of them has his own lamp and they know well by their lamps when anyone has to die, for the light begins to change and weaken. And if he was not worthy it remains out. Others have told me that the one who sang the mass for the dead monk found in writing on the altar after the mass the name of the one whom they had to elect as prelate.[101] I asked several of them about this; but they would tell me nothing, although I told them that they should not conceal the grace that God showed them, but that they ought to make it known to make people more devout, and that they sinned in concealing it, it seemed to me; for the miracle that God has performed and [those that he] still performs every day are the witnesses to his power, as David said in the Psalter: "*Mirabilia testimonia tua Domine.*"[102] And then they told me that both things had happened many times and I was not able to know any more about them.

---

99. The first record of this miracle, Thietmar's account of his 1217 pilgrimage, attributes it to the Virgin Mary, not birds, and connects it with the miracle of the flies and other insects as related in the text below.

100. Exod. 3:5, a rare scriptural quotation not given in Latin.

101. No previous work records this miracle.

102. "Miracles are your witnesses, O Lord." An echo of several psalms: e.g., Pss. 39:6, 93[92]:5, 118:29.

Into that abbey come neither flies nor gnats nor fleas nor any other such filth through God's and Our Lady's miracle, for there used to be so many kinds of flies and other such filth there that the monks wanted to leave the abbey. They did once go out and climb the mountain to flee the place, and Our Lady came there before them and told them to return, and from then on no fly nor other such filth would enter. So the monks went back and no such thing has entered there ever since.

Also, in front of the gate is the well where Moses struck the rock and water came out.[103] From this abbey one climbs the mountain of Moses by many steps, and there one finds first a church of Our Lady where she encountered the monks when they were running away from the flies. Higher up on this same mountain is the chapel of Elijah the prophet, and this place is called Horeb, of which Holy Scripture speaks: "*Et ambulavit in fortitudine cibi illius usque ad montem Dei Oreb.*"[104] And beside there is the vine that Saint John the Evangelist planted and the grapes are called *Scaphis*.[105] And a little higher up is the chapel of Moses and the rock where Moses fled in fear when he saw Our Lord face to face. In this rock the form of his body is impressed, for he struck the rock so hard that his whole body sunk into the rock through a miracle of God. And beside there is the place where Our Lord gave Moses the Ten Commandments of the Law. And the cave is there beneath the rock where Moses stayed when he fasted for forty days, but he died in the Promised Land, but no one knows where he was buried.

From this mountain one passes through a large valley to go to another mountain where Saint Catherine was buried by the angels of Our Lord. In this valley there is a church of [the] Forty Martyrs, and the monks of the abbey often sing there. And this valley is very cold. Then one goes up the mountain of Saint Catherine, which is much higher than the mountain of Moses.[106] And there where Saint Catherine was buried is neither a church nor a chapel nor any other dwelling. But there is a cairn of stones arranged around the spot where her body was placed by the angels. There used to be a chapel there, but it has been ruined; the stones are still lying there. Although the Collect of Saint Catherine[107] says that where Our Lord gave Moses the Ten Commandments and where the holy virgin [Saint Catherine] was buried are the same place,

---

103. Moses striking water: Exod. 1:.6; fearing God: Exod. 3:6; commandments and fasting: Exod. 24:12–18; his death: Deut. 34:1–8.

104. "And he walked in the strength of that food unto the mount of God, Horeb" (1 Kings 19:8), omitting "*quadraginta diebus et quadraginta noctibus*" (forty days and forty nights). Horeb: another name for Mount Sinai.

105. No other source mentions this odd legend.

106. Jebel Katharina is southwest of Jebel Musa (assumed to be Mount Sinai), and slightly higher.

107. A *collect* is a short prayer of a kind used in the Western Church since at least the fifth century.

this is to be understood as meaning in one country or in one place bearing one name; for both places are called Mount of Sinai. But it is a great way from one to the other, and there is a large and deep valley between them.

[Chapter 9]
About the Desert between the Church of Saint Catherine and Jerusalem. About the Dry Tree. And How Roses First Came into the World

Now after visiting those holy places, one wants to return to Jerusalem and wants to take leave of the monks and recommends oneself to their prayers. Then they give the pilgrims some of their food so that they can cross the deserts towards Syria. These deserts last for a good thirteen days' travel.

In this desert dwell many Arabs who are called Bedouins and Ascoparcz. These people lead a completely degraded life.[108] They have no houses except tents, which they make from the skins of animals such as camels and other animals that they eat, and they sleep under them and stay in places where they can find water, as by the Red Sea and elsewhere. For in this desert there is a great lack of water; and it often happens that where it is found in one season it is not found in another, and that is why they make no dwellings. This people that I have told you about, they do not cultivate or work the land, for they do not eat bread—except those who dwell near some good town where they go and eat occasionally—and they roast their meat and their fish on hot stones in the sun; and they are a very strong people and good fighters, and there are so many of this people that they are countless, and they do nothing except hunt animals to eat; and they value their lives as nothing, and therefore they fear neither the Sultan nor any other prince. But they readily dare go to war with him if he does something that upsets them; and they are often at war with the Sultan, and especially in the period when I was with him.[109] They carry only a shield and spear and no other arms and wrap their head and their neck with large white linen cloth, and they are extremely wild and filthy and of a wicked nature.

When one has crossed this desert going towards Jerusalem, one comes to Bersabee [Beersheba], which used to be a most beautiful and

---

108. *Ces sont gentz pleinz de toutes malveises condiciouns* ("these are people full of all wicked ways"). More negative here than WoB, the *Mandeville* author tries as usual to explain cultural difference rationally. "Ascoparcz": an Ethiopian people in Albert of Aachen's *History* of the First Crusade.
109. Which Sultan this might be is uncertain (see Appendix C.4). The first "Ogier" interpolation in the Liège Version occurs here (see Appendix A.2).

delightful Christian city, and there are still some churches there. In this city the patriarch Abraham lived for a long time. This city was founded by Bersabés [Bathsheba], who was Urie's [Uriah's] wife; on her David the king begot Salamon [Solomon] the Wise, who was king after David over the twelve Tribes of Israel, and he reigned for forty years.[110]

From there one goes to the city of Ebron [Hebron], which is a good two leagues away, which otherwise is called the Valley of Mambre and otherwise is called the Valley of Tears, because Adam wept for one hundred years in this valley for the death of his son Abel, whom Cain killed. Hebron used to be the main city of the Philistines and the giants lived there then. It was the sacerdotal city of the tribe of Judah, and it was so independent that they received there all those fleeing other places for their misdeeds. To Hebron Josué [Joshua], Calef [Caleb], and their company first came to spy out how they might win the Promised Land. In Hebron David reigned first for seven and a half years, and in Jerusalem he reigned for thirty-two and a half years.[111] All the tombs of the patriarchs Adam, Abraham, Isaac, and Jacob are there on the mountain slope, and [those] of their wives Eve, Sara, and Rebecca and Leah; and above them there is a beautiful crenelled[112] church in the shape of a castle that the Saracens guard very carefully, and they hold the place in great reverence because of the holy father patriarchs who lie there, and they do not allow Christians or Jews to enter unless they have special permission from the Sultan; for they regard the Christians and the Jews as dogs and say that they ought not to enter so holy a place. The place where they lie is called Double Spelunk, or Double Cave or Double Fosse, because one lies below the other. The Saracens call that place in their language *Karitarba,* which is as much as to say the place of the Patriarchs; and the Jews call that place *Arboch.*[113]

In the same place was Abraham's house, and it was there that he was sitting at his door and saw three persons and adored only one, just as Holy Scripture testifies, saying *"Tres vidit et unum adoravit."*[114] There too Abraham received the angels into his home, and quite close to this place there is a cave in the rock where Adam and Eve dwelt when they

---

110. Abraham: Gen. 21:28–34. David and Solomon: 2 Sam. 11. The name's etymology is fanciful.

111. Cain kills Abel: Gen. 4:8. Hebron: Josh. 20:1–9; sacerdotal city (E: "citee of prestez," WBJM 34): Josh. 21:10–11; and spying: Josh. 2:1–24 (in Jericho, not Hebron). David's reign: 2 Sam. 5:4–5.

112. Crenelles (or crenels): notches, like those in the battlements of castle walls.

113. Venerated by Jews, Christians, and Muslims, the Cave of Machpelah ("halved" or "double" tomb) was, in scripture (Gen. 23, and 49:29–50:13), the gravesite of Abraham, Sara, Isaac, Rebecca, Jacob, and Leah, and, in legend, of Adam and Eve. In the Vulgate text of Josh. 14:15, Adam was buried at Kiryat Arba, read in rabbinical tradition as Town (Kiryat) either of Arba or of Four.

114. The Latin is translated in the words introducing the quotation, which, though adapted from Gen. 18:2, comes from the liturgy rather than the Bible.

were cast out of Paradise and they conceived their children there.[115] In this same place Adam was created and formed, in the opinion of some people, for this place used to be called the Field of Damascus because it was in the lordship of Damascus. And from there he was translated to the Paradise of Delights, as they say; and after he was driven out of Paradise, he was put back there. And the very same day he was put in Paradise, he was cast out of it. The Valley of Hebron begins there that stretches to Jerusalem. There the angel ordered Adam to sleep with his wife, and he begot Seth, from whose descendants Jesus Christ was born.

In this valley there is a field where something reddish is extracted from the land that they call *Cambil* that people eat instead of spices, and it is taken away to sell. The pit cannot be made so deep or so wide that within a year's time it is not completely full again and just the same, by God's grace.[116]

Two leagues from Hebron is the tomb of Lot, who was the son of Abraham's brother. Quite close to Hebron is the Mount of Mamre from which the valley takes its name. There is an oak tree there that the Saracens call *Dirp;* it is from Abraham's time, and is called the Dry Tree.[117] This tree is said to have been there since the beginning of the world, and it was always green and leafy until Our Lord died on the cross; then it dried up, and so did all the trees that existed then in the whole world, or they withered, or their core inside dissolved and rotted, and they have remained entirely empty and hollow inside—of which [trees] there are many throughout the world. Some prophecies say that a lord prince from the West will win the Promised Land with the help of the Christians and have mass sung beneath this dry tree, and the tree will turn green again and bear leaf and fruit, through which miracle many Saracens and many Jews will be converted to the Christian law. Therefore the tree is greatly revered and watched over most carefully and lovingly. And although it is dry, it nevertheless has great powers, for

---

115. These and other legends of Adam and Eve circulated very widely; some are noted in other pilgrim accounts. Most are found in the early thirteenth-century Syriac *Book of the Bee*, a detailed tour of Christian history in its variants (trans. E. A. Wallis Budge [Oxford, 1886], Chs. 13–18).

116. Some pilgrims mention a red earth, but none calls it *cambil*, a name that Warner traces to an early fourteenth-century medical treatise, suggesting that it refers here to a red powder from the flowers of the kamala tree (*Mallotus Phillipensis*) and used medicinally (WBJM 176, n. to 34, l. 27).

117. Two legends are conflated: the Oak of Mamre, linked to Abraham's hospitality to the Lord (Gen. 18:1–18), and the Dry Tree, which may have biblical links (Ezek. 17:24 and Luke 23:31). The latter is noted by Marco Polo, who places it in Persia. The prophecy of the "lord prince" may come from a legend linked to the thirteenth-century emperor, Frederick II (LMT 1.48–49, n. 3), but a similar prophecy appears in the popular late thirteenth-century French encyclopedia, *The Book of Sydrach* (WBJM 176, n. to 35, l. 5).

whoever carries a little with him, it protects him from epilepsy and his horse cannot go lame; and there are many other virtues for which it is considered precious.

From Hebron one goes to Bethlehem in half a day, if one wants to, for it is only five leagues away, and there is a very fine and very pleasant road through plains and woods. Bethlehem is a small city, long and narrow and enclosed with good moats, and it used to be called Effrata, such that the Psalter says "*Ecce audivimus eam in Effrata.*"[118] Towards the end of the city to the east there is a most beautiful and very graceful church with towers, pinnacles, and crenellations made most skillfully, and inside the church there are forty-four pillars of marble.

Between the church and the city is *Campus Floridus,* which is called Field of Flowers because a young virgin was wrongly accused of fornication and she had to be burnt in that place. They lit the thorn bush, and this virgin said her prayer to Our Lord requesting that, since she was not guilty, He help her and make [her innocence] manifest before everyone. Thereupon she entered the fire, and the fire immediately went out and the branches that had been burning became bright red rose bushes and the branches that had not yet been lit became white rose bushes. These were the first-ever roses in the world and the first roses that had ever been seen to that day. Thus was that maiden set free by God's grace. This place is therefore called Field of Flowers, for it was full of rose flowers.[119]

Also, beside the choir of this above-mentioned church,[120] going down sixteen steps to the right side, is the place where Our Lord was born that is decorated most nobly in marble and most graciously painted in gold and azure and other colors. Thirteen steps from there is the manger of the ox and the ass, and quite near is the pit where the star fell that led the three kings, Jaspar [Caspar], Balthazar, and Melchior, all the way there. But the Jews name the three kings differently in Hebrew, for they call them *Appellius, Amerrius,* and *Damasus;* and the Greeks call them *Galgalath, Malgalath,* and *Saraphy.* These three kings offered Our Lord gold, incense, and myrrh. They did not come there by traveling for days, but by God's miracle, for they found each other in India in a city by the name of Cassak [Kashan], which is a fifty-three-day journey from Bethlehem, and they were there [in Bethlehem] on the thirteenth day; and this was already the fourth day since they had seen the star when

---

118. "Behold we have heard of it in Effrata" (Ps. 132[131]:6).

119. No other travelers tell this story, also found in a French poem about Mary (WBJM xx, n. 1).

120. The Church of the Nativity, built over a site traditionally associated with Jesus' birth (the Grotto of the Nativity). The wise men (*magi*) from the East are mentioned only in Matt. 2:1–12, but over time their story accreted details, and they became three named kings. The Hebrew and Greek names come from Peter Comestor, *Historia Scholastica* (Evang. 8), or the *Golden Legend* ("The Epiphany").

they found each other in this city, and so it took them nine days from that city to Bethlehem, and this was a great miracle.

Also, below the cloister of this church eighteen steps to the right is the Charnel of the Innocents,[121] where their bones lie. In front of that place where Our Lord was born is the tomb of Saint Jerome, who was a priest and a cardinal and translated the Bible and the Psalter from Hebrew into Latin.[122] And outside the minster is the chair on which he sat when he translated them. Quite close to this church, sixty fathoms away, is a Church of Saint Nicholas where Our Lady rested after having given birth; and because she had too much milk in her breasts and because they were sore, she squirted some [milk] there on the red marble stones such that the white spots are still there on the stones.[123]

Know that almost all those who dwell in Bethlehem are Christians, and there are beautiful vines all around the city and a great abundance of wine that the Christians have made; for the Saracens do not cultivate vines nor drink any wine, for the books of their law that Machomet gave them—which they call *Alkaron,* and the others call it *Meshaaf,* and in another language it is called *Harme*—and the said book prohibits them from drinking wine.[124] For in this book Machomet curses all those who drink wine, and wine, and all those who sell it, because one time he was accused of having drunkenly killed a hermit whom he much loved;[125] and therefore he cursed wine and wine-drinkers. But the curses would come back on him, just as David says in the Psalter: "*Et in verticam ipsius iniquita ejus descendet.*"[126]

---

121. According to Matt. 2:1–18, Herod, having learned of the birth of a new king from the Magi, ordered the deaths of all the children in Bethlehem less than two years old; the event is sometimes known as the Massacre of the Innocents. Charnel: a vault used to store bones, as the text makes clear.

122. One of the Latin Church Fathers, Jerome (d. 420) was a scholar whose translation of the Bible, known nowadays as the Vulgate, was widely used in Latin Christendom and recognized as authentic in 1546 by the Council of Trent (the Douay-Rheims Bible contains its English translation).

123. The so-called Milk Grotto can still be visited. Two translators of L responded very differently to this passage: Otto von Diemeringen, "And I have kissed the drops" (Crosby 1965, 178); Vulgate Latin, "And red stones are shown there spattered with white spots that the simple-minded say happened to the stones from the abundance of milk cast out of the Virgin's breasts" (Hakluyt 1589, 35).

124. This sentence unravels because the author tries to give too much information. *Mushaf:* the name of a complete Qur'an as physical object; *horme:* Arabic for "holy."

125. See Chapter 15.

126. "And his iniquity/unrighteousness shall come down upon him" (Ps. 7:17). For a medieval Christian, the Hebrew poet's prophetic words apply even to Muslims.

The Saracens do not raise pigs nor eat any pork at all, for they say that it is man's brother, and that it was prohibited in the Old Testament,[127] and they consider those who eat it to be hopeless. Also in the land of Palestine and in the land of Egypt they eat little veal or beef, unless the animal is so old that it can no longer work—not because it is prohibited to them, but because there are few of them—and they look after them and feed them to plow their lands.

In this city of Bethelem King David was born. King David had sixty wives, the first of whom had the name Michol, and he had three hundred concubines.[128] From Bethlehem to Jerusalem is only two leagues. On the route to Jerusalem half a league from Bethlehem there is a church where the angel announced to the shepherds the birth of Our Lord; and on this route is the tomb of Rachel (who was mother to Joseph the patriarch), who died as soon as she had given birth to Benjamin and was buried by Jacob her husband; and Jacob placed twelve large rocks on her [grave] as a sign that she had had twelve children.[129] On this same route, half a league from Jerusalem, the star appeared to the three kings that had come to rest near Herod. On this route there are many Christian churches that one goes past.

[Chapter 10]

About the Pilgrimages in Jerusalem and About the Holy Places around There

Next is Jerusalem the holy city, well situated between mountains; and there are no rivers or wells, but the water comes by pipe from Hebron. You can know that in the old days Jerusalem was called Jebus until the time of Melchisedech; and then it was called Salem until the time of King David, who joined the two names and called it Jebusalem; and then Solomon called it Jerosolimie, and then it was called Jerusalem.[130]

---

127. See Lev. 11:2–4, 7–8, and Deut. 14:8. The Qur'an forbids eating pork in suras 2.173, 5.3, 6.145, and 16.115.

128. Michol: 1 Sam. 18:19–28. The number of David's wives and concubines is not known. King, prophet, and supposed author of the Psalms, David was a popular figure in Latin Christendom, regarded as a forerunner of the Christ-King and, despite his failings, the model of a Christian prince.

129. Gen. 35:16–20, where Rachel's monument is called "a pillar." Since her son Joseph's life (Gen. 37–50) was read as anticipating the Messiah's life, and since her husband Jacob (Abraham's grandson) was the third great patriarch, Rachel was well known. The drama of her own life story (Gen. 29–35) also helped.

130. Jerusalem is holy in all three Abrahamic religions: Judaism, Christianity, and Islam. Its manifold fourteenth-century Latin Christian associations are the focus here. The origin of the city's name is uncertain; this explanation comes from Peter Comestor's *Historia Scholastica* (2 Kings 7).

Around Jerusalem is the kingdom of Syria, and near there is the land of Palestine, and near Ascalon is the land of Maritanie; but Jerusalem is in the land of Judea, and it is called Judea because Judas Maccabeus was king of that country. To the east it borders on the kingdom of Arabia, to the south on the land of Egypt, to the west on the Great Sea,[131] [and] to the north on the kingdom of Syria to the sea of Cyprus. Jerusalem used to have a patriarch and many archbishops and bishops in the country.

Around Jerusalem are these cities: Hebron seven leagues away, Jericho six leagues, Bersabee [Beersheba] eight leagues, Ascalon seventeen leagues, Jaffa sixteen leagues, Ramatha [Rama in Ephraim] three leagues, and Bethlehem two leagues. Two leagues south of Bethlehem is the church of Saint Karitot [Chariton], who was abbot there, for whom the monks grieved deeply when he was about to die; and they are still there grieving in a painting that is very sad to look at.

This country of Jerusalem has been in the hands of many different nations, and the country has often had to suffer for the sin of the people who dwell there; for the country has been in the hands of all nations, such as the Jews, the Cananees [Canaanites], the Assyrians, the Persians, the Medains [Medians], the Macedonians, the Greeks, the Romans, the Christians, the Saracens, the Barbarians, the Turks, the Tartarians [Mongols], and many other different peoples; for God does not allow traitorous peoples nor great sinners to rule for long in this Holy Land, be they Christians or other peoples. And now the misbelievers have held this land in their hands for the space of one hundred and forty years and more. But they will not hold it for long, if it please God.

You can know that when one is in Jerusalem one makes the first pilgrimage to the Church of the Holy Sepulcher,[132] which is outside the city towards the north side. But it is encompassed by the city and is a very beautiful round church, open above and covered about with lead; and there is a very beautiful tower, tall and strong, towards the west side for

---

131. The Mediterranean. Judea comes from Judah, Jacob and Leah's son (Gen. 29:35) and founder of the tribe of the same name, not from Judas Maccabeus, a central figure in the two books of Macabees.

132. The Holy Sepulcher, as the ostensible location of Jesus's burial and Resurrection, is Christianity's holiest site and, since its rediscovery around 325, the greatest goal of Christian pilgrims. Building around it began almost immediately under Constantine, the first Roman ruler to embrace Christianity, and it incorporated the nearby Golgotha (Calvary), site of the Crucifixion according to the four Gospels. The Persian invasion in 614 and the Fatimid Caliph al-Hakim's attack in 1009 caused serious damage to the complex, which was afterwards restored in each case. The structure was enlarged and unified in the twelfth century by the crusaders, whose Latin Kingdom of Jerusalem ended when Saladin captured the city in 1187. Columbus claimed to be seeking gold to refinance its conquest, or so says the surviving transcription of his log for December 26, 1492. A version of the crusaders' church still stands, having survived smaller and larger threats, including restoration, a fire in 1808, and an earthquake in 1927.

hanging bells. Inside this church in the middle there is a tabernacle just like a little house with a little door, and this tabernacle is made in the shape of a semicircle very nobly wrought with gold and azure and very well decorated with other colors. In this tabernacle to the right side is Our Lord's sepulcher, and the tabernacle is eight feet long and five feet wide and also the tabernacle is eleven feet high. It is not very long since the sepulcher was uncovered, such that it could be touched and kissed. But because everyone who went there strove to take either a piece of the rock or some rock dust, the Sultan therefore had it walled round so that it cannot be touched. But on the left side of the tabernacle wall at a man's height there is a rock the size of a man's head that came from the Holy Sepulcher, and the pilgrims kiss this rock. In this tabernacle there are no windows, but it is all lit with lamps. And there is a lamp that hangs in front of the sepulcher that is always burning, and on Good Friday it goes out by itself and then lights again on the day of the Resurrection, at the very hour when Our Lord rose again from death into life.[133]

Also, inside the church to the right side near the church choir is the mount of Calvary where Our Lord was placed on the cross, and it is a rock colored white with a little red mixed into it in some places. This rock is split and that cleft is called Golgotha.[134] There the blood from Our Lord's wounds dripped when He was hung on the cross, and this Golgotha is reached by steps. And there in this cleft Adam's head was found after Noah's Flood as a sign that Adam's sins would be redeemed in this same place. And on this rock Abraham made his sacrifice to Our Lord; and there is an altar there, and before this altar lie Godefroy [Godfrey] of Bouillon, Baudouin [Baldwin],[135] and others who were Christians and kings of Jerusalem. And beside the place where Our Lord was crucified is this writing in Greek: "*Otheos vasilion ysmon perseonas ergasa sothias emesotis gis,*" which is to say in Latin: "*Hic est Deus rex noster ante secula operatus est salutem in medio terre.*"[136] Also, on the rock where the cross was set is writ-

---

133. Other medieval pilgrims and historians also report this miracle, one of the high points of the Byzantine liturgy in the Holy Sepulcher. The Vulgate Latin casts doubt on it (Ch. 14 in Appendix A.5).

134. Golgotha, the name of the whole rock, means "skull" in Aramaic; it was translated as *calvaria* in Jerome's Latin Bible, hence Calvary. The rock serves here, as in other pilgrims' accounts, to combine the major events of Christian history into one story. Abraham's willingness to sacrifice his son Isaac, which Christians read as a typological anticipation of the Crucifixion, is depicted in Gen. 22:1–19. The legend of Adam's head goes back to at least the third century (when the biblical scholar Origen, for example, believed the site to be Adam's grave), and some pilgrims report having seen his skull on display.

135. Godfrey was elected first ruler of the Crusader Kingdom of Jerusalem and styled himself "advocate of the Holy Sepulcher." His brother Baldwin succeeded him after his death in 1100.

136. "Here God our king before the ages [i.e., before time] wrought salvation in the middle of the earth" (Ps. 74[73]:12). The garbled Greek (from the Septuagint,

ten in the rock: *"Cyos nyst ys basys tou pisteos they thesmosy,"* which is to say in Latin: *"Quod vides est fundamentum tocius fidei mundi hujus."*[137] I want you to know that when Our Lord was put to death He was thirty-three years and three months old, and David's prophecy said that He would be forty, there where he says: *"Quadringita annis proximus fui generacioni huic."*[138] Thus there it seems to some that the prophecy was not true. But both are true, for in the old days a year was made of ten months, the first of which was March and December was the last. But Caius Caesar, who was emperor of Rome, had two months added, January and February, and ordained the year of twelve months, that is of three hundred and sixty-five days without [counting] the bissextile day,[139] following the sun's own course; and thus all Christians hold that according to the ten-month year He [Jesus] was in his fortieth year, as the prophet said. According to the twelve-month year he was thirty-three years and three months old.[140]

Also, near the mount of Calvary to the right there is an altar where the column lies to which Our Lord was tied and [then] scourged. Near there, there are four stone columns that always drip water; and some say that they weep for Our Lord's death. Near this altar in a place underground forty-two steps down the True Cross was found through Saint Helen's wisdom beneath the rock where the Jews had hidden it. And she had the True Cross tested, for three crosses were found there: that is, Our Lord's and those of the two thieves. And Saint Helen had them tested on a dead body that was immediately resuscitated when the True Cross was placed on it. Beside there in the wall is the place where Our Lord's four nails were hidden, for He had two in His hands and two in His feet. And one of these nails the Emperor Constantine had made into a bit for his horse to wear in battle.[141] Through the sight of this bit he conquered all his enemies and won all the land of Asia Minor (that is, Turkey), greater and lesser Armenia, Syria, Jerusalem, Arabia, Persia, Mesopotamia, and the kingdom of Halappe [Aleppo], upper and lower Egypt, and all the other regions deep into Ethiopia [and]

---

a third-century-BCE Greek translation of Hebrew scriptures) probably comes from Peter Comestor's *Historia Scholastica.*

137. "What you see is the base of all the faith in the world." No known source (the Greek is even more garbled: see HMT 2.59 for corrected transcriptions).

138. "Forty years long was I neighbor to that generation." Cf. Ps. 94[95]:10, which has *offensus* ("offended by") instead of *proximus* ("neighbor to").

139. The extra day added in a Leap Year.

140. The Roman calendar was reformed by Julius Caesar, not Gaius, as some copies, including E, correctly note. This attempt to harmonize contradictory accounts is typical of the *Mandeville* author's syncretic imagination, which in Chapter 20 will accept that the earth is a sphere with Jerusalem "in the middle."

141. This story, already mentioned in Chapter 2, of the finding of the Cross comes from the *Golden Legend.*

into India Minor, such that at that time almost all were Christian and of the good faith.

There were after that time in those regions many worthy hermits, of whom the books of the *Lives of the Fathers* speak,[142] and now they are all Saracens and pagans. But when it pleases God, just as this land has been lost because of the sins of the Christians, so will it be won again because of their bravery with God's help.

Also, in the middle of the church choir there is a circle where Joseph of Arimathea laid the body of Our Lord when He was taken down from the cross, and in the same place he cleaned His wounds. It is said that this circle is right in the middle of the world.[143]

In the Church of the Holy Sepulcher towards the north is the place where Our Lord was imprisoned, for He was imprisoned in several places; and a piece of the chain with which He was bound is also there. And there Our Lord appeared first to Mary Magdalene after His Resurrection, and she thought that He was a gardener.[144]

In the Church of the Holy Sepulcher there used to be canons of the Order of Saint Augustine, and they had a prior, but the patriarch was their sovereign. Outside the church doors, climbing eighteen steps to the right, Our Lord said to His mother, "Behold your son," and He showed her Saint John the Evangelist and then said to Saint John, "Behold your mother,"[145] and He also said the same thing on the cross. Our Lord climbed those steps when He carried the cross on His shoulders. Beneath those steps there is a chapel, and in this chapel Indian priests sing, not according to our law but according to theirs, and nevertheless they make the sacrament of the altar out of bread, saying *Pater Noster*,[146] and little else with it, and the words with which the sacrament is consecrated, for they know nothing of the additions that several popes have made. But they sing very devoutly. And quite close to this is the place where Our Lord rested when He was tired from carrying the cross.

Know that near the Church of the Holy Sepulcher the city is weaker than in other parts because of the great plain that lies between the

---

142. The *Vitae Patrum* (*Lives of the Fathers*) collected the lives of early monks (fourth to sixth centuries), typically hermits, whose ascetic, spiritual heroism was celebrated, especially in Eastern Christendom.

143. Joseph of Arimathea is mentioned in all four Gospels (Matt. 27:57–60; Mark 15:42–47; Luke 23:50–55; John 19:38–40). See Chapter 20 for more on Jerusalem's centrality.

144. John 20:11–18.

145. John 19:26–27; quoted, unusually, in French only.

146. Sacrament of the altar: the Eucharist. *Pater Noster:* "Our Father" (see Matt. 6:9–13), the Lord's Prayer. The "Indian" Christians may have been Ethiopian, "rediscovered" in the crusading era after the earlier Arab expansion had effectively cut them off from the rest of Christendom.

church and the city. And near the eastern part outside the city walls is the valley of Jehoshaphat that reaches to the walls as if it were a large moat; and above this valley of Jehoshaphat outside the city is the Church of Saint Stephen, where he was stoned to death.[147] Beside there is the Golden Gate that cannot be opened. Our Lord entered through that gate on Palm Sunday on a she-ass,[148] and the gates opened for Him when He wanted to go to the Temple. The hoofprints of the she-ass are still visible in three places in the steps that are made of very hard stone.

In front of the Church of the Holy Sepulcher two hundred steps towards the south is the large Hospital of Saint John where the Hospitallers were founded.[149] Inside the palace for the sick[150] of this hospital there are one hundred and twenty-four pillars of stone. And in the walls of the house, not counting the number mentioned above, there are fifty-four pillars that hold up the house. From this hospital going east there is a very beautiful church that is called [the Church] of Our Lady the Great. And then there is another church quite nearby that is called Our Lady of the Latins. Mary Cleophas and Mary Magdalene were there and they tore their hair when Our Lord was on the cross.[151]

[Chapter 11]
About the Temple of Our Lord. About Herod's Cruelty. About Mount Sion. About the **Probatica Piscina** *and the* **Natatoria Siloe**

The Templum Domini,[152] which is one hundred and sixty steps east of the Church of Saint Stephen, is a very fine religious house, completely

---

147. Acts 7:58–59.

148. Jesus' entrance into Jerusalem is depicted in all four Gospels (Matt. 21:1–11; Mark 11:1–11; Luke 19:28–44; John 12:12–19), but without the legendary details. The Golden Gate: a Byzantine structure associated with both Jesus' entrance and the locked gate of Ezek. 44.1–3.

149. The pilgrim hospital goes back to the eighth century, but the Hospitallers (Knights of the Order of the Hospital of Saint John of Jerusalem) took it over in the eleventh century. See also Chapter 4, n. 35.

150. Great sickroom? Several copies have simply "in front of the house"; others, "this hospital for the sick has a palace and in front there are . . ."

151. Our Lady the Great: an abbey of Benedictine nuns founded in 1130 to receive female pilgrims. Our Lady of the Latins: the earliest Latin Christian church in Jerusalem, built in 1014 by the merchants of Amalfi, Italy. Two Marys: cf. John 9:25.

152. Temple of Our Lord: the Dome of the Rock (Qubbat al-Sakhra), built in the late seventh century by the Umayyad Caliph Abd al-Malik on Mount Moriah, where, in Islamic tradition, Muhammad ascended to Heaven. The site was also thought to be where Abraham prepared to sacrifice Isaac in Gen. 22.

round, quite large and quite high and covered with lead; and there is a large houseless square around it, and the square is well paved everywhere with white marble. The Saracens allow neither Christians nor Jews to enter, for they say that such foul people ought not to enter or rest in such a holy place.

But I went in there, and wherever else I wanted to, on the strength of letters from the Sultan, in which there was a special order to all of his subjects to allow me to see all the places and describe to me the places and the secrets of each place, and to guide me from one city to another if need be, and to receive me and my companions kindly, and to facilitate all my reasonable requests unless they were highly contrary to the royal dignity of the Sultan or of his law. To others who ask for his grace he gives only his seal, which they have borne before them hanging from a spear; and the people of the country greatly honor that seal and kneel just as we do before *Corpus Domini*.[153] Even incomparably greater respect is shown to these letters, for the emir and the other lords to whom they are shown, before they receive them, they bow down, and then they take them and put them on their heads, and then they kiss them, and then they read them while bowed right down and [they do so] with great respect, and then they offer to do whatever the bearers require.

In that Templum Domini there used to be canons regular and they had an abbot whom they obeyed. Charlemagne was in this Temple when the angel brought him Our Lord Jesus Christ's foreskin from the Circumcision, and he took it to Aix-la-Chapelle; and then Charles the Bald had it taken to Poitiers and then to Chartres.[154]

Also, know that this is not the same temple that Solomon made,[155] for that temple only lasted one thousand one hundred and two years, for Titus, the son of Vespasian, the emperor of Rome, laid siege to Jerusalem to destroy the Jews because they had put Our Lord to death without the emperor's leave; and when they had taken the city, they burnt the temple and knocked it down and took all the Jews and put

---

153. "The Lord's Body": the Eucharist. Christian pilgrims typically needed the Sultan's approval for safe passage. Cf. WoB (Ch. 4 in Appendix B.1).

154. Charroux, not Chartres, claimed to have the foreskin, but only one copy corrects this. Another places the relic in Rome: "And nevertheless it is said that it is in Rome in [the basilica of] Saint John Lateran." This copyist might have been recalling the *Golden Legend*, where the foreskin's travels are mentioned in a chapter on the significance of Jesus' circumcision (the Jewish custom being read through the lens of Christian theology). Charlemagne's fictional pilgrimage to Jerusalem, from which he brings back many relics, is told in a widely known *chanson de geste*, or heroic narrative.

155. This history of the temple, Judaism's most significant shrine, is a typical, unreliable mix of fact and fancy drawn from various sources to supplement WoB. Not Titus but Nebuchadnezzar destroyed the temple (c. 586 BCE). The story of Titus' role here derives from the *Golden Legend* on Saint James the Apostle. Hadrian (not a Trojan) *preceded* Julian, and so on.

eleven hundred thousand to death, and put the others in prison and sold them into slavery at thirty a penny; for he [Titus] said that they had sold Jesus Christ for thirty pennies and he would make a better bargain of them: he would offer them at thirty a penny. Then some time afterwards the Emperor Julius Apostata [Julian the Apostate] gave the Jews permission to rebuild the temple in Jerusalem, because he hated the Christians—and he was also a Christian but he abjured his faith. When the Jews had almost made the temple, an earthquake occurred, such as it pleased God, and knocked down what they had made. Then the Emperor Hadrian, who was of Trojan descent, remade the city of Jerusalem and the temple in the same way that Solomon had; and he did not want any Jews to live there, but only Christians, for although he was not Christian he preferred Christians to all other peoples after those of his own law. This emperor had the Church of the Holy Sepulcher enclosed and walled within the city, which before was far outside the city, and he wanted to change the name of Jerusalem, and they called it Helia [Aelia]. But that name barely lasted.

Also, know that the Saracens very greatly revere that Temple and indeed say that the place is most holy, and they enter shoeless and kneel often. When my companions and I saw that, we took our shoes off and thought that we ought to behave much better than the misbelievers, and we had great compunction in our hearts.

This Temple is sixty-four cubits wide and as many long, and one hundred and twenty cubits high,[156] and there are marble pillars all around, and in the middle of the Temple there are very high risers eighteen steps high, and good pillars all around. The Jews call that place *Sancta Sanctorum*.[157] No one entered there but the prelate who performed the rite of the sacrifice, and the people were all around separated on different levels according to their rank, so that they would all see the sacrifice performed. In this Temple there are four entryways and the doors are of well-crafted cypress, and inside the eastern doors Our Lord said: "Here is Jerusalem." In the northern part inside the doors there is a well, but it does not flow at all, of which Holy Scripture speaks: "*Vidi aquam egredientem de Templo, etc.*"[158] On the other side of the Temple there is a rock that used to be called Moriath [Moriah], but then it was called Bethel, where the Ark of God or the relics of the Jews used to be kept.[159] Titus had that Ark with the relics taken to the great Rome

---

156. On the cubit, see Chapter 2, n. 15.

157. Holy of Holies.

158. "I saw water flowing from the Temple, etc." (cf. Ezek. 47:1). "Here is Jerusalem": an echo of Ezek 5:5?

159. Ark of the Covenant: Exod. 25:10–22. Yahweh (God) orders Moses to make the Ark to contain His testimony to the Israelites, understood to be the Tables of the Law. Some of the other materials said here to be in the Ark are mentioned in Heb. 9:2–5.

when he had defeated all the Jews. In this Ark were the Tablets of the
Ten Commandments, and Aaron's rod and the rod with which Moses
parted the Red Sea when the people of Israel crossed dry-footed, and
with that rod he struck the rock and the waters flowed out, and with
that rod he performed many miracles. There was also a gold vessel full
of manna, and the vestments and the ornaments, and the tabernacle
of Aaron, and a square tabernacle made of gold with twelve precious
stones, and a box of green jasper with seven figures of the names of Our
Lord inside. And seven gold candlesticks and twelve gold pots and four
gold censers, and a gold altar, and four gold lions on which there were
four gold cherubim twelve palms high, and the circle of the zodiac with
a gold tabernacle and silver trumpets, and a silver table and seven loaves
of barley bread, and all the other relics that existed before the birth of
Our Lord Jesus Christ.

Also, Jacob was resting on this rock when he saw the angels climbing and descending by a ladder and said: "*Vere hic est locus sanctus et ego
ignorabam.*"[160] An angel held Jacob there, and changed Jacob's name
and called him Israel. And in this same place David saw an angel who
cut down the people with a sword and then replaced it all bloody in
the sheath.[161] On this rock Our Lord was presented to Saint Simeon;
and on this rock Our Lord often preached to the people, and He cast
the sellers and the buyers out of this Temple; and He set himself on
this rock when the Jews wanted to stone him, and the rock split in the
middle and He was hidden in that cleft; and a star came down to Him
there that gave Him light and served as a lamp. On this rock Our Lady
sat and learned her Psalter. There Our Lord pardoned the sins of the
woman taken in adultery, there He was circumcised, there the angel
announced to Zacharias the birth of his son John the Baptist, and there
he[162] first offered bread and wine to Our Lord as a sign of the sacrament
to come.

On this rock David deliberately prostrated himself in prayer to Our
Lord and to the angel that he saw slaying the people, so that Our Lord
would have pity on him and on the people, and Our Lord heard his
prayer. Therefore he wanted to found the temple in this place, but Our
Lord prohibited him with an angel because he [David] had acted trai-
torously when he had Uriah the brave knight slain because he coveted

160. "Indeed this place is holy and I did not know that" (cf. Gen. 28:16).
161. 2 Sam. 24:16.
162. The offering was made by Melchisedek, as several French copies and C, D,
and E correctly have it, and to "the most high God" (Gen. 14:18–20). Christians
saw in this event a type of the Eucharist; it is recalled in the Roman Catholic mass.
This paragraph contains a typical mix of biblical, apocryphal, and legendary
material. Mary's link to the Temple derives from the apocryphal second-century
Protevangelium of James, augmented by medieval assumptions about her learning
to read there. Other legends about Mary mentioned here and elsewhere share a
similar derivation.

his wife. And therefore all the groundwork that he had done and put in place for building the Temple, he gave to his son Solomon, [for him] to build the Temple; and so Solomon built it and asked Our Lord to hear the requests of all those who pray with a good heart in this place Bethel and help them and advise them in whatever just cause that they have asked assistance for in this place. And Our Lord granted him this and therefore Solomon called it the Temple of God's Counsel and Help.[163]

Outside the door of this Temple there is an altar where the Jews used to offer doves and turtledoves, and now the Saracens have made grooves on the altar[164] to observe what time of day it is with a pointer that is there. Between this altar and the temple Zakarie [Zacharias] was slain, and on the pinnacle of this Temple, which is quite high, Our Lord was taken to be tempted by the Devil. From the top of this pinnacle the Jews threw Saint James to the ground who was the first bishop of Jerusalem.[165] And at the entrance to the Temple, to the west, is the *Porta Speciosa,*[166] through which Saint John and Saint Peter passed when Saint Peter by God's grace made the lame man walk and come out of the Temple.[167] And quite close to this Temple, to the right, there is a church covered with lead that is called the School of Solomon. And quite close to this Temple towards the south is the Temple of Solomon, which is most beautiful and situated in a great square and on a fine plain. In this Temple dwelt the Knights of the Temple who used to be called Templars, and this was the foundation of their order such that knights dwelt here, and canons regular in the Temple Domini.[168]

From this Temple east one hundred and twenty paces in the corner of the city is Our Lord's bath. Into this bath used to come the water of Paradise and it still trickles there. Beside there is Our Lady's bed, and nearby is the tomb of Saint Simeon, and outside the cloister of the temple towards the north is a most beautiful church of Saint Anne, Our Lady's mother. Our Lady was conceived there, and in front of this church there is a large tree that began to grow that same night. Beneath this church going twenty-two steps down lies Saint Joachim, Our Lady's

---

163. 1 Chron. 22:7–19 and 2 Chron. 6:21–42.

164. Four French copies name the device: "made a clockface [*quadran*] on top of this altar."

165. Zacharias slain: 2 Chron. 24:20–22. Jesus tempted: Matt. 4:5–6; Luke 4:9–12. Saint James' martyrdom is recounted in the *Golden Legend.*

166. "Beautiful Gate," built in the twelfth century by the crusaders.

167. Acts 3:19.

168. Like the Hospitallers (see Ch. 4, n. 35), the Knights Templar were a military religious order; founded in 1118 in Jerusalem, they received papal recognition in 1128 and took up residence in the Temple, now the al-Aqsa Mosque (built originally in the eighth century, it was rebuilt as a church in the twelfth century under the Latin kings of Jerusalem, then restored as a mosque in 1218 after Saladin's conquest). The Templars were violently suppressed in 1312.

father, in a stone tomb, and beside there Saint Anne his wife used to lie, but Saint Helen had her taken to Constantinople. And in this church there is a well in the form of a cistern that is called *Probatica Piscina*[169] that had five entries. To this well the angels used to come down and bathe in it, and the first person who bathed afterwards was healed of whatever illness he had had. There Our Lord healed the paralytic man who had been ill for thirty-eight years and said to him: "*Tolle grabatum tuum et ambula.*"[170]

Beside there was Pilate's house and nearby is the house of Herod, the king who had the Innocents killed.[171] This Herod was truly evil and very cruel, for he first had his wife killed whom he loved very much and, because of the great love that he had in him, when he saw that she was dead he became furious and was out of his mind a great while. Then he came to himself again, and afterwards he had his two grown sons—two young gentlemen—killed whom he had with that wife, and then he had another of his wives killed plus a grown son he had with her. Then he had his own mother killed and he also wanted to kill his brother, but he [the brother] died suddenly. Then Herod did all the evil that he could, and when he approached the end [of his life], and realized that he could not escape his illness, he sent for his sister and all the great lords of the country; and when they were there, he had all the lords put in a tower and said to his sister that he knew well that no one in the country would mourn his death, and therefore he had her swear that she would have all the great lords beheaded as soon as he was dead so that the whole country would greatly mourn his death, and thus he made his testament. But his sister did not carry this out, for as soon as he was dead, she freed the lords from the tower and sent them to their homes and told them what her brother had planned for them, and so the king was not lamented as he had thought to be.

Know that there were in that time three Herods greatly renowned for their cruelty. This Herod of whom I have spoken was Herod Ascalonite, and the one who had John the Baptist's head cut off was Herod Antipas, and Herod Agrippa had Saint James killed and had Saint Peter put in prison.[172]

---

169. Pool of Bethesda: near the church, not in it. The story told here comes from John 5:1–9.

170. "Take up your bed and walk" (John 5:8).

171. Matt. 2:16. Herod's story as told here derives from the *Golden Legend* on the Feast of the Innocents and Peter Comestor's *Historia Scholastica* (2 Macc. 23; Evang. 13–18).

172. Herod Ascalonite, or Herod the Great, ruled Palestine 37–34 BCE. His son Herod Antipas (responsible for beheading John the Baptist in Matt. 14:1–12) was tetrarch of Galilee and Peraea 4 BCE–40 CE; and his grandson Herod Agrippa was king of Judea 41–44 CE (in Acts 12, Herod is responsible only for James' death). A fourth Herod, Agrippa II (son of Agrippa I), presides over Paul's trial in Acts 25:13–27.

Also, farther into the city is the Church of Saint Savior. The left arm of Saint John Chrysostom is there and the largest part of Saint Stephen's head. On the other side of the street towards the south, just as one goes towards Mount Sion, is the Church of Saint James, there where he was beheaded.

One hundred and twenty steps from this church is Mount Sion. There is a beautiful Church of Our Lady, there where she dwelt, and she died there. It used to have an abbey and canons regular.[173] From there she was carried by the Apostles all the way to the valley of Josaphat. The stone that the angels brought to Our Lady from Mount Sinai is there, and it is exactly the color of the rock of [Mount] Saint Catherine. And beside there is the gate where Our Lady left to go towards Bethlehem.

Also, at the entrance to Mount Sion, there is a chapel, and in this chapel is the large and broad rock with which the Holy Sepulcher was covered when Joseph of Arimathea had placed Our Lord inside. This is the stone that the three Marys saw rolled back when they came on the day of the Resurrection to the tomb and found the angel who told them that Jesus Christ had already risen from death to life. There is also a rock there, in the wall near the door, from the column at which Our Lord was scourged. And the house of Annas was there who was bishop of the Jews at that time, and there Our Lord was interrogated at night and scourged and struck and cruelly treated, and in the same place Saint Peter denied Him three times before cockcrow. And there too is a piece of the table on which Our Lord dined with His disciples when He gave them His flesh and His blood in the form of bread and wine. And thirty-two steps beneath that chapel is the place where Our Lord washed His disciples' feet, and the vessel where the water was is still there. And beside this vessel Saint Stephen was buried. And there is the altar where Our Lady heard the angels singing mass. There Our Lord first appeared to His disciples after His Resurrection at the locked doors and said to them: *"Pax vobis."*[174] On Mount Sion Our Lord appeared to Saint Thomas the apostle and had him touch his wounds one week after His Resurrection, and then Saint Thomas first believed in Him and said: *"Deus meus et Dominus meus."*[175] In this same chapel near the great altar the Apostles were gathered on the day of Pentecost when the Holy Spirit descended on them in the form of a flame. There Our Lord celebrated Passover with His disciples and there Saint John the Evangelist slept on Jesus Christ's chest, and while sleeping saw many of Heaven's secrets.[176]

---

173. Clergymen living together under a system of monastic rules.

174. "Peace unto you" (John 20:19, 21, 26). The four Gospels, occasionally supplemented by other sources, provide the details here of the story of Jesus and His disciples.

175. "My God and my Lord" (John 20:28).

176. Pentecost: Acts 2:1–4. John sleeping by Jesus: John 13:23–26, which mentions an unnamed disciple leaning on Jesus at the Last Supper; this may have given

Mount Sion is inside the city and is a little higher than the other part of the city, and thus the city is stronger on that side than on any other, for at the foot of Mount Sion there is a fine and strong castle that the Sultan had made. On Mount Sion King David and King Solomon and several other Jewish kings of Jerusalem were buried. And there is the place where the Jews wanted to cast the body of Our Lady when the Apostles brought it for burial in the valley of Josaphat.[177] And there is the place where Saint Peter wept very tenderly after he had denied Our Lord.

A stone's throw from that chapel mentioned above there is another chapel where Our Lord was sentenced to death. Caiaphas' house was there then. One hundred and forty steps eastwards from that chapel is a deep cave under the rock that is called Our Lord's Galilee. Saint Peter hid there when he had denied Our Lord. Also, between Mount Sion and the Temple of Solomon is the place where Our Lord resuscitated the virgin in her father's house.[178]

Beneath Mount Sion towards the valley of Josaphat there is a well that is called *Natatorium Siloe*.[179] There Our Lord was washed after baptism, there Our Lord made the blind man see, and there Isaiah the prophet was buried. Also, at the place of the *Natatorium Siloe* there is a stone image of ancient workmanship that Absalom had made and therefore it is called Absalom's Hand. And nearby is still the tree of Sohur where Judas hanged himself in despair that he had sold and betrayed Our Lord. Close to there is the synagogue where the bishops of the Jews and the Pharisees gathered and held their council. And there Judas threw the thirty deniers before them and said that he had sinned in betraying Our Lord. Nearby there was the house of the Apostles Philip and Jacob [James], son of Alpheus.

From the other side of Mount Sion towards the south, a stone's throw beyond the valley, is Acheldemak [Haceldama], that is to say the Field of Blood, which was bought for the thirty pennies for which Our Lord was sold.[180] In that field there are many graves of Christians, for dead pilgrims used to be buried [there]. And there are many oratories and chapels and hermitages where hermits used to dwell. One hundred steps farther towards the east is the charnel house of the Hospital of Saint John where the bones of the dead used to be placed.

Also, from Jerusalem one league towards the regions of the west there is a beautiful church where the tree of the cross grew. And two leagues from there, there is a beautiful church where Our Lady met and

---

rise to images and sculptures (especially popular in fourteenth-century female Dominican houses in the Upper Rhine) known as "Christ-John groups."

177. Another story from the *Golden Legend*, this time from the chapter on the Feast of the Assumption.

178. Matt. 9:18–27.

179. "The Pool of Siloe." Miracle of the blind man: John 9:1–7.

180. Judas' hanging, repentance, and Haceldama: cf. Matt. 27:1–10.

greeted Elizabeth, her cousin, the mother of Saint John the Baptist; and both were pregnant, and Saint John moved in his mother's womb and venerated his creator whom he could not yet see.[181] And beneath the altar of this church is the place where Saint John was born. From this church it is one league to the castle of Emmaus, where Our Lord also showed himself to His disciples after His Resurrection.[182] Also, from the other side, two hundred steps from Jerusalem, there is a church where the Cave of the Lion used to be. And beneath this church thirty steps down twelve thousand martyrs were buried in the time of King Cosdroe[183] that the lion brought all together in one night through the divine will.

Also, two leagues from Jerusalem is Mount Joy, a very beautiful place and most delightful, where Saint Samuel the prophet lies in a beautiful tomb, and this place is called Mount Joy because it gives joy to the hearts of pilgrims; for from this place the pilgrims coming from these regions first see the holy city of Jerusalem. Also, between Jerusalem and the Mount of Olives is the valley of Josaphat beneath the walls of the city, as I said before. And in the middle of this valley there is a small stream that one calls *Torrens Cedron* or the Stream of Cedron. And sideways above the stream lies the tree of the cross and one passes over [it]. And quite close to there, there is a small pit in the ground where the base of the column is still in the ground where Our Lord was first scourged, for he was scourged and cruelly treated in several places. Also, in the middle of this valley of Josaphat is the Church of Our Lady, and it is forty-four steps underground to Our Lady's tomb. Our Lady was seventy-two years of age when she died. And there beside Our Lady's tomb there is an altar where Our Lord pardoned Saint Peter of all his sins. And beside there towards the west under an altar there is a spring that comes from one of the rivers of Paradise. Know that this church is very low in the ground and almost all in the earth. But I think that it was not first built like this, but rather, because Jerusalem has been destroyed several times and the walls razed, the walls tumbled and fell into the valley, and they have been thus filled and the earth raised, and this is why the church is so low in the ground. Nevertheless it is commonly said thereabouts that the earth thus dug itself out when Our Lady was buried. And they still say that it grows every day without any doubt. In this church there used to be black monks[184] who had their own abbot.

---

181. The Visitation, a celebrated event in the cult of the Virgin Mary: Luke 1:39–56.

182. Luke 24:13–27.

183. This story about the Christian victims of Chosroes I (king of Persia 531–78/9) in the Byzantine-Persian wars is found in several twelfth-century Latin itineraries that the *Mandeville* author sometimes drew on.

184. That is, monks living according to the influential sixth-century Rule of Saint Benedict of Nursia.

Near this church is a chapel beside the rock with the name Gethsemane, where Our Lord was kissed by Judas, and where he was seized by the Jews. There Our Lord left His disciples when He went to pray before the Passion, and He prayed, saying "*Pater si fieri potest transeat a me calix iste.*"[185] When He returned to His disciples, He found them sleeping. And in the rock inside the chapel the fingers of Our Lord's hand are still visible where He leaned on the rock when the Jews forcefully seized him. A stone's throw beyond towards the south there is another chapel where Our Lord sweated drops of blood. And quite close to there is the tomb of the King Josaphat, whose name the valley bears. This Josaphat was king of that country and he was converted by a hermit and was a very worthy man and did much good.[186] Beyond there a bowshot towards the south is the church where Saint James and Zacharias the prophet were buried.

Above this valley is the Mount of Olives, and it has this name because many olive trees grow there. This mountain is higher than the city of Jerusalem is and therefore one can see from this mountain almost all the streets of the city; and between the mountain and the city there is only the valley of Josaphat, which is not very wide. From this mountain Our Lord rose to Heaven on Ascension Day and [the imprint of] His left foot is still visible in the rock.[187] There is a church there where there used to be an abbot and canons regular. And close to this spot, twenty-eight steps away, there is a chapel where the stone is on which Our Lord used to sit and preach the eight beatitudes: "*Beati pauperes spiritu.*"[188] There He taught His disciples the *Pater Noster* and wrote it in the rock with His finger. And nearby is a Church of Saint Mary the Egyptian and she lies there in a tomb.[189] Beyond towards the east at three bowshots is Bethphage where Our Lord sent Saint Peter and Saint James to fetch the she-ass on Palm Sunday, and He mounted the she-ass there. In coming down from the Mount of Olives towards the east there is a castle that

---

185. "Father, if it may be done, let this chalice go from me" (cf. Luke 22:42). The biblical context for the stories here is Matt. 26:36–56 and the other Gospels.

186. The first Josaphat is Jehoshaphat, king of Judah in the mid-ninth century BCE; the second is from a legend of the Buddha (unknown as such) that circulated as the story of Barlaam and Josaphat, retold, for example, in the *Golden Legend*.

187. Ascension: Acts 1:1–9. Seymour notes that a stone with the right footprint was at Westminster Abbey from 1249 until the Reformation, and suggests that the *Mandeville* author's *not* pointing out this connection stands against his claim to be English (2002, 146, n. to 40/9).

188. "Blessed are the poor in spirit" (Matt. 5:3–11). The Beatitudes are thought to have been preached closer to the Sea of Galilee, but after the late thirteenth century many Gospel stories came to be associated with Jerusalem (DLMM 223, n. 63). *Pater Noster:* see Chapter 10, n. 146.

189. Saint Pelagia, according to other pilgrims. The confusion may stem from the similarity of their stories, which involve a repentant turning away from a dissolute life.

has the name Bethany. Simon the Leper dwelt there, and he lodged Our
Lord there, and then he was baptized by the Apostles and was named
Julian and was made bishop.[190] It is this Julian to whom one prays to
be well housed because he provided Our Lord with lodgings in his
house. In this same place Our Lord forgave Mary Magdalene her sins,
[and] there she washed His feet with her tears and dried them with her
hair. There Saint Martha served Him. And there Our Lord resuscitated
the Lazarus who had been dead for four days who was the brother of
Mary Magdalene and Martha. And there too Mary Cleophe [Cleophas]
dwelt. This castle is a good league away from Jerusalem. Also, in coming down from the Mount of Olives is the place where Our Lord wept
for Jerusalem, and beside there is the place where Our Lady appeared
to Saint Thomas after [the] Assumption and gave him her girdle. And
nearby is the rock where Our Lord often sat and preached, and He will
be there too on Judgment Day, as He Himself said.[191]

Also, after the Mount of Olives is the Mount of Galilee, where the
Apostles were gathered when Mary Magdalene came to make the
Resurrection known to them, and halfway from the Mount of Olives to
the Mount of Galilee there is a church where the angel told Our Lady of
her death. Also, from Bethany to Jericho it is only five leagues. Jericho
used to be a beautiful city, but it was completely destroyed and now
there is only a small village. Joshua took this city by God's miracle and
on the angel's order, and destroyed it and cursed all those who would
ever rebuild it. From this city came Zacheus, who was a dwarf, who
climbed a sycamore to see Our Lord, for he was so small that he could
not see for the other people.[192] From that city Rahab, who was a common
woman,[193] escaped with only two of her family, for she had hidden and
fed the messengers of Israel and kept them from danger of death; and
so she received a good reward for this, just as Scripture says: "*Qui accepit
prophetam in nomine meo mercedem prophetae accipiet etc.*"[194] And so she did,
for she prophesied to his messengers, saying: "*Novi quod Dominus tradet
vobis terram hanc.*"[195] And so it was. Then Salomon [Salmon] the son of

190. Palm Sunday: Matt. 21:1–11. Simon (Mark 14:3–9) is assimilated to Julian in
the *Golden Legend*'s account of Saint Julian.

191. There is no biblical record of this claim. Mary Magdalene and Martha: John
12:1–3; the former is here confused with the sinner of Luke 7:36–50, a common
medieval confusion. Lazarus: John 11:1–44.

192. Mary Magdalene and Apostles: Matt. 28:1–8. Angel and Our Lady: apocryphal (well known through the *Golden Legend* on the Assumption). Destruction of
Jericho: Josh. 6:1–21. Zacheus: Luke 19:3–4.

193. Prostitute. Rahab's story: Josh. 2:1–21 and 6:22–26; her husband's name
(Salmon): Matt. 1:4–5.

194. "He that receives a prophet in my name, shall receive the reward of a prophet"
(cf. Matt. 10:41).

195. "I know that the Lord will give this land to you" (Josh. 2:9, which has *tradiderit,*
"hath given").

Nason [Nahasson] took her as his wife, and she was thereafter a worthy woman and served God well.

Also, from Bethany one goes to the River Jordan by a barren mountain, and the journey takes almost a day. From Bethany towards the east to the large mountain where Our Lord fasted forty days is six leagues. Our Lord was taken on to this mountain and there He was tempted by the Devil, who said to Him: "*Dic ut lapides isti panes fiant.*"[196] In this place on the mountain there used to be a beautiful church, but it was destroyed, and now there is only a hermitage held by a kind of Christians who are called Georgians because Saint George converted them.[197] On this mountain Abraham dwelt for a good while, and therefore it is called Abraham's Garden. Between the mountain and this garden runs a little stream of water and this water used to be bitter. But by the blessing of Helize [Elisha] the prophet it became sweet and good to drink,[198] and at the foot of this mountain towards the plain there is a large spring that goes into the River Jordan. From this mountain to Jericho about which I spoke above it is only a league, going towards the River Jordan. Also, on the road to Jericho the blind man sat and said: "*Jhesu, fili Dei, miserere mei,*"[199] and immediately he could see. Also, two leagues from Jericho and the River Jordan and half a league closer is a beautiful Church of Saint John the Baptist, there where he baptized Our Lord. And nearby is the house of Jeremiah the prophet.

[Chapter 12]

About the Dead Sea. About the River Jordan. About the Head That Exists[200] *and About the Practices of the Samaritans*

Three leagues from Jericho is the Dead Sea.[201] Around this sea much alum and alkatran[202] grows. Between Jericho and this sea is the land

---

196. "Command that these stones be made bread" (Matt. 4:3).

197. Georgian Christianity, an independent branch of the Eastern Orthodox Church, traces its origins to the Apostle Andrew. See also Chapter 13, n. 271.

198. Abraham's Garden: Gen. 13:10 (filtered through WoB). Elisha's blessing: 2 Kings 2:19–22.

199. "Jesus, son of God, have mercy on me" (adapted from Matt. 20:30–31). Jesus' baptism: Matt. 3:1–17. Both events are also related in the other Gospels.

200. *Del teste qe est.* C's rubric is clearer: "Of the Hed of Seynt John the Baptist."

201. Advised by his Muslim interpreter against visiting this memorial to God's vengeance against sin, WoB only briefly describes the Dead Sea (Ch. 8 in Appendix B.1), so the *Mandeville* author draws on other sources, some details of which go as far back as Josephus' first-century *Jewish Wars*. The name Dead Sea, in use by the second century BCE, is not biblical.

202. Alum: a whitish or colorless mineral salt once used to dress leather or help dye cloth. Alkatran: pitch.

of Engadde [Engeddi] where balm used to grow. But the shrubs were pulled up and taken to be planted in Babylon, and they are still called the vines of Engaddy [Engeddi]. On one side of this sea in coming down from Arabia is the Mount of [the] Moabites where there is a cave that is called Karna. Balac, the son of Boor [Zippor or Sephor], led Balaam the priest onto this mountain to excommunicate and curse the people of Israel. This Dead Sea separates the land of Judea and of Arabia, and this sea extends from Zoara all the way to Arabia.[203]

The water of this sea is very bitter and salty, and if the land is moistened with this water it will bear no fruit. The land there often changes its color and throws out of the water something that is called asphalt—pieces as big as a horse every day and on all sides. From Jerusalem to this sea is two hundred stades.[204] This sea is five hundred and eighty stades long and one hundred and fifty stades wide; and it is called Dead Sea because it does not flow at all. No living man or animal could die in this sea, and this has been proved many times, in that people are thrown in who have deserved death and they have remained three or four days, but they could not die, for it retains nothing that has life in it. Nor can anyone drink the water. Whoever puts iron in it, it swims on top, and whoever puts a feather in, it goes to the bottom—and these are things against nature. Thus the cities there perished because of sin against nature. And also trees grow nearby that bear very beautiful apples of a beautiful color to look at and seemingly fully ripe, but whoever breaks them open or slices them through the middle will find nothing inside but ashes as a sign that through God's wrath the cities and the land were burned with Hellfire. Some call this sea the Lake of Alfetide, others the Devil's River, and others the Stinking River, for the water is filthy and smelly.

Into this sea the five cities—that is, Sodom and Gomorrah, Aldama [Admah], Seboyn [Zeboiim], and Segor [Zoara]—collapsed through God's anger for the sin of sodomy that reigned in them. But Segor was largely spared through Lot's prayer, for it was situated beneath a mountain.[205] It is still partly visible under the water, and the walls can be seen when the weather is clear and calm.

---

203. Vines of Engeddi: cf. Song of Sol. 1:13. Despite Christian pilgrims' claims to the contrary, balm grew throughout the Near East. Balaam: Num. 22–24. Zoara is another name for Segor.

204. Stade: see Chapter 5, n. 49.

205. Gen. 19:1–29. The Dead Sea's extreme salinity accounts for its remarkable buoyancy and its highly limited flora and fauna; the "apples" may be the fruit of a local plant (*Calotropis procera*), but two others have been suggested (*Solanum sodomaeum; Citrullus colocynthis*). As such legends reveal, medieval Christians saw Nature (God's creation) as both a physical and a moral system. The lake's "unnatural" behavior thus mirrors the sins "against nature" (Rom. 1:24–27) committed in Sodom. "Sodomy" here probably means male homosexual activity, which was biblically proscribed (e.g., Lev. 8:22).

In this city Lot lived for a little while, and there he was made drunk by his daughters and he lay with them and begat Moab and Amon.²⁰⁶ The reason why the daughters got their father drunk to make him lie with them—it was because they saw no one around there except their father alone. They thought that God had destroyed the whole world, just as He did the cities near them and also as He did with Noah's flood. Therefore they wanted to lie with their father to have descendants, so that the world would afterwards be peopled by them; for they believed that there were no more people in the world, and had he not been drunk, he would not have lain with them.

The mountain above Segor was called Edom in those days, and then it was called Seir and then Idumea. Also, on the right side of this Dead Sea remained Lot's wife, upright like a rock of salt, because she looked back when the cities collapsed into the abyss. This Lot was the son of Aram [Haran], Abraham's brother. Sara (Abraham's wife) and Melcha [Milcha] (Nachor's [Nahor's] wife) were sisters of the said Lot, and this Sara was ninety years old when Isaac was begotten. Abraham had at that time another son Ishmael who was fourteen years old whom he had begotten on Agar his handmaid. When Isaac was eight days old Abraham had him circumcised and Ishmael with him who was fourteen years old.²⁰⁷ Therefore the Jews, who are descendants of Isaac, are circumcised at eight days, and the Saracens, who are descendants of Ishmael, are circumcised at fourteen years of age.²⁰⁸

The River Jordan flows into the Dead Sea and disappears there, for it flows no further. This is one league from the Church of Saint John the Baptist, a little towards the west from the place where the Christians commonly bathe. And one league from the River Jordan is the River of Laboch [Jabbok], which Jacob crossed when he came from Mesopotamia.²⁰⁹ This River Jordan is not a very broad river, but it has good fish. It comes from Mount Liban [Lebanon] from two sources that

206. Gen. 19:30–38. Lot's daughters' excuse is adapted from the biblical account.
207. Lot's wife: Gen. 19:26. Lot's family: Gen. 11:29–31 (Sara is not Lot's sister, however). Abraham, Agar, Ishmael: Gen. 16:15. Isaac conceived and circumcised: Gen. 21:1–4. Ishmael circumcised: Gen. 17:23–26.
208. In Gen. 17:9–13 male circumcision is the sign of God's covenant with Abraham; it is thus an important Judaic rite, normally performed eight days after birth. Not mentioned in the Qur'an, nor one of the five pillars of Islam, it is widely regarded as a necessary, traditional rite of purification (pre-Islamic Arabs practiced it), but there is no Islamic requirement for circumcision at fourteen. As a Jew, Jesus was circumcised at eight days of age (Luke 2:21), but early Christians abandoned the practice after some dissension, following Paul (cf. Acts 15, Gal. 2); the practice has been retained in some Christian traditions, however (e.g., Coptic and Ethiopian).
209. Gen. 32:22.

are called Jor and Dan.[210] From these sources it takes its name and its origin; and it passes through a lake that is called Maron [Merom], and then passes through the Sea of Tiberie [Tiberias], and passes under the mountains of Gelboe [Gilboa]. There is a very beautiful valley on both sides of the river, and the mountains of Lebanon all the way along to the desert of Pharan. These mountains divide the kingdom of Surie [Syria] and the country of Phenicie [Phoenicia]; on these mountains grow very tall cedar trees that bear long apples that are as big as a man's head. This River Jordan divides the land of Galilee and the land of Idumea and the land of Betron [Basra?]. It runs underground a ways to a beautiful and broad plain that is called *Meldan* in the Saracen language—that is to say *fair* or *market* in English, because there is often a fair on that plain—and in front of there the river becomes large and wide. On this plain is Job's tomb.[211]

In this River Jordan God was baptized, and the voice of the Father was heard saying: "*Hic est filius meus dilectus etc.*"[212] And the Holy Spirit descended on Him in the form of a dove. Thus the whole Trinity was at this baptism. And through this river the sons of Israel passed completely dry, and they placed stones in the middle as a sign of the miracle by which the water was drawn back. Also, in this River Jordan Naaman of Syria bathed who was a very rich man, and he was leprous and he was immediately healed. Around the River Jordan are many churches where many Christians dwell, and nearby is the city of Hay [Hai], which Joshua attacked and seized.[213]

Also, two leagues towards Galilee from the mountain about which I spoke above, where Our Lord fasted for forty days, there is a very high mountain where the Devil took Our Lord for the third time to tempt Him and he showed Him the full expanse of [the] country and said to Him: "Everything you see I shall give you if you fall to the ground and worship me."[214] Also, from the Dead Sea going towards the east outside the frontiers of the Promised Land there is a strong and beautiful castle in the mountain that has the name Carak [Krak] in Saracen: that is to say, Mount Royal in English. This castle was built for a king of France,

---

210. The Dan is one of the Jordan's tributaries, but there is no Jor. The river drops rapidly in elevation and its name (Nehar Hayarden in Hebrew) is thought to derive from a Hebrew verb meaning "to go down." The Sea of Tiberie [Tiberias] (mentioned in the next sentence) is also known as the Sea of Galilee.

211. The *"fair* or *market"* was held during a halt on the Hajj, or annual Islamic pilgrimage to Mecca. Job, from the biblical Book of Job, was the subject of contradictory traditions, but a site identified as his tomb was known to Christian pilgrims already in the fourth century.

212. "This is my beloved son" (Matt. 3:17). Jesus' baptism is recorded in all four Gospels.

213. Dry passage: Josh. 3:1–17. Naaman healed: 2 Kings 5:1–14. Siege of Hai: Josh. 8:14–18.

214. Matt. 4:9. Two manuscripts give the usual Latin with a French translation.

Baldwin, who had conquered that land, and he placed Christians there
to guard the country and that is why it was called Mount Royal.[215] Below
there is a town that has the name Sobach [Shobek], around which dwell
a great many Christians under tribute.

From there one goes to Nazareth, from which Our Lord took His
surname, and to there it is three days' travel from Jerusalem. One goes
through the province of Galilee by Ramatha, Sothim,[216] and the high
mountain of Effraym [Ephraim], where Elcana [Elkanah] and Anne
[Hannah], the mother of Samuel, dwelt. This prophet was born there
and after his death he was buried at Mount Joy, just as I have told you.[217]
Then one goes to Silo [Shiloh], where the Ark of God with the relics was long kept, under Helye [Eli] the prophet. There the people of
Hebron sacrificed to Our Lord, and there they gave Him their vows,
and there God first spoke to Samuel and revealed to him the change to
the priestly order and the mystery of the sacrament.[218] And quite close
to the left is Gabaon [Gibea] and Rama and Benjamin, about which
Scripture speaks.[219]

Then one goes through Sichem [Shechem], otherwise called Sichar,
which is in the province of [the] Samaritans. There is a very beautiful
and very fruitful valley [there], and there is a beautiful and good city
that is called Neopole [Nablus?], and it is one day's journey to there from
Jerusalem. There is the well where Our Lord spoke to the Samaritan
woman,[220] and it used to have a church, but it was destroyed. Beside this
well Roboas [Roboam][221] had two golden calves made and had them worshiped, and he placed one in Dan and the other in Bethel. One league
from Sichar is the city of Luze. In this city Abraham dwelt for a certain
time. Sichim [Shechem] is ten leagues from Jerusalem and is called
Neopole, that is to say new city. Nearby is the tomb of Joseph, Jacob's
son, who ruled Egypt, for the Jews carried those bones from Egypt and
buried them there. And the Jews often go there on pilgrimage with

---

215. Following WoB, the *Mandeville* author makes one crusader castle of two:
the Krak des Moabites and the Krak de Montréal (*karak*: "fortress" in Syriac).
The latter was built in 1115 by Baldwin I of Jerusalem to threaten the Islamic
pilgrimage route to Mecca and surrendered to Saladin in 1189. The former, in
the city of Karak, was begun in the 1140s by Pagan le Bouteiller (the Butler), lord
of Montréal and Transjordan, and lost to Saladin's brother in 1188.

216. Actually one town: Ramatha Sophim.

217. In Chapter 11.

218. Elcana, Anne, Samuel: 1 Sam. 1. Eli: 1 Sam. 4:3–6. God speaks to Samuel:
1 Sam. 3:1–14.

219. Cf. 1 Kings 15:22. Gabaon might be either Gibea or Gibeon. Ramah in
Benjamin is just one city. Such confusion was easy, as *rama* (height) and *gabaa*
(hill) are common biblical terms (DLMM 237, n. 27).

220. John 4:1–12.

221. Actually, Jeroboam (I Kings 12:28–33), as in E: "Jeroboam kyng of Israel"
(WBJM 53).

great devotion.[222] In this city Dyne [Dinah], Jacob's daughter, was raped, which is why her brothers killed many people in it and did great harm to the city. Beside there is the Mount of Garasoun [Gerizim] where the Samaritans perform their sacrifice. On this mount Abraham would have sacrificed his son Isaac. Beside there is the valley of Dotaym [Dothan]. And there is the cistern into which Joseph was thrown by his brothers before they sold him.[223] This is two leagues from Sichar.

From there one goes to Samaria, which is now called Sebaste [Sabastiyeh]; and this is the capital of that country and it is situated between mountains just as Jerusalem is. In this city were the seats of the ten tribes of Israel. But the city is now not so large as it used to be. There Saint John the Baptist was buried between two prophets, Heliseus [Elisha] and Abdian [Obadiah?]. But he was beheaded in the castle of Macheryn [Machaerus] near the Dead Sea, and then was translated by his disciples and buried in Samaria. And there Julius Apostata [Julian the Apostate] had his bones dug up and burned, for he was then emperor, and he had the ashes scattered in the wind. But the finger with which he [John the Baptist] pointed out Our Lord saying *"Ecce Agnus Dei"*[224] could not burn, but instead remained completely whole. This finger Saint Thecla the virgin had taken through the mountains, and a great celebration is held [in its honor]. In Sabastiyeh in this same place there used to be a beautiful church, and there were several others, but they are all destroyed. There the head of John the Baptist was enclosed in a wall. But the Emperor Theodosius had it removed and he found it wrapped in a very bloody cloth, and he had it taken like that to Constantinople. The whole back part of the head is still in Constantinople, and the front part to the upper jawbone is in Rome in the church of Saint Sylvester where there are Cordelier nuns,[225] and it is still thoroughly charred as if half-burnt. For that Emperor Julian mentioned above, because of his wickedness, had this part burnt with the other bones; and it can still be

---

222. Jews made pilgrimages to the Holy Land throughout the Middle Ages, and some, most notably Benjamin of Tudela in the mid-twelfth century, left written accounts of their pilgrimages. WoB mentions traveling with a German Jewish pilgrim (Ch. 8 in Appendix B.1).

223. Abraham in Sichem: Gen. 12:6–8 (Bethel and Luze are the same place: Gen. 28:19). Dinah: Gen. 34. Joseph: Gen. 37:24. Abraham and Isaac: Gen. 22.

224. "Behold the Lamb of God" (John 1:29). John's beheading is biblical (Matt. 14:10; Mark 6:28; Luke 9:9), but some details come from other sources: e.g., death in the castle from Josephus' *Jewish Antiquities* 18.5.1–2; the burial, Julian's role, and the finding of the head from the *Golden Legend* (Beheading of Saint John the Baptist); Thecla's role from other pilgrimage itineraries. Julian, nephew of Constantinople's founder and Roman emperor from 361 to 363, was the only fourth-century emperor who openly opposed Christianity and sought to restore earlier religious practices, hence his name.

225. Cordeliers: normally friars, Franciscans of the strict rule, named for a knotted cord they wore around the waist.

seen there, and this object has been verified by popes and by emperors. The jawbone below that attaches to the chin and a part of the ashes and the platter where the head was placed when it was cut off are in Genoa. The Genoese hold a great celebration for it, and so too do the Saracens hold a great celebration for it. Some say that the head of Saint John is in Amyas [Amiens] in Picardy, and others say that it is the head of Saint John the bishop. I do not know. God knows. But wherever one honors it, the good Saint John willingly accepts it.[226]

From this city of Sabaste [Sabastiyah] all the way to Jerusalem is twelve leagues. Between the mountains of this country there is a well that changes its color four times a year—sometimes it changes into green, sometimes red, one time clear, another time murky—and that well is called the fountain of Joel.[227]

The people of this country that are called Samaritans were converted and baptized by the Apostles, but they have not kept their teaching well, and yet they maintain a law of their own, differing from [that of] Christians, Saracens, Jews, [and] pagans. These Samaritans believe in only one God. And they say indeed that there is only one [God] that created everything and will judge everything, and they follow the Bible according to the letter and use the Psalter just as the Jews do. And they say that they are the true sons of God and amongst all peoples the most loved by God, and that the inheritance that God promised to his friends is their very own.[228] They also have different ways of dressing compared to other people, for they wrap their heads in red linen to distinguish themselves from others; and the Saracens wrap their head with a white cloth, and the Christians that dwell in the country [wrap their heads] with a blue or indigo cloth, and the Jews with a yellow cloth.[229]

In that country many Jews dwell paying tribute just as the Christians do. If you want to know the letters that the Jews use, they are these and the names that they call them are written below:

---

226. A typical remark valuing devout practice over doctrine as such.

227. No other writer uses this name.

228. Taking the Pentateuch (the first five biblical books) as their scripture, the Samaritans were said to practice a kind of Judaism characterized by its conservatism and strictness. Their name is known nowadays through the parable of the Good Samaritan (Luke 10:29–37). The *Mandeville* author's account derives mostly from WoB.

229. According to the fifteenth-century Arab historian al-Maqrisi, an edict issued in the Islamic year 700 (1300/1301) required Christians to wear blue turbans and Jews to wear yellow; before this it was the other way around (DLMM 237, n. 35).

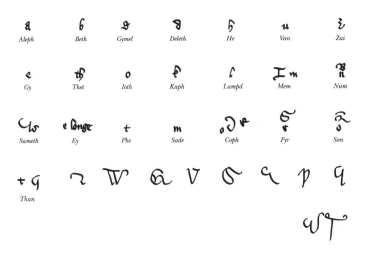

Aleph	Beth	Gymel	Deleth	He	Van	Zai
Gy	Thet	Ioth	Kaph	Lampd	Mem	Num
Sameth	Ey	Phe	Sade	Coph	Fyr	Son
Than						

[Chapter 13]

About the Province of Galilee and Where Antichrist Will Be Born. About Nazareth. About Our Lady's Age. About Judgment Day and About the Customs of the Jacobites, Syrians, and Georgians

From this country of Samaritans that I have spoken to you about one goes to the plains of Galilee and leaves the mountains to one side. Galilee is one of the provinces of the Promised Land, and in this province is the city of Naim and Capharnaum [Capernaum] and Corosaim [Chorozaim] and Bethsaida. From this Bethsaida came Saint Peter and Saint Andrew,[230] and three leagues away is Chorozaim, and five leagues from Chorozaim is the city of Cedar, about which the Psalter speaks: "*Et habitavi cum habitantibus Cedar.*"[231] In Chorozaim Antichrist will be born, as some say; and others say that he will be born in Babylon,[232] because the prophet says: "*De Babilone coluber exiet qe totum mundum devorabit.*"[233]

---

230. John 1:44.

231. "I have dwelt with the inhabitants of Cedar" (Ps. 120[119]:5).

232. These are the two main medieval views of Antichrist's birth (Emmerson 1981, 79–80). The rest of this account, however, follows only the Chorozaim tradition. On Antichrist, see also Chapter 29.

233. "Out of Babylon will come a serpent that will devour the whole world." Not scriptural, this prophecy recalls the medieval linking of Antichrist with the tribe of Dan, who, in Gen. 49:17, are associated with a serpent (Gow 1995, 110). The same words appear in Abbess Herrad of Hohenbourg's mid-twelfth-century *Hortus deliciarum* (*Garden of Delights*), in an entry on *idolatria:* "Idolatry is regarded as

This Antichrist will be raised in Bethsaida and reign in Chapharnaum and therefore Scripture says: "*Ve tibi Chorozaim ve tibi Bethsaida ve tibi Capharnaum.*"[234] All these cities are in the land of Galilee, and Cana of Galilee also, which is four leagues from Nazareth. Simon Cananeus was from this city, as was the woman of Canaan about whom the Holy Gospel speaks. There Our Lord performed His first miracle at Architriclin's wedding, when He turned water into wine.[235] At the end of Galilee in the mountains the Ark of God was captured. And on the other side is Mount Hendor [Endor] or Heremon [Hermon], and around there flows the stream of *Torrens Cison,* which is also called the *Radinim* Torrent. Near there Barac [Barak], Abimelech's [Abinoam's] son, with Delbore [Deborah] the prophetess' son, defeated the host of Idumea when Cisara [Sisera] the king was killed by Gebel [Jael], Aber's [Heber's] wife, and chased Jeb and Zebee and Zalmana [Zeeb, Zebah, and Zalmunna] across the River Jordan with the power of his sword the force, and killed them there.[236]

Also, five leagues from Naim is the city of Jesrael [Jezreel] and it is also called Zarim, from which came Jexabel [Jezebel] the wicked queen, who took Naboth's vineyard through her strength. Near that city is the field of Magedo [the plain of Megiddo] where the king Joras [Joas] was killed by the king of Samaria, and then was taken and buried on Mount Sion.[237] One league from Jesrael are the mountains of Gelboe [Gilboa] where Saul and Jonathas who were so handsome died—which is why Holy Scripture cursed them, saying, "*Montes Gelboe nec ros nec pluvia[e] etc.*"[238] One league from Mount Gelboe towards the east is the city of Scitople [Scythopolis] that is called Bethsaim [Bethshan]. On the walls of this city Saul's head was hung.[239]

Then one goes by the mountain near the plains of Galilee all the way to Nazareth, which used to be a great and beautiful city, but now is only

having taken hold in the city of Babylon. In this city too Antichrist will be brought to birth, as it said: out of Babylon . . ." (ed. Rosalie Green [London: Warburg Institute, 1979], 2 vols. at 2.59 [no. 126, fol. 33r]). Herrad's work survives in only one copy, so the *Mandeville* author is unlikely to have known it; both citations presumably derive from a third text.

234. "Woe to you Chorozaim, woe to you Bethsaida, woe to you Capharnaum" (cf. Matt. 11:21–23, Luke 10:13–15).

235. Simon: Matt. 27:32, where he comes from Cyrene. Woman of Canaan: Matt. 15:21–28. First miracle: John 2:1–12. Cana and Canaan are confused here; "Architriclin," from *architriclinus:* master of the feast.

236. Ark of God: 1 Sam. 4:1–11. Barak et al.: cf. Judg. 4 and 8:1–21. This narrative is confused both here and in its source, Eugesippus; scribal errors show that it was not well known (DLMM 250, n. 9).

237. Jezebel: 1 Kings 21:1–10. Joas: 2 Chron. 24:23–25.

238. "Ye mountains of Gelboe, let neither dew nor rain come upon you . . ." (2 Sam. 1:21).

239. 1 Kings 31:9–10.

a small town with houses scattered here and there. It is not walled, and is situated in a small valley and there are mountains all around. Our Lady was born there but she was conceived in Jerusalem, and because Our Lady was born in Nazareth therefore Our Lord bore the surname of that city. There Joseph wedded Mary when she was only fourteen years old. There the angel Gabriel greeted her, saying: "*Ave Maria gratia plena, Dominus tecum*"[240] in the place of a great altar in a beautiful church that used to be there; but it was completely destroyed, and a small house has been built beside a pillar of this church to receive pilgrims' offerings. The Saracens look after it very scrupulously because of the profit that they have, and they are far more wicked and far more cruel Saracens than in other parts, and they have destroyed all the churches. There is the Gabriel's Well where Our Lord used to bathe when He was little. From that well He often carried water to His mother, and in this well she often washed the clothes of her child Jesus Christ. From Jerusalem to there is a three-day journey. In Nazareth Our Lord was brought up. Nazareth means Garden Flower, and it is called flower with good reason, for there the flower of life was raised that was Jesus Christ.

Two leagues from Nazareth is the city of Sephor [Sepphoris, now Shefaram] on the road that goes from Nazareth to Acon [Acre]. Half a league from Nazareth is Our Lord's Leap; for the Jews led Him to a high rock to throw Him into the valley to kill Him, but Jesus passed through them and leapt onto another rock, and the footprints are still visible in the said rock. Therefore some people, when they are afraid of thieves on the road or of enemies, say "*Jhesu autem transiens per medium illorum ibat*"[241]—recalling the fact that, just as Our Lord passed safely amongst the cruel Jews and escaped from them, it is possible to pass securely by the perils of thieves. Then one says these two verses from the Psalter three times: "*Intret super eos formido et pavor in magnitudine brachii tui, Domine, fiant immobiles quasi lapis donec pertranseat populus tuus, Domine, donec pertranseat populus tuus iste quem possedisti.*"[242] And then one passes unhindered.

---

240. "Hail Mary full of grace, the Lord is with you" (Luke 1:28). Matthew (2) and Luke (2:4–5) differ on where Mary and Joseph lived before Jesus' birth but agree on Nazareth as His home. Details of Mary's life here likely come from the *Golden Legend* on "The Birth of the Blessed Virgin Mary." Gabriel's Well: also known as Mary's Well; its associations here derive ultimately from the apocryphal Syriac Infancy Gospel. The meaning of Nazareth is uncertain; the standard medieval Christian reading is given here.

241. "But Jesus passing through the midst of them went his way" (Luke 4:28–30, quoting 30).

242. "Let fear and dread come upon them, in the greatness of thy arm, O Lord: let them become unmovable as a stone, until thy people, O Lord, pass by: until this thy people pass by, which thou hast possessed" (Exod. 15:16, which has *inruat*, "fall," for *intret*, "reach, come"). A Middle English charm adapts this passage (Seymour 2002, 148, n. to 46/30).

Know that Our Lady gave birth in her fifteenth year and remained with her son for thirty-three years and three months; and after Our Lord's Passion, she lived twenty-three years.[243] Also, from Nazareth one goes to Mount Tabor, which is only three leagues away and is a very beautiful and very high mountain where there used to be a town and many churches. But they are all destroyed. But there is still a place that is called God's school where He used to teach His disciples and explained to them the Heavenly secrets.[244] At the foot of this mountain, Melchizedek—who was king of Salem (that now has the name Jerusalem) and was also a priest—while coming down from this mountain encountered Abraham, who was returning from the battle in which he had killed Amelech.[245] On this mountain Our Lord was transfigured in front of Saint Peter, Saint John, and Saint James, and there they saw spiritually Moses and Elyes [Elias] [the] prophets near them, and therefore Saint Peter said: *"Domine, bonum est nos hic esse, faciamus hic tria tabernacula."*[246] And there they heard the voice of the Father, who said: *"Hic est filius meus dilectus in quo bene complacui."*[247] Our Lord forbade them from telling this vision to anyone until He was raised from death to life again. On this mountain and in this same place on Judgment Day four angels will sound four trumpets and restore to life all those who have suffered death since the world was created. They will come in body and in soul to the Judgment before Our Lord's face in the valley of Josaphaz [Jehoshaphat], and this Judgment will be on Easter Day at the very hour when Our Lord rose from death to life at the Resurrection, and the Judgment will have begun at the very hour when Our Lord descended into Hell and plundered it.[248] For at such time He will plunder the world and lead His friends into glory and condemn the rest to perpetual pain. Thus everyone will have his reward as deserved, whether good or bad, unless God's great pity precede His justice.

---

243. Details from the *Golden Legend* on "The Assumption of the Blessed Virgin Mary."

244. "God's school": the *Mandeville* author's addition to WoB's account of Jesus teaching.

245. Gen. 14:17–24.

246. "Lord, it is good for us to be here: . . . let us make here three tabernacles" (Matt. 17:4). The Transfiguration (Matt. 17:1–9; Mark 9:2–10; Luke 9:28–36; 2 Pet. 1:16–18) was located on Mount Tabor from the fourth century.

247. "This is my beloved Son, in whom I am well pleased" (Matt. 17:5).

248. The timing of the Last Judgment (see Matt. 24–25; Rev. 20; 1 Thess. 4) was disputed in the medieval world, but some theologians advanced these claims. The descent into Hell has a less substantial biblical foundation (Matt. 27:50–54; Luke 23:43; 1 Pet. 3:18–20), but was elaborated in the apocryphal Gospel of Nicodemus (second or third century CE) and often re-imagined in both art and literature. E adds "as doctoures saise" (as learned men say [WBJM 56]) to the sentence linking the two events, a reminder that the account here also derives from medieval commentary.

Also, one league from Mount Thabor is Mount Heremon [Hermon]; the city of Naim was there. In front of the gates of this city Our Lord restored to life the son of the widow who had no other children.[249] Also, three leagues from Nazareth is the castle of Saffra, from which the sons of Zebedee and of Alphe[us] came.[250] Also, seven leagues from Nazareth is Mount Kayn [Cain], and below it there is a well, and beside that well Lameth [Lamech], Noah's father, killed Cain with an arrow. For this Cain went through the brambles and the bushes like a wild animal, and he had already lived from Adam's time to Noah's, and thus he lived more than two thousand years, and this Lameth was completely blind because of old age.[251]

From Saffra one goes to the Sea of Galilee and the city of Tiberias, which sits on this sea. Although it is called the sea, it is not a sea or an arm of the sea, for it is only a freshwater lake that is one hundred stades long and forty stades wide;[252] and there are many good fish in it and the River Jordan flows through it. The city is not very big but there are good baths. In the place where the River Jordan leaves the Sea of Galilee there is a large bridge by which one passes from the Promised Land to the land of King Baasan and the land of the Gerassenz [Gennesaret], which are in the vicinity of the River Jordan and the beginning of the sea of Tiberias. From there one can go to Damascus in three days through the region of Tracondye [Gaulonitis], which stretches from Mount Hermon to the Sea of Galilee, or the sea of Tiberias, or the sea of Jenazar [Gennesaret?]—it is all one sea. This is that lake that I told you about, but it changes its name like this because of the names of the cities that are beside it. On this sea Our Lord walked dry-footed, and there He raised Saint Peter who was almost drowned in the sea and said to him: "*Modice fidei, quare dubitasti.*"[253] After His Resurrection Our Lord appeared on this sea to His disciples and ordered them to fish and filled the whole net with large fish. In this sea Our Lord often went sailing; there He called Saint Peter, Saint Andrew, Saint James, and Saint John, the son of Zebedee.

In this city of Tiberias is the table at which Our Lord ate with His disciples after His Resurrection, and they recognized Him while breaking

249. Luke 7:11–17.

250. Saffra is Sephor mentioned above (DLMM 251, n. 25). Zebedee: said to be the father of the Apostles James and John (Matt. 4:21; Mark 1:19–20; Luke 5:10). Alpheus: called father of the Apostles James (Matt. 10:3; Mark 3:18; Luke 6:15; Acts 1:13) and Matthew Levi (Mark 2:14).

251. Cain's descendant Lamech claims to have killed someone, but not Cain (Gen. 4:23). Cf. E's more common explanation: "Lamech slew Cayn with ane arowe, supposing he had bene a wylde beste" (WBJM 57).

252. Stade: see Chapter 5, n. 49.

253. "O thou of little faith, why didst thou doubt?" (Matt. 14:31). Fish: John 21:1–25. Disciples called: Matt. 4:18–22; Mark 1:16–20; Luke 5:1–11.

the bread, about which the Gospel speaks: "*Et cognoverunt eum in fractione panis.*"[254] And near this city of Tiberias is the mountain where Our Lord satisfied five thousand people with five loaves and two fishes. In this city someone threw a burning brand in anger at Our Lord, and the top fell to the ground and turned green and grew and became a large tree that is still growing and the bark is all scorched.

Also, at the head of this sea of Galilee towards the north there is a strong and tall castle that has the name Saphor [Safed?], and it is quite close to the Capharnaum. Within the Promised Land there is no castle as strong, and there is a very good town below that also has the name Saphor. In this castle Saint Anne, Our Lady's mother, was born, and below it was [the] Centurion's house. This land is called the Galilee of the peoples; it was given to [the] tribes of Zabulon and Neptalim [Nephtali].[255] And thirty miles on the way back from this castle is the city of Dan, which is otherwise called Belynas or Caesarea Philippon [Philippi]. It sits at the foot of the mountain of Lebanon where the River Jordan begins. The Promised Land begins there and extends to Bersabee [Beersheba] in length going northwards all the way southwards,[256] and it takes in a good one hundred and eighty miles. Its width is from Jericho to Jaffa, and it takes in a good forty miles, counting in Lombard miles or those of our country, which are just as small. These are not the leagues of Gascony, Provence, or Germany, where there are large leagues.[257]

Know that the Promised Land is in Syria, for the kingdom of Syria lasts from the deserts of Arabia all the way to Cilicia, that is Greater Armenia, that is to say from south to north; and from east to west it lasts from the large deserts of Arabia right to the Western Sea.[258] But in the kingdom of Syria there is the kingdom of Judea and many other provinces, such as Palestine, Galilee, Cicilia, and many others.

In this country and in other countries over there, they have a custom when they wage war and a city or a castle is under siege and they dare not send messengers with letters from one lord to another to ask for help. They have the letters made and tie them to the neck of a pigeon and they let the pigeon fly, and the pigeons are trained so that they carry it [the letters] straight to where they are meant to go. For the pigeons are raised in that place to which they are sent, and they are sent

---

254. "And they knew him in the breaking of the bread" (Luke 24:35). Loaves and fishes: Matt. 14:13–21; Mark 6:30–44; Luke 9:10–17; John 6:1–13. The burning brand is mentioned in some thirteenth-century pilgrims' accounts.

255. Anne's traditional birthplace is Sephor (mentioned earlier), not Saphor. Centurion: Matt. 8:5. Zabulon and Neptalim: Josh. 19:10–16 and 32–39.

256. The text here (*vers bise jusques vers mydy*) must be in error.

257. See Chapter 5, nn. 48 and 49 on medieval measures of distance; "just as small": the same size.

258. Greater Armenia: actually Lesser Armenia. Western Sea: the Mediterranean.

out to carry letters, and the pigeons return to where they were raised, and they do this commonly. Know that here and there amongst these Saracens dwell many Christians of various kinds and different names, and all are baptized and have different laws and different customs, but all believe in God the Father and the Son and the Holy Spirit. But they always lack some articles of our faith.

Some are called Jacobites because Saint James converted them and Saint John the Evangelist baptized them.[259] They say that confession must be made to God alone and not to man, for we must declare ourselves guilty to the very man we have wronged. God neither ordained nor ever established in writing or by prophecy that confession be to anyone but God, as they say and as Moses wrote in the Bible.[260] Therefore David says in the Psalter:

Confitebor tibi, Domine, in toto corde meo.[261]

Delictum meum cognitum tibi feci.[262]

Deus meus es tu, et confitebor tibi, quoniam cogitacio hominis confitebitur tibi etc.[263]

For they know the whole Bible and the Psalter, and therefore they cite the letter like this. But they do not cite the authorities in Latin as well,[264] but very openly in their own language; and they say that David and the other prophets say this. Nevertheless Saint Augustine and Saint Gregory say:

Qui scelera sua cogitat et conversus fuerit, veniam sibi credat (Augustine).[265]

Domine potius mentem quam verba respicit (Gregory).[266]

---

259. Jacobite Christians, after Jacob Baradaeus, bishop of Edessa (d. 578), who held the Monophysite view that Christ had only one (divine) nature. They are today's Syrian Orthodox or Syrian Jacobite Church.

260. No such Mosaic passage exists, although one might read Num. 5:5–8 this way.

261. "I will praise thee, O Lord, with my whole heart" (Pss. 9:2, 110[111]:1, 137:1).

262. "I have acknowledged my sin to thee" (Ps. 31[32]:5).

263. "Thou art my God, and I will praise thee" (Ps. 117[118]:28); "For the thought of man shall give praise to thee" (Ps. 75:11).

264. Rather than *auxi en latin* ("in Latin as well") several French copies have *ensi en latin* ("like this in Latin"). The book's original readers would have felt this paragraph's local relevance, since there were vigorous contemporary debates over both the use of scripture in the vernacular and penance. A list of quotations hardly amounts to an argument, however.

265. "Whoever considers his own sins and will change may believe himself forgiven." Attributed to Augustine in the *Mandeville* author's source: Defensor de Ligugé, *Liber Scintillarum* (Book of Sparks), Chapter 9, sent. 13 (the printed text qualifies "will change" with "*statim*," at once). Cf. Proverbs 28:13.

266. "Lord, he looks more at my thoughts than at my words" (Defensor, *Liber*, Chapter 9, sent. 37, with no authorial attribution). The printed text reads:

And Saint Hilarius says: "*Longorum temporum crimina in ictu oculi pereunt, si cordis nata fuerit compunctio.*"[267] Because of such authorities they say that man must confess his misdeeds to God, declaring his guilt, and pleading for mercy, and promising to improve. Therefore when they want to confess they take fire and place it beside them and throw incense powder into it, and in the smoke they confess to God and plead for mercy. And the truth is that this confession is original and natural.[268]

But the holy apostolic fathers who have come since have decreed that confession be made to man, and with good reason; for they have seen that no illness can be cured, nor can any good medicine be given, if the nature of the evil is not known.[269] Likewise no one can give the proper medicine who does not know the nature of the deed; for the same sin is more serious for one person than for another and in one place and time rather than another. Therefore the nature of the deed must be known, and penance given for it.

There are others that are called Syrians. They hold a belief between us and the Greeks, and they all wear beards just as the Greeks do, and they make the sacrament of leavened bread, and in their language they use the Saracen letters. But for the rites of the church they use Greek letters, and make their confession just like the Jacobites. There are others that are called Georgians, whom Saint George converted, and they worship him more than all the other saints of Paradise and they always call him to their aid, and they come from the kingdom of Georgia. Those people all have shaved crowns; the clerics wear them round, the laity wear them square; and they hold to the Christian law just as the Greeks do about whom I have told you before. There are others that are called Christians "of the belt" because they are belted on top.[270] And there are others that are called Nestorians, others Arians, others Nubians, others Greek, and others Indians who are from the land of Prester John.[271]

"*Internum iudex potius mentem quam verba considerat*" (An inner judge had examined my thoughts more than my words).

267. "The sins of long ago vanish in the blink of an eye, should remorse arise in the heart." Attributed to Hilarius in Defensor, *Liber*, Chapter 9, sent. 26.

268. "Original" translates *primitive*, which here has a positive sense. One manuscript has *pleinere*, "full" or "complete."

269. The original puns on the etymological relation between *maladie* ("illness") and *mal* ("evil").

270. Presumably "on top" of their cloths, but *par dessure* could mean "in addition."

271. Syrians: the Jacobites mentioned above. Georgians: noticed also in Chapter 11, one of the oldest Christian communities, an independent branch of the Orthodox Church. "Of the belt": probably Coptic (Monophysite Orthodox) Christians centered in Egypt. Nestorians: named for Nestorius, an early fifth-century bishop of Constantinople who insisted on the independence of Christ's human and divine natures; from their eventual base in Persia, the Nestorians expanded east into India and China. Arians (probably a mistake for Armenians, another

They all have many articles of our faith, and they vary in others, and it would take too long to recount the variety so I will stop and say no more.

[Chapter 14]

About the City of Damascus. About the Three Ways to Jerusalem: One by Land and by Sea, the Other More by Land Than by Sea, and the Third All by Land

Now since I have described to you some part of the peoples who dwell in those farthest regions, I want to return to my route to return on this side. So now whoever wants to return from the land of Galilee (about which I have spoken to you) to come back over here comes back through Damascus, which is a very beautiful city, and most noble, and full of every kind of merchandise; and it is three days' journey from the sea and five from Jerusalem. But merchandise is taken there on camels, mules, horses, dromedaries, and on other animals, and the merchandise comes by sea from India, Persia, Chaldea, Armenia, and from many other regions. This city was founded by Eliseus [Eliezar] of Damascus who was Abraham's servant and steward before Isaac was born, and who thought he would be Abraham's heir, and he named the city with his surname Damaste. And in that place where Damascus was founded Cain killed his brother Abel,[272] and beside Damascus is Mount Seir. In this city there is a great abundance of wells, both inside the city and outside, and many beautiful gardens and different fruits. No other city can be compared to it with its beautiful gardens and beautiful pleasure spots. The city is large and very well populated and walled with double walls, and there are many physicians. Saint Paul himself was a physician in order to keep his body healthy before he was converted. But afterwards, he became a physician of souls; and Saint Luke the Evangelist was Saint Paul's disciple to learn medicine, and [so were] many others,

---

independent eastern Church with fourth-century roots): followers of Arius, a priest in Alexandria, who in the early fourth century insisted on the absolute oneness of Christ's divinity. Nubians: from Nubia, an ancient region in northeastern Africa, Christianized in the sixth century and loyal to the Orthodox patriarch of Alexandria; these communities dwindled after the Egyptian Mamluks began to Islamicize their kingdom and may have disappeared by the early sixteenth century. Indian Christians: sometimes called the Christians of Saint Thomas (because of a claim to have been originally converted by him), centered on the Malabar Coast (see Ch. 19), composed of four major groups, and possibly begun through Nestorian missionary efforts in the fourth and fifth centuries.

272. Eliezar: Gen. 15:2, properly corrected in E: "the son of the steward of Abraham the patriark." Mention of the city's foundation comes from Eugesippus. Cain: Gen. 4:8, which does not specify the place of the murder.

for Saint Paul held their schools of medicine. There near Damascus he
was converted, and after his conversion he remained in the city for three
days without seeing and eating and without drinking, and during these
three days he was ravished into Heaven and saw many of Our Lord's
secrets.[273] Quite close to Damascus is the castle of Arkes [Arqa], which
is a very strong castle.

From Damascus one returns past Our Lady of Sardenak [Saidenaya],
which is five leagues this side of Damascus. It sits on a rock and is a
very beautiful place, and it resembles a castle, for it used to be a castle.
There is quite a beautiful church there, and Christian monks and nuns
dwell therein, and there is a vault under the church where Christians
also dwell, and there are many good wines. In the church behind the
high altar in the wall there is a tablet of blackish wood where Our Lady's
image was once painted that turned into flesh, but now the image can
hardly be seen. But nevertheless by God's grace the said tablet oozes oil
just like olive oil, and there is a marble vessel below the tablet secured
well and wrapped with iron to receive the oil that oozes out, and some
of this oil is given to the pilgrims who come, for this oil comes by God's
miracle and heals many illnesses. It is said that this oil, well kept and
clean, after seven years becomes flesh and blood.[274]

From Sardenak [Saidenaya] one goes through the valley of Bochar
[Bekaa], which is a very beautiful valley and very fertile. It lies between
the mountains, and there are beautiful rivers and meadows and large pas-
tures for the animals. And one goes through the mountains of Lebanon,
which last from Greater Armenia north to Dan, which is towards the
south at the beginning of the Promised Land, as I told you above.[275]
These mountains are very fertile, and there are many beautiful wells and
cedar and cypress and many other different trees, and there are many
good and well-peopled cities. Towards the head of these mountains,
between the city of Arke [Arqa] and the city of Raphane [Rafineh], there
is a river called Sabataire, because it flows strong and rough on Saturdays
[the Sabbath], and the other six days of the week it does not flow at all
or hardly does. And there is another river between these mountains that
freezes very hard by night, and by day no ice can be seen.[276] In following

---

273. In Col. 4:14, Paul calls Luke "the beloved physician," presumably the source
of this (confused?) legend. Paul's conversion: Acts 9:1–9. Paul's vision: 2 Cor.
12:1–10.

274. Cf. WoB's more skeptical account of the icon (Ch. 10 in Appendix B.1), whose
miraculous oil is first mentioned in the early thirteenth century.

275. In Chapter 13. WoB's pilgrimage effectively ends in Beirut, and the *Mandeville*
author no longer uses his work as a template. The other routes come from a variety
of sources.

276. These legendary rivers are mentioned in Jacques de Vitry's early thirteenth-
century *Historia Orientalis* (Eastern History), but the first river goes back at least
to Pliny's first-century *Historia Naturalis* (Natural History).

the route back through these mountains there is a large and high mountain that is called the Great Mountain where there is a very beautiful city that is called Tripoli. In this city dwell many good Christians according to our faith.

From there one goes through Beruch [Beirut], where Saint George killed the dragon. There is a good city and a good and strong castle there, as I have told you before,[277] and it is three days' journey from Sardenak [Saidenaya] mentioned above. Near Beruch [Beirut] sixteen miles away in returning is the city of Sidon. In Beirut whoever wants to return towards Cyprus enters the sea, or one goes by land to the port of Sur or of Thyr [Tyre]. From there one goes to Cyprus in little time, or one comes from the port of Thyr more directly without going to Cyprus, for one turns and arrives at one of the ports of Greece, and then one comes into those regions by the routes that I already described to you.

Now I have told you about the route by which one first comes the farthest, as to Babylon and Mount Sinai and the other places that I described to you above, and by which route one returns towards the Promised Land. Now I want to describe to you the right way to go straight to the holy city of Jerusalem. For many go to Jerusalem who do not intend to go farther, whether because of poverty they lack the means, or because they do not have enough company, or because they cannot endure the hardships, or because they are too afraid to cross the desert, or because they are in a great hurry to return to their wives and their children, or for other good reasons.

I am going to tell you briefly where one can go without taking much time and without remaining too long. One goes from the western regions, as I said before,[278] through France, Burgonie [Burgundy], Lombardy, and to the port of Venice or Genoa or one of the other ports in those far places; and one goes by sea to the isle of Gref [Corfu], which belongs to the Genoese, and then one comes to a river in Greece at the port of Mirok [Mavrovo], or of Valona, or of Duras [Durazzo], or at one of the other ports. Then one goes ashore to prepare, and quite soon one puts to sea again, and one goes straight to Cyprus without going to the isle of Rhodes, for one leaves Rhodes aside, and one arrives at the port of Famagost [Famagusta], which is the main port of Cyprus, or at Limecyn [Limassol]. Then once again one goes into the sea, and passes by the port of Thyr [Tyre], and without going ashore one goes by sea, skirting all the ports of this coast, right to the city of Jaffa. There is the closest port to Jerusalem, for from this port it is only a day and a half's

---

277. Chapter 5, where the castle is not mentioned. The story of Saint George (who rescues a princess from the dragon and agrees to kill it if the local people convert, as some twenty thousand do) was well known (especially through the *Golden Legend*); it is not usually associated with Beirut. Sur and Thyr [Tyre] mentioned shortly are the same place.

278. In Chapters 1 and 8.

journey to Jerusalem, ⁹ for it is only sixteen leagues. At Jaffa one arrives and goes by land to the city of Rames [Ramleh], which is quite close to Jaffa, and it is a very beautiful city and most delightful and well populated. Past Rames to the south there is a church of Our Lady where Our Lord showed Himself to her in three shadows that signified the Trinity. And beside there is another city that has the name Diospole [Diospolis], and it used to be called Libda [Ludd?], and it is also well inhabited. There is a church of Saint George there where he was beheaded. From there one goes to the castle of Emaux [Emmaus], and then to Mount Joy where Samuel the prophet lies; from this place the pilgrims first see the holy city of Jerusalem and it is two leagues away, and then one goes to Jerusalem. Nearby is the route to Ramatha [Ramah] and the Mount Modein, where Mattathais was from, who was [Judas] Maccabeus' father, and there lie the Maccabees, and their tombs are there. Also, beyond Ramatha is the city of Teuke [Tekoa] where Amos the prophet was from, and his tomb is there.[279]

I told you before about the holy pilgrimages that one finds in Jerusalem, so I will go on without any further account. For those who cannot bear the sea crossing and who prefer to go as far as they can by land, even though they might have more hardships, I will return again to the other ways whereby one goes there more by land. One goes, as I have told you before, to one of the ports of Lombardy, or Genoa, or Venice, and reaches Greece at the port of Mirok [Mavrovo], or Valona, or Duras [Durazzo], or at other ports; and one goes by land to Constantinople, and one crosses the Arm of Saint George, which is an arm of the sea. From there one goes to Ruffinel, where there is a strong castle, and then one goes to Pulveral [Bafra?], and then to the castle of Sinople [Sinope]. From there one goes by Cappadocia, which is a large country where there are large mountains, and one goes through Turkey to the port of Chievetot [Civetot] and to the city of Nike [Nicea], which is seven leagues away. The Turks took this city from the emperor, and it is a much-fortified city with walls and towers on one side, and on the other side there is a large lake and there is a river that is called the Lay [Halys]. From there one goes through the Alps of Black Mount, and the valleys of the Malebruns, and the straight of Roches, and the city of Orimanx [Dorilay], or the cities on the Rechay [Heraclea] and on the Stancone [Konya], which are very good rivers. Then one comes to Antioch the Lesser,[280] which sits on the Rechay [Heraclea]. Around

---

279. There is no known source for the legend of the three shadows. Saint George's beheading is usually located in Nicomedia; his church, built by crusaders, is said to have been destroyed by Saladin. Samuel was buried in Ramah (1 Sam. 28:3). Mattathais: 1 Macc. 2:1–4, 9:19. Amos: Amos 1:1.

280. Antioch in Pisidia, rather. This route and that in the next paragraph are those of the First Crusade, as traced by Albert of Aachen in his early twelfth-century history of that campaign. The *Mandeville* author's retracing contains errors.

there are many beautiful wells and many beautiful woods, and a great abundance of wild animals for hunting and entertainment. Whoever wants to go by another way goes through the plains of Romany in following along the seacoast of Romany. On this coast there is a beautiful and strong tower that is called Florache. Farther up between the mountains is the city of Toursont [Tarsus], and the city of Logumaach [Longimas], and Asser [Adana], and Marmistre [Mopsuestia]. And when one is out of these rocks and these mountains, one goes through the city of Maresth [Marash] and through Artese [Artah], where there is a large bridge on the river Ferue, which is called Farfar [Pharphar or Orontes]. It is a very large river carrying ships, and it flows with great speed, and it comes from springs and from rocks from towards the city of Damascus. There is another river near Damascus that comes from the mountains of Lebanon that has the name Albane [Abana]. In crossing this river, Saint Eustace—who first had the name Placidas—lost his two children after having lost his wife.[281] But this river goes through the plain of Archades. Then one goes right to the Red Sea.

From the places mentioned above, one goes to the city of Phemynie [Philomelium?] where the place of hot springs is—these are hot baths—and then one goes to the city of Ferue [Ilgin?]; and between Phemynie and Ferue there are many beautiful woods. Then one goes to Antioch, which is ten leagues away. This city of Antioch is a most beautiful city, and well provided with walls and towers, for it is a very large city, and it used to be even larger, for it used to be two leagues long and a league and a half wide. Through the middle of the city flows that river of Ferue or Farfar. It used to have three hundred and fifty towers around the walls, and at each pier of the bridge there was a tower. This is the noblest city in the kingdom of Syria, and ten miles from this city is the port of Saint Simeon; there the river of Ferue flows into the sea.

From Antioch one goes to the city of Laouse [Latakia], and then to Gybel [Gebal], and then to Tortouse [Tortosa]. Beside there is the land of the Chanulee [Homs] where there is a strong castle that is called Maubok [Baalbek]. From Tortouse one goes to Triple [Tripoli] on the sea, and at the passage by the strait of the rocks is the city of Gybelet [Djebeil], and then Beruch [Beirut] on the sea. Then one goes to the city of Acre, and there there are two ways to go to Jerusalem. The left goes by Damaste [Damascus] and the River Jordan, and the right goes by sea, and through the land of Flagenne and beside the mountains to the city of Cayphas [Haifa?], of which Cayphas was lord. Some call it Castle Pilgrim,[282] and from there it is a good three days' journey to Jerusalem.

281. Saint Eustace's story is told in the *Golden Legend*. His name was originally Placidus.

282. Mentioned also in Chapter 5, Chateau Pèlerin, on the rocky promontory at Atlit, was a major citadel built by the Knights Templar (see Ch. 11, n. 168) during the Fifth Crusade (1217–1221).

Then one goes by Caesarea Philippi, and Jaffa, and Rames [Ramleh], and the castle of Emaux [Emmaus], and then to Jerusalem.

Now I have described for you some ways both by sea and by land that one can take to the Holy Promised Land. Although there are many other ways according to the different places from which one departs, nevertheless one route and the next all lead to the same destination. There is still another way by which one can go, all by land without a sea crossing, to Jerusalem, from Flanders or France. But the way is long, and hard, and dangerous, and full of hardships. Therefore few people go that way. It is to go through Germany, Bahaigne [Bohemia], and the other countries into Prussia, and then one goes through Tartary to Jerusalem.

This Tartary is accountable to the Great Chan, about whom I shall speak afterwards, for his lordship extends to there, and all the provinces of Tartary pay tribute to him.[283] It is a most miserable land, sandy and not very fertile, for few goods grow there: not wheat, not wine grapes, not fruit, not peas, not beans. But there is a great abundance of animals. Therefore they eat only meat without bread, and sip the broth, and drink milk from all animals; and they eat dogs, foxes, wolves, cats, and all other animals, wild and tame, and both rats and mice. Also, they have no wood or little, and therefore they heat and cook their meat with the dung of horses and other animals [that has been] dried in the sun. And princes and others eat only once a day and less, and they are an extremely filthy people and of a wicked nature. In summer throughout all this country storms and lightning and thunder often happen, and many times they kill the people, and the animals too. And all of a sudden it gets very hot, and just as suddenly it gets very cold, such that this is a vile country, both bad and poor. Their prince who rules the country who is called Batho [Batu] stays in the city of Orda.[284] Truly no worthy person ought to stay in this country, for the land and the country are not fit for a dog to enter. It would be a good land for sowing bracken, broom, and thorns, and brambles, for the country is worthless for anything else. Nevertheless, there is some good land in certain places, but it is not plentiful.

---

283. Tartary: the medieval name for the Central Asian steppes east of the Caspian Sea into which the Mongols (called Tartars: see Ch. 23, n. 444) expanded in the early thirteenth century under Chingiz (Genghis) Khan. The *Mandeville* author draws here on Vincent of Beauvais, *Speculum Historiale* 1.31, itself based on the records of John of Plano Carpini and Simon of Saint Quentin, papal envoys to the Mongols in 1245. Nomads and fierce warriors who burst unexpectedly into eastern Latin Christendom, the Mongols were initially viewed negatively (cf. the Bedouins in Ch. 9, but see also Chs. 23–26).

284. *Orda* is not a city; the name derives from the Turkic *ordu*, "camp" (cf. English *horde*). The settlement on the Volga River was called Sarai (Turkic for court or palace), capital of the Golden Horde, the westernmost Mongol khanate. When the papal envoys mentioned in n. 283 above wrote their reports, Chingiz Khan's grandson Batu ruled the Golden Horde.

I have not been by this route, and I have been in other lands bordering on this one, such as in the land of Russia, and the land of Niflan [Livonia], and the kingdom of Crake [Krakow] and of Leto [Lithuania], and the kingdom of Arasten,[285] and in many other places in that far land, but I never went by this route to Jerusalem, which is why I cannot describe it well. But if it is a subject that pleases any brave man who has been by this route, he may add it here if he pleases, so that those who would like to make this journey by this way might know what route there is.[286] For one cannot readily take this route except in winter, because of the wretched waters and because of the marshes that are in those regions, such that one cannot cross if it is not freezing hard, and if there is no frozen snow above. For if there were no snow, no one could cross the ice, neither man nor horse. It takes a good three days' journey by this route to pass through Prussia to the habitable land of the Saracens. The Christians who go there every year to fight with them[287] have to take all their food with them, for they will find nothing good there; and they have their food carried above the ice in wheel-less carts that they call *soleies*.[288] For as long as their food lasts they can stay there, and no longer, for they will find no one there who will sell them anything. When their spies see the Christians come on them, they run to the towns and cry in a loud voice: "*Kera, Kera, Kera,*"[289] and right away they arm themselves and gather together. Know that it freezes much harder in those parts than over here. Therefore everyone has stoves in their houses, and at those stoves they eat and fill their needs such as they are able. For this is in the northern regions: that is to say, towards the north where it is piercingly cold, for the sun does not come to those parts or very little. Therefore in the true north—that is, exactly north—the earth is so cold that no one can dwell there; and to the contrary towards the land of the

---

285. A far-eastern country known from the *chansons de geste,* or medieval epics (DLMM 271, n. 33).

286. Compare the similar request in the Prologue. No Latin Christian pilgrim would have traveled from France or Flanders through Tartary; only those coming from Central Asia (a small number of missionaries and merchants) would have done so. Mentioning Tartary, though, brings into the account the borderlands east of Latin Christendom to the north of the Balkans.

287. Likely a reference to the Baltic Crusades (early thirteenth to fifteenth centuries), led by the Teutonic Knights, who after Acre fell in 1291 made their headquarters in Marienburg (now Malbork, Poland).

288. "sleighs"; cf. E: "sleddes and carres withouten wheles" (WBJM 65).

289. DLMM (271, n. 36) derives *kera* from *houra,* originally a Russian war cry (not to be confused with *hourra,* or "hurrah"), whereas Seymour (2002, 150, n. 55/27) derives it from Persian *khar,* "trouble," dismissing the Arabic verb *karrah,* "attack," suggested by Moseley (1983, 104, n.). Deluz is presumably thinking of attacks on Islamicized Mongols in Russian territory, Seymour of a Persian-influenced Mongol Islam, and Moseley of crusades on Arabic-speaking Muslims.

south it is so hot that no one can dwell there, because the sun when it is in the south casts its ray straight down on that region.

[Chapter 15]

About the Customs of the Saracens and About Their Law. How the Sultan Questioned the Author of this Book. And About the Beginning of Machomet

Now, because I have spoken about the Saracens and their country, if you want to know a part of their law and their belief, I will describe them to you according to what their book that has the name *Alkoran* explains. Some call this book *Meshaf* and some call it *Harme*,²⁹⁰ according to the different languages of the country. Machomet gave them this book, in which is written, amongst other things, as I have often read and seen,²⁹¹ that the good will go to Paradise and the bad to hell, and this all Saracens believe.²⁹²

If they are asked what [sort of] Paradise they understand, they say that it is a place of delights where one will find all kinds of fruit in all seasons, and rivers flowing with milk and honey and wine and fresh water; and that there one will have beautiful and noble houses according to one's merits made of precious stones and gold and silver; and that each man will have ninety wives, all virgins, and will have relations with her [*sic*] every day, and will always find them virgins.²⁹³

290. DLMM has *Alkaron* throughout Chapter 15, but the most common scribal form (found in seven manuscripts) is *Alkoran* (272, textual n. b) followed here; the names *Meshaf* and *Harme* (defined in Ch. 9, n. 124) vary more.

291. This chapter derives mostly from the late thirteenth-century *Treatise on the State of the Saracens* attributed to William of Tripoli (see excerpts in Appendix B.2), supplemented by Vincent of Beauvais, *Speculum Historiale,* and Jacques de Vitry, *Historia Orientalis.* Given this and the romance flavor of his claim to have served the Sultan, the *Mandeville* author is unlikely to have read the Qur'an (his main source was apparently unacquainted with the Qur'an in Arabic: William 1992, 84–85). It is plausible, however, since two Latin translations of the Qur'an existed; the more widely circulated was part of an anti-Islamic translation project sponsored in the 1140s by Peter the Venerable, abbot of Cluny.

292. Just as I have not used "Muslim" for "Saracen," I have not given "Muhammad" for "Machomet," whose spelling signals the historically and culturally specific nature of this account (even more detailed, one might note, than that of Greek Christianity in Ch. 3).

293. Cf. (Pseudo-)William, *Tractatus* 52. Cf. also Qur'an, suras 2.25, 13.35, 55.54–56, 56.1–40, and 76.12–22. No Qur'anic mention is made of the number of *houris,* or virgins of Paradise, but seventy-two wives are mentioned in the *hadith* ("narrative" or "talk"), traditional accounts of Muhammad's deeds and utterances taken to be authoritative, after the Qur'an.

Also, they believe in and willingly speak about the Virgin Mary and about the Incarnation.[294] They say that Mary was instructed by the angels, and that Saint Gabriel told her that she was fore-chosen from the beginning of the world, that he announced to her the Incarnation of Jesus Christ, and that she would conceive and give virgin birth; and this their book truly testifies. They say also that Jesus spoke as soon as He was born, and that He was a holy and true prophet in deeds and in words, and meek, merciful, and just, and without any failings. They also say that when the angel announced the Incarnation to Saint Mary, she was young and very afraid, for there was in the country an enchanter or sorcerer that had the name Takina who through his sorcery made himself resemble an angel, and he would often go to bed with the virgins. So Mary was afraid that the angel was Takina, and that he wanted to deceive her along with the [other] virgins; and she entreated him to say whether he was that, and the angel answered that she had nothing to fear, for he was the true messenger of Jesus Christ. Also, their book says that when she gave birth under a palm tree she was ashamed to have a child, and she cried, and said that she wished she were dead; and right away the child spoke and comforted her and said: "Mother, do not be dismayed, for God has hidden in you his secret for the salvation of the world." In many other places their Alkoran says that Jesus Christ spoke as soon as He was born. This book also says that Jesus was sent by God Almighty to be a mirror and an example and a sign to all men.

The Alkoran also speaks about Judgment Day: how God will come to judge all classes of people, take the good to His side and place them in glory, and condemn the wicked to the pains of Hell.[295]

And [it says that] amongst all the prophets Jesus is the most excellent, and the closest to God, and that He made the Gospels in which there is good teaching and healthy guidance, clarity, truth, and true preaching to those who believe in God, and that He was a true prophet and more than a prophet, and lived without sin, and gave sight to the blind, and healed the leprous, and revived the dead, and that He ascended entirely alive to Heaven. When they can get hold of the book where the Gospels of Our Lord are written—especially *"Missus est Angelus Gabriel"*[296]—those

---

294. Cf. (Pseudo-)William, *Tractatus* 30–36. Behind the (distorted) story told here lies the Qur'anic account of Mary and the birth of Jesus in sura 19.16–33, where God's spirit (*ruh*), not a magician called Takina, appears. Mary is the only woman named in the Qur'an and its most prominent female figure: suras 3, 4, 5, 19, 21, 23, and 66. On Mary and Jesus as signs, cf. *Tractatus,* Chapter 36, and Qur'an 23.50.

295. Mentioned, like Paradise, several times in (Pseudo-)William's *Tractatus,* the Last Judgment is an important Qur'anic theme, and both are thus central to Islam.

296. "The angel Gabriel was sent" (Luke 1:26). This claim comes from a decidedly negative depiction of Islamic views of Christianity in Jacques de Vitry, *Historia Orientalis,* Bk. 3 (1611, 1137: Bk. 3 is now viewed as an unauthorial supplement:

who are literate say this Gospel in their prayers and they kiss it and honor it with great devotion.

They fast for a whole month in the year, and they only eat at night, and they keep themselves from their wives every day in that month, but the sick are not constrained to this fast.[297]

This book also speaks about the Jews, who it says are wicked because they will not believe that Jesus was sent by God, and they lie falsely about Mary and about her son Jesus Christ in saying that they have crucified Jesus, Mary's son, for He was not crucified, as they say, but rather God had Him ascend to Himself without [suffering] death and without being mutilated. But He transfigured His likeness into someone else who was Judas Iscariot, and the Jews crucified that one and believed that it was Jesus. But Jesus ascended to Heaven completely alive and He will also descend completely alive to judge the world. Therefore they say that the Christians have no knowledge of this, and that they foolishly and falsely believe that Jesus Christ was crucified. They further say that if He had been crucified God would have acted contrary to His justice, when He allowed Jesus Christ who was innocent to be put to death guiltless,[298] and they say that we fail in this article [of our faith], and God's great justice could not allow such a wrong to happen. In this their faith fails, for indeed they acknowledge the works of Jesus Christ to be good, and His words and His teachings and His Gospels to be true, and His miracles to be real, and the blessed Virgin Mary to be a good and holy virgin before and after the birth of Jesus Christ. And [they acknowledge] that those who believe perfectly in God will be saved.

Because they come so close to our faith they are easily converted to Christian law when one preaches to them and shows them clearly Jesus

---

2008, 8–9). On Jesus, cf. (Pseudo-)William, *Tractatus* 32, 41–42, 44. The Qur'an calls Jesus a prophet, mentions the Gospel (e.g., 5.46, 57.27), and accepts that He performed miracles and was raised by God to God's presence.

297. Ramadan, the ninth month in the Muslim lunar calendar, requires fasting (and sexual abstinence) from sunrise to sunset. This fast, one of the Five Pillars of Islam, commemorates the revelation of the Qur'an to Muhammad. Exemptions are made for the sick, amongst others, as correctly noted here. The claim comes from Jacques de Vitry (1611, 1059; 2008, 136), but without Jacques' comment that after sunset the Saracens eat and drink like animals, even to vomiting, and indulge in the pleasures of the flesh.

298. Cf. (Pseudo-)William, *Tractatus* 43–44. Behind this story lies Qur'an 4.157–59, elaborated by the addition of Judas. Traditional Islamic commentators accepted the idea that, although "the Jews" believed that they had crucified Jesus, it was in fact a likeness on the cross. Some Christian heresies (Docetism, Gnosticism) make a similar claim, as in the second-century Gnostic Apocalypse of Peter found at Nag Hammadi, but the exact source of the substitute Judas is unknown (the story is also found in the medieval Gospel of Barnabas, but its date is uncertain, either fourteenth or sixteenth century).

Christ's law and explains the prophecies to them.[299] They also say that they know by the prophecies that Machomet's law will fail, just like the Jews' law, which is a failure, and that the Christian people's law will last until the world's end. If anyone asks them what and how they believe, they answer: "We believe in God the maker of Heaven and of earth and of all other things, who made everything and without whom nothing is made, and we believe that on Judgment Day each will have justice according to his deeds, and we believe to be true everything that God has said through the mouths of all His holy prophets."[300]

Also, Machomet decreed in their book of Alkoran that every man may have two wives, or three, or four. But now they take up to nine, and as many concubines as they can maintain; and if any of their wives wrongs her husband he can cast her out of his house, and separate from her and take another, but he is required to give her a part of his goods.[301]

Also, when one speaks to them about the Father and the Son and the Holy Spirit, they say that there are three persons there and not one God, for their Alkoran does not speak at all of the Trinity. But they say truly that God has speech, for otherwise He would be mute, and God has a spirit, this they know well, for otherwise He would not be alive. Also, when they are told about the Incarnation—how through the angel's word God sent His wisdom to earth and was engendered in the Virgin Mary, and [how] by God's word the dead will be revived on Judgment Day—they say that this is true and that God's word has great power. They say that whoever does not know God's word, does not know God at all; and they further say that Jesus Christ is God's word. Thus says their Alkoran, where it says that the angel spoke to Mary and said to her: "Mary, God will preach the Word to you from his mouth and his name will be called Jesus Christ."[302] They also say that Abraham was God's friend, and Moses was God's spokesperson, Jesus was God's Word and Spirit, and Machomet was God's true messenger. They say indeed that of these four Jesus was the worthiest, and the most excellent, and the greatest, such that they have many good articles of our faith and of our belief, although they do not have perfect law and faith according to

---

299. Christianity has been a missionary religion since its founding (Latin Christendom itself was one of its results). By the mid-thirteenth century, influenced by crusading setbacks and the new mendicant orders (see Ch. 18, n. 358), the Latin Church increased its missionary activity, promoting conversion in the East, amongst Muslims and Mongols. This activity continued well into the fourteenth century, and Friar Odoric's *Relatio*, the *Mandeville* author's template for Chapters 16–34, is one record thereof.

300. Cf. (Pseudo-)William, *Tractatus* 48–50, 52. Cf. the similar Mongol prophecies in Chapter 26.

301. Cf. (Pseudo-)William, *Tractatus* 51.

302. Cf. (Pseudo-)William, *Tractatus* 31; for the rest of the material in this paragraph, cf. *Tractatus* 53–55.

Christians, and all those who know and understand the Scriptures and the prophecies are easily converted, for they have the Gospels and the prophecies and the Bible all written in their language, and they know much of Holy Scripture.

But they do not understand it except according to the letter; and the Jews do likewise, for they do not understand the letter spiritually, but bodily, and therefore they are persecutors of the true wise men who understand it spiritually. Therefore Saint Paul says: *"Littera enim occident, spiritus autem vivificat."*[303]

Also, the Saracens say that the Jews are wicked, for they have broken the law that God sent them through Moses,[304] and the Christians are wicked, as they say, for they do not keep the commands of the Gospels that Jesus set out for them.

Therefore I will tell you what the Sultan said to me one day in his personal quarters. He had everyone leave his chamber, lords and others, whatever their rank, because he wanted to speak to me in private. He asked me how the Christians behaved in our countries,[305] and I said well, thank God; and he told me that truly they did not.

"For," [he said,] "your priests are not concerned to serve God. They ought to set an example for lay folk to do well, and they set an example of doing ill. Therefore the common people, on holy days when they should go to church to serve their God, go then to the taverns to be in gluttony all day and all night, and they eat and drink like animals that do not know when they have had enough. And all the Christians also seek in every way they can to make trouble and to deceive one another. On top of this, they are so proud that they do not know how to dress, [wearing clothes that are] now long, now short, now narrow, now wide, now embroidered, now cut close,[306] and in all kinds of shapes and dress and other things. They ought to be simple and humble and true and charitable as was Jesus in whom they believe. But they are just the opposite and completely inclined to do wrong. And they are so greedy that for a little silver they sell their daughters, their sisters, their own wives into debauchery, and they seduce one another's wives, and they do not keep

---

303. "For the letter kills, but the spirit quickens" (2 Cor. 3:6).

304. Cf. (Pseudo-)William, *Tractatus* 43.

305. The plural is important. The text constitutes its audience not as English or French knights, but as (Latin) Christians. Like the claim to have read the Qur'an, this assertion is both plausible and unlikely. Dialogues of Christians with non-Christians occur not only in travel memoirs, sometimes as genuine records, but throughout medieval writing, often as moral fictions. They take various forms, including that used here, where the outsider is a mouthpiece for an insider's critique (cf. Alexander the Great's exchanges in Chapter 32). The likeliest source of this exchange is Caesarius of Heisterbach's early thirteenth-century *Dialogus miraculorum* (*Dialogue of Miracles*) 4.15.

306. *Cortealx: court taillez* ("cut short") in several French copies. C: "now swerded, now daggered" (HMT 1.89).

their word to one another. But they break their entire law that Jesus has given them and set out for their salvation. Thus for their sins they have lost all this land that we possess, for because of their sins your God has put them [the lands] in our hands—not through our strength, but for their sins. For indeed we know truly that when you serve God well and he wants to help you no one can counter you, and so we know well through our prophecies that Christians will win back this land when they serve their God more devoutly.[307] But as long as they are of such a foul life as they are right now, we have no fear of them whatsoever, for their God will not help them at all."

Then I asked him how he thus knew the state of the Christians, and he answered me that he knew the whole state of the courts of the Christian princes and the state of the commons by means of the people whom he sends through all countries in the guise of merchants of precious stones and other things, to know the behavior of each country. He had me call back the lords that he had sent out of the chamber, and he showed me four who were great lords of the country who described our countries to me, and the other countries of Christendom, as well as if they were from the country, and they spoke French very well, and so did the Sultan, at which I marveled greatly.

Alas, what a great scandal it is to our law and to our faith when people who have neither law nor faith rebuke us and reprimand our sins, and those who through our good examples and through our acceptable life ought to be converted to the law of Jesus Christ are through our evils and through us distanced and estranged from the holy and true belief. It is no wonder that they call us wicked, for they speak the truth. But Saracens are good, faithful, for they entirely keep the command of their holy book Alkoran that God sent them by His holy messenger their prophet Machomet, to whom they say Saint Gabriel the angel often spoke, and explained to him the divine will.

Know that Machomet was born in Arabia, and was at first a poor servant boy who looked after the camels and accompanied the merchants, until he went once with the merchants into Egypt. At that time they were Christian in those regions, and in the desert of Arabia he came to a chapel where there was a hermit, and when he entered the chapel— which was quite small, and had a small and low door—the entry then became as large and as high as if it had been a palace gate. This was the first miracle that the Saracens say that he performed in his youth.[308]

Afterwards Machomet began to become wise and rich, and he was a great astronomer. Then he was governor of the land of the prince of Corrodane [Khorosan], and he governed it most wisely, in such a way that when the prince died, he married the lady, who had the name

---

307. For the prophecies, cf. (Pseudo-)William, *Tractatus* 22–23, 49.

308. With this paragraph, cf. (Pseudo-)William, *Tractatus* 2.

Gadryge [Khadija].[309] Machomet often used to fall down with the great sickness—that is, with epilepsy—and so the lady was terribly angry that she had taken a husband. But Machomet gave her to understand that every time he fell down, Saint Gabriel came to speak to him, and he could not bear it because of the angel's great brightness, but had thus to fall down. Therefore the Saracens say that the angel Gabriel often came to speak to him.

This Machomet ruled in Arabia in the year of grace 610,[310] and he was a descendant of Ishmael, who was Abraham's son begotten on Hagar his chambermaid. Therefore there are Saracens who are called Ishmaelites; others call them Hagarenes, from Hagar. [There are] others who are properly called Saracens, from Sarra. There are others who are called Moabites, and others Ammonites, for Lot's two sons, Moab and Ammon, whom he begot on his daughters [and] who were afterwards great earthly princes.[311]

Also, Machomet very much loved a worthy hermit who dwelt in the desert one league from Mount Sinai, on the route by which one goes from Arabia towards Chaldea and towards India, one day's travel from the sea where the merchants of Venice often came to trade. Machomet so often went in the company of this worthy man that all the servants were very angry, for he willingly heard this worthy man speak and preach, and made his servants stay awake almost all night; and these servants thought that they would kill this worthy man. It happened one night that Machomet was terribly drunk—he had drunk that much wine— and the servants took Machomet's sword while he slept, and killed this worthy man and then put the sword, all bloody, back in its sheath. In the morning when Machomet found this worthy man dead he was exceedingly angry, and wanted to have justice done to the murderers. But all his servants by [prior] agreement said that he himself had done it when he was drunk, and they showed him his sword all bloody. When he saw this, he thought that they had spoken the truth, and he cursed wine and all those who sell or drink wine. Because of that curse the Saracens who are devout drink no wine whatsoever.[312] But there are those who freely drink it in secret—except that they know that they will be criticized. They drink a very good drink, both sweet and nourishing, that is made

---

309. Variously spelled in the manuscripts. This paragraph draws on Vincent of Beauvais, *Speculum Historiale* 23.39.

310. There is some scribal variation in the date, more often given as the year of Muhammad's first revelation (he is thought to have been born around 570). His emigration from Mecca to Medina, the *hijra*, occurred in 622, and his political power only expanded in the few years before his death in 632.

311. Gen. 19:31–38. For the Saracen names, cf. Jacques de Vitry, *Historia* 5 (1611, 1053; 2008, 108–10).

312. With this paragraph, cf. (Pseudo-)William, *Tractatus* 3.

from sugarcane—which is what sugar is made from—that tastes very good, and is good for the chest.

Also, it often happens that a Christian becomes Saracen, either out of simplemindedness or poverty, or out of wickedness; and the arch-flamens or flamens[313] when they receive them say this: "*La illec ella sila Machomet Roses Alla hec.*"[314] That is to say in English: "There is no God but one alone and Machomet [is] his prophet."

Since I have described for you part of their law and their customs, I will describe for you, if you like, what letters they have with the names that they call them:

Almoy Beth Cachi Deltoi Estoi Foithi Gaiepi Tothi Heth Iochi Kachi Lacm Milai Rabaloth Orthi Yrtho Zormich.

They have these four additional letters because of the difference of their language, because they speak thus in the throat, just as we in our speech in England have two letters more than they have in their abc: that is, þ and ȝ, which are called *thorn* and *yogh.*

[Chapter 16]

About the Lands of Albania and Libya. About the Wishes for the Safekeeping of a Sparrowhawk and About Noah's Ark

Since I have described for you and spoken above about the Holy Land and the countries nearby and the many ways to go into that land, and Mount Sinai and lesser Babylon, and the other places that I have spoken about before this, now it is time, if you like, to speak to you about the neighboring lands, the islands, and the diverse animals and diverse peoples beyond these boundaries. For in that country over there, there are many diverse countries and many great regions that are divided by the four rivers that come from [the] Earthly Paradise:[315] Mesopotamia and the kingdom of Chaldea and Arabia are between the two rivers Tigris and Euphrates; and the kingdom of Medea and of Persia are between the rivers Nile and Tigris; and the kingdom of Syria, about which I

---

313. Chief priests and priests (C: "as oure Erchebisshopp or Bisshopp"; E: "the cheeff maister and keper of thaire lawe"). Used of pagan priests, these terms may be meant pejoratively here.

314. The spelling of the *Shahada,* or Muslim profession of faith, taken from the *Tractatus* 8, varies greatly in the manuscripts, but is translated almost correctly ("there is no God but God . . ."). A current transcription might read, "*La ilah illâ Allâh wa Muhammad rasûl Illâh.*" The *Mandeville* author also adapted the *Tractatus'* unusual claim that the *Shahada* was in effect a baptismal formula.

315. Gen. 2:13; and see Chapter 33. Only three rivers are named here (missing is the Physon or Ganges). The geographical overview in the first two paragraphs represents received views and derives mainly from encyclopedias; many of the places are on the more detailed world maps: see Appendix C.1.

have spoken to you above, and Palestine and Phoenicia are between [the] Euphrates and the Mediterranean Sea. This Mediterranean Sea stretches from Morocco on the Sea of Spain right to the Great Sea,[316] so that it extends beyond Constantinople three thousand and forty Lombard leagues.

Towards the Ocean Sea in India is the kingdom of Sythie [Scythia], which is completely enclosed by mountains. Then below Sythie, and from the Caspian Sea to the River Thany [Don], is Amazonia. This is the land of Feminy where there are no men, only women. Next is Albania, a very great kingdom, and it is called Albania because the people are much whiter than in the other places around there; and there are such large and such strong dogs in this country that they attack and kill lions.[317] Then next is Hircania, Baccaria [Bactria], Hiberia, and many other regions. Between the Red Sea and the Ocean Sea towards the south is the region of Ethiopia and upper Libya. This land of Libya— that is, lower Libya, which begins at the Sea of Spain, where the Pillars of Hercules are[318]—extends towards Egypt and towards Ethiopia. In this country of Libya the sea is indeed higher than the land, and it seems that

---

316. The Black Sea. The Mediterranean measures about 3,860 kilometers (2,084 nautical miles) in length.

317. Ocean Sea: see Chapter 8, n. 95. Amazonia: see Chapter 17 (and n. 338), where it is placed "beside the land of Chaldea." Albania: Pliny's *Natural History* is the ultimate source (7.2, Albanians as white-*haired;* 8.61, as dogs). *Albus* is Latin for "white," but the name comes from Greek, drawing apparently on Indo-European *alb,* or mountain, and Albania here is Caucasian Albania in the Caucasus Mountains.

   Note that, as soon as he has left the biblical East, the *Mandeville* author refers to the unusual, often monstrous, peoples thought to dwell in the Far (marvelous) East, typically in the vaguely defined regions called India and Ethiopia (see Ch. 17, n. 344). On the major thirteenth-century world maps (Hereford and Ebstorf), though, they are mostly placed in Africa at the world's edge, if still within Christ's cosmos. Uncertain as to whether monstrous races as such existed, Augustine argued in his influential early fifth-century *City of God* 16.8 that, if they do, they too must descend from Adam (see Appendix C.1). Some fifty such peoples were "known" to Latin Christians, transmitted above all by Pliny, who much supplemented his Greek inheritance. Here as throughout the rest of *TBJM* (especially in Chs. 17, 21, 22, and 31), the *Mandeville* author interweaves this Greco-Roman inheritance (mostly from encyclopedias) with the latest information (mostly from Odoric). With a few exceptions (the Amazons in Ch. 17, the dog-heads in Ch. 21), the traditional races are merely named and do not receive the "anthropological" attention that the author gives to other eastern peoples and their *outré* customs; in Chapter 24 they are even said to descend from Noah's "cruel" son Cham after devils coupled with his female line. Two early studies remain fundamental: Wittkower 1942; Friedman 1981 (2000 reprint with updated bibliography).

318. The Strait of Gibraltar lies between Spain and both Monte Hache and the Jebel Musa in Morocco; these were sometimes considered the Pillars of Hercules, a boundary that was not fully breached until the fifteenth-century Portuguese and Spanish explorations. In Greek myth, Hercules (Greek: Heracles) had to perform

it should cover the land, and nevertheless it does not pass its bounds. Thus one sees in this country a mountain that one cannot approach. In this land of Libya, if one turns towards the East, the shadow of one's body is to the right, and in our regions the shadow is to the left.[319] In this sea of Libya there are no fish, for they cannot live or endure because of the sun's great heat, for the water is always boiling because of the great heat. There are so many other countries that it would make too long an account if one named them all, but I will speak to you more fully about some regions after this.

Whoever would like then to go towards Tartary, Persia, Chaldea, and India, puts to sea at Genoa or Venice or some other port that I have described to you before, and crosses the sea and arrives at Trapezonde [Trebizond], which is a good city and which used to be the port of Ponz [Pontus].[320] The ports of the Persians and the Medeans are there, and [the ports] of the border lands over there.

In this city lies Saint Athanasius, who was bishop of Alexandria who made the psalm "*Quicumque vult salvus esse etc.*"[321] This Athanasius was a great doctor of theology, and because he preached and spoke so deeply of divinity and the Godhead he was accused to the pope of Rome[322] of being a heretic, for which reason the pope sent for him and put him in prison. While he was in prison he made that psalm *Quicumque vult,* and sent it to the pope, and said to him that if he was a heretic, then it was because the articles of that psalm were not true and good, for thus he believed; and when the pope saw that psalm, he said that it was all our faith, and he ordered that it be sung every day at Prime,[323] and he considered the bishop a worthy man and a true Christian, and freed him

---

a series of labors to atone for killing his children; one labor took him to the far west, where he set up the Pillars at the end of his journey.

319. This places Libya in the southern hemisphere. In Chapter 20, the *Mandeville* author will first see the "Antarctic" star there.

320. Here the *Mandeville* author begins to use OP as his template, reworking it all the way to Chapter 34, even more freely than he uses WoB in Chapters 1–14.

321. "Whoever will be saved etc.": the opening words of the Athanasian Creed, not a psalm but a profession of faith focused especially on the Trinity and the Incarnation and widely used by Western Christians. No longer considered its author, Athanasius (d. 373) was Bishop of Alexandria; he was exiled several times for opposing Arianism, which denied Christ's full divinity and was declared heretical in the fourth century.

322. "Of Rome" is not necessarily redundant: *TBJM* was composed when the papacy was in Avignon and copies made between 1378 and 1417 were made during the Great Schism, when there were two (and for a time even three) popes, one of Avignon, the other of Rome.

323. The first of the daily offices (canonical hours of monastic prayer in the Roman Catholic Church), traditionally the early morning (6:00 a.m.). Does such knowledge make the *Mandeville* author a cleric? (See also Ch. 18, n. 351, and Ch. 33, n. 569.)

from prison. But he would never go back to his bishop[ric] because he had been accused of heresy out of jealousy.

Trapezonde used to belong to the emperor of Constantinople, but a rich man that the emperor sent to guard the country against the Turks usurped the land and took it for his own property and calls himself emperor.[324] From Trapezonde whoever wants to goes through little Armenia.

In this country there is an old castle that sits on a rock that is called the Castle of the Sparrowhawk—it is beyond the city of Layays [Laiazzo, now Ayas] near the city of Parsipee [Persembe], which belongs to the lord of Cruk [now Corycus], who is a rich man and a good Christian— where one finds a very handsome and very well-formed sparrowhawk on a perch, and a beautiful lady of Fairy who looks after it.[325] If anyone wanted to keep this sparrowhawk awake for seven days and seven nights (others say for three days and three nights), alone without company and without sleeping either a little or at all, this beautiful lady will come to him at the end of seven days (or of three days) and give him the first wish that he would wish of earthly things, and this has often been tried.

In particular, a king of Armenia who was a very brave prince once kept watch there, and at the end of seven days the lady came to him and told him that he should make a wish, for he had indeed accomplished his task. The king answered that he was a great enough lord and truly at peace and had riches enough, and that he wished for nothing but the body of that beautiful woman, to have it as he wanted; and she answered him that she [*sic*] did not know what he asked for, and that he was foolish and he could not have it, for he should ask only for something earthly, and she was not earthly but spiritual. The king said that he wished for nothing else, and the lady answered: "Since I cannot withdraw you from your foolish desire, I will give you [something] without [your] wishing for it, and to all your descendants [as well]. You shall have war without stable peace, and be continuously in subjection to your enemies for nine generations, and be in need of material goods." And ever since the king of Armenia has had neither peace nor abundant goods, and has always been under tribute to the Saracens.

Also, a poor man's son kept watch there as well and wished that he could be successful and fortunate in trade, and the lady granted him [his wish] and he became the richest and most famous merchant there could be at sea or on earth. He was so rich that he did not know the

---

324. The Empire of Trebizond (1204–1461) was, under the Grand Komnenoi, not only an important port, but also a thriving center of art and architecture.

325. Like the tale of Hippocrates' daughter in Chapter 4 (see n. 34), this tale has no known source. The pilgrim Willibrand of Oldenburg tells a very brief version of it in 1211 (Laurent 1864, 179–80), but nothing suggests that the *Mandeville* author read it (DLMM 297, n. 7), and its next occurrence (in Jean d'Arras' prose romance *Melusine*, 1392–1393) clearly derives from the Mandevillean version.

thousandth part of what he had, and he was wiser in wishing than the king was.

Also, a knight of the Temple[326] likewise kept watch there and wished for a purse always full of gold and the lady granted him [his wish]. But she told him that he had asked for the destruction of their order because of their faith in this purse and because of the great pride that they would have, and so it was. Nevertheless, let anyone who wants to keep watch take good care of himself, for if he sleeps he will be lost and no one will see him any more. This is not the right way to go to the regions that I named above, but whoever wants to see these wonders can take it.

Therefore whoever wants to go the right way goes from Trapezonde towards Greater Armenia to a city that has the name Artiton [Erzerum]. This city used to be very good and most abundant, but the Turks have utterly destroyed it. Around this place little or no wine or fruit grows. In this country the land is higher than elsewhere and it is very cold, and there are many good waters and good wells that come underground from the river of Paradise that has the name Euphrates, which is a day's travel from this city; this river comes towards India underground, and comes out again in the land of Altazar. One goes through this Armenia and enters the sea of Persia.

From this city of Artiron [Erzerum] one goes to a mountain that has the name Sabissacole, and near there is another mountain that has the name Ararath, but the Jews call it Thanez, where Noah's ark came to rest. It is still on that mountain, and one sees it from afar when the weather is fair. This mountain is a good seven leagues high, and some say that they have been [there], seen and touched the ark, and stuck their finger in the hole where the Devil came out when Noah said *"Benedicite."*[327] But those who tell such tales talk nonsense, for no one can climb that mountain because of the great abundance of snow that is always on that mountain, both in summer and in winter, so that no one can climb, and no one has climbed the mountain since Noah's time, except one monk who by God's grace brought back one of the planks, which is still in a monastery at the foot of the mountain. Nearby is the city of Dayne [Dvin], which Noah founded, and quite close is the city of Any [Ani], in which there used to be a thousand churches. But this monk greatly desired to climb that mountain, and one day he attempted to climb. When he was a third of the way up the mountain he was so weary that he could go no further, and so he rested and slept; and when he woke, he found himself there right at the foot of the mountain, and he prayed devoutly to Our Lord to allow him to climb, and an angel came and told

---

326. On the Knights Templar, see Chapter 11, n. 168.

327. "Bless you," used here against evil. This particular anecdote has no known source.

him that he would climb it and he did, and no one [has done so] ever since. Which is why one ought not to believe such tales.[328]

From this mountain one goes to the city of Thamise [Tabriz], which used to be called Faxis, which is a very beautiful and large city and is one of the best there is in the world for trade. All merchants go there to buy goods sold by weight. It is in the land of the emperor of Persia, and they say that the emperor takes in more in that city as a result of trade than does the richest Christian king in the world, for they tax an incalculable amount from all the goods.

Near this city there is a mountain of salt and everyone takes as much of this salt as they want to salt everything. Many Christians dwell there under tribute to the Saracens. From this city one goes through many cities and past many castles in heading towards India to the city of Sadony [Isphahan?], which is ten day's travel from Thamise and is a most noble city and very large. The emperor of the Persians dwells there in summer, for the country is quite cold, and there are good rivers carrying ships. Then one takes the way towards India through many days' travel and through many countries all the way to a city that has the name Cassat [Kashan], which is a most noble city and very abundant in wheat, in wine, and in all other goods. This is the city where the three kings met and gathered by God's grace to go to Bethlehem to see Our Lord and to adore him and to make him presents of gold, of incense, and of myrrh,[329] and from that city to Bethlehem is fifty-three days' travel.

From this city one comes to another city that has the name Geth [Yezd], which is one day's journey from the Sandy Sea.[330] This is the best city that the emperor of Persia has in all his land, and there they call meat *Dabago* and wine *Vapa*.[331] The pagans say that Christians cannot dwell in this city, nor endure there, nor live without soon dying, and no one knows for what reason.

Then one goes through many cities and many towns that would be too long to recount all the way to the city of Cornaa [Kinara, near the ruins of Persepolis], which used to be so large that the walls stretched about twenty-five leagues in circumference. The walls can still be seen but the city is completely uninhabited. From Cornaa one goes through many lands and many cities to the land of Job, and there the land of the emperor of Persia ends.

---

328. Versions of this tale are also found in William of Rubruck, *Journey* (Ch. 38) and Simon of Saint-Quentin, *History of the Tartars* 31.97. OP claims that he wanted to climb the mountain (Ch. 1 in Appendix B.3).

329. Matt. 2:1–12. See also Chapter 9, n. 120.

330. On the Sandy Sea, see Chapter 30.

331. This odd bit of information may be the result of scribal confusion: see Appendix A.3 (16/94).

If you want to know the letters of the Persians and what they are called, know that they are these:[332]

Alim Boin Doin Ethin Fiochina Gith Hith Iothim Kanuncein Lathim Moim Nichom Oriph Phisoun Gumuch Pi Eth Thoich Vith Ya Zozim.

[Chapter 17]

About the Land of Job and About His Age. About the Clothing of the People of Chaldea. About the Land Where Women Dwell without Men's Company. About the Growth and the Powers of the True Diamond

Then on leaving from the city of Cornaa [Kinara], one comes into the land of Job, which is a most beautiful country and abundant in all goods, and the land of Job is called Sweze. In this land is the city of Theman.

Job was pagan and was Are of Gosra's son, and he held this land as prince of the country and was so rich that he did not know the hundredth part of what he had. Although he was pagan he nevertheless served Our Lord well according to his law, and Our Lord indeed found his service good. When he fell into poverty he was seventy-eight years of age, and afterwards, when Our Lord had seen his patience, which was so great, He restored him to wealth and rank once again, and then he was king of Idumea, after the king Esau, and when he was king he was called Jobab. He then lived one hundred and seventy years in that kingdom, and thus when he died he was two hundred and forty-eight years old.[333]

In this land of Job there is no lack of anything that the human body needs. There are mountains there where one finds great plenty of manna, more abundantly and better than one finds elsewhere. Manna is called angels' bread: it is something white, very sweet and most delicious, and much sweeter than honey or other sugar, and it comes from the dew of Heaven that falls on the grass in that country, and it thickens and becomes white and sweet. They put it into medicines for the rich, to loosen the belly and to purge bad blood, for it purifies the blood and dispels melancholy.[334]

---

332. This alphabet is missing in many French manuscripts.

333. Following Gregory the Great's sixth-century *Moralia in Job,* Latin Christians saw the biblical Job as a type of Christ, the Church, and the good Christian, but the *Mandeville* author emphasizes his service as a good pagan here and in Chapter 32. The account likely comes from Isidore of Seville (570–636), whose *De ortu et obitu Patrum* (*On the Patriarchs' Origins and Deaths,* Ch. 34), also identifies Job with Jobab, son of Zara of Bosra in Gen. 36:33. The *Mandeville* author locates the land of Job farther east than do most pilgrimage accounts.

334. The manna mentioned by OP is from either the manna ash (flowering ash, *Fraxinus ornus*), whose cut bark exudes a sugary substance used medicinally, or

This land of Job borders on the kingdom of Chaldea. This land of Chaldea is very large, and it is the language that is greater[335] than any other beyond the sea. To go there one goes past the Tower of Babylon, which is the great Babylon that I told you about earlier where the languages were first changed;[336] it is four days' travel from Chaldea. In the kingdom of Chaldea the men are handsome, and they go about very nobly dressed with golden scarves, and their clothes too are very nobly adorned with gold embroidery and large pearls and precious stones. The women are very ugly and badly dressed, and they all walk barefoot and wearing a miserable, baggy garment, cut off at the knees, and the sleeves are long and baggy in the manner of a monk's habit, and they have the sleeves hanging right to their feet; and they have their hair long and black, hanging all around their shoulders; and the women are quite dark, ugly, and hideous, and they are certainly not at all beautiful, but they lack graciousness.

In this kingdom of Chaldea, in a city that has the name Hur [Ur], dwelt Thare [Terah], Abraham's father, and there Abraham was born. This was in that time when Ninus was king of Babylon, Arabia, and Egypt. Ninus completed the city of Nineveh that Noah had begun to build, and because Ninus completed it, he called it Nineveh from his name. There lies Tobit the prophet about whom Holy Scripture speaks. From this city of Ur by God's command Abraham went away after his father's death, and took Sarah his wife and Lot, his brother's son, with him because he had no child; and he went to dwell in the land of Canaan in a place that had the name Sichem [Shechem]. And this was that Lot who was saved when Sodom and Gomorrah and the other cities were burnt and collapsed into the abyss there where the Dead Sea is, as I have told you previously. In this land of Chaldea they have their own language and their own letters such as are here.[337]

Next beside the land of Chaldea is Amazonia, that is the land of Feminy, which is the kingdom where there are only women: not, as some say, that men cannot live in this country, but rather that they do not want

---

camel's thorn (manna plant, *Alhagi camelorum*), which exudes a sugary substance used in sweets. The *Mandeville* author conflates it with the biblical manna ("bread from Heaven") that the Israelites miraculously received during their forty years in the wilderness (Exod. 16:4–36; Num. 11:7–9); Vincent of Beauvais, *Speculum Naturale* 4.84–85, notes its medicinal properties.

335. This makes no better sense in the original. "Greater": "more widely used"? If so, the claim is false, for Persian was more widely used than Chaldean.

336. Tower of Babel (Gen. 11: 1–9), in Chapter 6.

337. Abraham's origins: Gen. 11:22–27. In classical tradition (not biblical), Ninus founds Nineveh. The city's link with Noah is through his grandson Ashur: Gen. 10:11, 22. Tobit: Tob. 13:1. From Ur to Sichem: Gen. 11:31–32; 12:4–6. Lot and Sodom: Gen. 19 (and Ch. 12). The Chaldean alphabet is lacking in most Insular French manuscripts (DLMM 302, textual note c) and thus not given here.

the men to have lordship over them.[338] For in former times there was a king in this country and married men dwelt there as elsewhere; and it happened that this king had war with the Scythians, and he had the name Colopeus, and he was killed in the battle with all the other noble families of his kingdom. When the queen and the other noble ladies saw that they were all widows and that all the noble blood[339] was lost, they took up arms and, as if in despair, they killed all the men of that country who were left, for they wanted all the women to be widows such as they were. Since then they have never wanted a man to dwell amongst them for more than seven days, or a male child to be raised amongst them. But when they want male company, they head out towards the neighboring lands, and they have their lovers whom they visit, and they remain with them for eight days or ten, and then they return. If they have a child and it is male, either they send it to the father when it knows how to walk and eat by itself, or they kill it; and if it is female, they remove one breast with a hot iron, and if this is a noble woman [they remove] the left for better carrying of the shield, and if this is a common woman[340] the right so that she is not hindered in drawing the bow. In this land there is a queen who governs the whole country and all are obedient to her; and they always choose the queen by electing the one who is bravest in arms. They are good, brave warrioresses, wise and bold, and they go very often for pay to the aid of other kings to earn money and they acquit themselves most forcefully. This land of Amazonia, it is an island completely surrounded by water except in two places where there are two ways in; and beyond this water live the men who are their lovers where they go to take pleasure when they wish.

Beside Amazonia is the land of Termegite [Terra Margine], which is a very good and most delightful country; and because of the country's abundance, King Alexander built his first city of Alexandria there; he built twelve cities by this name, but this one is now called Celsite [Selucia, now Merv].

From the other part of Chaldea towards the south is Ethiopia, a large country that extends all the way to the end of Egypt. Ethiopia is divided into two main parts: that is, into the eastern part and the northern part; the northern part is called Moretane [Mauretania] and there the people are very much blacker than elsewhere. In this region there is a spring

---

338. OP never mentions the Amazons, thought by the Greeks to live at the known world's limits in Asia. Their name is of uncertain origin, but was interpreted as Greek for "breastless" (*a*, lacking + *mazos*, breast). This account combines several sources: Brunetto Latini, *Tresor* 1.30 and 1.22; Vincent of Beauvais, *Speculum Historiale* 1.96; the Alexander Romances; and the *Letter of Prester John* (Deluz 1988, 230–33).

339. "noble families" in the preceding sentence and "noble blood" here are both *bon sanc* in the original.

340. *femme de pié*, foot woman, presumably as in "foot soldier."

whose water in the day is so cold that one cannot drink it and in the night is so hot that one cannot keep one's hand in it. Beyond this region towards the south, in crossing over the Ocean Sea, there is [a] large land and [a] large country. But no one can live there because of the sun's great heat, so hot is it in that land. In Ethiopia all the rivers and all the waters are murky, and they are a little salty because of the great heat that is there. The people of this country get drunk easily, and they do not have a very great appetite for eating and they commonly have a flux of the belly[341] and do not live long. In Ethiopia are many diverse peoples and Ethiopia is called Cusys [Cush]. There is a people [there] that have only one foot and they move so quickly it is a wonder, and the foot is so large that it shades the whole body from the sun when they are lying down. In Ethiopia when the children are small they are all grey-haired, and when they become grown up their hair is all black. In Ethiopia is the city of Saba and the land ruled by one of the three kings who came to seek Our Lord in Bethlehem.[342]

From Ethiopia one goes into India through many different countries, and upper India is called Evilat.[343] India is divided into three main parts:[344] into India Major, which is a very hot country; and India Minor, which is a temperate country, which touches the land of Medea; and the third part towards the north that is very cold, such that because of the sheer cold and the continual freezing the water becomes crystal.

On these crystal rocks grow the good diamonds that seem to be the color of opaque yellowish crystal resembling the color of oil, and they are so hard that no one can polish them, and these diamonds are called *Hamese* in this country.[345] Other diamonds are found in Arabia that are

---

341. Diarrhea.

342. Ethiopia was vaguely located in medieval thought, blurring into India, with which it shared some of the so-called monstrous races (on which see Ch. 16, n. 317). The one-footed Sciopods appear again in Chapter 22. One of the three magi (Matt. 2:1–12) was linked with Ethiopia through medieval commentaries on Pss. 68[67]:31 and 72[71]:9–10; by the mid-fourteenth century he was therefore being depicted visually as black.

343. Named in Gen. 2:11–12 as a land "where gold groweth," Hevilat was sometimes thought to be in or be India, as in Chapter 33, and in Peter Comestor, *Historia Scholastica* (Gen. 14).

344. Medieval sources generally agree on India's tripartite geography, but divide it variously; the division given here probably derives from the Apocryphal Acts of Thomas (as noted in Ch. 19, Thomas was believed to have carried Christianity to India). Like Ethiopia, India was vaguely located, representing above all the marvelous strangeness at the world's end (see Ch. 16, n. 317). It is instructive to compare the *Mandeville* author's account of India (which lasts to Ch. 19) not only with OP's but also with Marco Polo's (1928, 177–202; 1958, 260–94), which presents much the same material in a somewhat different light.

345. Cf. *almâs,* Arabic for diamond. Ancient and medieval authors attributed medicinal and other powers to gemstones, cataloguing them in lapidaries and

not so good, and they are browner and softer; and others are found on the island of Cyprus that are even softer and can be well polished; and they are also found in the land of Macedonia, but the best and the most precious are in India. Very hard diamonds are often found in the mass that comes out where gold is refined from the mine, when this mass is broken into small pieces; and it sometimes happens that one is found as big as a pea, and sometimes smaller, and they are to some extent as hard as those of India, and cut steel and glass easily. Although one finds good diamonds in India on crystal rocks, nevertheless one finds them more commonly on the adamant rocks in the sea and on mountains where there are gold mines, and they grow several together, one small, the other large, and there are some the size of a bean, and there are some as big as a hazelnut, and they are all of square form and with their natural points both above and below without any shaping by a human hand. They grow together male and female, and they feed on the dew from Heaven, and they conceive and beget and make their little children beside them that multiply and grow every year.

I have many times demonstrated that if they are kept with a little of the rock, and not separated from their root, and wet often with May dew, they grow visibly every year, and the small ones become quite big. For just as the fine pearl comes together and forms itself and becomes large with the dew of Heaven, so does the true diamond; and just as the pearl by its nature grows round, so the diamond by divine power grows square.

One should carry all diamonds on the left side, and it is of greater power than on the right, for the strength of their birth comes from the north, which is the left side of the world, and to a man's left side when he turns his face eastwards. If it pleases you to know the powers of the diamond, although you have them in your lapidaries, I will set them down here for you—because not everyone knows them—according to what is asserted by those overseas from whom all knowledge and philosophy have come. The diamond gives to its bearer boldness and high spirits, and keeps the body's limbs whole, and gives victory over enemies in legal disputes and war, if the cause is just, and keeps the bearer in his right mind, and keeps him from quarrels and fights and from bad dreams and fantasies and [the] illusion of evil spirits. If any wicked person wants to bewitch or enchant the bearer, the spells and the enchantments will rebound on him who wanted to harm the bearer through the power of the stone, and likewise no wild animal will dare attack a person who carries the diamond on him. Also, the diamond must be given without

---

encyclopedias. The *Mandeville* author here draws mainly on Vincent of Beauvais, *Speculum Naturale* 8.40, supplemented and dramatized by inference and imagination. Brunetto Latini notes that pearls are created by dew being sunbaked in a seashell (*Tresor* 1.133), and the *Mandeville* author could well have seen crystals form in a liquid supersaturated with salts: hence the inference that crystals are alive.

greed in buying or selling, and then it is of much greater power, and makes one stronger and more steadfast against the enemies,[346] and it heals lunatics and those whom the Devil follows and torments, and if one brings venom or poison into the presence of the diamond, it grows moist right away and begins to sweat.

There are diamonds in India that are purplish or more brown than purplish that are very hard and very precious. But some people do not like them as much as the others. But as for me I would like them as much as the others, for I have seen them tested. There is also another kind that are as white as crystal, but they are a little more opaque and are good and of great power, and are all square and have their natural points, and some are six-cornered and some are four-cornered and some are three-cornered such as nature forms them.

Because the great lords and the young knights who seek honor in arms willingly carry them, I will speak a little more about diamonds, although I prolong my subject, so that they will not be deceived by cheats who go through countries and sell them. For whoever wants to buy diamonds has to know how to recognize them, because they are often counterfeited from yellow crystal and lemon-yellow sapphire and flawed sapphire,[347] and from many other stones. But in all cases these counterfeit diamonds are not so hard and the points break easily, and they can be polished well. But some workers out of malice do not polish them at all, so that the people think that they cannot be polished. But one can test them in this way. First, one tests them by cutting into sapphire or into other precious stones and crystal and steel. Next, one takes adamant, which is the sailors' stone that attracts the needle, and if the diamond is real and powerful the adamant will not attract the needle at all while the diamond is there.[348] This is the proof that those overseas use. Nevertheless, it sometimes happens that good diamonds do lose their power through the incontinence of those who carry them, and then it is necessary to make the stone regain its power, or else it will be of less worth and of less value.

---

346. Or "devils."

347. *Saphir loupe.*

348. Medieval writers sometimes called the diamond "adamant" (Greek *adamas*, "unbreakable"), as here, but because they derived its name from the Latin *adamare* ("to fall in love with, be drawn to") they used it more often for the loadstone, or magnetized iron: its magnetic properties are also discussed in Chapters 18 and 30.

[Chapter 18]

About the Customs in the Islands around India. About the Difference between Idols and Simulacra. About the Three Kinds of Pepper Growing on One Tree and About the Well Whose Scent Changes Every Hour of the Day

In India there are many different lands and many different countries, and it is called India because of a river that flows through the lands that has the name India [Indus]. In this river one finds eels that are more than thirty feet long, and the people beside the river are ill-colored, green and yellow. In India and around India are more than five thousand habitable islands, fine and large, without counting those that are uninhabitable and without counting other small islands, and on each island there is a great abundance of cities, and countless towns and people, for Indians are of such nature that they do not leave their country.

Therefore there is a great multitude of people, for they are not mobile at all, because they dwell in the first climate, which is Saturn's, and Saturn is slow and barely mobile, for it takes thirty years to make its circuit through the twelve signs, and the moon passes through all twelve signs in a month.[349] Because Saturn is of such slow movement, therefore the people of its climate have a nature and will that they do not wish to move. In our country it is just the opposite, for we are in the seventh climate, which is of the moon, and the moon moves easily and is the planet of travel. Therefore it gives us the nature and will to move easily and travel by different routes and seek foreign things and the diversities of the world, for it goes around the earth more quickly than any other planet.

Also, one goes through India through many different countries all the way to the great Ocean Sea, and then one finds an island with the name Orynes [Hormuz], where the merchants from Venice and Genoa and other distant places come to buy goods. But it is so hot on this island that, because of the heat's great force, men's hangers, *videlicet testiculi*,[350] come out of their bodies halfway down the leg, because of the body's great dissipation. But the local people and those who know nature prescribe that they be bound very tightly and smeared with astringent and cooling ointment to keep them in the body, or else they [the men]

---

349. Twelve signs: the zodiac. Following Ptolemy, medieval writers divided the earth's habitable regions north of the equator into seven climates, or parallel bands, each of which could affect national or regional character, as here (England lies just north of the seventh climate: cf. end of Ch. 20). See Appendix C.1.

350. I.e., testicles. "Hangers" translates *perpendicles:* in the singular a mason's plumb line. This odd anecdote comes from OP; Yule hid it untranslated in a footnote (1913, 112, n. 4).

could not live or endure. In this country and Ethiopia and many other countries the people lie completely naked at the water's edge, men and women all together, from terce until none.[351] They always lie in the water except for the face because of the great heat that there is there, and the women have no shame in front of the men, but they lie publicly side-by-side until the heat abates. One can see many ugly figures gathered there, especially near the good towns. On this island the boats are all of wood without iron strapping or nails because of the rocks of adamant, of which there are so many in the sea around there that it is a wonder. And if a ship passed through these far regions that had iron nails or strapping it would be immediately wrecked, for the adamant by its nature attracts iron and the ship because of the iron would be drawn to the adamant and it could never get away.[352]

From this island one goes by sea to another island that has the name Chana [Thana] where there is great plenty of wheat and wine, and it used to be a very great island and a very fine port. But the sea has now badly ravaged and shrunken it. The king of this island used to be so powerful that he would fight against King Alexander.[353] The people of this land have [a] different law, for some worship the sun, and some fire, others trees, others snakes, or the first thing that they meet in the morning; and some worship simulacra, and some worship idols.

But between simulacra and idols there is a difference,[354] for simulacra are images made to look like some natural object, such as the likeness of a man or a woman, or the moon, or some animal, or some other natural object; and [an] idol is some image made through man's foolish will that one cannot find amongst natural objects, such as an image with four heads, or a man with a horse's head or an ox's or some [other] animal's head that no one has seen in the natural order. Know that those who worship simulacra honor them on account of

---

351. That is, from mid-morning until late afternoon. Terce: the "third" hour of the day (about 9:00 a.m.); none: the "ninth" hour (about 3:00 p.m.). See also Chapter 16, n. 323, and Chapter 33, n. 569.

352. On adamant, see Chapter 17, n. 348. This power of loadstone is noted in several medieval encyclopedias (and in the *Arabian Nights*) and invoked here to explain something that OP only describes (1913, 113–14). Polo's longer account of ironless ships refers to the local lack of the material (1928, 30; 1958, 66).

353. See Chapters 29 and 32 for more of the medieval Alexander legends.

354. *simulacrum:* "likeness" (Latin). This unusual distinction between mimetic representation and the made-up was first articulated in Chapter 6; it will return in Chapter 34, in the comparative summary of eastern religious practices and beliefs. It is *not* based on Isidore of Seville, *Etymologies* 8.9.11 (2006, 183–84), as DLMM suggests (324, n. 8), but rather, as Salih notes, resembles Thomas Aquinas' commentary on 1 Cor. 8:4, "an idol is nothing in the world" (2003, 119; 131, n. 31). Also unusual, but typical of *TBJM*, is the long rationalizing explanation. Like most Latin Christian travelers, OP here as elsewhere simply condemns alien practices as "idolatry" without reflecting on what he reports (1913, 114).

some worthy man who once existed, such as Hercul‹
ers who did many wonders in their time; for they say
know that they [the simulacra] are not gods, for the
of Nature who made all things who is in Heaven. But
that this [hero] could not have done the wonders that
by God's special grace, and because he was well with
them [simulacra]. They say this of the sun too, because it changes uн
seasons and gives heat and nourishment to all things on earth, and
because it is of such great use they know indeed that it cannot be that
God does not love it more than he does the other things. Therefore He
has given it the greatest powers in the world, and so it is quite reasonable, as they say, that one honor it and show it reverence. Thus they give
their explanations for the other planets and for fire also, because it is
so useful. About the idols, they say that the ox is the holiest animal that
exists on earth, and more patient and useful than any other, for it does
much good and does no evil, and they indeed know that this could not
be without God's special grace. Therefore they make their god partly
from an ox, and the other part they make from man, because man is
the noblest creature on earth; and because he has lordship over all
animals, they therefore make half of the idol out of man and the other
half out of ox.[355]

Snakes and other things that they meet first in the morning, they worship them—especially all those things that are good to meet and that
do them good on the day that they meet them, such as they have proved
by long experience. Therefore they say that this good meeting cannot
come about without God's grace, and therefore they make the images
as likenesses to look at them and worship them first thing in the morning before they meet something contrary. There are also Christians
who say that some animals are good to meet and some bad, and it has
been proved many times that the hare is bad to meet and the pig and
many other animals as well. And as for a sparrowhawk or another bird
of prey, when it flies after its prey ahead of armed men and catches it,
that is a good sign, and if it fails, that is a bad one. Also to such people
it is bad to meet ravens. There are many people who believe in these
things and in other such things because it has often happened thus,
but a good many people do not believe. Since the Christians, who are
immersed in all holy doctrine, have such belief, it is no wonder that the
pagans, who have no good doctrine at all except their nature, believe
more generally in such things because of their simplicity. Truly I have
seen pagans and Saracens who are called augurs who, when we rode
out in arms somewhere against our enemies, would by the flight of the
birds predict everything that we afterwards found [to be true], and this

---

355. This rationalizing explanation comes *before* the negative portraits, both
adapted from OP, of ox worship and sacrifice to the ox-man god: see n. 365 in
this chapter.

y did many times and pledged their lives that it would be so. But one should not therefore put all one's faith in such things, but should always have hope in Our Lord.[356] This island of Cana [Thana] was won by the Saracens, and they hold it.[357] There are on this island many lions and other wild animals; and there the rats of this island are as big as dogs here, and they are caught with large mastiffs, for the cats cannot catch them. On this island and on many others the dead are not buried, for the heat is so great that in a little while the flesh is completely consumed right to the bone.

From there one goes by sea towards India Major to a city that has the name Zarchee [Bharuch], which is very beautiful and very good; and many Christians of good faith live there, and there are many members of religious orders, especially the Mendicants.[358] Then one goes by sea to the land of Lombe. In this land pepper grows in a forest that has the name Combar; and it grows nowhere else in the whole world except in this forest, which is a good eighteen days' travel in length. In this forest there are two good cities—one has the name Fflandrine [Fandaraina, or Bandinanah] and the other Zinglanz [Cranganur]—and in each of them a great many Christians and Jews dwell, for there is much good and fertile country, but the great heat there is excessive.[359]

---

356. Divination or fortune-telling (including augury, using birds), though condemned biblically (1 Sam. 15:23; Acts 19:19) and by early Christians like Augustine and understood less systematically in Latin Christendom than in Antiquity, still persisted in the medieval world. More positive Arabic-Islamic views influenced Latin Christians after the thirteenth century (as here), but "casual superstitions" also persisted (Kieckhefer 1989, 85–90). Again, the *Mandeville* author paradoxically collapses and keeps distinctions between Latin Christians and others. Cf. Polo's briefer mention of augury in India (1928, 183; 1958, 267).

357. The Islamic conquest of India began in the eleventh century: the small Hindu capital of Delhi was taken in 1193 and became a powerful Sultanate in the thirteenth century, expanding well south by the early 1330s, when the Sultan Muhammad Tughluq ruled most of India. The great Moroccan traveler Ibn Battuta arrived in India in the 1330s, and his *Rihla* offers a fascinating account of Muslim India as seen by a Muslim; he shows little interest in the "infidels" (Hindus), however.

358. Mendicants (Latin "begging"): members of Latin Christian religious orders (Dominicans, Franciscans, etc.) formed in the thirteenth century and devoted to communal poverty. Like OP, who collected the bones of four Franciscans martyred in Thana, they were much involved in eastern missionary work, establishing themselves in India and China from the later thirteenth century on (see Ch. 22, n. 434, and Ch. 31, n. 536). OP here offers a lengthy report on his fellow friars' deaths, but the *Mandeville* author omits it, moving on to the account of pepper.

359. Lombe: Quilon (now Kollam), a city on the Malabar coast of southwestern India, once an important port linking east and west. Pepper, native to southern India but also grown in Sri Lanka, Thailand, and Sumatra, was its most important product, and the most important spice traded in the medieval world, outranking cardamom, cinnamon, cloves, ginger, and nutmeg. The Malabar coast was also an important religious center, home to Hindus, Muslims, Jews, and Christians.

You can know that pepper grows in the same way as a wild vine that is planted beside the trees of a forest to support it just like the grapevine. The fruit hangs in the same way as grapes, and the tree is so thickly laden that it seems as if it must break; and when it is ripe it is completely green, just like the berries of the plant that we call *ivy* in English.[360] They are thus harvested just as grapes are, and then they are dried in the sun, and then in an oven, and they become black and wrinkled. There are three kinds of pepper all on one tree: long pepper, black pepper, and white pepper. The long pepper is called *sorbetin,* and the black is called *ffulful,* and the white *bano.* The long pepper comes first, when the foliage begins to come out, and it looks something like the flower of the hazel tree that comes out before the leaf and it hangs down. Then comes the black pepper with the foliage in the manner of clusters of very green grapes; and when it has been gathered, the white pepper comes that is somewhat smaller than the black; none or few of those are brought to these parts, for those people over there keep them for themselves because the white pepper is better and of a more moderate nature than the black, and it is not so plentiful as the black.[361]

In this country there are many kinds of snakes and other worms because of the great heat of the country, and some people say[362] that when they wish to gather the pepper they make a fire and burn round about so as to make the snakes and crocodiles flee. But with all due respect to those who say this, if they burned around the trees that bear the pepper, they would burn them and wither everything and anything, and they would do much harm. They would never set fire [to the pepper groves], but [instead] they smear their feet and their hands with

---

The so-called Cochin or Black Jews, said by tradition to have settled there after the Roman destruction of the Temple in 70 CE, were well established by the sixth century. So too probably were the Malabar Christians, communities of the Syriac rite sometimes associated with Saint Thomas' supposed mission to India (see Ch. 19, n. 369).

360. Like the reference to the thorn and the yogh at the end of Chapter 15, the mention of an English plant name fits (if only rhetorically) with the author's claim to be English.

361. Pepper is the fruit of the tropical vine *Piper nigrum.* Black pepper is made by drying the unripe peppercorns with their skin on, white pepper by soaking the ripe fruit and rubbing the skin off. The more pungent long pepper is the dried unripe fruit (formed on a catkin-like flower) of the related *Piper retrofractum;* it was known earlier in the West, and its name, from Sanskrit *pippali,* came to be applied to the now more familiar black and white pepper. *Fulful* is the Arabic for pepper; the other two names have not been identified.

362. In fact, the *LPJ* makes this claim (paragraph 25); the apparently more reasonable counterexplanation given next has no known source, and is presumably the *Mandeville* author's own invention, derived from a remedy against leeches mentioned by OP (see Ch. 21).

the juice of lemons[363] and of other things whose scent the snakes fear, and thus the snakes flee before them because of the scent, and they go harvesting in complete safety, for then they do not have to watch out for any worms approaching them.

Also, towards the head of this forest is the city of Polombe, and above the city there is a large mountain that also has the [same] name, and from this mountain of Polombe the city takes its name. At the foot of this mountain there is a large and beautiful well that has the scent and taste of all spices, and at each hour of the day it changes scent and taste variously. Whoever drinks three times from this well while fasting is cured of whatever illness he might have, and those who stay and drink often are never sick and always seem to be young. I drank from it three or four times, and it still seems to me that I feel better. Some call it the Fountain of Youth, because whoever drinks often from it seems to be always young and lively without any illness, and they say that this spring comes from Paradise and that is why it is so powerful.[364]

Throughout this entire country good ginger grows, and many merchants go there to find spices. In this country the people worship an ox for its simplicity and good disposition and for the usefulness that is in it, and they say that it is the holiest animal that there is on earth.[365] For it seems to them there that whoever is simple and meek and patient and useful is sanctified, for to them it seems that he has all virtues in himself. The king of this country always has such an ox with him, and its keeper everyday catches the dung and the urine in two gold vessels and then gives it to their great prelate that they call *Archiprothopapaton*.[366] The

---

363. Lemons were barely known in northern Latin Christendom (the name, from Arabic *laimun* or Persian *limun*, entered French only in the mid-fourteenth century), as one can see from translators' responses. Both the German Velser (Morrall 1974, 107) and E (WBJM 84) translate by explaining: "a fruit they call lemons" (the first English use, according to the *OED*). C is more ingenious, reading *limaces* for *lymons:* "an oyn[t]ement made of snayles" (HMT 1.112).

364. Fountain of Youth: one of three magical fountains in the Far East described in the Alexander Romances. This simpler reference comes from the *LPJ*, where it immediately follows the mention of fire used to scare snakes before harvesting pepper and whose Mount Olympus becomes Mount Polombe (paragraphs 25–28). How one might read the *Mandeville* author's claim here is uncertain (cf. E's version in Appendix A.3), but one should note that in contrast to the *LPJ* this account clearly limits the spring's powers, making them more medicinal than magical.

365. Cf. OP's version of ox worship and sacrifice (Ch. 10 in Appendix B.3). These accounts show some acquaintance with the reverence for cows central to Hindu life in India for about three thousand years.

366. Added to OP's account, *Archiprothopapaton* (*archi-*, "chief" + the Byzantine Greek *protopapas*, "senior priest") comes from *LPJ* (paragraph 74), where he is one of the emperor's regular dining companions. *Gaul,* in the sentence following, may well be gall or bile rather than urine (both are used in traditional Hindu medicine): see "ox-bile," "ox-gaul," and "urine" in the index in K. M. Nadkarni, *Indian Materia Medica,* 3rd ed. (1954; rpt. Mumbai: Popular Prakashan, 1982),

prelate takes it before the king and makes a great blessing over it, and then the king wets his hands in the urine that they call *gaul,* and wets his brow and his chest, and then rubs himself with great reverence in the dung with the aim of being filled with the above-mentioned virtues that the ox has, and of being sanctified by the power of this holy thing that is worth nothing. After the king the great lords do this, and after the lords, the other ministers.

In this country they make idols [that are] half man and half ox, and in these idols the evil spirits speak to them and answer them about whatever they want to ask. Before these idols they frequently kill their children and sprinkle the idols with blood and thus they perform their sacrifice.

When any man dies in the country they burn the body in the name of penance so that he will not suffer pain in the earth when the worms eat him. If his wife has no children they burn her with him[367] and say that this is reasonable that she should accompany him in the other world as she did in this one; but if she has children by him, they let her live to raise the children, if she wishes to; and if she would rather live with the children than die with her husband, they consider her false and wicked, and she will always be regarded as nothing, nor will anyone trust her. If the wife dies before her master, the man is burned with her if he wishes, and if he does not, no one compels him to, but he can be married again without criticism.

In this country many strong wines grow, and the women drink wine and the men do not, and also the women shave their beards and the men do not.

[Chapter 19]

About the Judgments Made by Saint Thomas the Apostle's Hand in the City of Calamie. About the Devotion and Sacrifice That Are Made to the Idols There and About the Procession around the Said City

From this country one passes through many distant regions towards a country ten days' travel away that is called Mabaron,[368] and it is a very large kingdom and there are many fine cities and fine towns. In

---

vol. 2. Wild ox dung and gall were also in medical use in the *Mandeville* author's own world (cf. Bartholomaeus 1975, 1151). In Mal. 2:3 anointing with dung is God's curse against His wayward priests.

367. The Hindu custom known in English as "suttee" (Sanskrit *sati,* "true" or "virtuous wife"). Polo mentions it (1928, 181; 1958, 264–65), as do many later Western travelers to India.

368. Mabaron (Maliapur, now Mylapur, a suburb of Madras): a city on the Coromandel Coast of southeastern India. This chapter rewrites OP, Chapters

this kingdom in a beautiful tomb lies the body of Saint Thomas the Apostle, in flesh and in bone, in the city of Calamie [Mylapur], for he was martyred and buried there. But the Assyrians [Syrians] had his body taken to Mesopotamia to the city of Edisse [Edessa], and then he was taken back there [to India]. And the arm and the hand that he thrust into Our Lord's wounds when Our Lord appeared to him after His Resurrection and said to him: *"Noli esse incredulus sed fidelis"*[369]—it still lies outside in a vessel. With this hand they make judgments in this country to know who is wrong or right. For when there are disputes between two parties and each maintains that he is right, they put each case in writing, and then they put the writing in Saint Thomas' hand, and immediately the hand casts the wrong and the false away and the hand keeps the right and the true. So they come from quite far to have judgment of uncertain cases.[370]

Also, the church where Saint Thomas lies is a very large and beautiful church and completely full of large simulacra:[371] these are large images that they call their gods, the smallest of which is as large as two men. Amongst the others there is a very large image, bigger than all the others, which is all covered with gold and precious stones and pearls, and this is the idol of false Christians and it sits most nobly in a chair. Around its neck there are large belts worked from gold, precious stones, and pearls. This church is very nobly made and all gilded on the inside.

To this idol one comes on pilgrimage as often and with as great devotion as Christians here make to Saint James of Galicia.[372] Many people who go towards this idol from distant lands—because of the great devotion they have—always look at the ground and dare not raise their heads to look around them for fear of seeing something that will put them out of their devotion. And others go there on pilgrimage who carry knives in their hands, and they stab and wound themselves in the arms and the

---

10–11 (Latin), 10 (French), which especially in Long John's translation is much more negative (see Appendix B.3).

369. "Be not faithless but believing" (John 20:27). Named in all four Gospels, Thomas also figures as the author of or central actor in several apocryphal works, including the Gnostic Acts of Thomas: probably first written in Syriac, this work was largely responsible for the medieval belief in Thomas' mission and martyrdom in India. In Latin Christendom the *Golden Legend* was the best-known source (from it the *Mandeville* author took the saint's body's translation to Edessa, but little else). The Syrian Christians of Malabar see themselves as descendants of Thomas' supposed mission (see Ch. 18, n. 359), but the medieval Christian community in Mylapur was probably Nestorian.

370. This anecdote has no known source. WBJM (199–200, n. to 86, Ch. 19) notes two partial analogues in Gervase of Tilbury's *Otia Imperiala*.

371. On simulacra (as against idols), see Chapter 18 (and n. 354 there).

372. The cathedral dedicated to Saint James *matamoros* (Moor-killer) in Santiago de Compostela (northwest Spain), the most important pilgrimage site in Latin Christendom (see Melczer 1993).

legs and the thighs and spill their blood for love of this idol; and they say that he who dies for love of his god is blessed. And there are others who bring their children to kill and sacrifice before this idol and then sprinkle the idol with the children's blood. And others go there who from the moment they leave their houses kneel at every third step until they are at the idol; and when they have come there, they have incense and other aromatics with which they cense [the idol] as if it were the body of Our Lord. Thus they come to worship this idol from more than one hundred leagues away.

There is in front of the church of this idol as it were a fishpond or a lake entirely full of water; and into this fishpond the pilgrims throw gold, silver, pearls, and countless precious stones instead of an offering. Therefore, when the ministers of the idols need to repair something in the church, they go straight to the fishpond and take what they need for the repair of the church, such that nothing is lacking that is not fixed immediately.

Know that when the great festivals of this idol occur, such as the dedication of the church or the enthroning of the idol, the whole country roundabout gathers. They set this idol with great reverence on a chariot adorned with cloths of gold, tartar, and camaca,[373] and they lead it with great solemnity around the city. In front of the chariot first in the procession go all the maidens of the country in a very orderly fashion, in pairs, and after the maidens go the pilgrims who have come from far regions. Of these pilgrims some let themselves fall under the wheels of the chariot and let the chariot pass over them so that some die right away, others have their arms and their legs all broken, and some their sides. And all this they do out of love for their god in great devotion, and they think that insofar as they suffer more pain and more tribulation for love of this idol, so the closer to God they will be and in greater joy in the other world. In short, they perform such great acts of penance and suffer such great bodily martyrdoms for love of their idols that no Christian would scarcely dare undertake to do a tenth as much for love of his Christ. Then, I tell you, right in front of the chariot go the almost countless minstrels of the country with different instruments, and they make amongst themselves loud music. When they have gone around the whole city, they return to the church and set the idol back in its place.

Then out of honor for the idol and out of reverence for the festival two or three hundred people kill themselves with sharp knives, and their bodies are taken and placed before the idol, and they are said to be holy, because they killed themselves with their own goodwill out of love for their god.[374] And just as a family over here would consider itself

---

373. Tartar, camaca: probably rich silk cloths. Cf. E: "clathez of gold and of silke" (WBJM 87).

374. Polo's account of India mentions devout suicide, but committed to enact a death sentence for a capital crime (1928, 181; 1958, 264).

honored by a saint or two—if they were kin, and if the good deeds and the miracles that they had done so as to have them canonized were set down in writing[375]—so over there they consider themselves honored by those who kill themselves out of love for their god, and they put them in writing and in their litanies, and they boast and say to one another: "I have more saints in my family than you have in yours."

The custom is such that when they plan to kill themselves for their god, they inform all their friends and have a large number of minstrels and go before the idol in a great celebration. The one who must kill himself has a very sharp knife in his hand and he cuts a small piece of his flesh and throws it in the idol's face while saying his prayers and recommending himself to his god; and then he stabs and wounds [himself] here and there until he falls down dead. Then his friends present the body to the idol and say chanting: "See, god, what your loyal servant has done for you. He has given up wives and children, riches and all worldly goods, and his own life out of love for you; he has sacrificed his flesh and his blood. Place him if you wish beside you amongst your most beloved in your glory of Paradise, for he is very deserving." Then they make a big fire and burn the body, and then each of them takes some of the ash and keeps it instead of relics, and they say that this is a very holy thing and that they do not worry about any danger so long as they have some of that ash with them.

[Chapter 20]

About the Evil Customs Used in the Isle of Lamory. And How the Earth and the Sea are of Round Form by Proof of the Antarctic Star

From this country one goes by the Ocean Sea and many diverse islands and many countries that would be too long to name and describe; and fifty-two days' travel from this land that I have spoken about, there is another land that is quite large and has the name Lamory.[376]

In this land there is a very great heat, and the custom is such that the men and the women all go naked. They jeer when they see any foreigner who is clothed, and they say that God who made Adam was naked—and [that] both Adam and Eve were made naked—and that people should not be ashamed to show themselves as God has made

---

375. The *Mandeville* author has added to OP this discussion of canonization (the official recognition of a saint as such by the Church after examination of the evidence of sainthood), explicitly linking Latin Christian and other religious practices.

376. A kingdom on Sumatra in Indonesia, whose islands straddle the equator.

them, for nothing is ugly that comes from nature.[377] And they say that those who are clothed are people of another era,[378] or they are people who do not believe in God; and indeed they say that they believe in God who created the world and made Adam and Eve and all other things.

Since they have no married women, all the women of the country are thus common and refuse no man; and they say that they sin if they refuse men and that God commanded it of Adam and his descendants where he said: "*Crescite et multiplicamini et replete terram.*"[379] Therefore no man in all this country can say: "this is my wife." Nor can any woman say: "this is my husband." And when the women have children, they give them to those they like who have had sexual relations with them. The land is also common, for some hold it in one year and others in another, and each takes whatever part he wants; and also all the goods of the country are common, wheat and other things, for nothing is enclosed, nothing is locked up at all; each takes what he likes without restriction and one person is as rich as another. But they have an evil custom, for they more willingly eat human flesh than any other flesh. And the country abounds in wheat, meat, fish, gold, silver, and other goods. The merchants go there and take children with them for sale to the inhabitants, and the latter buy them; and if they are fat, they eat them right away, and if they are lean, they fatten them, and they say that this is the best and sweetest meat in the world.

In this land and in many others over there the Tramontane star cannot be seen at all. It is the star of the sea that does not move which is towards the north. But one can see another star opposite it, towards the south, which is called Antarctic.[380] And just as sailors here take their bearings and steer themselves by that star to the north, so the sailors over there use this star to the south, which is never visible to us, and the one to the north is not visible to them.

Through this we can perceive that the earth and the sea are of round form, for the part of the firmament that appears in one country does not appear in another. And it can be easily discovered by experience

---

377. Because nature is God's creation: cf. Chapter 26, n. 493. This account elaborates on a briefer anecdote in OP (Ch. 12 in Appendix B.3).

378. *siècle* (Latin *saeculum*) can also mean "world." Travel eastwards in *TBJM* is almost time travel, towards the inaccessible origin of Paradise (Ch. 33) in a world that knows natural or Mosaic law but not Christian.

379. "Be fruitful and multiply and fill the earth" (Gen. 1:28). Added to OP. Cf. the Calonakians in Chapter 21.

380. Tramontane: the North Star. No "Antarctic" star exists, but this may be Canopus, mentioned in Chapter 33 (on which see Appendix C.1). Using Sacrobosco's *De Sphera* and Brunetto's *Tresor* (1.109, 112, 119), this account elaborates OP's passing remark on the North Star's disappearance (Ch. 12 in Appendix B.3). Polo notes the same thing and says "that will indeed seem to everyone a marvelous thing" (1928, 171; cf. 1958, 252–53), presumably because the torrid zone was often considered uninhabitable (see Appendix C.1).

and by clever research that, if a man found passage by ship and people who wanted to go explore the world, he could sail all around the world, both above and below.[381] This thing I prove according to what I have seen, for I have been towards the regions of Brabant and seen with the astrolabe that the Tramontane is 53 degrees high. And farther forward in Germany and Bohemia it is 58 degrees, and farther forward towards the northern regions it is 62 degrees and several minutes high, for I myself have measured it with the astrolabe.[382]

Now you ought to know that opposite this Tramontane is the other star that is called Antarctic, as I have said above. And these two stars are not very mobile, and the whole firmament turns on them as a wheel turns on its axle, such that these stars divide the firmament into two equal parts so that there is as much below as above.

Afterwards, I went towards the meridional regions—that is, towards the south—and found that the Antarctic star is first seen in Libya,[383] and the farther forward I went in those parts the higher I found this star, such that towards upper Libya it was 18 degrees and several minutes high (60 minutes make one degree). Then in going by sea and by land towards those regions that I have spoken about and to other islands and lands beyond this country, I found the Antarctic star 33 degrees and several minutes high.

If I had found company and ship to go farther, I believe it to be certain that we would have seen the whole roundness of the firmament all around. For, as I told you above, half of the firmament is between these two stars. I have seen all of this half; and of the other half to the north under the Tramontane, I have seen 62 degrees and 10 minutes, and towards the meridional [southern] parts under the Antarctic I have seen 33 degrees and 16 minutes.[384] Now half of the firmament in total has only 180 degrees, and of these 180 I have seen 62 of one part and 33 of the other, which is 95 degrees and almost half a degree. Thus I have not seen only 94 degrees and half a degree of the whole firmament; and

---

381. Unlike OP and Polo, two actual travelers, the *Mandeville* author uses the North Star's disappearance for speculation. The boldest claims are that the earthly sphere could be circumnavigated and that the author has measurements to prove it. See Higgins 1997, 132–39; Ridder 1996; and Deluz 1988, 147–52.

382. See Appendix C.2 for more on the astrolabe and the plausibility (or not) of these European measurements (the celestial measurements in the southern hemisphere given shortly must have been made up). Like Sacrobosco's treatise, astrolabes were used in university teaching, evidence perhaps of the *Mandeville* author's education.

383. According to Chapter 16, Libya lies south of the equator. With this paragraph's claims cf. those about the "Antarctic" Star in "How to Mount a Crusade Overseas" (Appendix B.4).

384. This account is unclear. The author seems to be talking about quarters even as he uses "half," imagining each hemisphere (north and south between two pole stars) in its east-west dimension: by quarters.

that is not one quarter of the firmament, for a quarter of the roundness of the firmament is 90 degrees, and lacks 5 and a half degrees of the quarter. So I have seen three quarters of all the roundness of the firmament and 5 and a half degrees more. For this reason I say for certain that a man could travel around all the land in the world, both below and above, and return to his own country, if he had company and shipping and always found men, lands, and islands just as in this country.

For you know that those who are in the place of the Antarctic are exactly foot against foot[385] with those who live beneath the Tramontane, just as we and those who live under us are foot against foot: for all the parts of sea and land have their habitable and navigable opposites, and islands here as well as there. Know that according to what I can perceive and understand, the lands of Prester John, emperor of India, are under us. For in going from Scotland or England towards Jerusalem one is always climbing; for our land is in the low part of the earth to the west, and Prester John's Land is the low part of the earth to the east, and they have day there when we have night, and just the opposite: they have night when we have day. For the earth and the sea are of round form, as I told you above, and as one climbs on one side one descends on the other.[386]

Now you have heard said before that Jerusalem is in the middle of the world,[387] and this can be shown over there by a spear—fixed in the ground at the hour of noon at the equinox—that casts no shadow on any side.[388] That it is in the middle of the world David testifies in the Psalter, where he says *"Deus operatus est salutem in medio terre."*[389] Thus those who leave from these parts of the west to go towards Jerusalem take as many days of climbing to go all the way there as they would take from Jerusalem to the other ends of the earth's surface over there. And when one takes more days towards India and the farther islands, one is going around all the roundness of the land and the sea under our countries over here.

---

385. The literal meaning of the word "antipodes," used of the opposite (southern) hemisphere. See Appendix C.1.

386. The author is imagining a T-O world map (see Appendix C.1) as a hemisphere, such that to look at it is to look down on the top half of a ball seen as a planar surface: a central Jerusalem must be the highest point, eastern and western extremities the lowest. It is hard to believe that the author really means that pilgrims travel uphill to Jerusalem, but if so it would be evidence against his having traveled even to the Holy Land.

387. In the Prologue (see n. 6) and Chapter 10.

388. This "proof" (which would place Jerusalem on the Tropic of Cancer) is first mentioned in Arculf's record from about 680 of a Jerusalem pilgrimage (Adamnan 1958, 56–57). Mark Twain satirizes it in *Innocents Abroad* (1869; see Higgins 1997b, 29–31).

389. "God worked salvation in the middle of the earth" (Ps. 74[73]:12).

For this reason I have often recalled a thing I heard told when I was young: how a brave man once left from our regions to go explore the world.[390] He passed India and the islands beyond India, where there are more than five thousand islands, and he went so far by sea and by land, and he went round so much of the world through many seasons that he found an island where he heard his own language spoken and the oxen called with the same words as in his own country. This amazed him very much. For he did not know how it could be. But I say that he had gone so far by land and by sea that he had gone around the whole earth, that he came back having gone right round to his own borderlands—and if he had gone forward he would have found his own country and his own knowledge. But he went back by the way he had come and lost much effort, as he himself said a great while after he had returned. For it happened afterwards that he was in Norway, and a storm on the sea caught him and he came to an island, and when he was on that island he recognized it as the island where he had heard his own language spoken in guiding the oxen pulling the plow.

That was indeed a possible thing, although it seems to simple people that no one could go beneath the earth and that one must fall into the sky below. But this cannot be, any more than we could fall into the sky from the land where we are. For in whatever part of the earth one dwells, either above or below, it always seems to those living there that they walk more upright than any other people; and just as it seems to us that they are under us, so it seems to them that we are under them.[391] For if one could fall from the earth to the firmament, [there is] all the more reason [to believe that] the earth and the sea—that are so large and so heavy—ought to fall right to the firmament. But that could not be, and this is why Our Lord says *"Non timeas me qe suspendi terram ex nichilo."*[392]

Although this is a possible thing that one could thus go around the whole world, nevertheless not one person in a thousand would travel the right way so as to return to his own country. For because of the large size of the earth and the sea, one could go by thousands of other ways,

---

390. No known source. Gervase of Tilbury (*Otia Imperialia* 3.45) says that he heard from a very religious man about a British swineherd who went into a hillside cave looking for a pregnant lost sheep; a long journey in darkness brought him to another land where, amidst the harvest, he found his sheep, then returned home to the late winter he had left. Gervase deduces that the sun does not shine everywhere at once, but the tale reads like the more fanciful stories about the other world (2002, 644–45, n. 4), like that in Gerald of Wales, *Journey through Wales* 1.8. The *Mandeville* author's more realistic anecdote uses chance quite differently.

391. The author knows that in a spherical universe "up" is always outwards from the center; therefore everyone everywhere is upright. This passage closely echoes Pliny's *Natural History* 2.64.

392. "Do not fear me, who hung the earth from nothing" (Ps. 104[103]:5). The earth cannot fall because, as the heaviest object in the universe, it must be located at the bottom: see Appendix C.1.

such that no one could return exactly to the regions from which he left, except by chance or God's true grace.

For the earth is very broad and very big, and is 20,425 miles in roundness and all around, above and below, according to the opinion of the ancients. I do not reject their word, but according to my small intelligence, it seems to me that with all due respect it is larger. The better to understand what I mean, let there be imagined a figure of a large circle, and around the point of this large circle (the part called the center), let there be another smaller circle. Then let the large circle be divided by lines into many parts, and let all the lines come together in the center such that the small circle that is around the center will be divided into as many parts as the large circle, although the spaces will be smaller. Now let the large circle stand for the firmament and the little circle for the earth. The firmament is divided by astronomers into twelve signs, and each sign is divided into thirty degrees; around the whole firmament there are 360 degrees. Now let the earth be divided into as many parts as the firmament, and each part will correspond to a degree of the firmament.[393] Know that according to the authorities in astronomy, 600 stades[394] of the earth correspond to one degree of the firmament; there are 87,004 stades. Now let this be multiplied by 340 [360]; there will be 31,600 miles, each of eight stades, according to the miles of our country. Such is the earth in roundness and all around, according to my opinion and my understanding.

Know that, according to the opinion of the wise ancient philosophers and astronomers, our country, Ireland, Wales, Scotland, England, Norway, and the other islands bordering them are not on the earth's surface calculated above, as it appears in all the books of astronomy. For the surface of the earth is divided into seven parts by the seven planets, and these parts are called climates, and our parts are not in the seven climates.[395] For they descend to the west owing to the roundness of the

---

393. This awkward explanation merely asks one to imagine two concentric circles divided into 360 degrees by lines running out from their joint center.

394. Stade: see Chapter 5, n. 49. Determining the earth's size was made difficult by the lack of a standard measure and the variation of Roman numerals in copying; the answer varied according to the calculation derived from Ptolemy or Eratosthenes. The rejected smaller figure here is Ptolemy's, which the *Mandeville* author would have found in *leagues* in Brunetto's *Tresor* 1.109; the accepted larger figure is (roughly) Eratosthenes', which he would have found in *stades* in Sacrobosco's *Sphere* (Ch. 1). See Taylor 1935, especially the helpful comparative table (66). Contemporary scientists almost split the difference, measuring the earth's equatorial circumference at about 24,900 miles. Columbus accepted the smaller number, which helped motivate his *westward* journey to the East.

395. On medieval climates, see Chapter 18, n. 349 and Appendix C.1. The Ptolemaic climates extended no farther north than about 51 degrees, so this claim is not only correct, it also contradicts the one made near the start of Chapter 18 placing England in the seventh climate.

world, and the islands of India are there, and they are opposite us who are in the low part, and the seven climates extend all around the world. [*And if there were signs or fixed stars eastwards and westwards by which they [east and west] could be measured, as are the regions of the north and the south by the two unmoving stars, one would certainly find the islands and the land of Prester John quite far outside the climates, and going around under the earth [such] that the region of the north and the south are not visible. And I well know that I have taken many more days' travel to go towards the islands of India than I took to go straight from the true north to the true south. And since the earth is round, there is as much from north to south as from true east to true west—which is why I say that what one passes through beyond this measure is under us in going around the earth, as I said.*][396]

[Chapter 21]

About the Palace of the King of the Island of Java. About the Trees That Bear Flour, Honey, Wine, and Poison, and About Other Wonders and Customs on the Islands Nearby

Beside this island that I have told you about there is another island that is called Sumobor [Sumatra]. It is quite a large island and the king is very powerful. The people of this island always have themselves marked on the face with a hot iron, men and women, out of great nobility and to be recognized by other peoples, for they consider themselves to be nobler and braver than any other people in the whole world. And they are always at war with that people that I told you about who go about completely naked.

Quite close there is another island that is called Betingna,[397] which is a very good island and very plentiful; and there are many other islands around there with many diverse people about whom it would take too long to say everything.

But quite close to this island in going by sea there is a large island and large country that is called Java, and it is nearly two thousands leagues in circumference. The king of this country is a very great lord, both rich and powerful, and he has under him the seven other kings of seven

396. The bracketed italicized passage (translated as edited by de Poerck 1955, 136–37; cf. LMT 2.335) is found only in the Continental French Version (see Appendix A.1). De Poerck, however, makes a good case that it belongs in the Insular Version (after the remarks about the western regions outside the seven climates), having become separated in the early copies, such that both versions end incompletely. In the Continental manuscripts the preceding (Insular) part is absent and the bracketed passage follows what might be an interpolated remark (given in Appendix A.1).

397. Mentioned only in OP's Latin, which shows that the *Mandeville* author consulted both it and the French. He returns to OP for his template here.

islands round about. This island is very well inhabited and well peopled. All spices grow more abundantly there than in other places: such as ginger, cloves of gillyflower, cinnamon, setwall, nutmeg, and mace.[398] And know that the nutmeg bears the mace, for just as the hazelnut has a husk on the outside in which it is wrapped until it is ripe and then it falls out, so it is with the nutmeg and the mace. Many other spices and many other goods grow there on this island, for they have plenty of all goods but wine; and there is a great abundance of gold and silver. The king of the country has a most noble and most wonderful palace, and richer than any other in the world. For all the steps that rise to the halls and the rooms are of alternating gold and silver; and also the floors of the halls and the rooms are of alternating squares of gold and silver; and all the walls on the inside are covered with gold and silver plating, and on these plates are engraved histories and battles of knights, and all the circles around their heads are of precious stones and large pearls. And the halls and the rooms on the inside of the palace are covered with gold and silver, such that no one would believe the richness or the nobility that is in that palace who had not seen it. Know that the king of this island is so powerful that on the [battle]field he has often defeated the Great Chan of Cathay, who is the most powerful emperor there is under the firmament, whether on this side of the sea or the other. For they are often at war with each other, because the Great Chan would like to compel him to hold the land from him,[399] but the other has always defended himself well.

After this island in going by sea one finds another fine and large island, which is called Thalamassy, and in another language it is called Paten.[400] This is a large kingdom, and the king has many beautiful cities and beautiful towns in his land. In this land grow trees that bear flour with which one makes good bread, white and tasty, and it seems to be of wheat, but it does not have quite the same flavor. There are other trees that bear good and sweet honey, and others that bear wine, and others that bear poison[401] against which there is only one medicine: that is, to take some of one's own feces[402] and stir with water and then drink this,

---

398. Cloves of gillyflower: the familiar culinary cloves. Setwall (zedoary): the bitter-tasting root of an Indian plant (*Curcuma zedoaria*) of the ginger family; used as a drug.

399. I.e., be his subject. In 1293 Qubilai Khan led an unsuccessful campaign against Java.

400. Probably Borneo, east of Sumatra and north of Java.

401. Flour-bearing tree: probably the sago palm (*Metroxylon sagu*), from whose trunk a starch is extracted, though not as described here. Several trees are known as sugar and toddy palms for obvious reasons. The upas tree (*Antiaris toxicaria*) produces poisonous latex once used on arrows.

402. Some ten French copies read *foilles* ("leaves"), not *fiens* ("feces"). L has "urine" (Deluz 1997, 1409).

or otherwise whoever has had any of this poison will die quickly. No antidote or other medicine is of any use. The Jews in recent years sent [someone] in search of this toxin to poison all Christendom, as I have heard them say in their confession at death. But thank God, they failed in their aim, but they nevertheless caused much death.[403]

If it pleases you to know how the flour is made from the trees I will tell you. The tree is struck with a hatchet all around the base so that the bark is pierced in many places, and then a thick fluid oozes out that they catch in vessels and place in the sun and let dry, and then they grind it in the mill and it becomes beautiful and white flour. The honey and the wine and the poison are drawn out of other trees in the same way and put in vessels for storage.

On this island there is a dead sea, which is a lake where there is no bottom, and if anyone throws something into this lake, it will never be found. In this lake grow reeds: these are canes that they call *thaby* that are thirty fathoms or more long, and with these canes they make beautiful houses. There are other canes that are not so long that grow near the land, and they have such long roots that they extend for four acres or more, and at the base of these roots are found precious stones that have many great powers, for whoever carries one with him, iron or steel will not injure or wound him or draw blood. Because they have the stone they fight boldly at sea and on land, for one cannot harm them with any weapon. Therefore those that have to go and fight them and know how to, shoot arrows and quarrels[404] without iron at them and thus they injure and kill them. With those canes they make houses, ships, and other things, just as we do here with great oaks and other trees. And let no one suppose that I say this deceitfully, for I have seen with my own eyes canes lying on the shore of that lake that twenty of our companions could not carry or lift off the ground.

After this island one goes by sea to another island that has the name Calonak,[405] and there is much beautiful land there and great plenty of goods. The king of the country has as many wives as he wants, for he has the most beautiful women sought out throughout all his country and all the country round about, and he has them brought before him and he takes one on one night, and another on another night, and so on, such that he has a thousand or more wives, and he only ever sleeps once with each wife if she does not please him much more than the

---

403. This anti-Jewish remark (which, unlike most of the author's testimonials, lacks the air of romance) is not in OP, but echoes the widespread Latin Christian hostility to Jews, especially in the fourteenth century: after the Black Death of 1348–1349 Jews were accused of poisoning wells (Marcus 1938, 43–48).

404. "quarrels": square-headed heavy arrows shot from a crossbow. The canes are bamboo, and the stones may be *tabashir* ("bamboo salt"), a silica produced in the bamboo joints and used medicinally.

405. Possibly Champa in what is now southern Vietnam.

others. And the king has a large number of children—sometimes there are one hundred, sometimes there are two hundred, and sometimes there are more. And he has a good fourteen thousand or more tame elephants that he has fed by his servants in the towns, for in case he goes to war with some other king thereabouts, he has people mounted in castles on his elephants to fight his adversaries and so do all the other kings around there. For the way in which they go to war over there is not at all the order of battle over here. And the elephants are called *barkes*.[406]

There is moreover a great wonder on this island that is nowhere else in the world. For all the kinds of fish of the sea come once a year, one species after another, and they cast themselves on the shore of that island, such that no fish are seen in the sea, and they stay there for three days, and everyone in the country takes as many of them as they want. Then that one species of fish goes away, and another kind comes and does the same, and thus one kind [comes] after another until all the species of fish have been there. Thus they follow this arrangement one after the other for three days, such that everyone of the country takes as many of them as they like of each kind, and no one knows the reason why this can be. But those of the country say that it is to revere their king, who is the worthiest there is, as they say, and because he fulfilled what God said to Adam, *"Crescite et multiplicamini et replete terram,"*[407] and because he thus multiplied the world with his children, therefore God sends the fish of the whole sea freely for him and for his country. Thus all the fish give themselves to him, paying homage as if to the most excellent and best beloved of God, as they say. I do not know the reason why this is—God knows it who knows everything—but this thing seems to me a greater wonder than anything that I have ever seen. For Nature makes[408] very many different things and very many wonders, but this marvel is not of nature; rather, it is entirely against nature that the fish which have the freedom to go all around the world should come to give themselves up to death of their own will and without any compulsion. Therefore I am certain that it cannot be without great significance.

There are also in this country large snails that are so large that several people could dwell inside the shell, just as one would do in a little

---

406. *Warkes* or *karkes* in some copies. Not in OP, the name may derive from Isidore, *Etymologies* 12.2.14, who gives *barrus* as the Indian name for elephant.

407. "Increase and multiply, and fill the earth" (cf. Gen. 1:28). Are these people (and the Lamorians in Ch. 20) to be judged as interpreters of scripture? Margery Kempe, asked by "a gret clerk" in York how to understand this passage, insisted on its spiritual meaning as well (the "purchasyng of vertu"), and received his approval (Kempe 1996, 121–22, Ch. 52). Either shoaling or spawning could lie behind the "unnatural" wonder described here.

408. *fait*: also "does/performs."

house,[409] and there are other snails that are much smaller. With these snails and with the large white worms that have black heads that are as big as a man's thigh (and some are smaller) that are found in rotten wood, one makes a royal dish for the king and for the other great lords. If a married man dies in this country, his wife is buried completely alive with him, and they say that it is reasonable that she accompany him in the other world just as she has done in this.

From this country one goes by the Ocean Sea by way of an island that has the name Caffoles.[410] The people of this island, when their friends are sick, they hang them from a tree, and say that they would rather that the birds, which are God's angels, eat them than that the worms, which are so filthy, should eat them in the earth.

From this island one goes towards another island where there are people of the most evil nature who raise large dogs and train them to strangle their friends when they are sick, for they do not want to die a natural death, for they say that they would suffer too much pain. When they are thus choked to death, they eat the flesh instead of venison.

Then one goes ahead by way of many islands of the sea to an island that has the name Milke [Malacca?]. There is also a very evil people there, for they take pleasure in nothing so much as to fight and kill people, for they freely drink human blood (this blood they call God) and whoever can kill the most is the most honored amongst them. If two persons who hate each other are reconciled by friends, or if some make an alliance amongst themselves, each one of them must drink the other's blood, or else the agreement and the alliance are worthless. Nor would anyone who acted against such an agreement or such an alliance be condemned.

From this island one goes by sea from island to island to an island that has the name Tracoda, where there is a completely animal-like people and as if without reason. They dwell in caves that they make in the ground, for they do not have enough understanding to know how to make houses, and when they see any people pass through this land, they hide themselves in their caves. They eat snake meat, and they eat little, and they do not speak but hiss to one another like snakes, and they do not care about any goods or any riches except only a precious stone that has sixty colors and that, because of the name of the island, has the name Tracoda. They very much love this stone that has the name Tracoda and do not know what power it has, but they covet it for its beauty alone.

409. OP saw "a snail . . . larger than the bell-tower of Saint-Martin's [Anthony's] in Padua" (1891, 188; "tortoise" in Latin). A tortoise shell once used as Henry IV's crib is now in Pau castle (DLMM 355, n. 13).

410. The author here interrupts OP's itinerary with a list, possibly from Vincent of Beauvais, *Speculum Historiale* 1.87, of imaginary islands with odd customs. On strange peoples see Chapter 16, n. 317.

After this island, one goes by the Ocean Sea through many islands to an island that has the name Nacumera,[411] which is a very large island and good and beautiful, and it is more than one thousand leagues in circumference. All the men and the women of this island have dog's heads and they are called Canopholez,[412] and they are people possessed of reason and good understanding, and they worship an ox for their god. Thus each of them wears on his forehead a gold or silver ox as a sign that they do indeed love their god; and they go about completely naked except for a small cloth with which they cover their knees and their genitals. They are large people and good warriors, and they have a large shield that covers their whole body and a spear to fight with, and if they take anyone in battle, they eat him. The king of this island is very rich and very powerful and very devout according to his law. He has around his neck three hundred very large orient pearls knotted in the fashion of an amber paternoster; and in the way that we say *Pater Noster* and *Ave Maria* while counting the paternosters,[413] so this king every day devoutly says three hundred prayers to his god before he eats; and he also wears around his neck a fine and noble orient ruby that is a good foot long and five fingers wide. For, when they choose their king, they give him that ruby to bear in his hand, and thus they lead him on horseback all around the city and from then on they are all obedient to him. And he always wears this ruby around his neck, for if he did not have this ruby no one would consider him king. The Great Chan of Cathay has much coveted this ruby, but he has never been able to have it, neither by war, nor for any price. This king is very just according to his law and a very good ruler, so one can go safely throughout his whole country and carry all that one wishes, since no one is so bold as to rob another, for the king will have justice done right away.

From this land one goes to another island that has the name Silha [Ceylon] and that is a good eight hundred leagues in circumference. In this land there is much uncultivated land[414] where there are so many snakes and dragons and crocodiles that one dare not remain there. These crocodiles are snakes, yellow and striped above, and they have

---

411. One of the Nicobar Islands in the Bay of Bengal. The *Mandeville* author returns to OP here.

412. *Cynocephali*, "dog-heads" in Greek. OP (Ch. 17) says that the people have dog's faces; he does not call them by their classical name or give them reason. Their mention presumably inspired the above list, which moves from unusual customs to bodily deformity. Polo mentions a people with dog's heads, teeth, and eyes, and calls them cannibals, but also does not use the classical name (1928, 176; 1958, 258).

413. "amber paternoster": Roman Catholic prayer beads. On the *Pater Noster:* see ch. Chapter 10, n. 146. *Ave Maria* ("Hail Mary"): a prayer derived from the salutations to Mary in Luke 1:42 and 1:28.

414. *terre gaste:* anything from ruined land through uncultivated land to wilderness.

four feet and short legs and large claws. There are some five fathoms long, and some six and some eight, and some ten; and when they go through a sandy place, it seems as though someone had pulled a large tree through the sand. There are many wild animals there, especially elephants.

On this island there is a large mountain,[415] and in the middle of this mountain at the top there is a large lake on a fine plain and there is a great abundance of water. Those of the country say that Adam and Eve wept on this mountain for one hundred years when they were cast out of Paradise, and this water they say is their tears, for they wept so much on this mountain that this lake was thus created. At the bottom of this lake are found many precious stones and large pearls. In this lake grow many reeds and irises,[416] and in it there are many crocodiles and snakes and leeches. The king of the country once a year gives the poor permission to enter the lake and gather those stones as alms and for the love of Adam's God, and every year enough are found. Because of the vermin that are in it, they smear their arms and legs with the juice of lemons (it is a kind of fruit like small peaches),[417] and then they do not worry about crocodiles or other vermin. This water flows and descends on one side of the mountain, and in this stream one finds a great abundance of stones and pearls. It is commonly said on this island that the snakes and the wild animals of the country never touch nor do any harm to any foreigner who enters the country, but only to those born in the country.

In this country and in others roundabout there are wild geese that have two heads, and there are lions completely white and as big as oxen, and many other diverse animals, and there are birds that are not on this side of the sea. Know that in this country and other islands around there the sea is so high that it seems to hang from the clouds and should cover all the earth. It is a great wonder how it can be held up thus, except by the will of God who holds up the air, and therefore David says in the Psalter: "*Mirabiles elaciones maris.*"[418]

---

415. Adam's Peak (Samanala or Sri Pada) in Sri Lanka, revered as holy by Buddhists, Hindus, Muslims, and Christians. Its link with Adam derives from Muslim tradition. Like OP, whose account the *Mandeville* author elaborates, Polo mentions the site, but recounts its Buddhist links (1928, 192–94; 1958, 281–83).

416. *glageux,* or *glaiol:* some sort of iris or sword grass (cf. gladiola).

417. See Chapter 18, nn. 362, 363.

418. "Wonderful are the surges of the sea" (Ps. 93[92]:4).

[Chapter 22]

How It Is Known by the Idol Whether the Sick Will Die or Not. About Peoples Who Look Different and Much Disfigured. And About Monks Who Give Their Leftovers[419] to Baboons, Apes, and Marmots

From that island in going southwards by sea there is another large and broad island that has the name Dondia.[420] On this island are people of diverse natures, such that the father eats the son, and the son the father, and the husband the wife, and the wife her husband. If it happens that the father or the mother or any friends are sick, the son goes right away to the priest of their law and requests that he ask their idol whether his father will die of this illness or not. Then the priest and the son go together before the idol and kneel most devoutly and put their question, and the devil that is inside the idol answers and says that he will not die this time and teaches them how they should heal him. Then the son returns and serves the father and does for him what the idol explained to him so that he [the father] will be healed; and the wives do this for their husbands, and the husbands for the wives, and the friends for one another. If the idol says that he must die, then the priest goes with the son or the wife to the sick man and places a cloth over the mouth to stop the breath and thus they suffocate and kill him; then they cut the whole body up into pieces and invite all their friends to come and eat some of the dead man, and they make all the minstrels come that they can have, and they eat him at a great feast and with great ceremony. When they have eaten the flesh, they take the bones and bury them and sing and make loud music, and all the relatives and the friends who were not at the feast are criticized and shamed, and they are deeply hurt, for forever after no one considers them friends; and the friends say that they eat the flesh like this to free him [the dead man] from pain, for if the worms were to eat him in the ground, the soul would suffer great pain, as they say.[421] When the flesh is too lean, then the friends say that they have committed a great sin in having allowed him to languish for so long and to suffer so much pain without cause; and when they find the flesh fat, they say that it was well done to have sent him straight to Paradise and not allowed him to suffer too much pain.

---

419. *Relef,* which, as in English, can mean "leftovers," "feudal payment," or "alms."

420. Possibly one of the Andaman Isles, north of the Nicobar Islands in the Bay of Bengal.

421. In OP, this explanation follows the friar's rebuke to the local people for this custom (1913, 175–76; 1929, 456–57; 1891, 238–39). He says nothing about the quality of the flesh.

The king of this island is a very great lord and most powerful, and he has under him fifty-four large islands that all answer to him; and on each of these islands there is a crowned king and all are obedient to the other king, and there are on these islands many different peoples.[422]

On one of these islands dwell people of large nature like giants, and they are hideous to see, and they have only one eye in the middle of the forehead and they eat nothing but fish and meat completely raw. On another island towards the south dwell people of ugly shape and evil nature who have no head and have their ears in their shoulders and their mouth twisted like a horseshoe in the middle of their chest. And on another island there are also headless people and they have their eyes and their mouth behind their shoulders.[423] And on another island there are people who have a completely flat and completely level face, noseless and eyeless, except for two small round holes instead of eyes, and a mouth as flat as a lipless slit. And on another island there are people of ugly form whose lower lip is so large that when they want to sleep in the sun they cover their whole face with their lip. And on another island there are small people like dwarves; however, they are twice as big as the Pygmies, and they have a little hole instead of a mouth, and therefore they have to take what they eat and drink with a pipe of lead or other material; and they have no tongue whatsoever and do not talk at all, except that they hiss and make signs to one another just like monks or the mute and thus they understand each other's meaning. And on another island there are people who have big ears hanging right to their knees. And on another there are people who have horses' feet and they are strong and powerful and great runners, for they catch wild animals on the run and eat them. And on another there are people who walk on their hands and feet like an animal and they are all hairy and steal as easily through the trees as a monkey does. And on another there are [people] who are man and woman and have the nature of both, and they have a breast on one side and none on the other, and they have the members of generation of man and of woman and use whichever they wish, one once and the other another time, and they beget children

---

422. OP notes that he does not write about many other local wonders since no one who had not seen them would believe them (1913, 176; 1929, 457; 1891, 239). Drawing as in Chapter 21 mostly on Vincent of Beauvais, *Speculum Historiale* 1.92–93, and interweaving traditional information with the latest news, the *Mandeville* author uses the mention of fifty-four islands to insert a list of marvelous peoples (see Ch. 16, n. 317) formally analogous to the visual catalogues (in Africa) on the Ebstorf and Hereford world maps. Their insular habitats presumably explain why the peoples remain morphologically distinct.

423. In his *Discovery of . . . Guiana* (1595–1596), Walter Raleigh mentions "a nation of [South American] people, whose heades appeare not above their shoulders," and notes that they were also "written of by Maundeville," perhaps making his "fables . . . true" (1848, 85–86). They appear too in Othello's "travel's history" (*Othello* [1603–1604] 1.3.143–44).

when they do the male work, and when they do the female work they conceive and bear children. And on another island there are people who always walk on their knees most amazingly and it seems that at every step they ought to fall and they have eight toes on each foot.

There are many other kinds of people on the other islands around there about whom a long account could be made, but my material would be rendered too lengthy, and so I will move on quite quickly.

From these islands in going through the Ocean Sea eastwards by many days' travel one finds a large country and large kingdom that is called Mancy. It is in India Major[424] and is the best land and most beautiful and the most delightful and most abundant in all goods that are in man's power. In this land dwell many Christians and Saracens as well, for there is good and large country, and there are more than two thousand big cities without [counting] other towns. The population is very large, and it is more than in any other [country] of India because of the bounty of the country; and in this country no one asks for bread for God,[425] for in the whole country there are no poor. There are many good-looking people, but they are very pale, and the men have very sparse beards with few hairs and quite long—but a man has scarcely fifty hairs in his beard, but just one hair here and another there, like a leopard's or a cat's beard. In this country there are more very beautiful women than in any other country beyond the sea, and therefore some call this land Albania because there are white people [there].[426]

The first city of this country, which is one day's travel from the sea, has the name Lacorni [Canton?] and it is quite a bit larger than is Paris.[427] In this city there is a large river carrying ships that goes right to the sea. No city in the world is so well supplied with ships as it is, and all those of the city and the country worship idols. In this country all the birds are twice as big as here. There are geese there [that are] white and red around the throat and have a large knob on the head[428] and they are twice as big as over here, and all live animals[429] are cheap.

---

424. Manzi, southern China, was considered ethnically distinct from Cathay (northern China: see Chs. 23–27); the name may derive from either *man-tseu,* "barbarians," or *Nanchao,* "southern states" (DLMM 367, n. 4). That Manzi lies in Greater India (Upper India in OP) shows both the vagueness of medieval notions of the Far East and the desire to fit new information into existing frameworks. India: see Chapter 17 (esp. n. 344). Cathay: see Chapter 23, n. 442.

425. No one begs for food as alms.

426. This account of local physiognomy and beauty is only in the OP's Latin (1913, 179; 1929, 458; cf. 1891, 246). Albania: see Chapter 16, n. 317.

427. OP Latin: "as big as three Venices" (1913, 179–78; 1929, 458); French: "twice as big as Rome" (1891, 264).

428. The swan goose (*Anser cygnoides*) is domesticated rather than wild, as the knob and the size reveal.

429. "*vivres*" could mean either "provisions" or "live animals"; the latter seems better here.

There is a great abundance of large snakes, for which a great celebration is held, and they are eaten with great ceremony; for if someone held a great feast and offered all the dishes that one knows how to make, if he did not offer a course of those snakes, he would have done nothing, for whatever he had done would be regarded as nothing. There are many good cities in this country and provisions are cheap. In this country there are many churches and monks of their law, and there are in these churches idols as big as giants, and on their feast days they give food to these idols to eat in this fashion: they bring before them all the dishes thoroughly cooked as hot as they come from the cooker and let the steam rise towards the idols; then they say that the idols have eaten and then the monks eat the dishes afterwards.

In this country there are white hens that have no feathers, but have white wool like sheep.[430] And the married women in this country wear a sign of horn on their heads so as to be distinguished from unmarried women. In this country they train animals that one calls *loyres*[431] that go around the waters and eat the fish. This animal they throw into ponds, or into pools, or into deep rivers, and right away this animal brings out of the water as many large fish as one wants. And whoever wishes to have more throws it back again as many times as one likes.

In passing through this country many days' travel from this city there is another city, the largest in the world, which has the name Casaie: that is to say, City of Heaven.[432] This city is a good fifty leagues in circumference and is so densely inhabited that a good ten houses are made in one house. In this city there are twelve main gates and in front of each gate, three or four leagues away, there is a quite large town or city. This city sits on a lagoon just as Venice does. And there are in this city more than twelve thousand bridges, and on each bridge there are fine towers where the guards dwell who guard the city from the Great Chan, because this land borders on the Great Chan's land. On one side of the city a large river flows the whole length of the city. Christians and many merchants and others from many nations dwell there, because the country is so good and so abundant; and a very good wine called *bigoun*[433] grows that is quite strong and most pleasing to drink. This is a royal city where the

---

430. The silk fowl (*Phasianus lanatus, Gallus lanatus*), also known as *coq-à-duvet*.

431. "otters": OP speaks of diving birds (1913, 190; 1929, 462; 1891, 266): cormorants were traditionally used; the *Mandeville* author "corrects" OP from Vincent of Beauvais, *Speculum Naturale* 19.89.

432. Mongol Kinsay (Hangchow/Hangzhou).

433. *bigin* or *bigum* in OP (1929, 462; 1891, 302), "probably the Persian *bagni*, 'malt liquor or beer,' though this is not a good description of the Chinese beverage," a rice wine (1913, 199, n. 5).

king of Mancy used to dwell and where many Christian monks of the Mendicant orders dwell.[434]

From this city one goes by water, merrily and delightedly, to an abbey of monks that is quite near who are very pious according to their law. In this abbey there is a large and beautiful garden where there are many trees with different kinds of fruit, and in this garden there is a large hill all full of trees. On this hill and in this garden dwell many different animals such as baboons, monkeys, marmots, and other different animals. When the community of this abbey has eaten, the alms-giver has the leftovers brought to the garden and he rings a small silver bell that he holds in his hand, and right away a good three thousand or four thousand of such animals as I have told you about come down from the hill, and they circle round like the poor, and they are given leftovers in beautiful vessels gilded with silver. When they have eaten, another small bell is sounded and they immediately go back to their places from which they came. The monks say that these are the souls of noble men that have entered those noble animals and they give them something to eat out of the love of God; and they also say that the souls of the peasants enter servile animals after their death, and they believe this and no one can turn them away from that opinion. They have these above-mentioned animals caught when young and feed them like this with as many alms as they can find.

I asked them whether it would not be more worthy to give the leftovers to the poor,[435] and they answered me that there are no poor in the country—and even if there had been poor, it seems to them that the alms are better used for these souls that do their penance there and that lack the know-how or the ability to earn anything or work; that they should not be used for poor people who have the intelligence and the capacity to earn their living expenses. There are many other wonders in this city and around the country, but I do not intend to describe them all.

From this city one goes through the country, and after six days' travel there is another city that has the name Chilenfo [Nanking], whose walls are twenty leagues in circumference, and in this city there are sixty stone bridges as beautiful as any can be. In this city was the first seat of the king of Mancy, for it is a most beautiful city and very abundant in all goods.

---

434. Mendicant missions began in the thirteenth century (Ch. 18, n. 358). In 1313 John of Monte Corvino was invested as Archbishop of Khanbaliq (Beijing) and set up six Cathayan bishoprics (none outlasted the mid-fourteenth century). First made up of Italian merchants, the Christian community there grew through baptism.

435. This anecdote is slightly simpler than OP's (Ch. 22 in Appendix B.3), but the *Mandeville* author has radically changed the friar's response: a question of belief has become one of practice.

Then one crosses a large river that has the name Dalay.[436] It is the largest freshwater river in the world, for where it is narrowest it is more than four leagues wide. Then one comes back into the Great Chan's land. This river goes through the land of the Pygmies. These are people of small stature who are only three spans high,[437] and they are beautiful and elegant according to their smallness, both men and women. They get married at half a year old, and they have children and live only six or seven years and whoever lives eight years is considered to be terribly old. These little people are the best workers in silk and cotton and all things that are made from them that could be in the world, and they are often at war with the birds of the country that catch them and eat them. These little people do not work land or vines, but there is a big people amongst them such as we are who cultivate and work the lands as is appropriate; and the little people mock these big people and scorn them just as we would large giants if they were amongst us. There is a good city amongst the others where a large number of these little people dwell, and the city is most beautiful and very big. And the large men who dwell amongst them, when they have children, they are as small as the Pygmies. Therefore they are all somewhat Pygmies, for such is the nature of the land. The Great Chan has this city well guarded, for it belongs to him. Although the Pygmies are small, they are entirely reasonable according to their age and they can distinguish well enough between wisdom and evil.[438]

From this city one goes through the country through many cities and through many towns to a city that has the name Jamchay [Yangchow, or Yangzhou] and it is a most noble city and very rich and highly profitable. One goes there in search of all goods. This city is worth very much to the lord of the country, for there is revenue from this city every year, as the citizens say: fifty thousand *cumans* of gold florins. For they all count there by *cumans*, and each *cuman* is worth ten thousand florins[439]—now one could calculate how much that might be. The king of this country is very powerful and nevertheless he is under the Great Chan; and the Great Chan has under him twelve such provinces. In this country in good towns there is a good custom, for whoever wants to hold a feast with his friends, there are certain inns in each town where one would say

---

436. Talay, "the sea": Mongol name for the Yangtze.

437. Span: traditionally from the tip of the thumb to the tip of the little finger on the outspread hand (about nine inches). This account derives from Long John's reworking of OP's Latin. The battle with birds mentioned shortly (traditionally cranes) goes back to Homer (*Iliad* 3.1–6) but was known through Pliny, *Natural History* 7.26, which, like the Ebstorf and Hereford world maps, places the Pygmies in India; the *Catalan Atlas* places them in Cathay.

438. "reasonable": capable of rational thought, unlike animals; "wisdom" translates "*sen*" and "evil," "*malice.*"

439. *cuman:* the Mongol *tümen,* meaning 10,000. Florin: see Chapter 6, n. 64.

to the innkeeper: "Fix me a feast tomorrow for so many people," and the number is said, and the dishes described, and then one says: "I want to spend this much and no more." Right away the innkeeper makes things so right and ready that nothing is lacking—and better and more quickly and at considerably less cost than one could do in one's own house.

Ten leagues from this city towards the head of the River Dalay, there is a city that has the name Menke.[440] In this city there is a very large fleet of ships and all the ships are white as snow from the nature of the wood itself, and they are very fine ships and large and well kept—just as well as if they had been houses on land with clean rooms and other conveniences.

From there one goes through the country through many towns and many cities to a city that has the name Lanteryn, and it is eight days' travel from the city mentioned above [Menke]. This city sits on a large and wide river that is called Caramoran.[441] This river passes through Cathay and it often does great harm when it grows too big.

[Chapter 23]

About the Great Chan of Cathay. About the Royal Dignity of His Palace. And How He Sits to Eat and About the Large Number of Servants Who Serve Him

Cathay is a large country and beautiful and good and rich and well suited to trade.[442] Merchants go there every year to look for spices and all other goods, and more commonly than they go anywhere else; and

---

440. Possibly what is now Yizheng (DLMM 368, n. 22).

441. Lanteryn: Linching in the Mongol era, today Xuzhou. Caramoran ("Black River"): Mongol name for the Hwang-ho, "Yellow River"; the city actually sits on the Great Canal.

442. Manzi is southern China (Ch. 22, n. 424), Cathay, northern China. Its medieval name (from the nomadic Khitai, who ruled from the tenth to the twelfth centuries as the Liao Dynasty) was first used in the mid-thirteenth century by Franciscan travelers (Ch. 18, n. 358). None ventured farther than Karakorum in Mongolia, however, and Marco Polo recorded the first eyewitness European account half a century later. Eurasia was opened to such extensive travel by the rise of the Mongol Empire (see Ch. 24, esp. n. 459, and Appendix C.5). The China of Polo, OP, and Mandeville (the three most widely known medieval authors on the subject) is thus that of the Mongol or Yüan emperors (1270s–1368). Unlike India, Cathay had almost no Greco-Roman lore; the ancients had known only vaguely about the Sinae and the Seres (silk people). News about it really was new. It does not appear on any world map before the *Catalan Atlas* of about 1375 (see Appendix C.1). William of Rubruck did recognize, though, that Cathay was the land of the Seres and also knew that *Catai* was the name of a people (Chs. 17, 26; 1980, 121, 143–44; 1929, 206, 236), but his insights were little known. Latin Christian contact with Cathay fell off quickly in the later fourteenth and fifteenth

know that the merchants who come from Genoa, or Venice, or another part of Lombardy or from Romany [Byzantium], go by sea and by land for eleven or twelve months, or sometimes more, before they are able to enter the island of Cathay, which is the main region of all territories over there and it belongs to the Great Chan.[443]

From Cathay one goes east by many days' travel and finds a good city amongst the others that is called Sugarmago [Jining]. It is one of the best-supplied cities in the whole world for silk and for many other goods. Then one goes east again to another ancient city that is in the province of Cathay, and beside this city the Tartars have built another city that has the name Caidoun;[444] it has twelve gates, and between two gates there is always a large league such that the two cities—that is to say, the old and the new—have a circumference of more than twenty leagues.[445]

In this city is the Great Chan's throne, in a very beautiful and large palace whose walls are more than two leagues in circumference, and inside these walls it is completely full of other palaces. In the garden of the great palace there is a mountain on which there is another palace, and it is the finest and richest that one could imagine; and all around the palace and the small mountain, there are many different trees bearing many different fruits, and all around this small mountain there are large and deep ditches. Beside it there are large ponds on one side and another and there is a beautiful bridge to pass over the ditches; and in these ponds there are so many wild geese and ducks and swans and herons that they cannot be counted; and all around these ditches and these ponds is the great garden completely full of wild animals, such that when the Great Chan wants leisure or to catch wild animals

---

centuries, because of the rise of the nativist Ming dynasty in China, the adoption of Islam in the Mongol world, and the growth of the Ottoman Empire.

443. This title is (erroneously) explained in Chapter 24. OP was in China from about 1323 to 1328, a time of great political instability (the *Mandeville* author was almost certainly never there); in 1323 the fifth Yüan emperor, Shidebala (fourth successor to Qubilai, the Great Khan who became the first Yüan emperor), was assassinated and several figures briefly occupied the imperial throne until 1333, when Toghon Temür took over (until 1368 when he was forcibly displaced by the first Ming emperor). It is thus not clear which Khan(s) OP might have seen. The rest of this chapter rewrites OP.

444. Ta-tu, the Great Court, in the Mongol era, often known as Khanbaliq, on the site of Beijing. "Tartar" (possibly from "Tatar," the name of a Turko-Mongol people): the common Latin Christian term for Mongol, perhaps because it recalled Tartarus, the Hell of Greco-Roman mythology, and thus suited a people who first made themselves known in Latin Christendom as ferocious warriors, sacking Krakow in 1241. After about 1300, however, and the appearance of Polo's book, the Mongol world came to be depicted much more positively, as here, Cathayan riches contrasting with Tartar miseries (Ch. 14, n. 283).

445. League: see Chapter 5, n. 48.

or birds, he can hunt them and take them from his windows without leaving his room.

This palace where the throne is, is very large and very beautiful. Inside the palace in the hall there are twenty-four columns of fine gold, and all the walls are covered with red skins that are from animals called *pacies* [panthers], which are beautiful and pleasant-smelling animals, such that because of the scent of the skins no foul air can enter the palace. These skins are as red as blood, and so shiny in the sun that one can barely look at them. Many people worship these animals when they see them because of the great power and the fine scent that they have; and they value these skins as much as or more than they do gold plate.

In the middle of the palace there is a raised platform[446] for the Great Chan that is adorned everywhere with gold and precious stones and large pearls, and at the four corners of this dais there are four snakes, and all around there are large gold nets, and cloths made of silk and gold hang everywhere from this platform. Under this platform is the pipe for the drinks that they drink in the emperor's court; and beside this pipe are many gold vessels with which those of the [royal] household drink from the pipe.

The palace hall is most nobly and most wonderfully decorated and well furnished with everything with which a hall can be furnished. First of all, at the head of the hall is the emperor's throne—very high up, where he sits at table—which is made of fine precious stones bordered all around with fine gold, and this border is full of precious stones and large pearls. The steps to the platform are all made of different precious stones and set in gold. To the left side of the emperor's throne is his first wife's throne, one step lower than the emperor's, and it is also made of jasper bordered with gold and of precious stones; and his second wife's throne is a further step lower and is also made of jasper and bordered like the other one; and his third wife's throne is a further step lower than his second wife's, for he always has three wives with him, wherever he might be; and after these wives, on the same side, the ladies and maidens of his family sit a further step lower according to their rank. All those who are married have a likeness of a man's foot on their heads a cubit long[447] and all wrought with large orient pearls, and on top it is adorned with shiny peacock or crane feathers as if [it were] a peak or a crest of a helmet, as a sign that they are subject and under a man's foot, and those who are not married do not wear one. Then to the emperor's right side sits first of all his eldest son who is supposed to reign after him, and he also sits one step below the emperor in a throne made like those of the empresses; and then those of his family sit according to their rank. The emperor has his table all to himself that is made of

---

446. *mountour:* in OP (1929, 473; 1891, 368; 1913, 220–21) the "platform" is a container of some sort, a *pigna*, or a *grant vaissel.*

447. Cubit: see Chapter 2, n. 15.

gold and precious stones and white or yellow crystal bordered with gold and stones, whether with amethyst, or with *lignum aloes,* which comes from Paradise,[448] or with ivory set in and bordered with gold. Each of his wives also has her table near her and his sons and the other great lords that sit lower too, and there is no table that is not worth a large fortune. Below the emperor's table at his feet sit four clerks who set down in writing whatever the emperor says, whether good or bad, for whatever he says there must be conformed to there, for he cannot change or call back his words.

In front of the emperor's table, at great feasts, gold tables are brought in with gold peacocks or other kinds of birds all made of gold and enameled and very nobly wrought, and they are made to dance and flutter and beat their wings, and great tricks are done with them. Whether it is by art or by black magic I do not know, but they put on a fine show, and it is a great puzzle how that can be. But I can say this much: that they are the subtlest people in all forms of knowledge with which they concern themselves, and in all arts that could exist in the universal world; for in subtlety and in wickedness and in ingenuity they surpass all others in the world, and they well know it. Therefore they say that they see with two eyes and the Christians see with only one, because they are the subtlest after them. But all other nations, they say, are blind in both knowledge and practice.[449] I went to much trouble to find out [how they do such things], but the master told me that he had vowed to his god that he would teach no one but the eldest of his sons.

Also, above the emperor's table and the other tables and above part of the hall, there is a vine made of fine gold that extends above everything, and there are many bunches of grapes, white, yellow, red, green, and black, all of precious stones. The white [grapes] are made of crystal and beryl and iris; the yellow are of topazes; the red of rubies, garnets, and alamandines; the green are of emeralds, peridots, and chrysolites; and the black are of onyxes and geracites; and they are all so accurately made that it seems that they are all actual grapes.[450]

In front of the emperor's table were [*sic*] all the great lords and the others who serve him. But no one is so bold as to speak a word unless the lord [the Chan] speaks to him—unless they are minstrels who sing songs and stories or other amusements to relax the emperor. All the vessels with which [food] is served in his halls and his rooms are made

---

448. *lignum aloes:* see Chapter 8, n. 93.

449. OP says only that the birds were the work either of science or "diabolical art." This and the previous sentence are from Hayton, who gives this view to the "Cathayans" (1906, 121, 261). Cf. Vulgate Latin (Ch. 36 in Appendix A.5).

450. OP does not mention the vine, which comes from King Porus' palace in the Alexander Romances. Iris: a prismatic crystal; alamandine, or almandine: a purplish garnet; peridot and chrysolite: green gemstones; geracite, also known as *hieracites* (Greek *hierax:* "hawk," presumably for the bird's coloring).

of precious stones, especially at the large tables, whether of jasper, crystal, amethyst, or fine gold; and all their goblets are of emeralds and sapphires, of topazes, peridots, and many other stones. There is not a single vessel of silver, for they do not value silver enough to make vessels [from it], but they use it to make steps and pillars and paved floors in the halls and rooms.

In front of the hall door are stationed many lords and many knights to see that no one enters without the ruler's consent and command, whether they be servants or minstrels of the [royal] household, and no one else is so bold as to come to the hall door.

You can know that my companions and I with our men served him as soldiers for the space of fifteen months against the king of Mancy with whom he was at war.[451] The reason was that we had such a great desire to see whether his nobility and the state of his court and its order and government were such as we had heard tell—and indeed we found great order and nobility, excellence, wealth, and wonders in his court, more than we had been told; and we would never have believed it if we had not seen it, for no one who had not seen it could believe the nobility, the wealth, and the multitude of people that are in his court.

For it is not at all like over here, for the lords over here have the smallest number of people they can, and the Great Chan every day has a seemingly countless number of people at his expense. But one cannot even compare the arrangements, cost of provisions, decorum, or cleanliness to the manner over here. For all the common people eat without a cloth on their knees and they eat all kinds of meat and little bread, and after eating they clean their hands in their laps,[452] and they eat only once a day. But the lords' state is very great, very rich, and very noble.

Although some people will not want to believe me, and they will regard as a fiction any description made for them of the nobility of his [the Chan's] person and his estate and his court and the great multitude of people that he commands, nevertheless I will say something about him and about his people—the manner and the order—according to what I saw in part and many times. Those who want to may believe me if they please, and those who do not may ignore it, for I well know that if anyone had been in that country over there, even if he had not been as far as the place where the Great Chan dwells, he would have heard so much said about him and his estate that he would readily believe me; and those that have been in that country and in the Great

---

451. This passage replaces OP's own testimonial (Ch. 26), and its main claim (echoing the supposed military service to the Sultan noted in Ch. 6) is false: the wars took place in the later thirteenth century!

452. "laps": *girouns* or *geruns* can also mean "folds" or "pleats." In John of Plano Carpini, the source of this observation through Vincent of Beauvais (see Ch. 26, n. 483), the Mongols wipe their hands on their *ocreas* ("leggings") or on the grass (1929, 48; 1980, 16).

Chan's household know well whether I speak the truth. I will not leave off describing something about him and the retinue that he leads when he goes from one country to another and when he makes his official feasts, just because of those who know nothing and believe nothing unless they see it.

[Chapter 24]

Why He Is Called Great Chan. About the Style of His Letters and the Inscription around His Seals, the Large and the Small

I will tell you first of all why he is called Great Chan.[453] You ought to know that the whole world was destroyed by Noah's flood except for Noah and his wife and their children. Noah had three sons: Sem [Shem], Cha[m] [Ham], and Japhez [Japheth]. This Cham was the one who saw his sleeping father's uncovered back and pointed at it with his finger and mocked him; therefore he was cursed and Japhez turned his face away and covered it.[454] These three brothers took possession of all the earth, and this Cham because of his cruelty took the largest part and the best eastern part, which is called Asia, and Sem took Africa, and Japhez took Europe.[455] Therefore the earth is divided into three parts. Of these three brothers, Cham was the biggest and the strongest, and from him more generations have descended than from the others, and from his son Chus [Cush] was born Nembroth [Nimrod] the giant, who was the first king that ever was in the world, who began to found the Tower of Babylon.[456] With that the devils of Hell often came to sleep with women related to him and engendered diverse monstrous peoples and disfigured peoples, some headless, some with large ears, some with one eye, some giants, some with horses' feet, and others with other

453. *Khan:* a Turkic word meaning "ruler"; "Great Khan": effectively "supreme ruler." The following biblical explanation is thus incorrect, as the *Mandeville* author admits (although he may have invented it, since it has no known source or analogue), but so too is the "truth" he supplies instead: see n. 459 in this chapter. Note that he *does* endorse the claim that Asian peoples are Hamitic. Nothing in this chapter derives from OP, to whose account of Khan the author returns again in Chapter 25.

454. Noah's flood: Gen. 6:5–8:19. Noah's sons: Gen. 9:18–27 (in Jerome's Vulgate translation, Cham sees his father's nakedness: Gen. 9:22).

455. This allocation of the three continents is the standard Latin Christian reading of Gen. 9:19 and 10:1–32, although the texts scarcely support it and the *Mandeville* author switches Ham's and Shem's inheritances (so-called Noachid maps depict this genealogical geography visually: see Appendix C.1). See Braude 1997.

456. On Nimrod and the Tower of Babel (not Babylon), see Chapter 6, n. 68.

deformed limbs,[457] and from that generation of Cham have come the pagan people, and the diverse peoples that exist in the islands of the sea throughout all India, and because he was the strongest and no one could oppose him, he called himself son of God and ruler of the whole world. That is why this emperor the Cham calls himself Cham and ruler of everyone. From the generation of Sem have come the Saracens, and from the generation of Japhez has come the people of Israel, and then we who dwell in Europe.

This is the opinion that the Syrians and Samaritans have and that they gave me to understand before I went towards India, but then I found it entirely otherwise. Nevertheless, the truth is that the Tartars and those who dwell in greater Asia descend from Cham, but the emperor of Cathay is not called Cham, but Chan, and I will tell you the truth how.

It is not more than one hundred and sixty years since all of Tartary was in subjection and servitude to other peoples roundabout, for they were all animal-like and did nothing but keep animals and lead them to pasture. But amongst themselves, they had seven principal nations that were sovereign over all of them, the first of which nations or clans is called Tartar; they are the most noble and the most highly regarded. The second clan is called Tanghot, the third Eurath, the fourth Valair, the fifth Semoch, the sixth Mengly, the seventh Cobooch.[458]

Now it so happened that there was a old worthy man of the first family who was not rich, who had the name Chan Guys.[459] This man was lying in his bed one night and saw a vision in which there came before him a knight completely white and armed with white arms and sitting

---

457. On these peoples, see Chapter 16, n. 317, plus the examples in Chapters 17, 21, 22 (esp.), and 31.

458. From this paragraph on, Chapter 24 rewrites Hayton, *Flor* 3.1–26, composed about 1307, a quarter of a century before OP's memoir. Some 160 years before 1356 (about when *TBJM* was compiled) is 1196, and Chingiz (or Genghis) Khan is considered to have unified the Mongols by about 1206. After the Tatars/Tartars (see Ch. 23, n. 444), the kin-groups in question are, respectively, the Tanguts, Oirats, Jalairs (as in Hayton 3.1), Sünits, Merkits, and Tumuts (T[h]ebet in Hayton).

459. Chingiz (possibly meaning "oceanic") does not contain "Khan." This false etymology is based on an accident of spelling. Chingiz was joined to Khan to form the title (likely meaning "universal ruler") taken by the warrior Temüchin who unified the Mongol tribes and founded their Empire, making him the first "Great Chan." He died in 1227 campaigning in northwestern China, but expansion continued under his successors, starting with his sons, for whom he effectively divided his empire into four khanates (see the dynasties listed in Appendix C.5). By the later thirteenth century the Empire stretched from the Volga River to the Pacific, taking in Russia, Persia, China, the silk routes, and the steppes: the largest land empire ever. Attempts to reach farther into Europe and into Syria, India, and Japan failed, and the Empire did not survive the fourteenth century. See Morgan 1986, Chapter 3. The account of Chingiz Khan's rise given here derives from Hayton (3.1–8; cf. the excerpt in Appendix B.5).

(handwritten margin note: white knight? story? from whom did he steal this)

on a white horse and he said to him: "Chan, are you sleeping?[460] The immortal God sent me to you, and it is his will that you say to the seven families that you are to be their emperor. For you will conquer the surrounding countries, and the bordering areas will be subject to you as you have been subject to them. For this is the will of immortal God." When it came to the morning, Changuys [*sic*] got up and went to tell the seven families, who mocked him and said that he was foolish, and he went away all ashamed. On the following night, this white knight came to the seven families and ordered them on behalf of immortal God to make Chan their emperor, and [told them] that their subjection would end and they would hold the other regions around them in their servitude—such that on the day after they chose Changuys [*sic*] as emperor and made him sit on black felt and then with the felt they raised him with great ceremony and set him on a chair and they all honored him and called him Chan, just as the white knight had called him.

When he was thus chosen he wanted to test whether he could trust them and whether they would be obedient, and so he made several statutes and decrees that they call *Ysa Chan*.[461] The first statute was that they obey and believe in immortal and all-powerful God who would cast them out of slavery and that they would always call him to their aid in all needs. The second statute was that all the men of the country who could bear arms should be counted, and to every ten he entrusted a master, and to one hundred a master, and to one thousand a master, and to ten thousand a master. Afterwards he ordered all the heads of the seven families to give up and renounce whatever inheritance they had, and to consider themselves paid from then on with what he would give them out of his grace, and they did this right away. Afterwards he ordered each of the above-mentioned leaders to summon his eldest son and with his own hands to cut off his son's head without hesitation, and right away the order was fulfilled. When the Chan saw that they would place no obstacles before anything that he commanded, he thought that he could trust them, and right away he gave orders that they be outfitted to serve [under] his banner. Then the Chan subjected all the surrounding lands.

Afterwards a day came when the Chan was out riding with a few companions to see the strength of the countries that he had won, and he came upon a great multitude of his enemies and to give a good example to his people he attacked his enemies first, and there he was knocked off his horse and his horse [was] killed. When the people saw their lord on the ground they were all terrified and believed that he was dead,

---

460. In the French, the knight addresses Chan Guys with the familiar *tu* rather the more formal *vous*.

461. *Yasa*: a code of laws supposedly laid down by Chingiz Khan. It has not survived except in quoted fragments; its exact nature is uncertain (Morgan 1986, 96–99).

and they all took flight and the enemies pursued them, for they did not know that the emperor had stayed behind. When they had gone far in pursuit of the others, the emperor went and hid himself in a thick wood, and when they [the enemies] had returned from the pursuit, they went looking in this wood to see whether anyone was hiding, and they found several and put them to death. When they went to look near the place where the Chan was, he saw an owl that is called *bubo* sitting on a tree above him,[462] and they said amongst themselves that there was no one there, since this owl was on that tree, and thus they returned elsewhere and the emperor was saved from death. He left secretly at night and went to his people, who were very glad of his coming and showed their gratitude to immortal God and to this bird through which their lord was saved. Therefore above all other owls of the world, they honor this owl, and whoever can have a feather keeps it most preciously instead of relics, and they carry it over their heads most reverently, and think themselves blessed and saved from all dangers, and this is why they all wear feathers on their heads.

After this, the Chan readied and gathered his people and went against those who had attacked him and destroyed them and made them slaves. When the Chan had won and placed in subjection all the lands and the countries on this side of Mount Belyan [Baljuna], the white knight came to him another time in his sleep and said to him: "Chan, the will of immortal and all-powerful God is that you go beyond Mount Belyan, and win the land and make more nations subject to you. And because you will find no good passage to go towards that country, go to Mount Belyan, which is on the sea, and kneel nine times to the east in honor of God immortal, and he will show you the way through which you will pass." The Chan did this, and right away the sea that reached to the mountain began to withdraw and showed a fine passage nine feet wide, and thus he passed through with his people and won the land of Cathay, which is the largest kingdom there is in the world.

Because of those nine genuflections and because of the nine feet of route, the Chan and all the Tartars since greatly revere the number nine, and that is why whoever wishes to make a gift—whether of horses, or birds, or bows, or arrows, or fruit, or something else—always sends the number nine, and the gift is more graciously received than if there were one or two hundred. For it seems to them that this number is holy, because the messenger of immortal God determined it.

Also, when the Chan had won the country of Cathay and subjected many surrounding countries, he fell ill and knew well that he had to die. He told his twelve sons to bring him one arrow each and they did this right away. Then he said that they should be tied together with three bands, and then he handed them to the eldest of his sons and told him

---

462. *bubo:* "owl" in Latin. The name is used only in Hayton's Latin, not his French (3.4).

to break all of them together, and the son tried but he could not break them. Then the Chan told him to give them to the second [son] and then to the others one after another, but none of them was able to break them. And the Chan said to the youngest: "Take them apart and break each one by itself," and so he did. Then the Chan said to the eldest and to the others, why had he not broken them? And they answered that they could not because they were bound together. "And why," he said, "did your little brother break them?" "Because," they said, "they had been taken apart." Then the Chan said: "My children, it is the same with you, for so long as you are bound together by the three bonds of love, loyalty, and harmony, no one can harm you. But if you should be apart from those bonds such that you do not help one another, you will be destroyed and reduced to nothing. If you remember this and love one another, then you will be lords and rulers of everyone."

When he had made these arrangements, he died, and after him reigned Ettocha Chan [Ögedai], his eldest son, and the other brothers went to win many countries and many regions all the way to the land of Prussia and of Russia and they had themselves called Chan. But they were all obedient to their eldest brother, and this is why he was called Great Chan, and ever since they are called this.[463]

After Ettocha reigned Guyo Chan [Güyük], and then Mango Chan [Möngke], who was a good baptized Christian and gave letters of perpetual peace to all Christians;[464] and he sent his son Halaon [Hülegü] with a great multitude of people to win the Holy Land and to place it in the hands of Christians and to destroy Machometh's law and to capture the Caliph of Baldak [Baghdad], who was emperor and lord of all the Saracens.[465] When this Caliph was captured they found so much

---

463. On Chingiz Khan's successors and the four main khanates, see Appendix C.5.

464. According to Hayton 3.16–17, Möngke's baptism and protection of Christians resulted from a request by the Armenian king, but there is no evidence that he became a Christian. On his visit to Möngke, William of Rubruck wondered whether the Khan's wife Cotota was a Nestorian (1929, 258–59; 1980, 162); that was plausible, given the many Nestorians in central Asia and the fact that some Mongols did convert. Traditionally, though, the Mongols were Shamanists, and Shamanism never disappeared entirely in any Mongol territory. Still, the early Empire was open to all religions, including Christianity, and Latin Christian writers reported that the Khans believed in one god (cf. the end of Ch. 25). Of the four major khanates named in Appendix C.5, the Great Khanate favored Buddhism and the western three eventually became Muslim. None was ever officially Christian.

465. This story comes from Hayton 3.18–19: a reminder that a major source of Latin Christian interest in the Mongols was seeing them as potential allies against Islam. Hülegü, Möngke's younger brother, was sent west by Möngke in 1253 partly to demand the submission of the Abbasid Caliph al-Musta'sim, not to fulfill the Christian fantasy narrated here. Al-Musta'sim surrendered in 1258, and Hülegü had Baghdad brutally sacked, ending the Abbasid Caliphate. The Caliph was

treasure that in all the rest of the world one would scarcely have had so much, and Halaon made him come before him and asked him why, with a part of this treasure, he had not hired enough soldiers to defend his country. The Caliph answered that he had thought that he had enough of his own men. Then Halaon said: "You were like God to the Saracens, and gods ought not to eat mortal food, and therefore you will eat nothing but precious stones and pearls and the treasure that you loved so much." And he had him put in prison and all his treasure with him, and there he died of hunger and thirst. Then Halaon won all the Promised Land and placed it in the hands of the Christians, but the Great Chan died, and the whole business was botched.

After Mango Chan reigned Cobila Chan [Qubilai], who was also Christian and ruled for forty-two years. He founded the great city of Jong in Cathay, which is much bigger than Rome is. The next Great Chan who came after him became pagan,[466] and all the others too.

The kingdom of Cathay is the largest kingdom there is in the world, and also the Great Chan is the strongest emperor there is under the firmament. This is how he names himself in his letters: *"Chan filius dei excelsi omnium universam terram colencium summus Imperator et dominus omnium dominacium."*[467] And the writing around his small seal [privy seal] is this: *"Dei fortitudo omnium hominum Imperatoris sigillum."*[468] And this is the inscription on his great seal: *"Deus in celo et Chan super terram ejus fortitudo omnium hominum Imperatoris sigillum."*[469] Although they are not now Christians, nevertheless the emperors and all the Tartars believe in immortal God, and when they wish to threaten anyone they say: "God indeed knows that I will do such a thing to you." You have heard why he is called Great Chan.

---

put to death: probably wrapped in a carpet and trampled, a Mongol practice used to avoid spilling royal blood. The starvation story has been more popular, however: Marco Polo also tells it (1928, 18–19; 1958, 52–53). On Hülegü's western campaign, see Morgan 1986, 147–58.

466. Qubilai Khan (who ruled for thirty-four years) was not a Christian; like his successors Temür Öljeitü (r. 1294–1307) and others, he favored Buddhism (Morgan 1986, 123–26). Jong is Khanbaliq, the Mongol capital (Ch. 23, n. 444), probably from Yen King, its Chinese name.

467. "We, Chan, son of God on high, are Emperor of all of the entire earth's inhabitants and lord of all lordships." No known source, but its elements are in Vincent of Beauvais, *Speculum Historiale* 29.74. The official imperial language was Mongolian (in Uighur script), not Latin, but Latin presumably reinforces the imperial aura of the quotations and may reflect the fact that imperial letters to the pope and others would have been translated into Latin.

468. "God's strength. Seal of the Emperor of all men."

469. "God in Heaven and Chan his strength on earth. The seal of the Emperor of all men." Like the previous quotation, almost verbatim from John of Plano Carpini, *History of the Mongols* (1929, 93; 1980, 43–44), the second echoed in Vincent of Beauvais, *Speculum Historiale* 31.52. See also Chapter 26, n. 492.

[Chapter 25]

About the Government of the Great Chan's Court When He Holds His Official Feasts. About His Philosophers. And About His Entourage When He Rides through the Country

Now I will tell you about the government of the Great Chan's court when he holds official celebrations. This is mainly four times a year. The first feast is that of his birth, the next that of his presentation in their Moseach (that is, in their temple, where they perform a kind of circumcision);[470] and the other two feasts are of his idols: the first is when the idol was first placed in their Moseach and enthroned, the second when the idol first began to speak or perform miracles. He celebrates no other official feasts unless he marries off his children.

Now know that at each of these feasts there is a large number of people and very well ordered and well arranged in thousands, hundreds, and tens, and everyone knows well how they are supposed to serve and understands so well what they must do that nothing is lacking. There are in the first place four thousand rich and powerful lords appointed to supervise, govern, and arrange the feast and to serve the emperor; and these official feasts are held outside in tents most nobly made of gold cloth and tartar. These lords all have on their heads very noble and very rich gold crowns with precious stones and large orient pearls, and they are all dressed in clothes of gold or tartar or camaca[471] more beautifully than anyone in the world can describe; and these robes are embroidered all over with gold and very richly sewn with precious stones and pearls— and they can indeed do this, for gold and silk clothes are considerably cheaper than are woolen clothes here. These four thousand lords are divided into four companies, and each thousand is dressed in clothes all of the same color and so well adorned and so richly dressed that it is a wonder to see. The first thousand, which is made up of dukes, counts, and marquises and commanders, are all dressed in gold clothes woven with green silk and embroidered with gold and precious stones, as I told you. The second thousand is all dressed in decorated clothes of bright red silk adorned with gold and gold embroidery and very nobly adorned with pearls. The third thousand [is dressed] in clothes of purple or indigo silk, and the fourth thousand in yellow clothes. All their clothes are so nobly and so richly adorned with gold and stones and pearls that if someone from this country had just one of their robes, it could indeed be said that he was not poor; for the gold, the stones, and the pearls are worth a great fortune over here, more than they are over there. When

(margin, handwritten) military explanation

---

470. Perhaps an error for "coronation": the Mongols did not practice circumcision. This chapter returns to OP, supplemented by Hayton and Vincent of Beauvais.
471. See Chapter 19, n. 373.

they are thus dressed they go arranged in pairs before the emperor without saying a word, just bowing to him, and each carries in front of him a tablet of jasper or ivory or crystal, and the minstrels come before him playing many different instruments, and when the first thousand has thus passed by and shown itself for inspection, it moves aside. Then the second thousand enters and does the same thing, and then the third, and then the fourth, and none of them says a single word.

To one side of the emperor's table sit many philosophers learned in many sciences such as astronomy, necromancy, geomancy, pyromancy, hydromancy, augury, and many other sciences; and some have gold astrolabes in front of them, or spheres, some a dead man's skull, others gold vessels full of sand, others vessels full of burning coals, others gold vessels full of water and oil, and others very nobly made clocks and many other kinds of instruments suited to their sciences, and at certain hours, when it seems to them that it is time, they say to the assistants in front of them who are assigned to carry out their order, "Let there be silence." Then the assistants say, "Silence now—and listen." Then one of the philosophers says, "Everyone make obeisance and bow to the emperor, who is the son of God and sovereign lord of all others in the world, for it is now time." Then everyone lowers his head towards the ground, and then this philosopher says, "Arise. . . ." Then at another time another philosopher will say, "Put your little finger in your ear," and they do it right away; and then at another time another philosopher says, "Put your hand in front of your mouth," and they do it; and then another says, "Put your hand on your head," and they do it; and then they are told to take it away and it is done. Thus from one hour to the next, they say different things, and say that these things have a great hidden meaning.

I asked them privately what hidden meaning and what significance these things have, and one of the masters answered me that bowing one's head at this hour has the following hidden meaning: that all those who have bowed their heads will always be more obedient and loyal to the emperor, that they can never be corrupted either by gifts or by promises, nor tempted by any wealth to betray him. About the finger placed in the ear, they say that none of them would be able to hear said or say anything against the emperor that he would not stop it right away, even if it were his father or his brother who had said it. Thus they give different meanings to everything that they say and that they do. [You can] be sure that no one does anything pertaining to the emperor—not clothes, nor bread, nor bath, nor anything else—except always at specific times that the philosophers determine, and if war arises anywhere against the emperor, or if someone does anything contrary in all his land, these philosophers go straight to him and tell the emperor and his council, "Sire, someone is right now doing such a thing in your land and in these regions"; and the emperor immediately sends [men] to those regions.

When the said philosophers have thus fulfilled their duty, the minstrels begin to play, each on his own instrument one after another, and they make a loud music, and when they have played their instruments for a while, one of the emperor's ministers climbs up on an intricately made stage and calls out and says, "Let there be silence." Then everyone falls silent and then all the emperor's relatives are dressed most nobly in gold clothes and everyone is outfitted with as many white horses as he can pay for. Then the court steward says, "*N* of *D*," and names the most noble first, "Be outfitted with such and such a number of white horses to serve your lord the sovereign emperor." And to another such person, "*N* of *D* also be outfitted with so many," and so on. Thus he names all of the emperor's kin one after the other, and when he has named them all, they enter one after another and present their white horses to the emperor and leave. Then after all this each of the other lords gives him a present, or jewel, or something else according to their rank, and then afterwards all the chief priests of their law, both monks and others, each give him something, and then when everyone has made his offering to the emperor, the greatest of their priests gives the blessing, saying a prayer from their law.

Then the minstrels begin once again to play, and when they have played for a while, they are made to be quiet; and tame lions and other animals and eagles and vultures and many kinds of birds, fishes, and snakes are brought before the emperor to honor him, for they say that every living creature must obey him and honor him. Afterwards there come entertainers and magicians who perform plenty of wonders, for they make the sun and the moon seem to appear in the air to honor him, and these give off such a bright light that one person can scarcely see another, and then they make it night so that one can see almost nothing, and then they make the day return. They make dance the most beautiful young women in the world, as it seems to the people, and then they make other young women appear carrying gold cups full of mare's milk, and this they give to the lords and the ladies to drink. They make knights appear jousting most skillfully in their arms of cuirasses and other gear that belongs to jousting, and they shatter their lances so well and violently that the broken pieces fly across all the tables; and they make hunts in pursuit of stags and boars appear and running dogs, and they do so many different things that it is a wonder to see. Such entertainments are performed until the tables are cleared away.

This Great Chan has many people to serve him, as I have told you before, for he has servants numbering thirteen *cumans*[472] who all belong to him; but they do not all stay with him, for all the servants who come before him, from whatever nation they come, he has them retained in his royal household and has them registered in writing. Therefore, although they may go through every land, they always claim to be his, and that is why there are such a great number. [He has] officials who keep birds: ostriches, gyrfalcons, sparrowhawks, peregrine falcons,

472. See Chapter 22, n. 439.

lanners, sakerets,[473] talking parrots, and singing birds, and also wild animals and tame elephants and other [animals], baboons, monkeys, marmots, and other diversities, and there are fifteen *cumans* of officials. He has two hundred Christian physicians, and he has two hundred and ten Christian medics and also two hundred Saracen, for they put much more faith in the work of Christians than of Saracens; and his other common courtiers are also a countless number, and they get everything they need at the emperor's court. There are in his court many lords and servants who are Christian and converts to the good faith through the preaching of the Christian monks who dwell there, but there are more who do not wish it to be known that they are Christian.

This emperor can spend as much as he likes, an incalculable amount, for he neither spends nor produces any money except that printed on bark or paper, and there is of such money a greater or a lesser value according to the difference in the sign that there is.[474] When this money has circulated so much that it is all worn out, then one takes it to the emperor's treasury and he gives them new money for the old, and this money goes throughout his whole country and through all his provinces, for over there they make no money out of gold or silver. Therefore he can spend enough and with the gold and the silver that is brought into his country he always decorates his palace and has diverse things made and changes and alters [them] as it pleases him. He has in his chamber in one of his gold pillars a ruby carbuncle a foot long that lights up the whole room at night. There are many other precious stones and many other rubies, but that is the largest and the most precious.

In the summer this emperor dwells in a city that is towards the north that has the name Saduz [Shangtu], and it is quite cold there; and in winter, he dwells in the city of Camaalech [Khanbaliq], which is a very hot country; but the country where he dwells more commonly, that is in Caydo [Ta-tu] or in Jong [Yen-king],[475] which is a good country and quite temperate in accordance with the country over there, but for those of this [i.e., the *Mandeville* author's] country it would be too hot.

When the said emperor wants to ride from one country to another, he has four armies of his people drawn up, the first army of which goes one day ahead of him, for this army spends the night where the emperor spends the following night, and there everyone finds what he needs. In this first army there are fifty *cumans* of people, whether on horseback or on foot, each *cuman* of which amounts to ten thousand, as I have told you previously.[476] Another army goes on his right side half a day away,

---

473. "lanners": a species of falcon; "sakerets": male falcons.

474. The *Mandeville* author's unfamiliarity with paper money reveals itself in this paragraph.

475. These last three names are all variant names of the same city: see Chapter 23, n. 444, and Chapter 24, n. 466.

476. In Chapter 22.

and another goes on his left, and in each army there are as many people as in the first army; and then [there] is the fourth army, which is larger still than any of the others and goes with him a bowshot behind. Each army has its appointed days in certain places where they are to spend the night and there they find whatever they need; and if it happens that anyone in the army dies, another immediately replaces him so that the number is always maintained.

Know that the emperor himself never rides, nor do the other great lords over there, unless they wish to go somewhere secretly with few people so as not to be recognized. For he goes in a four-wheeled chariot on which there is a beautiful room made of a kind of wood that comes from [the] Earthly Paradise that is called *lignum aloes,* which the rivers of Paradise carry out in season, as I have told you previously;[477] and this room is very pleasant-smelling because of this wood, and the room is all covered inside with fine gold plate, precious stones, and large pearls. Four elephants and four large white chargers covered with rich caparisons pull this chariot, and four or five or six of the greatest lords ride around the chariot mounted and [are] outfitted most nobly, so that no one may approach the chariot but those lords, unless the emperor summons someone to speak to him. On the room in the chariot in which he sits are four or five or six gyrfalcons seated on a perch so that the emperor, should he see a wild bird that he wants to capture or if he wants to see the quarry, lets fly one of his gyrfalcons and then afterwards another when it pleases him, and thus he captures the quarry while passing through the country. None of his company rides ahead of him but always behind him, nor does anyone dare approach the chariot by [closer than] a bowshot except those lords who are around him, and the whole army comes handsomely after him where there is a great multitude. Also, to one side in another such chariot and with an army arranged in the same way go the empresses, each having with her four armies just like the emperor, but not with such a great multitude of people; and his eldest son goes by another route in another chariot in this same manner. There are amongst them so many people that it is a wonder to see and no one would believe the number if he did not see them. Sometimes it happens when he does not go far that the empresses and the children all go together, and their people are all joined and divided into only four parties.

Also, this Great Chan's empire is divided into twelve provinces, and in each province there are more than two thousand cities and count-less towns. This country is very large, for there are twelve main kings in these twelve provinces, and each of these kings has many kings under him, and all are obedient to the Great Chan. His land and his lordship extend so far that to go from one end to the other both by sea and by land would take more than seven years.

---

477. In Chapter 8 (see n. 93). *Lignum aloes* is mentioned only in OP's Latin.

Throughout the desert where one finds no towns, there are hostels placed a day's travel apart where those crossing find everything they need to go through the country. There is a wonderful custom throughout the country, but it is effective: that when something contrary or something new concerning the emperor comes into the country, the emperor knows this news in a day from three or more days' travel away, for immediately the ambassadors mount their dromedaries or their horses and ride as fast as they can right to one of these hostels, and when they approach this hostel they sound a horn, and right away those in the hostel understand well that some news is coming, and right away another prepares to take the letters and race ahead to the other hostels, just as the first had raced there; and the first remains there, and he and his animal rest and refresh themselves, and they do this from hostel to hostel until they come to the emperor, and thus he has the news right away. Also, when the emperor sends his couriers quickly through the country, each has a large strap full of little bells, and when they thus approach the hostels of other couriers that are also placed a day's travel apart, they ring their little bells and right away the other gets ready and speeds his way to another hostel, and thus one races very quickly to the other, and these couriers are called *Chydydo* in their language:[478] that is to say messenger.

Also, when the emperor thus goes from one country to another, as I have told you, and he passes through the cities and the towns, everyone makes a fire in front of their house and puts into it powders of pleasant-smelling things to give a good smell to the lord, and all the people kneel towards him and make their obeisance. Where the Christian monks dwell just as they do in many cities in the land, they walk ahead in procession with the cross and the holy water, and chant "*Veni Creator Spiritus etc.*"[479] in a loud voice, and go towards him; and when he hears them, he orders his lords who are riding beside him to make the monks come; and when they approach and he sees the cross he takes off his *galahoth*—which sits on his head like a felt hat, [and] which is made of gold and precious stones and large pearls, and it is so rich that it would be worth a kingdom in this country—and bows to the cross. Then the chief priest of these monks says his prayers in front of him and then blesses him with the cross and he bows most devoutly to the blessing; and then he [the head monk] gives him some fruit in the number of nine on a silver platter, whether pears or apples or some other fruit, and he [the emperor] takes one of them and gives [the rest] to the other lords who

---

478. From *ghichkiku* ("to walk") or *kiku pu ping* ("messenger on foot"): DLMM 404, n. 11. On the *yām*, or postal system, see Morgan 1986, 103–7.

479. "Come, Creator Spirit." A hymn dating perhaps from the ninth century, used especially during Pentecost. OP claims to have taken part in this ceremony; the *Mandeville* author's account follows the French in its placement, but the Latin in its details (see Ch. 38 in Appendix B.3).

are around him, for the custom is such that no foreigner may come
before him without giving him something according to the ancient law
that says: "*Non accedat in conspectus meo vacuum.*"[480] Then the emperor
tells these monks to withdraw so that they will not be stepped on by the
great multitude of horses that are coming from behind. Also those that
dwell where the empresses come past do the same thing, and they do so
for his eldest son as well, and so to each they present some fruit.

Know that these people—of whom there are so many in his armies
around him and around his wives and his son—do not remain continuously with him, but whenever it pleases him he has them come and then
they return to their lodgings, except only those who stay with him to
serve him and his wives and his children and to manage the court; and
even though all the others have gone, there remain with him at court,
decisively and continuously, fifty thousand men on horseback and two
hundred thousand on foot, without [counting] servants and those who
look after wild animals and diverse birds, the number of which I told
you about above.

Under the firmament there is no lord so great or so strong as is
the Great Chan, neither above earth nor below,[481] for neither Prester
John, who is emperor of high India, nor the Sultan of Babylon, nor the
emperor of Persia, compares to him in power, in nobility, or in wealth,
for in all this he surpasses all the earthly princes—which is why it is a
great harm that he does not steadfastly believe in God.[482] Nevertheless,
he very willingly hears God spoken about and certainly allows that there
are Christians who go throughout his whole country, for no one is prohibited from holding such law [religion] as he likes. In this country one
man has one hundred wives, another sixty, another more, and another
fewer; and they take their kin as wives except their mothers, their daughters, and their sisters on their mother's side, but they can take their
sisters on their father's side by another wife, and their brothers' wives
after their [brothers'] death, and their stepmothers as well.

---

480. "He shall not appear before me empty-handed." Some copies have *nemo
accedat* ("no one shall appear"). Cf. Exod. 23:15 (quoted correctly in OP's Latin
text; it is not in the French).
481. I.e., "in neither the northern nor the southern hemisphere."
482. This does not quite agree with the remarks at the end of Chapter 24 about
belief in "immortal God."

[Chapter 26]

About the Law and the Customs of the Tartars Dwelling in Cathay and What They Do When the Great Chan Will Die and How He Is Chosen

The people of this country all wear wide clothes without fur trim and are dressed in purpure, tartar,[483] [and] gold clothes, and their clothes are slit at the side and fastened with silk laces, and they wear fur cloaks with the hide facing out, and they do not wear or put on hoods or head coverings. The women are dressed in the same way as the men are dressed, such that one cannot distinguish the one from the other except for the married women, who wear a sign on their head;[484] and their wives do not dwell together, since each dwells by herself and the husband comes to sleep with her when he wants to. Everyone has their own house, both men and women, and they are round houses made with staves, and there is a round window above that gives them light and through which the smoke escapes, and the covering of the house and the wall[s] and the door are all of felt.[485] When they go to war, they take their houses with them on carts just as one does tents and pavilions, and they make their fire in the center of their houses. They have a very large multitude of all kinds of animals except pigs, which they do not raise. They do believe in a god that created and made everything, and nevertheless they have idols of gold and silver and felt and cloth; and to these idols they always offer their first milk from their animals and also some of their meat and some of their drinks before they consume them, and they often offer horses and animals. They also call God of Nature *Yroga*.[486]

Whatever name their emperor has they always add Chan, and when I was there the emperor had the name Thiaut, and he was called Thiaut Chan. His eldest son had the name Tossué, and when he is emperor he will be called Tossué Chan. He also had twelve sons in addition to these whose names were Cunuc, Ordu, Chahaday, Buryn, Nengu, Nocab, Cadu, Siban, Cuten, Balac, Babilan, [and] Garagan. Of his three wives the first and the foremost (who was Prester John's daughter) had the

---

483. Purpure: a rich purple cloth. Tartar: see Chapter 19, n. 373. The *Mandeville* author leaves OP aside in this chapter, drawing on Simon of Saint-Quentin's and John of Plano Carpini's mid-thirteenth-century reports from Vincent of Beauvais, *Speculum Historiale* 29 and 31 (with a few details from Hayton's *Flor*).

484. A feathered foot: see Chapter 23.

485. The *yurt* or *ger,* a portable tent-like dwelling still used in Central Asia.

486. John of Plano Carpini mentions *Itoga*, a god (1980, 12; 1929, 41); it is not in Vincent of Beauvais' extract in *Speculum Historiale* 29.73, so the author may have used both texts. God of Nature: the god known "naturally," as distinct from the God of Revelation known to Jews, Christians, and Muslims.

name Serioch Chan, and the next Borak Chan, and the next Carauke Chan.[487]

The people of this country begin everything they have to do in the new moon, and they greatly revere the moon and the sun and often kneel to them. All the people of this country commonly ride without spurs, but they always carry a whip in their hands to drive their horses. They are morally very scrupulous and consider it a very great sin to stick a knife in the fire, and take meat from the pot with a knife, and lean on the whip with which they strike the horses, or strike a horse with the reins, and break a bone with another bone, and throw on the ground milk or other liquid that one could drink, and kill and capture small children; and the greatest sin is to piss in their houses where they dwell, and whoever should piss will certainly be killed. They must confess each of these sins to their priest and pay a large sum of money for their penance, and the place where someone has pissed must be blessed, or else no one would dare go in; and when they have paid their penance, they are made to pass through a fire or through two fires to cleanse themselves of their sins, and also when any messenger comes and brings a present to the emperor, he must pass, with the things he is bringing, through two burning fires to purify them so that he will not bring poison or other bad thing that might harm the lord. Also, if any man is taken in adultery or woman in fornication, they are killed, and if anyone steals anything he is killed.

They are all good archers and shoot very well, and the women also ride and run as well as the men. The women do everything, and they do all the trades—silk cloths and other things—and they drive the carts and the chariots, and make the houses and all the other essentials, except bows and arrows and armor, which the men make; and all the women wear trousers just like the men.

All the people of this country are very obedient to their sovereign, and they do not fight with or scold one another; and there are no thieves in the country and they greatly respect one another, but they show no respect to foreigners, even if they are great princes. They eat dogs, lions, foxes, mares, foals, asses, rats, and mice, and all other animals, large and small, except pigs and animals that were prohibited in the Old

---

487. On *"Chan"* ("Khan"), see Chapter 24, n. 453. The *Mandeville* author was "there" in 1246, then: this account comes from John of Plano Carpini (1980, 26; 1929, 65–67) via Vincent of Beauvais, *Speculum Historiale* 31.13. Thiaut: Güyük. Tossué: Chingiz's eldest son Jochi (see Appendix C.5). The other names are of Chingiz's other sons and grandsons (John of Plano Carpini, 1980, xl–xli [Table 1], and 26, n. 2). Serioch Chan: Sorocan (Sorghaghtani Beki), wife of Tolui, Chingiz's youngest son and mother of Möngke, the fourth Great Khan. The last two names may derive from those of Ögedai's first and second wives (WBJM 209, n. to 121, l.17). The marriage alliance is briefly explained in Chapter 30.

Testament;[488] and they eat the whole animal, inside and out, such that they throw nothing away except the dung. They eat very little bread, except at the great lords' courts, and in many places they have neither peas nor beans nor other soups except the broth of meat, for they eat little else besides meat and broth. When they have eaten they wipe their hands in their laps,[489] for they do not use any tablecloths or napkins, except in front of the great lords, but the common people have none, and when they have eaten, they put their bowls unwashed into the pot or the cauldron with the leftover meat and broth, until they want to eat again. The rich men drink mares' milk, or camels' or asses' milk, or that of other animals, and they get good and drunk from this milk or from another drink that is made of honey and water brewed together, for they have no wine or ale in the country. They live very wretchedly and eat only once a day and very little indeed, whether at court or elsewhere, and one single person from this country [over here] would certainly eat more in one day than one of them would eat in three days. If a foreign messenger comes to the lord, they give him something to eat only once a day, and very little.

When they go to war, they make war very wisely and always take pains to surround their enemies. Everyone has two or three bows and a great many arrows and a large axe, and the noblemen have swords that are short and broad and sharp on one edge, and they have armor and helmets of *cuir-bouilli,* and trappers for their horses.[490] Whoever flees from the battle is killed. When they besiege a castle or walled town, they promise to those inside to do so many good things that it is a wonder, and everything that those inside ask for they grant, and when they have surrendered they kill them all and cut off their ears and put them in vinegar to steep and with them they make food for the great lords.[491] Their goal is to place all lands under them and they say that they know well through prophecies that they will be conquered by the power of archers and that they will be converted to the law of those who will conquer them; but they do not know which people or which law will conquer them,[492] and therefore they allow the peoples of all laws [religions] to dwell peacefully in their land. When they wish to make their idols or the image of some of their friends to commemorate them, they always

---

488. The Mongols were not bound by Jewish dietary laws, of course, and no other work makes this claim.

489. See Chapter 23, n. 452.

490. *cuir-bouilli:* boiled leather, molded when wet and soft; trappers: armored covers for horses.

491. This story, here made a custom, concerns only one event in Vincent of Beauvais, *Speculum Historiale* 29.83.

492. From John of Plano Carpini (1980, 64; 1929, 25–26), where the mention of world domination introduces the Khan's seals described at the end of Chapter 24. Cf. the Saracen prophecies in Chapter 15.

make them entirely naked without any kind of clothing; for they say that in good love there is no concealment and that no one should love on account of fine clothing or beautiful adornment, but only on account of the body such as God made it and the good virtues with which the body was naturally provided, and not on account of the fine clothing, which is not from nature.[493]

It is very dangerous to pursue the Tartars when they flee in battle, for in fleeing they shoot behind them and kill men and horses. And when they want to fight they are so close together that if there were twenty thousand men one would not believe that there are ten thousand. They readily capture other land, but they do not know how to hold it, for they know better how to lie in tents outside than in towns or castles. They rate the understanding of other nations at nothing, and amongst them the olive is very costly, for they consider it a most noble medicine.

All the Tartars have small eyes and not much of a beard and very sparse. They are false and treacherous and they keep none of their promises. They are a very hardy people and can endure much more pain and hardship than any other people, for they are well trained in their own country and they spend nothing.

When someone is about to die, they place a spear beside him, and when he draws towards his death, everyone flees the house until he is dead, and then they bury him in the fields. When the emperor dies, they seat him in a throne in the middle of his tent, and they place a table in front of him with a tablecloth and meat and food, and a goblet full of mare's milk; and they put a mare beside him with her foal, and a horse saddled and bridled, and they place gold and silver on the horse, and they place straw around it. They make a deep and wide pit, and with the tent and with all the other things they place him in the ground and say that when he will go to the other world he will not be homeless, nor horseless, nor without gold, nor without silver, and the mare will give him milk and bear him other horses until he is well supplied in the other world. For they say that after death they are in the other world eating and drinking and enjoying themselves with their wives just as they do here. After he is placed in the ground, no one is ever so bold as to talk about him in front of any of his friends, and yet they sometimes have them [the dead] buried secretly at night in the wildest places and they put the grass back to grow on the grave, or they cover it very well with sand and gravel so that no one knows where the grave is, so that he [the dead person] will never return in memory to any of his friends. Then they say that he was seized into the other world, and that he is a greater lord over there than he was over here.

Thus after the emperor's death the seven clans gather and choose his son or his next of kin and they say this to him, "We desire and entreat and decree that you be our lord and our emperor." And he

---

493. Cf. the Lamorians' defense of nakedness in Chapter 20.

answers, "If you wish me to rule over you, each of you will do what I order you to, whether to remain or to go, and the one I order killed will be killed immediately." And they all answer with one voice, "Whatever you command will be done." Then the emperor says, "Then know that henceforth my word is as sharp as my sword." Then they seat him on black felt and they place him in his throne and crown him, and then all the good towns send him presents until that day he has more than sixty chariots laden with gold and silver without [mentioning] all the jewels from lords, the gold and the precious stones beyond counting, and without [mentioning] horses, and without [mentioning] gold cloth and camaca and tartar that are countless.

[Chapter 27]

About the Kingdom of Thars [Tarshish] and the Lands and Kingdoms Towards the Northern Regions in Descending from the Land of Cathay

This land of Cathay is in the depths of Asia, and next on this side is Asia Major. The kingdom of Cathay borders to the west on the kingdom of Thars [Tarshish], which belonged to one of the kings who went to seek Our Lord in Bethlehem and those that are of this king's line are all somewhat Christian.[494] In Thars they do not eat meat or drink wine. And on this side towards the West is the kingdom of Turkestan, which extends westwards to the kingdom of Persia and northwards all the way to the kingdom of Chorasme [Khwarezm]. In this country of Turkestan there are few good cities; the best city of the kingdom has the name Occorar [Otrar]. There are broad grazing lands and little wheat, and therefore they are all herders of a sort, and they lie in tents and drink ale made from honey. Next on this side is the kingdom of Chorasme, which is a good land and fertile without wine; it has to the east a desert that lasts more than one hundred days' travel, and the best city of the country has the name Chorasme, and from this city the country takes its name. The people of the country are good warriors and bold.

On this side is the kingdom of Comanie [Cumania], where the Cumans, who dwell in Greece, were formerly driven. It is one of the largest kingdoms in the world, but it is not all inhabited, for in one of

---

494. Based on a misreading of Ps. 71[72]:10: "The kings of Tharsis and the islands shall offer presents." Drawing on Hayton's overview of eastern lands (*Flor* 1), the *Mandeville* author continues his long departure from OP's itinerary. He mostly leaves out Hayton's negative remarks: e.g., that "nearly all" Turkestanis "believe in the false teachings of Machomet's law" (1.3; 1906, 123). The Central Asian territories mentioned here came under Mongol rule in the thirteenth and fourteenth centuries.

its regions it gets so cold that no one could dwell there, and in another part it gets so hot that no one could bear it, and there are so many flies that one would not know which way to turn. In this country there are few fruit-bearing trees, or any others. They lie in tents and burn animal dung for lack of bushes. This kingdom descends towards us, towards Prussia, and towards Russia. Through this country flows the River Ethil [Volga], which is one of the largest rivers in the world, and every year it freezes so hard that many battles have been fought on the ice by a conscript army[495] on horseback and on foot of more than one hundred thousand persons on each side. Between this river and the great Ocean Sea, which they call the Maure [Black] Sea, lie all these kingdoms. Towards the upper end of this kingdom is the Mount Cochaz [Caucasus], which is the highest in the world, and it is between the Maure Sea and the Caspian Sea.

There is a very narrow pass there to go towards India, and therefore Alexander had a city built there that they call Alexandria to guard the country so that no one would cross through without permission; and now this city is called the Iron Gate. The capital city of Comania has the name Sarak [Sarai]. It is one of the three ways to go to India, but on this route one would not pass many people except in winter, and this passage is called the Derbent.[496] The other way is to go from the kingdom of Turkestan through Persia, and on this route there are many days' travel in the desert. And the third way is that one goes from Comania and goes by way of the Great [Black] Sea and the kingdom of Abchaz [Abkhasia].

Know that all these kingdoms and all these lands mentioned above as far as Prussia and Russia all obey the Great Chan of Cathay, and many other countries and borderlands on the other side [do as well], which is why his power and his lordship are so great.

---

495. *Host banniz:* or army summoned by a ban, presumably meaning here an especially large army.

496. Alexander the Great, on his eastern campaigns, which began in Persia in 334 BCE and took him across the Indus River into India in 326, founded some twenty Alexandrias, but probably not this one. According to legend, he built a barrier against the northern nomads, who in medieval accounts became Gog and Magog (see Ch. 29, where another gate is mentioned but not called the Iron Gate; see Ch. 32 for the Alexander in India). This barrier was sometimes identified with Derbent (Persian *dar-band,* "gate" or "narrow passage"), between the Caucasus Mountains and the Caspian Sea, founded in the fifth century CE on a major caravan route between Europe and Asia.

[Chapter 28]

About the Empire of Persia. About the Land of Darkness and About Other Kingdoms from Cathay All the Way to the Greek Sea

Now, since I have described for you the land and the kingdoms towards the northern regions descending from the land of Cathay all the way to the land of the Christians towards Prussia and towards Russia, I will describe for you the other lands and kingdoms descending on the other side towards the right all the way to the Greek Sea towards the land of the Christians.[497] And because after [the emperor of] India and after [the emperor of] Cathay, the emperor of Persia is the greatest lord, I will speak first about the kingdom of Persia, where there are two kingdoms.

The first kingdom begins eastwards towards the kingdom of Turkestan and extends westwards right to the River Physoun [Phison], which is one of the four rivers that come from Paradise,[498] and northwards it extends right to the Caspian Sea, and southwards right to the desert of India. This land is good and level and well populated, and there are several good cities, but the two main ones are Boccura [Bokhara] and Seornegant [Samarkand], which some call Sormagant. The other kingdom of Persia extends by way of the River Physoun westwards right to the kingdom of Mede [Media] and to Greater Armenia, and northwards to the Caspian Sea, and southwards to the land of India. It is also a good country and fertile, and there are three main cities: Nessabor [Nishapur] and Saphaon [Ispahan] and Sarmassane.[499]

Next is Armenia, in which there used to be four kingdoms. It is a noble country and full of goods, and it begins at Persia and extends westwards in length right to Turkey, and in breadth it extends from the city of Alexandria—which is now called the Iron Gate, about which I spoke above[500]—to the kingdom of Mede. In this Armenia there are many good cities, but Tauriso [Tabriz] is the best known.

Next is the kingdom of Mede, which is very long but is not so wide, which begins eastwards at the land of Persia and at the land of India

---

497. Greek Sea: presumably the Black Sea. The *Mandeville* author here seems to be imagining a sphere (modeled on the T-O map discussed in Appendix C.1) with Cathay in the east, which would leave north to the left (Prussia and Russia) and south to the right (Persia); this is partly consistent with the views given in Chapter 20. Note that he does not speak of "Europe," but rather of Christendom. As in Chapter 27, he draws on Hayton, *Flor* 1.

498. On the rivers of Paradise, see Chapter 6, n. 74, and Chapter 33.

499. Sarmassane: not from Hayton but from a long poem about the First Crusade, the *Chanson d'Antioche* (DLMM 425, n. 4).

500. In Chapter 27.

Minor, and it extends westwards towards the kingdom of Caldee [Chaldea], and northwards it descends to Lesser Armenia. In this region of Mede there are many tall mountains and little flat land. There the Saracens dwell and a kind of people that are called Cordins [Kurds]. The two best cities of this kingdom are Saras [Shiraz] and Karemen [Kermanshah].

Next is the kingdom of Georgia, which begins eastwards at a large mountain that is called Abzor [Elbruz], where there dwell many different peoples of different nations, and the country is called Alamo [Alania]. This kingdom extends towards Turkey and the Great Sea, and northwards it borders on Greater Armenia. There are two kingdoms in this country: one is this kingdom of Georgia, and the other is the kingdom of Abchas [Abkhazia]. There are always two kings in the country and both [of them are] Christians, but the king of Georgia is subject to the Great Chan, and the king of Abchas has the stronger country and has always forcefully defended it against all those who have attacked it, so that they can never be made subject to anyone.

In this kingdom of Abchaz there is a great wonder, for one province of the country—which is a good three days' travel in circumference, and is called Hanyson [Hampasi]—is all covered in darkness without any light, such that no one can see and no one dares enter it. Nevertheless, those of the country say that sometimes peoples' voices can be heard, and horses whinnying, and cocks singing, and they indeed know for certain that there are people dwelling there, but no one knows which people. And they say that this darkness happened through God's miracle, for a wicked emperor of Persia who had the name Saures [Shapur II] used to persecute all Christians to sacrifice to his idols and used to ride everywhere with a conscript army to overthrow all Christians. In this country dwelt many good Christians who left all their goods and decided to flee to Greece. When they were on a plain that had the name Megon [Moghan], then the emperor came before them with all his army through a valley to slaughter all the Christians, and the Christians went down on their knees and made their prayer to God. Right away a thick cloud came and covered the emperor and all his army, and they endured there a very long time in such a manner that they could move neither forwards nor backwards, and they thus dwelt covered in this darkness such that they could never get out; and the Christians went away where they pleased, and their enemies dwelt enclosed and overthrown without a blow having been struck.[501]

---

501. Hayton not only concludes this story differently, leaving the Christians safely in darkness, he also introduces it differently: "In this kingdom of Georgia a great wonder can be seen that I would not dare to tell if I had not seen it. And because I was there and saw it, I dare to say and tell that in Georgia . . ." (1906, 129). The historical details of his story Hayton attributes to reading Armenian and Georgian histories.

We can well say indeed, "*A Domino factum est istud et est mirabile in oculis nostris.*"[502] This was a great miracle that God performed for them, and it is still visible there, which is why all Christians ought to be more devout towards Our Lord than they are, for without a doubt if there were no wickedness and sin amongst Christians, they would be lords of all the world. For the banner of Jesus Christ is always unfurled and ready to help his good servants. One true worthy man could put to flight one thousand wicked men, just as David says in the Psalter: "*Quomodo persequebatur unus mille et duo fugarent decem millia.*[503] *Et cadent a latere tuo mille et decem millia a dextris tuis.*"[504] And how this can be, that one person can put one thousand to flight, David himself says the following: "*Quia manus Domini fecit hec omnia.*"[505] And Our Lord Himself says through the mouth of the prophet: "*Si in viis mei ambulaveritis, super tribulantes vos mississem manum meam.*"[506] Such that we can see clearly that if we would be good, no enemy could last against us.

Also, out of this land of darkness comes a large river that indeed shows through signs that people dwell there, but no one dares enter. Know that in these kingdoms of Georgia, Abchaz [Abkhazia], and Lesser Armenia, they are good Christians and very devout, for they confess and take communion once or twice a week, and there are many who take communion every day and we do not do this over here, although Saint Paul commanded, "*Omnibus diebus dominicis ad communicandum hortor.*"[507] They keep this precept, but we do not keep it at all.

---

502. "This is the Lord's doing: and it is wonderful in our eyes" (Ps. 118[117]:23). This appended moral, which returns to *TBJM*'s concern with Christendom's shrunken state, is not in Hayton. The rapid marshalling of scriptural evidence suggests that the *Mandeville* author had religious training.

503. "How did one pursue after a thousand, and two chase ten thousand?" Not from the Psalter, nor from 1 Sam. 18:7 (as DLMM suggests, 425, n. 9), but adapted from Deut. 32:30, where the verb tenses are different (How should one pursue . . . ?).

504. "A thousand shall fall at thy side, and ten thousand at thy right hand" (Ps. 91[90]:7).

505. "Because the hand of the Lord hath made all these things." Cf. Job 12:9 ("*quis ignorat quod omnia haec manus Domini fecerit*"; "who is ignorant that the hand of the Lord hath made all these things?"). DLMM (425, n. 10) suggests Ps. 118[117]:16, which is less apropos.

506. "If you had walked in my ways, I would have laid my hand on those troubling you." DLMM (425, n. 11) cites Deut. 11:22–23. The closest sources seem to be Lev. 26:3 ("*si in praeceptis meis ambulaveritis et mandata mea custodieritis et feceritis ea dabo vobis pluvias temporibus suis*": "if you walk in my precepts, and keep my commandments, and do them, I will give you rain in due seasons"); and Ps. 80:15 ("*pro nihilo forsitan inimicos eorum humiliassem et super tribulantes eos misissem manum meam*": "I should soon have humbled their enemies, and laid my hand on them that troubled them").

507. "I urge you to take communion every Lord's Day [Sunday]." Not Paul but, as DLMM notes (425, n. 12), Gratian, *Decretum* 11.13: "*Cottidie eucharistiae communionem*

Also, after this [region] is Turkey, which borders on Greater Armenia, and there are many provinces: Liconie [Lycaonia], Capadoche [Cappadocia], Saure [Isauria], Questyon [Saruhanli?], Bryque [Phrygia], Pytan [Kemah?], and Gemyech [Paphlagonia].[508] And in each there are very fine cities. This Turkey extends right to the city of Sathala [Adalia], which is situated on the Greek Sea, and it borders on Syria. Syria is a large and fine country, as I have told you previously.

In addition, upwards towards India, there is the kingdom of Chaldea, which extends from the mountains of Chaldea eastwards right to the city of Nineveh, which is situated on the Tigris River, and in width it begins northwards at the city of Maraga [Maragheh] and extends southwards right to the Ocean Sea. In Chaldea there is level country and few mountains and few rivers. Next is the kingdom of Mesopotamia, which begins eastwards at the Tigris River at a city that has the name Mosel [Mosul], and it extends westwards right to the Euphrates River at a city that has the name Roaiz [Roha, or Edessa], and in breadth it goes from the mount of Armenia right to the desert of India Minor. It is a fine country, and flat, but there are few rivers. There are only two mountains in this country, one of which has the name Symar [Sindjar] and the other Lyson [Behsend?]. And this land borders on the kingdom of Chaldea.

In addition, there are towards the southern parts many countries and many regions, such as the land of Ethiopia, which borders to the east on large deserts, to the west on the kingdom of Nubia, and to the south on the kingdom of Moretane [Mauretania], and to the north on the Red Sea. Next is Moretane, which lasts from the mountains of Ethiopia right to Upper Libya, and this country lies all along the Ocean Sea to the south, and to the north it borders on Nubia and Upper Libya. Next is Nubia, where they are Christians, and it borders on these lands mentioned above and on the desert of Egypt, and this is the Egypt that I previously told you about. Then Upper Libya and then Lower Libya, which descends down towards the Great Sea of Spain, in the which countries there are many kingdoms and many diverse people.

Now have I described for you many countries on this side of the great kingdom of Cathay, many of which are obedient to the Great Chan.

---

accipere nec laudo, nec uitupero, omnibus tamen dominicis diebus communicandum hortor"; "I neither praise nor condemn receiving the communion of the Eucharist every day, yet I urge it every Lord's Day" (*Corpus Iuiris Canonici . . .* , ed. A. Friedberg [Leipzig, 1879], col. 1318). Gratian cites Augustine, *De ecclesiasticis dogmatibus* [*On Church Teachings*] 53, now attributed to Gennadius of Marseilles.

508. See DLMM (425, n. 13) on these places, most of which were provinces of the Seljuk Sultanate of Rum. Moseley (1983, 164) suggests Questyon: Lydia; Pytan: Bythnia; Gemyech: Paphlagonia.

[Chapter 29]

About the Countries and the Islands That Are Beyond the Land of Cathay and the Diverse Fruits There. About the Twenty-Two Kings Enclosed between Mountains

Now I will tell you in what follows about some countries and some islands that are over there, and I tell you that in passing through the land of Cathay towards upper India and Bachcharie [Bactria?] one passes through a region that is called Cadilhe [Kao-li, or Korea?], which is a very beautiful and large country.[509] A kind of fruit grows there like gourds, and when they are ripe they are split open in the middle and inside is found an animal of flesh and bone and blood—just like a little lamb without wool—that is eaten, both the fruit and the animal. It is indeed a great wonder, this fruit, and it is a great work of nature. Nevertheless, I said to them that I did not consider it a very great wonder, for there are also trees in our country that bear fruit which become flying birds and are good to eat; and those that fall into the water live, and those that fall to the ground die right away, and they were much amazed by this.[510]

In this country there are long apples that smell good and taste good, of which there are more than one hundred in a bunch and just as many in another [bunch], and they have large leaves, long and broad, of two feet long and more. In this country and in other countries roundabout grow many trees that bear clove-gillyflowers and nutmegs and large nuts of India and cinnamon and many other spices; and there are vines that bear such large grapes that a strong man would have considerable work to carry a single bunch of grapes in the whole cluster.[511]

In this same region are the mountains of Caspye that they call *Uber* in the country,[512] and between these mountains are enclosed the Jews of the Ten Tribes, who are called Goth and Magoth [Gog and Magog],[513]

---

509. The *Mandeville* author continues his digression from OP (used only for the legends discussed in n. 510 below).

510. OP's version is simpler (Ch. 27 in Appendix B.3); details added here come from Vincent of Beauvais, *Speculum Naturale* 16.40. The Vegetable Lamb may be cotton, a fern, or the fan mussel (Appleby 1997, supplementing WBJM 212–13, n. to 130, Ch. 29). The tree-born birds, often called Barnacle Geese, were well known: e.g., Gerald of Wales, *Topography of Ireland* 1.11, who says that here nature is acting *"contra naturam"* (see too WBJM 213–14, n. to 130, l. 18).

511. Long apples: plantains; clove-gillyflowers: cloves; "nuts of India": probably coconuts.

512. The Caspian Mountains were sometimes called *Ubera aquilonis* (Breasts of the North [Wind]).

513. This bizarre tale, a characteristic Latin Christian fusion of apocalypticism and anti-Semitism, is the *Mandeville* author's idiosyncratic version of a story that

and they cannot get out by any route. Twenty-two kings with their people were enclosed there who used to dwell between the mountains of Scythia. King Alexander drove them there between these mountains and thought to enclose them through the work of his men,[514] but when he saw that could not bring it to an end, he prayed to God of Nature that he would fulfill what he had begun, and although he was not worthy to be heard, nevertheless God with His grace closed the mountains together, such that they all dwell there locked up and completely enclosed by high mountains all around except on one side, and on that side is the sea of Caspye [Caspian Sea].

Now someone might ask, since the sea is on one side, why they do not leave by this sea to go where they would want to go, but to this I answer that this sea of Caspie comes out of the ground under these mountains and flows through the desert on one side of this country and then it stretches all the way to the ends of Asia. Although it is called a sea, it is not a sea and it touches no other sea; therefore it is a lake, the largest in the world. And even if they set out on this sea, they would not know where they would arrive, for they know no language but their own and therefore they cannot leave.

Know that the Jews do not have their own land [anywhere] in the whole world except this land between the mountains; and in addition they pay tribute from this land to the Queen of Amazonia, who keeps a very careful eye on them so that they do not come out towards her side of the land, for her land borders on these mountains. It has happened many times that some of these Jews have climbed there and come down through the mountains, but a large number of people could not climb out. For the mountains are high and steep so that they are there despite them,[515] for they have no way out but along a small path that was made by human effort and lasts for a good four leagues. And there is still more

---

uses several biblical and classical legends: Alexander the Great's enclosure of northern barbarians (Ch. 27, n. 496), traditionally under twenty-two kings; the Amazons (Ch. 17, n. 338); the ten "lost" tribes of northern Israel; and Gog and Magog. Ten of biblical Israel's original twelve tribes were led into captivity by the Assyrian king Salmanassar in the eight century BCE (2 Kings 17); they then disappeared from the record. Belief in their existence persisted in Jewish and Christian traditions, often in messianic thought. Usually placed vaguely in Ethiopia or Asia, they were from the thirteenth century on sometimes linked to the Mongols and Gog and Magog. The latter are biblical names (Ezek. 38–39 and Rev. 20:7–8) that were given various historical and allegorical meanings, often complex and contradictory (Westrem 1998); they too found their way into the Alexander legends (even into the Qur'an, 18.83–108) and apocalyptic thought. On this tale, see Akbari 2009, 136–40; DiMarco 1991; and Higgins 1997, 181–85.

514. This enclosure, called a gate below, was sometimes associated with the Iron Gate (Ch. 27 and n. 496 there), but not by the *Mandeville* author. Polo also mentions the Iron Gate, but corrects "the book of Alexander's" claim that it shut in the Tartars: it was the *Comains,* Cumans (1928, 16–17; 1958, 49).

515. Despite their efforts?

desert land where one cannot find water, either by digging a well or in any other way, which is why one cannot live in this place; and there are so many dragons, snakes, and poisonous animals in this place that no one can pass through, unless it is during a very fierce winter. They call this narrow passage Cliroun in the country, and it is the path that the Queen of Amazonia has guarded. Although some sometimes get out, they know no language but Hebrew and do not know how to speak to [other] people.

Nevertheless, it is said that they will come out in Antichrist's time and that they will slaughter a great many Christians. Therefore all the Jews that dwell throughout all lands always learn to speak Hebrew, in this hope that, when those of the mountains of Caspie come out, the other Jews know how to speak to them and lead them into Christendom to destroy Christians. For the other Jews say that they know well through their prophecies that those of Caspie will come out and spread throughout the world, and that furthermore Christians will be subject to them for as long as and longer than they have been subject to Christians.

If you want to know how they will find the way out, I will tell you according to what I have heard. In Antichrist's time a fox will make his den in that place where King Alexander had the gates made, and it will dig so much and pierce the earth that it will pass right through towards these people, and when they see this fox they will be amazed, because they have never before seen such an animal, for they have all other animals enclosed amongst them but foxes, and they will hunt it and pursue it until it goes back into its den. Then they will dig and pierce after [the fox], always following the den, until they find the gates that Alexander had built from large, well-cemented stones, and this gate, they will smash it and thus find their way out.[516]

From this land one goes towards the land of Bacherie [Bactria], where there is a very wicked and very cruel people. In this land there are trees that bear wool just like sheep from which one makes clothes to wear.[517] In this country there are many ypothames [hippopotamuses] that dwell sometimes on land, sometimes in water, and are half-man, half-horse, as I have told you previously, and they eat people when they can take them. And there are rivers and waters that are three times more bitter than sea water. In this country there are more griffons than elsewhere. Some people say that they have the body in front like an eagle and behind like a lion, and they speak the truth, because they are of this shape. But

---

516. This folktale ending has both literary and historical analogues (DLMM 432, n. 4); it may come from an apocryphal Latin letter of the 1230s or 1240s about the enclosed tribes (Burnett 1984; Burnett and Dalché 1991). In the thirteenth and fourteenth centuries, through an allegorical reading of Song of Sol. 2:15, foxes were often associated with heretics.

517. Cotton. The natural marvels come from the Alexander legends, with details from the encyclopedias.

a griffon has a body bigger and stronger than eight lions—of the lions over here—and more size and strength than one hundred eagles, for indeed it carries flying to its nest a large horse and takes it up, if it just finds [the horse], or two oxen harnessed together as one harnesses them to a cart, for it has talons on its front feet as big and as long as an ox's or a cow's horns, and one makes drinking goblets [from them] just like [those] one makes from the horns of wild oxen, and from the sides of the wing feathers one makes large and strong bows to shoot arrows.

From there one goes by many days' travel through the land of Prester John, the great emperor of India, and his kingdom is called the island of Pentoxoire.

[Chapter 30]

About Prester John's Royal Estate.[518] And About a Rich Man Who Made a Wonderful Castle and Called It Paradise

This Emperor Prester John possesses much land and many good cities and good towns in his kingdom and many diverse islands, large and wide, for this country of India is all divided by islands because of the large rivers that come from Paradise that divide all the land into many regions. And also in the sea there are many islands. The best city of the island of Pentoxoire[519] has the name Nyse, which is the royal city, very noble and very rich. Prester John has under him many kings and many islands and many diverse peoples, and his country is very good and very rich, but not so rich as that of the Great Chan; for the merchants do not go there as commonly to buy merchandise as they do in the Great Chan's Land, for it is too far, and on the other hand they find in the island of Cathay all that they need: silk, and spices, and gold cloth, and all goods sold by weight.[520]

---

518. *Estat:* "estate, status, standing, or condition." Prester John: the name of a legendary eastern priest-king ("prester" from "priest": cf. the explanation in Ch. 32) who enters the historical record in 1145 in Otto, Bishop of Freising's world history as a descendant of the Magi (Ch. 9, n. 120) who had hoped to liberate Jerusalem from Muslim rule. More influential than Otto's account was the Latin *LPJ,* probably written in the 1160s, recounting the wonders of his Christian kingdom (recently translated in *LPJ* 2005). *LPJ* develops the long-lived tradition of the Marvels of the East by bringing them under the sign of Christianity.

519. This name is from Long John's OP, which, like the Latin, notes that the Land does not live up to its reputation (Ch. 28 in Appendix B.3). The *Mandeville* author draws on *LPJ* and offers a more extensive account than any thirteenth- or fourteenth-century traveler, most of whom were also disappointed like Odoric.

520. *Toute avoir du poys:* "other riche thinges" in D and E (Seymour 2002, 114; WBJM 133).

Therefore, although they would get a better bargain in Prester John's Land, they are nevertheless afraid of the long way and the great dangers that are in the sea in these regions; for there are in many places in the sea large rocks of adamant stone, which has the property of drawing iron to it, and for that reason if any ship passes that had nails or iron strapping, right away those rocks would draw it to them and it could never get away from there.[521] I myself saw in this sea from afar what seemed a large island where there was a great abundance of shrubs and thorns and brambles. The sailors told us that this was all ships that had been thus stopped by the adamant rocks, and from the decay that was in the ships grows the great abundance of these shrubs and thorns and brambles and grass. There are such rocks in many places around there, and therefore the merchants dare not pass, unless they know the passages very well or have good pilots.

Also, they are very much afraid of the long route, and thus they take to the island of Cathay, which is closer; and it is not so close that it does not take eleven or twelve months to go by sea and by land from Genoa or Venice all the way to Cathay—and Prester John's Land is still many days' travel farther. The merchants pass through the kingdom of Persia and go to a city that has the name Hermes [Hormuz], for Hermes the philosopher founded it.[522] Then they cross an arm of the sea and then they go to another city that has the name Golbach [Cambaye], and there they find all [kinds of] merchandise—parrots as abundant as larks are here—and if they want to pass beyond they can go completely safely. In this country there is little wheat or barley, and so they eat only rice and honey and milk and cheese and fruit.

This Emperor Prester John always takes the Great Chan's daughter as his wife, and the Great Chan [takes] Prester John's daughter as well.[523] In Prester John's Land there are many diverse things and many precious stones so big and so broad that one makes dishes, plates, bowls, and goblets, and many other wonders that it would take too many words to put into writing. But I will tell you something about some main islands and about his estate and about his law [religion]. This Emperor Prester John is a Christian and a large part of his country as well, but all the same they do not have all the articles of the faith such as we have. They indeed believe in the Father and the Son and the Holy Spirit and are very devout and truly loyal to one another, but they do not care for disputes, or tricks, or fraud. There are under him seventy-two provinces, and in each province there is a king, and these kings have under them still other kings and all of them have to pay him tribute.

---

521. Adamant: see Chapter 17, n. 348. Not part of the Prester John legend.

522. Hormuz: mentioned as "Orynes" in Chapter 18.

523. OP mentions Prester John's marriage; the *Mandeville* author has it reciprocated (see also Ch. 26).

There are in his country many wonders, for in his country is the Sandy Sea, which is all sand and gravel without a drop of water, and it comes and goes in larger waves just as the other sea does. At no time and in no season does it stay calm or peaceful, and no one can cross this sea, whether by ship or otherwise, and therefore no one can know what land there is beyond this sea. Although it has no water, nevertheless good fish are found on the shores different in kind and shape from those that are found in other seas, and they are good tasting and delicious to eat. Three days' travel from this sea there are large mountains out of which flows a river that comes from Paradise, and it is entirely of precious stones without water, and it flows down through the desert in waves just as the Sandy Sea does, and it runs into that sea and disappears there. This river flows like that three days a week and brings with it large stones from the rocks that make a very loud noise, and as soon as they enter the Sandy Sea, they disappear and are all lost. On these three days that the river flows no one dares go into it, but on the other days one indeed goes in.

Also, beyond this river farther on in the deserts there is between the mountains a great plain [that is] completely sandy. On this plain every day at sunrise small shrubs begin to grow and they grow until noon and they bear fruit. But no one dares take this fruit, for it is like something bewitched. After midday they shrink and go back into the ground, such that at sunset they are no longer visible, and they do this every day and it is a great wonder. There are in this desert many wild men, horned, ugly, and they do not speak, but grumble like pigs. There is also a great abundance of wild dogs, and there are many parrots that they call *psytak* in their language,[524] and there are some that speak naturally and that greet the people who go through the deserts, and they speak almost as clearly as a person does: the ones that speak well have a large tongue and have five toes on each foot. There is another kind that have only three toes per foot and these do not speak at all or only a little and incomprehensibly and can do nothing but squawk.

This Emperor Prester John, when he goes into battle against some other lord, has no banners carried but rather has thirteen crosses made of fine gold borne ahead of him, large and tall, full of precious stones; and each of these crosses is set in a cart, and to guard each there are ten thousand men-at-arms and more than one hundred thousand foot soldiers in the manner that the standard is guarded in these regions when one goes to war. And this number of people is without [counting] the main army and the troops in battle formation. When he is not at war and when he rides in private company, he has only a simple unpainted wooden cross borne ahead of him, without gold and precious stones, in remembrance that Jesus Christ suffered death on a wooden cross. And he also has a gold plate full of earth borne ahead of him, to remind

---

524. *Psittacus:* Latin for parrot.

him that his nobility, his power, and his flesh will become earth and return to it; and another vessel made of silver with noble gold jewels and precious stones is carried along as a sign of his lordship and his nobility and his power.

He generally dwells in the city of Suse, and his chief palace is there which is so rich and so noble that its value cannot be calculated. Above the master tower of the palace are two round pommels of gold, and in each there are two large and wide carbuncles that shine very brightly at night.[525] And the main gates of this palace are [made] of a precious stone that is called sardonyx, the edges and the bars of ivory, and the windows of the halls and the rooms are of crystal. The tables where they eat, some are [made] of emeralds, others of amethyst, others of gold with precious stones; and the legs that hold up the tables are of the same stones. The steps to climb to the throne where he sits, the first is of onyx, the next of crystal, the next of green variegated jasper, the next of amethyst, the next of sardonyx, the next of cornelian, and the seventh on which he places his feet is of chrysolite; and all these steps are bordered with fine gold with other precious stones and large orient pearls. The sides of his seat are of emeralds both bordered with gold and most nobly adorned with other precious stones and large pearls. And all the pillars of his room are of fine gold with precious stones and carbuncles that give much light at night. Although the carbuncle gives enough light, nevertheless a crystal vessel full of balm is always burning to provide a good scent and drive away the bad air. The frame of his bed is of fine sapphires trimmed with gold to make him sleep better and to restrain his lust, for he will sleep with his wives only four times a year according to the four seasons, and that is only to beget children.

There is also a very beautiful and noble palace in the city of Nise where he stays when he likes, but the air is not so temperate as it is in the city of Suse. Throughout his country, and in all the countries around there, they eat only once a day, just as one does at the Great Chan's court. More than thirty thousand people dine every day at his court without [counting] guests and visitors, but the thirty thousand of his country or of the Great Chan's country do not consume as many goods as would twelve thousand from the country over here. He always has seven kings with him to serve him, and they leave monthly and others come back; and with these kings there always serve seventy-two dukes and three hundred and sixty counts, and every day there eat at his court twelve archbishops and twenty bishops. The patriarch of Saint Thomas is just like a pope, and the archbishops are all kings in that country, and so are the bishops and the abbots. Of his great lords, each knows

---

525. Carbuncle: a shiny red gemstone, including the ruby and the mythical stone here (see Ch. 25 for a ruby carbuncle). Details from King Porus' palace in the Alexander legends have been added to *LPJ*'s account.

how he should serve: one is chief steward, the next is chamberlain, the next serves the bowl, the next the cup, the next is seneschal, the next is marshal, the next prince of the shields,[526] and thus he is most nobly served. His lordship extends in breadth for four months' travel and in length without measure: namely, [to] all the islands under [the] earth that we call under.[527]

Beside the island of Pentoxoire that belongs to Prester John, there is a large, long, and wide island that is called Milstorak and it is in Prester John's lordship. On this island there is a great abundance of goods. There used to be there a rich man there, not very long ago, who was called Gathalonabez,[528] who was very rich and very well off, and he had a most beautiful castle on a mountain, as strong and as noble as anyone could design. He had the whole mountain encircled with very fine walls, and inside those walls he had the most beautiful garden that one might see where he had trees bearing all kinds of fruit that could be found nowhere else, and he had all sweet-smelling herbs planted [there] as well as all plants that bear beautiful flowers. There were, and still are, many beautiful fountains, and beside those fountains he had beautiful halls and beautiful rooms built, all painted in gold and azure, and he had many diverse things and diverse entertainments made, stories and diverse animals and birds that sang and revolved on their own[529] as if they were all alive. He put in that garden all kinds of birds that he could find and all the animals that one could take pleasure or delight in watching, and he put the most beautiful maidens under fifteen years old that he could find, and the most beautiful young men of the same age, and all were dressed in gold clothes, and he said that they were angels. He had three beautiful and noble fountains made all surrounded by stones of jasper and crystal and adorned with gold and precious stones

---

526. Meaning "master of the guard"?

527. This phrase is puzzling; in some Continental copies it reads "that we call the heavens" (DLMM 443, n. 10).

528. Perhaps from Arabic *Shaykh al-Jabal:* "Old Man [Chief] of the Mountain," as he appears in OP (Ch. 30 in Appendix B.3). Cf. Marco Polo's version (1928, 32–35; 1958, 70–73), which may have supplied some details (the piped drinks: wine in Long John's OP; wine and milk in the Latin OP; wine, milk, honey, and water in Polo); but if so the author has not followed Polo in making the Islamic context clear. This tale is a version of the Assassins legend, itself a distorted picture of the Nizari Isma'ilis, a sect born in the 1090s from dynastic strife amongst the Shi'ite Fatimids in North Africa that used assassination as a political weapon. "Milstorak" (from OP, in many scribal variants) may derive from Arabic *mulhid* (plural *mulahidah*), or "heretic," as other Muslims called the Isma'ilis. Historically, the fortress was Alamut, a mountain castle in Persia south of the Caspian Sea, captured in 1090 by Hasan-i Sabbah, the original "rich man" (his name may lie behind "Gathalonabez," but one scholar wants to link it to Arabic *qatala*, to kill: Metlitzki 1997, 298, n. 35).

529. *par engyn:* by means of some trick or mechanical aid.

and pearls, and he had pipes made under ground so that these three fountains [would flow] when he desired: he made one run with milk, the other with wine, and the other with honey.

This place he called Paradise, and when some good young knight who was worthy and bold came to see him, he led him into his Paradise and showed him the diverse things, and the amusements, and the diverse birdsongs, and the beautiful maidens, and the beautiful fountains of milk and wine and honey, and he had diverse musical instruments played in a high tower where the minstrels could not be seen, and he said that these were God's angels and that this was Paradise, which God had promised to those he loves, saying: *"Dabo vobis terram fluentem lacte et melle."*[530] Then he had them drink a beverage that made them drunk right away, and then it seemed to them a still greater pleasure than before. Then he told them that if they were willing to die for love of him they would come into this paradise after death and be at the age of these maidens and enjoy love-play with them and they [the maidens] would always remain virgins, and afterwards he would place them in a still more beautiful paradise where they would see God of Nature visibly in his majesty and in his glory. At that moment they would offer to do all his will, and then he told them that they should go and kill such [and such] lords who were his opponents and that they should not be afraid to be killed themselves for love of him, for he would place them after death in another paradise a hundred times more beautiful and they would remain there forever with the most beautiful maidens. Thus these young knights went and killed great lords of the country and were themselves killed in the hope of going into that Paradise, and thus this man avenged himself on his adversaries through these grand deceits.

When the rich men of the country perceived the treachery and the malice of this Gathalonobez, they gathered together and went to attack his castle, and they killed him, and destroyed all the beautiful places and all the splendors that were in this Paradise. The place still has fountains and some other things, and the walls, but the riches are gone, and it is not long since that the place was destroyed.[531]

---

530. "I will give you . . . a land flowing with milk and honey" (cf. Lev. 20:24; Exod. 33:3). This originally Islamic Paradise has now been given a Christian dimension.

531. Alamut, as OP and Polo both know, was taken by the Mongols: captured in 1256 by Hülegü's forces (Ch. 24, n. 465), but only partly destroyed. The Nizari Isma'ilis are known today through organizations named "Aga Khan . . ." (from the title of their hereditary ruler).

[Chapter 31]

About the Devil's Head in the Perilous Valley. And About the Peoples' Customs in Different Isles around There

Beside this isle of Milstorak on the left beside the River Phison,[532] there is a marvelous thing: it is a valley between the mountains that lasts for almost four leagues. Some call it the Enchanted Valley, some call it the Devil's Valley, and some the Perilous Valley. In this valley storms and great noises and uproars are often heard, every day and every night, and great sounds and great resounding noises of drums and kettledrums and trumpets, as if there were a great celebration.

This valley is completely full of devils and always has been, and people say that it is one of the entrances to Hell. In this valley there is much gold and much silver, and that is why many pagans, and many Christians too, often go into it to seek the treasure that is there. But few of them return—especially the pagans, and also the Christians who go because they are greedy to have things—for they are soon strangled by the Devil. In the middle of this valley under a rock are the head and the face of a devil most terrible to see, and only the head is visible, down to shoulders. But there is no one in the world so bold, Christian or other, who is not afraid when he sees it; and it seems to the onlooker that he must die, so hideous is it to see and so piercingly does it look at everyone; and it has such shifting and such flashing eyes, and it changes and shifts its expression and appearance so often that no one dare approach it; and from it come fire and smoke, and so much stench that one can hardly stand it. But all the same, the good Christians who are in good standing[533] and stable in the faith enter without danger, for they confess and make the sign of the cross over themselves so that the devils have no power over them. But although they are not in danger, they are not therefore without fear when they see the devils visible all around them, making many different assaults on them and threats both in the air and on the ground, and blows, and thunders, and storms; and people always fear that God might take vengeance for misdeeds done against His will.[534]

---

532. One of the four rivers of Eden, often identified with the Ganges (Ch. 6, n. 74, and Ch. 33). This story is from OP (Ch. 32 in Appendix B.3). Polo calls a "Desert of Lop" a "wonder" because it disoriented nocturnal travelers; his account has some details in common with OP's, but no Christian moral (1928, 43; 1958, 84–85). See also Seymour 2002, 167–68, n. to 120/15.

533. With God, as defined next. The head described above recalls the Leviathan's head in Job 41.

534. Michel Velser intervened here and below to authenticate this story in his German translation of *TBJM* (see Appendix A.4).

Know that when my companions and I were in this valley, we thought long and hard about whether we dared venture our bodies[535] and enter under God's protection, and some of [my] companions agreed, and some were opposed. There were with us there two worthy Friars Minor, who were from Lombardy,[536] who said that if there were any of us who wanted to enter, they would put us in good standing [with God] and go in with us. When these worthy men told us this, trusting in God and in them, we had mass sung and were confessed and took communion and entered, [all] fourteen [of us]. But on coming out there were only nine of us, and we did not know whether our companions had been lost, or whether they had returned and come out ahead [of us]. But nevertheless we have not seen them since, and they were two Greeks and three Spaniards. Our other companions who did not want to enter went by another route so as to be ahead of us, and so they were.

Thus we passed through the said valley, and in many places there saw gold and silver and precious stones and jewels in abundance on every side, as it seemed to us. But whether it was as it seemed to us, I do not know, for I never touched [anything], because the devils are so cunning that they often make nonexistent things appear so as to deceive people. For this reason I did not want to touch [anything], and also because I did not want to put myself out of my devout state; for I was more devout then than I have ever been since, as much out of terrible fear of the devils that I saw in many forms as because of the many dead bodies that I saw lying throughout the whole valley—so many that if there had been an all-out war between the two most powerful kings in the country, and the greater part were routed, there scarcely would have been as many dead as there were in this valley, which was a very hideous thing to see. I wondered at how many there were, and how the bodies of so many were still intact, for most seemed not to have rotted at all, but I believe the devils made them seem intact, for in my view it could not be because they had entered so recently, nor could there have been so many newly dead without rotting. Many were dressed as Christians, but I think that they had been deceived by the treasure they saw, because of great greed, or their hearts were too weak and they could not stand the fear.

---

535. The phrase *mettre le corps en aventure* evokes the world of chivalric romance (the Grail story especially): this is one of the few places where the author's claim to be a knight matters (as also when he claims to have served the Sultan and the Great Khan as a soldier).

536. Friars Minor: members of the mendicant Franciscan Order, founded early in the thirteenth century by Francis of Assisi; they were deeply involved in Asian missionary work (Ch. 18, n. 358). OP was a friar from northern Italy near Lombardy, so this may be a veiled "thank-you" from the *Mandeville* author, who has stolen the story from him.

Therefore we were much more devout,[537] and we were beaten to the ground many times by wind and thunder and storms, but God helped us the whole time. Thus we passed through the said valley without danger, thanks be to God.

[*This valley*[538] *has quite a beautiful entry and a beautiful route at the start, and the route is continually descending between the rocks, while narrowing now here, now there, and it is quite light there for the distance of half a league. Then it begins to darken, as between day and night, and when we had gone a long league, it became so dull and so dark that we could not see except as at night when the moon and the stars do not shine. Then we entered into total darkness that lasted a good league, and there we endured much and thought for certain we were lost, and we were in this situation, both the monks and others. For know that if any of us had been lord and ruler of all the earth, he would freely have renounced all worldly things, even if he had been out of danger, for truly we did not expect ever to report [this] news to the world. In this darkness, we were knocked to the ground more than a thousand times in many ways, such that we had hardly gotten up again before we were immediately knocked to the ground again, for there was such a great multitude of animals. But we could not see what animals they were, but all [were] like bears or black pigs and lots of other kinds [of animals] that ran through our legs that made us fall, sometimes face to face, sometimes beside each other, now to one side, and at other times head first as into a pit. Then we were knocked down by thunder, by lightning, by storms, and by great winds, and at times it seemed to us that we had been struck by a bar across the lower back; and we found so many dead under our feet who lamented that we passed overtop of them that it was a terrible thing to hear. I am sure that if we had not received the* Corpus Domini,[539] *we would all have been lost and remained [there].*

In this place each of us had a mark, for there each of us was struck hard and so much that we long remained in swoons. But in these swoons we saw spiritually many wonders about which I dare not speak, for the monks who were with

---

537. Between this word and the next, Continental has considerable additional material, given in bracketed italics immediately following this Insular close. Up to here, Insular as edited by Deluz differs only in a few insignificant details from the critical text of Continental in de Poerck 1955, 140–54.

538. From de Poerck 1955, 140–54; his text varies somewhat from that in DLMM 485–86. This is the most important textual difference between Continental and Insular (on which see Appendix A.1). On the available evidence it is impossible to know whether it is authorial (thus deliberately cut or inadvertently omitted from Insular) or whether it was added by an early intermediary. A close reading suggests the latter: the visionary climax in particular is uncharacteristic (Higgins 1997, 206–16). DLMM considers it scribal (455, n. 3; cf. also 486).

539. "Our Lord's body": the Eucharist. The dead lamenting underfoot recall Dante, *Inferno* 23, where Virgil and Dante, walking like Friars Minor and descending surrounded by devils, meet the hypocrites who, weighed down by gold cloaks, walk over Caiaphas' outstretched body (the high priest who in the Gospels allows Jesus to be crucified: see Ch. 2).

us prohibited all of us from speaking except about what we saw bodily, so as to conceal Our Lord's secrets. We were struck in many places, and in this place each of us had a black spot as big as a hand, one person in the face, another on the chest, another on the side, and on the neck. I was struck on the neck in such a way that I thought my head had been severed from my neck, and I bore the mark black as coal for more than eighteen years. But after I repented of my sins and took pains to serve God according to my weakness, that stain vanished and the skin is whiter in this place than anywhere else. But yet the blow is clearly visible there, and will be visible there so long as the flesh lasts. This is why I advise no one to go into this valley, for in my opinion it is not pleasing to Our Lord that anyone go in there.

Also, when we were as if in the middle of this darkness, we saw that hideous figure quite deep under the rock, one time near, another time far away, which burned and sparked, and the fire that was all around it did not glow at all. But nevertheless we found it so hideous that we dared not look at it, and we had there so much stench that we almost died and barely succeeded in staying alive. We passed beyond this great hardship when we passed through the darkness, and we came back to the light. We were much relieved, although we had been much bothered and tormented by devils that attacked us in many forms. I would not know how to say or tell what we saw, for I was too concerned with prayers and devotions. Then we were again knocked to the ground many times by wind, by thunder, and by storm[s], but God through his grace always helped us and thus we passed through the said valley without harm and without hindrance, thanks to God.]

Later beyond this valley there is a large island where the people are quite as big as giants twenty-eight or thirty feet tall,[540] and they have no clothes but animal skins that they hang on them, and they eat no bread except raw flesh, and they drink milk, for they have enough animals, and they have no houses, and they eat human flesh more willingly than any other flesh. No one willingly enters there nor approaches the island, for if they see a ship and people in it, they go into the sea right afterwards to catch it. Yet we were told that on another island over there, there were considerably bigger giants, such as forty-five or fifty feet tall, and some said fifty cubits tall,[541] but I never saw them nor did I have any desire to go there, for no one goes to one island or another there who would not be devoured. Amongst these giants there are sheep as big as oxen are here, and they have very thick wool to match; I have seen some of them many times. And these giants have many times been seen catching people in the sea and carrying them to land, two in one hand and two in the other, and eating them completely raw while walking.

---

540. The catalogue that follows (see Ch. 16, n. 317) mostly adapts material from Vincent of Beauvais, *Speculum Historiale* 1.88–93. The personal testimony is thus as fictional as the journey above. For helpful notes on the wonders, see Seymour 2002, 168–69.

541. Cubit: see Chapter 2, n. 15.

There is another island southwards in the Ocean Sea where there are many wicked and very cruel women, and they have precious stones in their eyes, and their nature is such that if they look at someone in anger, they kill him just by looking, as the basilisk does.

There is another island, very beautiful and good, and large and well-populated, where the custom is such that on the first night that they are married they have another man lie with their wives to take their virginity and they give them a good reward for this. There are certain officials in each town who perform no other service whom they call *Cadebiriz*—that is to say, hopeless fools—for those of the country consider it such a great task and so dangerous to take a wife's virginity that it seems to them that those who take wives' virginity put themselves at risk of death. If the husband finds his wife a virgin on the next night, after the other has not taken her virginity because of drunkenness or for some other reason, he will lodge a complaint against the official for not having done his duty, as if the official wished to kill him. But after the first night that they lose their virginity, the wives are watched so closely that they are never so bold as to dare speak to anyone. But I asked about the reason why such a custom was kept, and they told me that a long time ago some men had died taking the virginity of their wives, who had snakes in their body; therefore they keep this custom and they always have someone else try out the passage before they endanger themselves.

After there is another island where the women mourn a great deal when their children are born, and when they [the children] die they celebrate with great revelry and great joy and throw them into a large fire and burn them; and those who really loved their husbands, if their husbands are dead, they throw themselves into the fire with their children and burn themselves, and they say that the fire cleanses them of all filth and all vices, and they go pure and clean into the other world to their husbands, and they bring their children with them. The reason why they cry when the child is born, and why they rejoice when it dies, is that when the child is born, it comes into this world to work, pain, and sorrow, and when it dies it goes into paradise, they say, where the rivers are of milk and honey, where one lives in joy and an abundance of goods without work and without pain.

On this island they always make their king by election, and they never choose the noblest and the richest, but the one who has been morally good and righteous, and who is of a great age, and who has no children. On this island they are very just and they judge everyone rightfully, both the great and the small, according to the misdeed that he has done, and the king cannot put a man to death without his barons' advice, and the whole court must agree. If the king himself commits a murder or some other crime, he must die just like any other man. Not that someone kills him, but they forbid anyone to be so bold as to associate with him, or speak with him, nor would anyone sell him anything, nor would anyone serve him or give him anything to eat or to drink, and thus he must die in misery. They spare no one who has committed a misdeed, not out of love, nor goodwill, nor wealth, nor nobility, so that one faces justice according to the deed.

Beyond this island there is another island where there is a great abundance of people and they do not eat for anything the flesh of the hare, the hen, or the goose, and they raise them in that case only to see them and look at them; and they eat the flesh of all other animals and drink milk. In this country they take their daughters and their sisters as wives, and their other relatives, and if there are ten or twelve or more men in a house, the wife of each will be common to all those of the household, such that each man will sleep with the woman he chooses, one night with one, and another night with another. If there is any child begotten on any of them, she will give the child to the one who first slept with her, such that no one knows whether the child is his or another's, and if they are told that they thus bring up others' children, they answer that others do the same with theirs.

In this country and throughout all of India there is a great abundance of crocodiles, which is a kind of long snake, as I told you earlier,[542] and by night they dwell in the water, and by day on land in rocks and in caves, and they do not eat at all throughout the whole winter, but rather lie in distress[543] as the snakes do. This snake kills people and cries while eating them, and when they eat they move the upper jaw and not the lower, and they have no tongue whatsoever. In this country and in many others over there, and also in many over here, cotton seed is prepared and sown every year, and small bushes grow that bear the cotton, and this is done every year, and there is cotton everywhere in great abundance. Also, on this island and on many others there is a kind of hard and strong wood. Whoever covers the coals of this wood under the ashes, the coals will keep and last completely live for a year or more, and this tree has many leaves like the juniper. There are also many trees of a wood[544] that cannot burn or rot in any way, and there are nut trees that bear nuts as big as a man's head. There are also many giraffes there; in Arabia they call them *gerfancz*. It is a spotted animal, which is not taller than a warhorse, but it has a neck a good twenty cubits long, and it has the crupper and the tail like a stag, and it can look over quite a high house.[545] In this country there are many chameleons. It is a small animal like a wild goat and it always walks open-mouthed because it lives on air and never eats or drinks and often changes and transforms its color, for it is seen at

---

542. In Chapter 21. Moving to marvelous natural history, the *Mandeville* author turns to other sources: Brunetto Latin, *Tresor;* Jacques de Vitry, *Historia Orientalis;* Vincent of Beauvais, *Speculum Naturale.*

543. This is hibernation from a human point of view. Cf. C: "as in a drem" (HMT 1.192); and E: "as thai ware half deed" (WBJM 142).

544. *de bonnis:* uncertain; "wood" is an inference from the context.

545. Displaced from WoB's account of Cairo (Ch. 3 in Appendix B.1).

one time in one color and at another time in another, and it can change itself into any color it wants except red and white.

There are also large and thick snakes there one hundred and twenty feet long, and they are of different colors: striped, red, green, yellow, indigo, black, and all spotted. There are others that have crested heads and walk on their feet almost upright, and they are a good four fathoms big or more, and they always live in the rocks and in the mountains, and they always have their mouths open from which they always drool poison. There are wild pigs of many colors as big as the big oxen of this country are, and they are spotted in the manner of young fawns; and there are also hedgehogs as big as wild pigs are here; we call them porcupines.[546] There are completely white lions, large and powerful, and there are other animals as large as and larger than large warhorses, and they are called *loherans,* and others call them *odenthos.* They have a very black head and three large horns on the forehead as sharp as a sword, and the body is dun-colored, and it is a very cruel beast and it chases and kills the elephants.[547] There are still other very malign and very cruel animals that are not bigger than a bear and have the head like a boar's; and they have six feet, and on each foot two large and sharp talons, and they have the body like a bear's and the tail like a lion's. There are mice as big as dogs and bats as big as ravens, and there are red geese three times as big as ours over here, and they have the head, the neck, and the breast all black. There are many other kinds of animal in this country and elsewhere around there and many diverse birds, a full account of which would take too many words.

[Chapter 32]

About the Goodness of the People on the Island of Bragmey.
About King Alexander, and How Prester John Got His Name

Beyond this island there is another large and good and bountiful island where there are good and trustworthy people, and of a good way of life according to their belief and of good faith, and although they are not Christians and do not have perfect law, nevertheless through natural law[548] they are full of all virtues and they flee all vices and all wickedness and all sins. For they are not proud, nor greedy, nor slothful, nor

---

546. The marvelous bestiary here comes from the Alexander legends.

547. Presumably a rhinoceros.

548. "Natural law" inhered in God's created world and could thus be known by human reason; it stands in contrast to "perfect law," the religion fulfilled by the revelation of Jesus Christ known through the Gospels (the Ten Commandments, accepted by Christians, are here regarded as part of Mosaic law: God's revelation to the Israelites through Moses).

envious, nor angry, nor gluttonous, nor lustful, and they do unto others only what they want done unto them, and in this custom they fulfill the Ten Commandments. They are not concerned with goods or wealth, and they do not lie at all, and they do not swear oaths for any reason, but simply say yes and no. For they say that whoever swears wants to deceive his neighbor, and therefore whatever they do they do it without oaths. This island is called the island of Bragmey, and others call it the Land of Faith.[549] Through it flows a large river that has the name Thebe. Generally all the peoples of the islands there around those far countries are more trustworthy and just than they are anywhere else. On this island there is no robber, no murderer, no loose woman, no poor beggar, nor has anyone ever killed in this land, and they are so chaste and lead such a good life that no monks could do it, and they fast every day. Because they are so trustworthy and so just and full of such good qualities, there have never been storms or lightning, nor hail, nor any plague, nor war, nor famine, nor other tribulation such as we have many times had over here for our sins.[550]

This is why it appears that God loves them and favorably accepts their belief and their good works. They indeed believe in God who created and made all things and they worship him, and value as nothing all earthly goods, and they are all just, and live so reasonably and so moderately in eating and drinking that they live very long, and most of them die without having been sick when nature fails in them because of old age.

In the distant past King Alexander sent [someone] to reconnoiter these islanders because he wanted to win their country, and they sent him messengers bearing letters through the country that said this: "What could be enough for the man for whom the whole world does not suffice? You will find nothing in us for which you should make war against us, for we have no wealth, nor do we desire any, and all the goods of our country are common. Our wealth lies in what we eat to sustain our bodies and, instead of gold or silver treasure, we make a treasure of

---

549. Leaving OP aside again, the *Mandeville* author adds material deriving ultimately from Antiquity. Likely sources: Vincent of Beauvais, *Speculum Historiale* 4.66–71, and *Speculum Naturale* 31.129; Jacques de Vitry, *Historia Orientalis* 3; the thirteenth-century *Prose Alexander Romance*. The account of Bragmey, Oxidrate, and Gynosophe (see n. 551 in this chapter) is elaborated from the Alexander legends to fit his concern with religious practice (Higgins 1997, 228–31).

550. If *TBJM* was written in the later 1350s, this claim would have resonated with the original readers. The Black Death had killed perhaps one third of the population in the later 1340s, greatly altering economic and social relations. The Hundred Years' War between England and France had begun in the late 1330s. A peasants' rebellion (the Jacquerie) had occurred in northern France in 1358, the first of several in Latin Christendom. Serious famines occurred early in the century and global temperatures had begun to cool, the beginning, according to some climate scientists, of the Little Ice Age.

harmony and peace and love of one another, and for bodily adornment we use a poor cloth to wrap our carrion flesh. Our wives are not adorned to please, but rather they consider beautiful adornment foolish, when pains are taken to beautify the body to make it seem more beautiful than God has made it. They do not know how to ask for more beauty than God gave them at birth. The earth provides us with two things: the necessities of life while we live, and our graves after death. We have had perpetual peace until now, of which you want to dispossess us, and we have a king, not to do justice, for he would find no wrongdoers, but to maintain nobility and to teach us to be obedient, for justice has no place amongst us, for we do unto others what we would want them to do unto us. Justice and vengeance have nothing to do amongst us, such that you can deprive us of nothing but good peace, which has always been there." When Alexander read these letters, he thought that he would do too much harm if he disturbed them, and he sent them written assurances that they did not have to guard against him and that he would maintain their good customs and their good peace to which they had been accustomed.

There is another island that is called Oxidrate and another that is called Gynosophe,[551] where there is also a good and trustworthy people and full of good faith, and they follow a good many of the customs and the good habits that those mentioned above do, and they always go about completely naked. King Alexander came to these islands, and when he saw their good faith and their great loyalty he told them that he would not harm them and that they should ask for what they wanted, wealth or something else. They answered that whoever had something to eat and drink to sustain the body was rich enough, and that the riches of this transitory world were worth nothing, but if he could make them immortal, they would thank him. Alexander answered that he could not do that, for he was mortal as they were. "Why then," they said, "are you so arrogant and so proud that you want to make the whole world subject to you as if you were God? You do not have [the] end to your life, neither [the] day nor [the] hour, and [yet you] want to collect everything in the world, which will leave you swiftly when you leave it. Just as things were to others before you, so will they be to others after you. You will

---

551. In the Punjab in 326 BCE Alexander the Great encountered "naked philosophers," gymnosophists. In the Alexander legends they became a people, also called Brahmans (the Hindu priestly caste), and *Oxydorkai* or *Oxydrakai,* the Greek name for the Khshudrakas, a warrior people of the Indus. The *Mandeville* author gives these names to three islands, but follows a common tradition in recording *two* encounters between Alexander and Indian ascetics. In them the author offers his interpretation of a well-known imaginary correspondence between Alexander and Dindimus (Dandamis), king of the Brahmans, in which ascetic and worldly values are debated. See Cary 1956, 13–14, 91–95; Hahn 1978; Ross 1988, 30–32; and Stoneman 2008, 91–106. Cf. also Polo on the "*Abraiaman*" (1928, 189–91; 1958, 277–79).

take nothing with you, but just as you were born naked, your body will be covered completely naked in the earth from which it was made. You ought to consider that no one is immortal except God who created everything."[552] Alexander was completely amazed by this answer.

Although this people do not have the articles of the faith such as we have, nevertheless for their natural good faith and for their goodwill I believe it to be certain that God loves them and that God favorably receives their service just as He did from Job, who was pagan; all the same, He accepted him as his loyal servant. Therefore although there are many diverse laws [religions] throughout the world, I believe that God always loves those who love him and serve humbly in virtue and loyalty and who do not value the vainglory of this world, just as these people do, and as Job likewise did.[553] That is why Our Lord said through the mouth of His prophet Hosea: "*Ponam eis multiplices leges meas.*"[554] And elsewhere: "*Qui totum orbem subdit suis legibus.*"[555] Also, Our Lord says in the Gospel: "*Alias oves habeo qe non sunt ex hoc ovili.*"[556] That is to say that He had other servants than [those] under Christian law.

This accords with the vision that Saint Peter the Apostle saw in Jaffa, how the angel came down from Heaven and brought before him a great abundance of all kinds of diverse animals and snakes and other reptiles of earth, and said to Saint Peter: "Take and eat." And Saint Peter answered: "I will never eat unclean animals." And the angel said to him: "*Non dicas immunda que Deus mundavit.*"[557] And this was a sign that one ought not to despise any earthly people for their diverse laws, nor any one person. For we do not know whom God loves and whom he hates. Because of these examples some people, when they say the *De profundis,*

---

552. This pious response seems to be the *Mandeville* author's own elaboration: Alexander is usually asked why he goes about doing wicked deeds. Cf. Sir John's exchange with the Sultan (Ch. 15).

553. Job: see Chapter 17. See Chapter 34 for an elaboration of the claims made here.

554. "I shall place my many laws on them." Cf. Hos. 8:12: "*scribam ei [Ephraim]*" ("I shall write to him").

555. "He who places the whole world under his laws." Lengeler (1992, 95–96) suggests that this may paraphrase Esther 13:2, a deuterocanonical passage translated by Jerome, but it appears almost verbatim in three texts: the weekly Office of Mary in the *Officium Marianum Ordinis Sancte Birgitte per hebdomadam* (Copenhagen, Royal Library CMB MS Thott 4° 538, fol. 4 [probably made in Utrecht, c. 1485–1490]; see http://www.chd.dk/thott/thott538.html); and the responsories of the *De Trinitate* (under *in tercio nocturno*) in two other manuscripts (Perugia, Biblioteca Comunale "Augusta," MS 2787, fol. 46v; and State Library of Victoria, MS *096.1 R66A: The Poissy Antiphonal, fol. 156v; see www.lib.latrobe.edu.au/MMDB/Feasts/l09011000.htm). Sites revisited May 11, 2009.

556. "And other sheep I have, that are not of this fold" (John 10:16).

557. "Do not call unclean what God has made clean" (Acts 10:11–15).

they say in joining together with the Christians "*Pro animabus omnium defunctorum pro quibus sit exorandum.*"[558]

Therefore I say of this people that they are so faithful that God loves them, for there are amongst them many prophets and there always have been; and on these islands they prophesied the Incarnation of Our Lord Jesus Christ, how he would be born of a virgin three thousand or more years before Our Lord was born of the Virgin Mary. They believe perfectly well in the Incarnation, but they do not well know the way in which He suffered passion and death for us.[559]

Beyond these islands there is another island that has the name Pytan. The people of this island neither cultivate nor work the land, for they do not eat, and they are of good color and beautiful shape according to their size, but they are small as dwarves, but not so small as the Pygmies are.[560] They live on the scent of wild apples and, when they go somewhere far, they take some wild apples with them, for if they lost their scent, they would die right away. They have little capacity for reason, but are very simple and completely animal-like. Then there is another island where the people are all hairy except for the face and the hands. This people move as well under the sea as they do on dry land, and they eat meat and fish completely raw. On this island there is a large river that is a good two and a half leagues wide that is called Buemar.

Fifteen days' travel away from this river through the deserts on the other side of the river—whoever might go there, for I was not there,[561] but we were told by those of the country that within this desert are the Tree of the Sun and [that] of the Moon that spoke to King Alexander and described his death to him. It is said that the people who look after these trees and eat the fruit of these trees and the balm that grows there live for a good four or five hundred years through the power of the fruit and the balm. For it is said there that a great abundance of balm grows

558. "For the souls of all the dead for whom prayers are to be offered": no known source. *De profundis:* "out of the depths" (Ps. 129[130]:1), used as a penitential psalm, chanted in funeral processions, and read in the Office of the Dead at Lauds and Vespers.

559. Cf. Hermes the Wise's similar prophecy in Chapter 3. The twelfth-century philosopher Abelard considered Dindimus one of four royal pre-Christian prophets of Christ (Cary 1956, 93). The argument that culminates here partly contradicts the Fourth Lateran Council (1215) whose first canon declared: "there is one universal church, outside of which there is no salvation." As the Latin Christian sense of the world's vastness expanded, some writers (e.g., William Langland, likely author of *Piers Plowman,* Julian of Norwich, and Margery Kempe) wondered at the possible injustice of so many damned souls.

560. Pygmies: see Chapter 22. Except for the small people, who belong to the wonders of India, the material of this paragraph and the next comes from the Alexander legends.

561. The *Mandeville* author declines here (as also in Ch. 33) to place himself on Alexander the Great's level as a traveler.

there and nowhere else except Babylon, as I told you previously.[562] We would have very willingly gone towards these trees, if we had been able to, but I do not believe that one hundred thousand armed men could safely cross those deserts there because of the great multitude of wild animals and large dragons and large snakes that are there and that kill and devour whatever they can catch. In this country there are countless white and grey elephants, and unicorns and lions of several kinds, and many animals such as I have described before and countless others that are very ugly. There are many other islands in Prester John's Land and many wonders that it would be too long to recount, and there is much wealth and nobility and a great abundance of precious stones.

I believe that you indeed know and have heard it said why this emperor is called Prester John, but yet for those who do not know I will briefly set down the reason. There was once an emperor who was a very brave prince and had Christian knights in his company like those that he has now, and he desired to see the manner of the service in the church of the Christians. At that time Christendom extended beyond the sea: all Turkey, Syria, Tartary, Jerusalem, Palestine, Arabia, Aleppo, and all the land of Egypt. This emperor came with a Christian knight into a church of Egypt, and it was a Saturday after Pentecost when the bishop performed the ordinations; and he watched and heard the service and asked what people they might be that the prelate had in front of him where he had so many great rites to perform. The knight answered him that they were priests; and he said that he would no longer be called king or emperor, but priest, and he wished to have the name of the first priest who came out [of the church], the one who had the name John. Ever since he has been called Prester John.[563]

In his land there are many Christians of good faith and good law and in particular those of the same country [as Prester John], and they all commonly have their chaplains who sing the mass and make the sacrament of the altar from bread as the Greeks do.[564] But they do not say as many things at the mass as one does over here, for they say only what Our Lord's Apostles taught them, such as Saint Peter and Saint Thomas and the other Apostles sung the mass, saying *Pater Noster*[565] and the words with which Our Lord's body is consecrated. But we have many additions that the popes have since made about which they know nothing.

---

562. In Chapter 7.

563. *Priest:* post-classical Latin *presbyter,* elder, via French, where it could be spelled *prestre:* hence "Prester" John. No source has been found for this explanation. See Appendix A.2 for L's different explanation.

564. See Chapter 3.

565. See Chapter 10, n. 146.

[Chapter 33]

About the Mountains of Gold That the Ants Guard and the Four Rivers That Come from [the] Earthly Paradise

Towards the eastern part of Prester John's Land there is a good and large island that is called Taprobane,[566] which is very noble and very fertile. The very rich king here is under Prester John's authority, and the king is always made by election. On this island there are two summers and two winters, and the grain is harvested twice a year, and the gardens flourish in all seasons of the year. Good people capable of reason dwell there and many Christians with them who are so rich that they do not know how much they have. In the old days when one crossed in the old ships from Prester John's Land to this island, it took twenty-three days or more to cross, and in the ships that are now made it takes seven days to cross the water. The bottom of the water can be seen in many places, for it is not very deep at all.

Beside this island towards the east there are two other islands that are called Orille (the first one) and Argite (the other one), whose entire land consists of a gold and silver mine, and these islands are at the place where the Red Sea separates from the Ocean Sea. On these islands no stars can be seen that appear clearly there, except one bright star that they call Canapos,[567] and the moon cannot be seen at all except in the second quarter of its cycle.

On the island of Taprobane there are also large mountains of gold that the ants guard carefully, and they refine and separate the pure from the impure; and the ants are as big as dogs, such that the people dare not approach these mountains, for the ants would attack them, and they cannot have any of this gold unless it is through a great ruse.[568] Therefore, when it is intensely hot, the ants hide in the ground from terce until none,[569] and at this time the people take camels, dromedaries, mares, and other animals and they go to load them very stealthily and then they flee before the ants come out of the ground. At other times when it is not so hot and the ants do not hide at all, they do this

---

566. Taprobane (possibly from the Sanskrit *Tamraparni*): the Greek name for Sri Lanka, which, following OP, the *Mandeville* author already described in Chapter 21 as Silha (presumably from the ancient Indian name for the island, *Sihala-dipa*). He seems unaware that they are the same place.

567. Canopus: see Appendix C.1.

568. This legend goes back to Herodotus (fifth century BCE), but is mentioned in most of the *Mandeville* author's encyclopedic sources (see Gervase 2002, 698, n. 5). The first ruse appears in *LPJ* (D redaction: 1879, 911), the second in Guillaume Le Clerc's early thirteenth-century *Bestiary* (1852, 222–23; 1892, 264–66).

569. "Terce": mid-morning; "none": mid-afternoon (see Ch. 16, n. 323, and Ch. 18, n. 351).

in another way. They take mares that have small foals and place on the mares two empty containers like small coffers, and these are open on top and hang almost to the ground. Then they send these mares to graze around these mountains and they hold the foals back, and when the ants see these vessels they leap up and climb in. Their nature is such that they leave nothing empty around them, whether a hole in the ground or anything else, and these ants fill these vessels with this gold. When the people think that the mares are loaded with enough of it, they let the foals out and make them whinny, and right away the mares come fleeing back towards the foals, and they unload the mare, and thus they have plenty of gold, for these ants allow other animals amongst them, but they will not allow human beings.

Beyond the land and the islands and the desert of Prester John's lordship in going straight towards the east, one finds nothing but mountains and large rocks and the dark region, where one cannot see by night or by day, as those of the country testify. This desert and this dark place last from this side all the way to [the] Earthly Paradise, where Adam our first father and Eve (who were barely there) were placed, which is eastwards at the beginning of the earth.[570] But this is not our east over here that we call east, where the sun rises on us, for when the sun is east towards those regions of Paradise, it is then midnight in our regions over here because of the roundness of the earth, [a subject] that I have previously spoken to you about.[571] For Our Lord made the earth round in the middle of the firmament, and that it should have mountains and valleys, this is only because Noah's Flood destroyed the soft and delicate earth and the hard earth and rock remained mountains.[572]

About Paradise I would not know how to speak to you properly, for I was not so far forward, because I was not worthy.[573] But what I have heard said by the wisest men over there I will willingly tell you. Earthly Paradise—they say this is the highest land in the world, and it is so high that it almost touches the circle of the moon by which the moon makes its turn, for it is so high that Noah's Flood (which covered all the land in the world all around both above and below, except only Paradise)

---

570. Adam's creation outside Paradise (in Damascus) is mentioned by Gervase of Tilbury (*Otia* 1.10) and Peter Comestor (*Historia Scholastica,* Gen. 14); both may also have supplied other details of this composite account of Paradise. The claim that the earth has a beginning need not imply a flat earth.

571. In Chapter 20. Discussing the sun's course, Brunetto Latini makes the same point about east having a relational rather than fixed location (*Tresor* 1.112).

572. Located in the sub-lunar realm of change and sin, the earth is the one imperfect sphere in the Ptolemaic cosmos (see Appendix C.1).

573. As in Chapter 32, the *Mandeville* author declines to equal Alexander the Great's achievements, even as he borrows details from his legends (in this case, that the general reached Paradise).

was not able to reach it.[574] Paradise is enclosed all around by a wall—no one knows what it is made of—and the walls are all covered with moss, it seems, and no stone or anything else of which the wall might be made can be seen, and the wall stretches from north to south, and there is only one entrance, which is closed by a burning flame, so that no mortal human being might enter.[575] In the highest place in Paradise right in the middle is the spring that casts out the four rivers that flow through diverse lands, of which the first has the name Physon or Ganges—it is the same [river]—and it flows through India or Evilat; in this river there are many precious stones and much *lignum aloes* and much gold gravel.[576] The next river has the name Nilus or Gyon; it flows through Ethiopia and then Egypt. And the next has the name Tigris; it flows through Assyria and Greater Armenia. And the next has the name Euphrates; it also flows through Mede [Medea?], Armenia, and Persia. Over there it is said that all the fresh waters of the world above and below have their origin in this well of Paradise, and from this spring they all come and flow out.

The first river has the name Physon, that is to say *gathering* in their language, for many other rivers join together and flow into this river; and some call it Ganges because of a king who was in India who had the name Gangares, for it flowed through his land. This river is clear in some places, and murky in some places, hot in some places, and cold in some places. The second river has the name Nilus or Gion, for it is always murky; and Gion in the language of Ethiopia means *murky;* also, Nile in the language of Egypt is to say *murky.* The third river has the name Tigris, which in their language means *fast-flowing,* for it flows faster than any other, and an animal is also called Tigris because it is fast-running. The fourth river has the name Euphrates, that is to say *well-bearing,* for many goods grow on that river, both grains and fruits and all other goods.

Know that no mortal human being can go to or approach this Paradise, for no one may go by land because of the wild animals that are in the wild places, and because of the mountains and because of the rocks where no one may pass through the dark places, of which there are many. And no one may go by the rivers, for the water flows so violently because it comes from high up, and it comes in such large waves that no ship may move against it, and the water roars and makes such a loud noise and so great a storm that one person could not hear another in the

---

574. The wise men's information is found in Gervase (n. 570 above), who, to forestall surprise, adds the story about Olympus' thin air related in Chapter 3 (*Otia* 1.11).

575. A flaming sword in Gen. 3:24. Moss-covered wall: from the legend of Alexander's journey to Paradise.

576. Four rivers: Gen. 2:10–14. India or Evilat: see Chapter 17, n. 343. *Lignum aloes:* see Chapter 8, n. 93.

ship, even if one shouted to another as loud as they could. Many great and very willful lords have many times attempted to go by these rivers towards Paradise and with large companies, but they were never able to complete their journey; rather, many died of fatigue from the movement against the waves and many others went blind and many deaf because of the noise of the water, and many were drowned and lost in the waves, such that no mortal can approach [Paradise] unless it were with God's special grace.[577] Such that about this place I would not know how to tell you more or describe more and therefore I will stop speaking with this and return to what I have seen.

[Chapter 34]

About the Customs of the Kings and Others Dwelling on the Islands near Prester John's Land. And about the Honour that the Son Does to His Dead Father

From these islands about which I spoke to you before in Prester John's Land (which is under the earth relative to us over here), and from other islands farther forward, those who want to do so can return to the regions they came from and thus go all the way around the earth. But as much because of the islands as because of the sea as because of provisions, few people attempt this journey, although someone who could take a direct route could indeed do it, as I told you before.[578]

   Therefore one returns from the above-mentioned islands by way of other islands near Prester John's Land, and on returning one comes to an island that has the name Casson, and this country is a good forty days' travel in length and more than fifty in breadth.[579] It is the best island and the best kingdom there is in these regions, Cathay excepted, and if the merchants were to visit this country before they do Cathay, it would be rather better than Cathay is. This country is well inhabited and so full of cities and towns and people that, when one comes out of a city, one sees another city right ahead in whatever direction one happens to be going. On this island there is a great abundance of all life's essentials and of every kind of spice, and there are great forests all of chestnut trees. The king of this island is very rich and very powerful, and all the same he has his land from the Great Chan and is his subject,

---

577. The obstacles detailed here derive mostly from the legend of Alexander's *successful* journey to Paradise (see Krantz 1991, xxxii–xxxiv, 127–34; and Stoneman 2008, 164–69).

578. In Chapter 20.

579. With Casson, probably Gansu in northwestern China, the *Mandeville* author returns to OP (Chs. 32–34 [Latin], 28–29 [French]), whose account he reorganizes as well as reworks.

for this is one of the twelve provinces that the Great Chan has under him, without [counting] his own land and the smaller islands, of which he has many.

From this kingdom one comes on the return journey to another kingdom that is called Byboth [Tibet], and it too is under the Great Chan. It is a very good country and very abundant in wheat, wine, and other goods. And the people of this country have no houses; rather, throughout the whole country they dwell and sleep under tents of black felt. And the royal and chief city is all walled with black and white stones, and all the streets are well paved with such stones. In this city there is no one so bold as to dare spill either human or animal blood out of reverence for an idol that is worshiped there. In this city dwells the pope of their law who is called *Lobassy*.[580] This *Lobassy* distributes all the benefices and the other honors and all the things that pertain to the idols, and all those who receive anything from their church, monks and others, all obey him as the people of Holy Church here obey the pope.

On this island they have a custom throughout the whole country that when someone's father dies and he wishes to greatly honor his father, he sends for all his friends and relatives and monks and priests and a great many minstrels. Then the body is carried onto a mountain with great ceremony and great joy, and when they have carried [it] all the way there, the greatest priest cuts off the head and sets it on a large platter made of gold or silver, if he is a rich man, and then delivers the head to the son, and the son and the other relatives chant many prayers to God. Then the priests and the monks cut all the flesh of the body into pieces, and then they say their prayers, and the birds of the country, which have long known this custom, come flying above—such as vultures, eagles, and all other birds that eat flesh—and the priests throw pieces of the flesh to them, and they carry it not far away and eat it. Then just as the chaplains over here chant "*Subvenite sancti Dei etc.*"[581] for the dead, so these priests there at this point chant aloud in their language, "See how worthy a man he was that God's angels seek him out and carry him to Paradise." At this point it seems to the son that he is very much honored when the birds have eaten his father, and whoever has the greatest number of birds is the most honored. Then the son takes his relatives and his friends back to his house and makes a great feast for them, and all the friends tell their story of how the birds came—five here, ten there, twenty here—and enjoy themselves most abundantly in the telling. When they are at the house the son has his father's head cooked and gives each of his most special friends a little

---

580. Possibly from *ulug bakshi*, an eastern Turkic term meaning "great lama" (chief monk).

581. "Come to aid [him], saints of God, etc.": from the *Ordo commendationis animae* (Service for the commendation of a soul [to God]), used in the Latin Church since at least the fourth century.

of the flesh from it instead of a dish of something else, and from the skull he has a goblet made, and he drinks from it—and his kinfolk do too—with great devotion in memory of the holy man whom the birds have eaten. And the son will keep this goblet and drink from it all his life in his father's memory.

From this island after ten days on the return journey through the Great Chan's land, there is another very good island and large kingdom where there is a rich and strong king, and amongst the rich men of his country there is a very rich man who is neither prince, duke, commander, or count. But there are many who have their lands from him, and he is extremely rich, for each year he has in payment a good three thousand horses laden with wheat and rice, and he leads a very noble life according to the custom over there, for he has fifty maiden ladies-in-waiting who always serve him at meals and in going to bed and do whatever he likes. When he is eating a meal, they bring him his food five dishes at a time, and while carrying it in they sing a song. Then they cut his food up for him and put it in his mouth, for he touches nothing but just holds his hands in front of him on the table, for he has such long nails that he could not grasp or hold anything. It is a noble thing for men to have long nails and to let them always grow and be looked after as much as they can. There are many men in the country who let them grow so much that they encircle the whole hand, and it is a very noble thing; and the noble thing for women in this country is to have small feet. Therefore as soon as they are born, they have their feet bound so tightly that they grow only half as long as they should grow. These ladies-in-waiting always sing while he eats, and when he is no longer eating any of these [five] dishes, they bring him another five dishes and sing as before, and they do this right to the end of the meal. It is done this way every day, and this is how he spends his life, and so did his ancestors and so will those who come after him, without [anyone doing] a fair deed of arms, but he always lives likes this in comfort like a pig that is being fattened. He has a very fine and very rich palace where he lives whose walls are a good two leagues in circumference, and he has inside it many beautiful gardens, and all the floors of the halls and the rooms are paved with gold and silver. In the middle of one of the gardens there is a small mountain where there is a meadow and in this meadow there is a little church with towers and pinnacles all of gold, and he often likes to sit in this little church both to take the air and to enjoy himself, for this church was made for no other purpose than for his pleasure alone.

From this country one goes by land through the Great Chan's land, about which I told you before, so no further account is needed.

Know that in all these countries about which I have spoken, and on all these islands, and amongst all these diverse peoples that I have described to you, and the diverse laws and the diverse beliefs they have, there is no people—because they have reason and understanding—who do not have some articles of our faith and some good points of our belief, and who do not believe in God who made the world, whom they call God of Nature, according to the prophet, who said: *"Et metuent eum omnes fines terre."* And elsewhere: *"Omnes gentes servient ei."*[582]

But they do not know how to speak perfectly,[583] for they have no one to explain it to them, except insofar as they understand it with their natural understanding. They do not know how to speak about the Son, nor about the Holy Spirit. But they all know how to speak about the Bible, especially about Genesis, the sayings of the prophets, and the books of Moses.

Indeed, they say that the creatures that they worship are not gods at all, but they worship them for the virtue[584] that is in them, which could not exist without God's grace. About simulacra and idols, they say that there is no people who do not have simulacra, and they say this because we Christians have images of Our Lady and other saints that we worship. But they do not know what we worship: not the images of wood or stone, but the saints in whose name they are made. For just as the letter instructs and teaches the clergy what and how they should believe, so the images and the depictions teach the laity to think about and worship the saints in whose name they are made.[585]

They say also that God's angels speak to them in those idols, and that they perform great miracles; and they speak the truth that there is an angel within. But there are two kinds of angel, good and bad: *Cacho* and *Calo,* as the Greeks say, and *Cacho* is bad and *Calo* is good.[586] But it is not the good angel, but the bad that is in the idols, to deceive them and keep them in their error.

There are many other diverse countries and many other wonders over there that I have not seen at all, and do not know how to speak properly about; and even in countries where I have been there are many diversities of which I have made no mention, for it would be a long thing to describe everything. Therefore what I have described for you about some countries should do you for now. For if I described as many things as there are over there, someone else who took the trouble and

---

582. "And all the ends of the earth shall fear him" (Ps. 96[95]:9). "All nations shall serve him" (Ps. 72[71]:11). This paragraph begins a conclusion that, like the Prologue, represents an independent composition, not a rewriting of sources.

583. Without error.

584. "virtue": "power" as well as "good qualities"; both senses are relevant here.

585. Idols and simulacra: see Chapter 18, n. 354. This defense ultimately comes from Pope Gregory the Great's remarks in two letters written around 600 to Serenus, Bishop of Marseilles. In the later 1300s in England there was vigorous debate over religious images; the *Mandeville* author's interest perhaps supports his claim to be English by birth.

586. Greek *kakos:* "bad," "ugly," or "worthless"; *kalos:* "beautiful," "fair," or "good."

labored bodily to go into those far places and find out about the country would be hindered by my words from reporting on anything foreign, for he would have nothing new to say in which the listeners could take pleasure, and it is always said that new things give pleasure.[587] Thus I shall keep quiet now without recounting any more diversities that exist over there, so that whoever wishes to go into those parts might find there enough to say.

And I John Mandeville abovesaid,—who left our countries and crossed the sea in the year of grace 1322, who has since sought out many lands and many journeys and many countries, and who has been in much good company and in many a fine undertaking (although I never did any fair deed nor fine adventure) and now have come to rest despite myself because of arthritic gouts, which constrain me—while taking pleasure in my miserable rest, in recording the time past, have compiled[588] these things and put them into writing, such as I can remember, in the year of grace 1356, in the thirty-fourth year since I left our countries.

I ask all the readers that they please pray to God for me and I shall pray for them; and all those who will say a *Pater Noster* for me, that God might grant me remission of my sins, I make them partners and grant them part of all the good pilgrimages I ever made and all the good deeds I ever did and shall do, if it please God, right to my end.[589] And I pray to God, from whom all good and all grace descends, that He will fill all the Christian readers and listeners with His grace and save their bodies and their souls. To the glory and praise of Him, who is three and one, without beginning and without end, without good quality, without great quantity,[590] present in all places, and containing all things and whom no good can improve nor any evil harm. Who lives perfectly in the Trinity and reigns in all eras and at all times. Amen.

---

587. A claim first made in the Prologue and at the start of Chapter 4.

588. Like many medieval authors, the *Mandeville* author presents himself as a compiler, not an inventor.

589. *Pater Noster:* see Chapter 10, n. 146. This partnership depends on the doctrine that one person's prayers and good deeds could help another sinner spend less time in Purgatory after death.

590. That is, God is beyond description in such human terms.

Appendix A:

Variants and Versions

Because scribes and translators made mistakes or deliberate changes, and sometimes authors even revised their originals, any copy of a medieval work is a snapshot of a text in motion. Deliberate changes reveal intermediaries' assumptions, attitudes, and (mis)understandings. If authorized texts like scripture were normally reproduced with care, others were "open," more subject to error and intervention. An open work could even become a "multitext," circulating in variously weighted versions, or "isotopes." Such is *TBJM*, whose text changed in transmission, usually silently; rarely did intermediaries explain their changes ("in that boke is moche thing / That nedeth naught in this talkinge").[1] Scholarly editions and studies by Higgins (1997a) and Tzanaki (2003) document the isotopic textual variety, a small sampling of which is given here.

1. The Insular and Continental French Versions

The original French text exists in three main forms, two possibly authorial, one not. All three gave rise to widely circulated translations, further shaping medieval and later understandings. Scholars generally call these three forms Insular, Continental, and Interpolated Continental (also known as Liège or Ogier).[2] It is not certain which of the first two is prior and authorial: a plausible case can be made for both. Liège, though, is clearly someone else's redaction of Continental. Continental differs from Insular in three main ways: (1) a longer account of Sir John's passage through the Perilous Valley; (2) another conclusion to the account of the earth's shape and size; and (3) a pair of minor variants (mentions of Liège and ivy). The first two differences are presented in context (see Chs. 31 and 20); the third is given below.[3]

---

1. Seymour 1973, 3–4 (ll. 35–36).

2. Insular survives in 25 manuscripts (14 in Anglo-French, 11 in Continental French); Continental survives in 30. See Higgins 2004, 103–5, for further details and citations of the relevant textual scholarship.

3. Chs. 11 (Liège/Aix) and 16 (ivy). All variants are from DLMM, an edition of Insular. Individual manuscripts are named only for unique variants using the standard abbreviations given in de Poerck 1955, 127 (e.g., Du2). No critical edition of Continental exists: Paris, Bibliothèque Nationale MS nouv. acq. fr. 4515, the earliest dated copy (1371) in any language, is transcribed in LMT vol. 2.

6/23:[4] *"and became Sultan."* Seemingly rewriting the Battle of Hattin
(July 1187), Du2 adds: "And the first Sultan of Egypt was Salhadins,
the which Salhadins came into Christendom and brought Hiron of
Thabaria [Tiberias] there who was a Christian convert, and he was an
exceptionally good knight in his time, and was king of Thabaria. But the
said Salhadins captured him and would have killed him if he had not
brought him into Christendom. Then this Hiron guided him there, but
he took him by such a route that he could not get through except by way
of a narrow passage between rock[s], and where only three or four men
could pass through abreast. And thus the said Hiron led them such that
they were all routed. And the said Hiron went to a Christian, to the lords
of France, and to the king of England named King Richard, and they
went to the said country and guarded it so well that the Saracens were
routed, and the twelve peers of France were there, the nail of Chevigny
William Longsword, King Richard of England, and many other lords of
France and elsewhere. And after Salhadins reigned . . ."

6/25: *"Sultan when I left there."* A Latin **Letter from the Sultan's
Son to the Pope** is inserted here in three Insular copies and two of its
Latin translation. Vogels' edition (1886, 15) is reprinted in Hamelius
(1919–1923, 2.40–42), who calls "the text . . . corrupt and [his] translation doubtful." My translation adapts Hamelius, but follows Deluz's text
(2000, 484–85), except where Vogels (signaled by italics) makes better
sense. "Malechnasser's son sent letters to the pope of Rome in this form:
Balthazarday—son of the illustrious king, the Sultan of the Babylonians,
Assyrians, Egyptians, Amaritans, Medes, Alexandrinians, Parthians,
and Ethiopians, Constantine of Jericho, provost of the Earthly Paradise
and guardian of the Sepulcher of the Crucified, king of Jerusalem,
Africa, and Asia, lord of Barbary from East to West, king of kings and
prince of princes, descendant of the gods, banner of Machomet, lord
from the Dry Tree to the river of Paradise and to the high hill of Ararat,
terror and threat to enemies, killer of Christians, comfort of pagans,
piercer of armor—to the High Priest of the Romans [sends] *the grace
that rattles anyone who has to request it and the greeting deserved by anyone to
be visited.* The foundation of the true faith of Christians, the mainstay
of the cautious, the bravery of the discreet: all these rest like a treasure
in the deceit [*hollow*] of your head. Yet your memory resounds, beginning to shake; stupidity devours you *who are called father and plot such
unheard-of evils against your sons.* For you and king Philip of the Franks
and other powers [*petty kings*] put your trust in a reedy scepter, raising
for yourselves a hope that vanishes like burning tow and is snuffed out
in a single breath. For through mature deliberation we always foresee
whatever you might plan against us to enfeeble us, and are not afraid.
What kind of father are you, then, who all but force your sons not to a
natural but a sudden death? Do you think we lack arrows and quivers,

---

4. 6/23: Chapter 6, p. 23, and so on.

against which you do not fear to send your sons so that they might vanish in them and thus surrender their living souls to death? By whom has the most precious city of Jerusalem been overthrown? By whom has the most powerful city of Acre been razed to its foundations? By whom has renowned Tripoli been laid waste and ruined? Have we not subjected three hundred and fifty-five cities that the Crucified man's vassals once ruled? You force your sons into a violent sea, where streams rage, but you yourself do not follow. You stand on dry land and drown the poor fools in the stream. Truly you mislead the simple-minded, but do not yourself go ahead. *Father* is what you are called in name, but not in deed. Let it suffice you therefore to threaten thus in the Turkish way. If however you want all the land, then look: we will open Acre and Tripoli to your sons and let them restore them, so long as they are our perpetual tributaries. We thus advise you first to call on your Lord, if you can, to complete the number of those martyred by us and to resuscitate the young men who, in avenging the murders of their fathers, may rush to us to receive a similar punishment. For we seek nothing but the blood of Christians: we are thirsty for it. Be advised, therefore, you who are called wise, and save those now abandoned to death, or else you will be a murderer and seducer of the simple. Even the spirit *of nature* earnestly entreats you to do this. Who do you think can resist us, since all your people, compared to our multitude, are barely a drop in the sea? Given at Babylon [Cairo] in the 39th year of our birth, and in the 20th of our reign."

6/27: *"the city of Methon [Mecca]."* Four copies: "which the pagans call Iathint." Deluz (DLMM 147, n. 17) hears an echo of "Iathrib," Medina's pre-Islamic name.

8/39: *"deep valley between them."* Lo9: "Also there where the body of Saint Catherine was first placed by the angels is a large and long and very hard rock on which the angels put the body, and the body sunk into the hard rock such that the form of the body remains in the rock (that is, from the head to the body's buttocks without the legs) right to this day, and this the pilgrims have seen. The rock is so hard that it cannot be pierced by any tool, for the pilgrims have tried with the points of their staves and could not pierce the rock at all, nor get a piece of it. And that is a great miracle how the body of Saint Catherine sunk into the said rock that is so hard, as I said before."

11/50: *"Jesus Christ's foreskin."* Variants for *prepuce* ("foreskin") include "present," "presence," "promise" (*premice*), "prophecy," and "navel" (*nombril*).

11/50: *"to Aix-la-Chapelle."* P12, Be3: "seven leagues from Liège." Found only in some copies of Continental and in Liège (de Poerck 1955, 131–32), is this the trace of an original Anglo-Norman composition in L (DLMM 81) or a later Continental addition that L takes over?

16/92: *"an old castle."* P12: "the walls of which are covered with ivy." Be3: "ivy that we call *rebun*." Some Continental copies have "ivy" in English where B3 has *"rebun."* Further minor variants exist; the passage helps distinguish Continental from Insular (de Poerck 1955, 132–34).

20/110: *"God who made Adam was naked."* Other French copies lack this oddly worded passage, and usually have something like "God made Adam [*or:* Adam and Eve] naked."

20/116: *"signs or fixed stars."* "And let what I have said not displease readers: that a part of India is under our country, and that our country is also under those to the opposite of the true west. And so too is the northern region [opposite] to the southern region. I have told you before about these regions. And it is true (for I have measured it with the astrolabe) that those who dwell in the southern region are foot against foot with the others in the other region opposite the south, and so are we and a part of the islands of India" (de Poerck 1955, 135). These words precede the final sentences of Chapter 20 in Continental, whose closing paragraph differs from Insular's. De Poerck considers them a likely interpolation, suggesting that the other words probably belonged to the Insular ending (as given above in Ch. 20; see also n. 396).

25/143: *"with the gold and the silver that is brought into his country he always decorates his palace."* In DLMM (397), the sentence ends with *"his country."* *"He always decorates"* begins a new sentence and a new paragraph, but the passage makes better sense, I think, with no break. Translated as in DLMM, the first sentence contradicts its predecessor: ". . . over there they make no money out of gold or silver, and therefore he can spend enough both of the gold and the silver that are brought into his country. He always decorates his palace. . . ." DLMM (397, n. l) records that two copies read, "And therefore he spends no gold or silver except to decorate his palace . . . ," and that ten copies omit *"He always decorates his palace,"* which would likewise allow the two sentences to run together. My reading is found in L (Deluz 1997, 1420). C translates the passage as I have (HMT 1.157), and E renders it similarly (WBJM 117).

30/164: *"very well off."* *"Mult catelous"* (DLMM 440), the sole example in the *Anglo-Norman Dictionary* of *[chastelouz], catelous,* defined as "wealthy, owner of chattels" (www.anglo-norman.net [AND2 supplementary entry, created after the print version went to press[:] vcd, February 2, 2007]). This is the likeliest meaning (*catel,* from Latin *capitalis,* cognate with "cattle/chattel"), but "very cunning" might be a plausible rendering, since both C and E read it as *cautelous* (*cautele,* "trick, ruse, ploy"), a variant not listed by Deluz, but anticipating the story's outcome. C: "full of cauteles [tricks]" (HMT 1.184–85); E: "wonder wyly [amazingly cunning]" (WBJM 137). *"Et mult catelous"* is lacking in ten copies (DLMM 440, textual note j).

31/168: *"in these swoons."* 1371 copy: "and in these swoons we saw in particular [*especialment* for *espirituelement*] many wonders about which I dare not speak. For the friars of religion who were with us prohibited us from speaking about them, but allowed us to say that from afar we had seen a fire burning that did not stop, and nevertheless we saw it bodily. But they prohibited us from speaking about it, so as to conceal Our Lord's secrets" (LMT 2.392).

32/175: *"this was a sign."* The 1371 copy has an additional biblical citation and different wording: "And this is to say that no one should despise or judge any earthly people for their diverse laws, but should pray for them. For we do not know those whom God loves more or hates, for He hates no creature that he has made. And therefore Saint Peter said this when he understood the meaning of the vision: '*Nunc in veritate comperi quia non est acceptor personarum Deus, nec distinguit inter Iudeos et gentes, sed in omni gente que timet illum et operatur iusticiam acceptus est illi*'.[5] And for these examples I say '*De profundis*' for the trespasses. And I say commonly with the Christians, '*Pro animabus . . .*' For I say that God loves this people for their faithfulness and their humility. . . . But they do not know the way that He suffered death for us, nor His Gospels, nor His deeds, as we indeed do" (LMT 2.400).

33/179: *"for I was not so far forward, because I was not worthy."* Twelve copies: "for I was not there. It grieves me that I was not worthy." L, C, D, and E are all closer to this version.

34/184: *"worship the saints in whose name they are made."* Three copies add: "for man's and woman's thought is often corrupted by many worldly things because of which they might often forget God and his Mother and the saints to pray to the figures made in God's name while not remembering them."

34/185: *"into writing, such as I can remember."* Three copies add: "by the abridged records [*memoires abregés*] made by me about this and on each country." Cf. Vulgate Latin, Chapter 50 (p. 217 below).

A Dedication to the King of England. Ten related Insular copies contain at the *end* (not at the beginning, as one would expect) a royal dedication. Closer study of the copies (see DLMM 36–46) and the royal titles might make it possible to date or locate this probably scribal dedication: "To the most excellent Prince [who is] to be especially revered before all mortals, Lord Edward, through Divine Providence most serene King of the French and the English, Lord of Ireland, Duke of Aquitaine, master of the sea and its western islands, repute and distinction of Christians, as well as protector of all those who bear arms and model of integrity and action; and also to the unconquered Prince, follower of the wonderful Alexander, [who is] to be feared by whole world, the things contained here are offered not with a reverence that is fitting, because they would stand out as insufficient to such and so great a Reverence, but as far as the sender's and giver's smallness and power reach" (DLMM 483).

---

5. "Now in truth I perceive that God is not a respecter of persons, nor does he distinguish between Jews and Gentiles, but in every nation whoever fears Him and works justice is acceptable to Him." Cf. Acts 10:34–35.

2. The Interpolated Continental (Liège) Version

Made possibly around 1390, definitely before 1396 (the date of Paris, Bibliothèque Nationale MS fonds fr. 24436), Liège survives in only seven manuscripts, but was highly influential,[6] being adapted into two widely circulated translations: the Latin Vulgate and Otto von Diemeringen's German. It differs from Continental and Insular in six main ways: (1) some twenty-five mentions of Ogier the Dane, many assigning him Sir John's deeds from the other French versions;[7] (2) two extra alphabets (Cathay and Prester John's Land);[8] (3) specific variations (e.g., a different etymology of the Great Khan's name); (4) the elaboration of two short passages near *TBJM*'s end; (5) an epilogue detailing *TBJM*'s composition at Hennequin le Volt's inn on Rue Basse Sauvenière in Liège; and (6) the addition in one copy (Musée Condé MS 699) of four "books":[9] Bk. 2 about "the earth's form"; Bk. 3 "about the form of the heavens and . . . our Lord God's throne"; Bk. 4 about "plants according to the Indians and the philosophers over there"; Bk. 5, "the lapidary . . . according to the opinion of the Indians from whom all the sciences of stones come." This version appears to have been conceived as a single work, since Books 2 and 5 are anticipated in the text (see Chs. 17 and 33 below), and the account of the diamond is displaced to the latter. This fifth "book" had an independent existence in the fifteenth and sixteenth centuries, one of several French and Latin lapidaries attributed to John Mandeville.[10]

9/39: "*when I was with him.*" "When I served the Sultan as a soldier, they used to attack us and I fought several battles against them with the Sultan" (1402). "Also, they say in the country of Egypt that Ogier the Dane, a valiant Duke of France, who formerly conquered fifteen kingdoms on a single expedition and twelve on another in that country over there, killed all these wicked people about whom I speak and destroyed

---

6. See Ridder 1991, 147–64. An edition is in preparation (Tyssens 2005).

7. In Chantilly, Musée Condé MS 699: listed in de Poerck 1961, 43–44; transcribed in Crosby 1965, lxix–lxxxvii; translated below (for English renderings of the Ogier passages in Otto and the Vulgate Latin, see LMT 2.483–98; and Ch. 29 in this Appendix in Sec. 5). Fewer Ogier interpolations are found in the other six copies (de Kock 1965, esp. 524–25). Ogier was a warrior hero first mentioned in the influential eleventh-century *Chanson de Roland,* or *Song of Roland;* he also appears in other well-known Charlemagne legends.

8. See Appendix C.3.

9. "Titles" translated from de Poerck 1961, 32–33. *TBJM* "proper" occupies folios 1–75r; the four other books, folios 75r–108v. See Bennett 1954, 110–34; and de Poerck 1961.

10. Bennett thought the lapidary a spurious attribution (1954, 133); de Poerck thought it possible (1961, 38). The Chantilly lapidary is edited, with another "by" John Mandeville, in Mourin 1955. See Goosse 1960.

them. But they cost him more trouble than all the battles that he had against the Saracens. Now the Devil of Hell has multiplied them such that they are more of them today than they ever were before" (lxix).[11]

11/50: "*and then to Chartres.*" "Also, in this Temple of the Lord, King Charles the Great, formerly king of France and the emperor of Rome, was one day in great devotion. With him were Naimes, the Duke of Bavaria, Ogier the Dane, Roland, Oliver, and many others of his peers of France who had come there on pilgrimage. And the angel brought to King Charles Our Lord Jesus Christ's foreskin from his circumcision, which Charles took and placed in Aix-la-Chapelle. But Charles the Bald (of whom Charlemagne was grandfather, since he was father of King Louis, himself Charles the Bald's father) removed it from Aix and had it taken to Poitiers, and then it was taken to Chartres" (lxix–lxx).

12/66: "*The people of this country.*" "The people of this country that are called Samaritans were first baptized and converted by the Apostles, but they were then destroyed by the Sultan and returned to their law. And in the time of Charles the Great, king of France and emperor of Rome, Ogier the Dane reconverted them and had them baptized: he was one of the twelve peers of France and conquered, as I told you already, fifteen overseas kingdoms on one occasion, and twelve on another. Of the lands and countries that he conquered this was one. This Ogier, as they say over there and as their chronicles also often mention, was a powerful knight, and they call him God's Champion, and no one was able to hold out against him, as I will tell you about him more fully when I come to India and to the great countries that he conquered, where fittingly they believe more in him than in God. These people of the Samaritans have not kept his religion and his teaching well; they have their own religion, different from that of the Christians, the Saracens, and the Jews . . ." (lxx–lxxi; last sentence from Deluz 1997, 1403).

13/74: "*the land of Prester John.*" "And you should know that Ogier the Dane ultimately converted all these regions by the sword, as is contained in their histories. And the first Prester John was set up in India through this Ogier, for when he conquered India, he gave it to Prester John, his cousin, who was its first Christian king, as I will tell you more fully when I speak about Prester John's Land" (lxxi).

15/89: "*called thorn and yogh.*" L ends differently: "You should know that when Mahomet died he was placed in a shrine of gold, silver, and precious stones, in a city called Galdara, where it remained for two hundred and sixty years. Then it was taken to the city of Mecca, where it still lies. Mecca was very strongly rebuilt after it had been destroyed by the French because of Ogier the Dane, who was imprisoned there, and the Templars of Acre had sold it [*or:* him] to king Ysore, king Bréhier's son, whom Ogier had killed near the city of Laon in France. And know

---

11. Select Ogier passages are translated from Crosby's transcriptions of Chantilly (1965, lxix–lxxxvii, supplemented, as needed, from Deluz 1997, 1399–1435).

that they say astonishing things about this Ogier's prowess. And they say that he will return and thus conquer all their country and convert it to the Christian law. You must know that in Tartary, Russia, and Prussia, they have their own alphabet with names for the letters and they have four more letters than we do, for their language is different from ours" (lxxxvii; 1404).

17/99: "*the most precious are in India.*" "If you want to know all the kinds of diamonds and their properties, you can find them further on in my *Lapidary* (which is the last of the five books that I have composed), according to the views of the Indians, who are the most learned and most experienced in these matters" (1405).

18/104: "*city . . . Zarchee.*" "There are many fine churches of monks there that Ogier the Dane founded, and they are still called Danish churches. Next one comes by sea to [. . .] Lombe where pepper grows. [. . .] And in this forest are two fine cities that Ogier the Dane founded when he conquered this country. He named one Flandrine after the queen (his father Geoffrey of Denmark's mother), who was called Flandrine, and she was Doon of Mayence's wife; and the city is still called Flandrine. The other city he named Florence after the other queen (his mother's mother Beatrice, wife of king John Mullebron of Hungary), who was called Florentine, daughter of the emperor Sanche (called Lion) and sister of Bertha, King Charlemagne's mother. But now the city of Flandrine is more commonly called Zinglans, and many Christians and Jews dwell there, for there is much good and fertile country there, but it is very hot" (lxxi–lxxii).

19/108: "*buried there.*" "He remained there for eight hundred years until the time when Ogier the Dane conquered this kingdom who founded a fine city there and a church, and had Saint Thomas raised and placed in a gold and silver reliquary adorned with precious stones" (lxxiii).

21/117: "*precious stones and large pearls.*" This clause and the next sentence are lacking in L, which reads ". . . and the whole wall inside is covered with gold and silver tiles on which are written and depicted histories and battles of knights and, in the great main hall, the whole history and the life of the Danish Ogier are written and depicted, how he was born right until the time when he returned from Syria [Cairo?] to France. And they know his history over there better than we do over here, even about what he did in France. And they know it through his cousins, who were kings of the regions of India and around there, and of this island of Java itself. And they have chronicles about him and they say that he will return and conquer and destroy all Mahommet's law, and thus the Saracens are very afraid of him, for they say that he will never die. And they say so much about him that it would take too long to recount. Know that the king of this island . . ." (lxxiv–lxxv; cf. Vulgate Latin, Ch. 29, in Sec. 5 below).

21/118: "*in vessels for storage.*" "Also, the people on this island say that the trees give such fruits through a miracle that God once performed for Ogier the Dane when he conquered this island and his army had such a great hunger in that it was going to have to leave, when Our Lord's angel brought him the news of these trees, which had never before this time borne such fruit. Thus they hold a great celebration of it, and the food trees are named after Ogier the Dane, for he conquered this island" (lxxvii–lxxviii; cf. Vulgate Latin, Ch. 29, in Sec. 5 in this Appendix).

21/119: "*a great wonder on this island.*" "There is on this island a great wonder that no one, I believe, has seen anywhere. Every species of fish of the sea comes once a year to cast itself one after another on the shore in such numbers that one can no longer see the water, only the fish. They remain there for three days and everyone takes as much as they want. On the third day, they withdraw and are replaced by others that do the same thing. And thus in succession until all have gone. I caught many of them. And those of the country say that they do not know by what cause it might be, except that they have in their histories that when Ogier the Dane conquered this island God sent him these fish in a famine that he had, as I told you, when he took flour, wine, and honey from the trees on the island of Calamach. I do not know the cause other than I am telling you, but this seems to me the greatest wonder that I have ever seen. For Nature does indeed make [*or:* do] many different things, but it is against Nature that the fish, which have the whole world to go around in their freedom, come to give themselves to death of their own free will. And certainly that could not be except through a great miracle from God. And since God loved the Duke Ogier the Dane so much, I quite easily believe what they say about it. And also all this is found in their chronicles and in those of our countries of England and elsewhere" (lxxviii–lxxix; initial sentences 1410–1411; cf. Vulgate Latin, Ch. 29, in Sec. 5 below).

21/121: "*if he did not have this ruby.*" "I have seen it three times; I will tell you how. When the people of this country chose a king, they give him this ruby and lead him on horseback through the city and from that day on they submit to him. But he has to wear this ruby instead of a crown each time he has to appear crowned and, if he is not wearing it, he will not be recognized as king. This is how I have seen him wearing it three times" (1412).

22/125: "*many Christians.*" "And there are more than two thousand large cities, not including the other towns, and they are all Christians, believing closer to our law than any others over there, for this is one of the lands conquered by Ogier the Dane, as they say. This country is more populous than all the others through its abundance, but no one asks for bread [i.e., begs], for all are rich. They are good Christians. But they are pale . . ." (lxxix; supplemented from 1414–15).

22/126: "*many good cities.*" Instead of this paragraph, L has: "In the cities of this country there are many beautiful churches that Ogier the Dane founded and many beautiful monasteries" (lxxix).

23/132: "*minstrels who sing songs . . .* " "Except the minstrels who sing certain songs and recite heroic stories, especially about Ogier the Dane and his kin" (lxxx).

25/145: "*they walk ahead.*" "And the Christian monks of the monasteries that Ogier the Dane founded, as is said, go towards him in a large procession with the cross . . ." (lxxxi).

28/156: "*to the Great Chan.*" "You should know that all these countries are part of Ogier the Dane's conquests, as those of the countries say, and they are subject to the Great Can" (lxxxi).

30/161: "*The sailors told us.*" "the sailors said that . . . the shrubs and the brambles grow on the decay of the bodies of the lost seamen" (1424).

30/164: "*how he should serve.*" The paragraph ends thus: "Each of his great lords knows what service he must provide and each has a specific role. This emperor's country is so big that its dimensions cannot be given. All the islands that we say are under us on the earth belong to him. The breadth of his empire extends for more than four month's travel, walking without stopping and moderately every day. Prester John holds quite a few more lands than the Great Chan and rules over more countries and great lords. He has more precious stones and jewels than the Great Chan and his land is more beautiful. But there are more trade goods in Cathay than on Pentexoire, and Cathay is therefore richer in gold and silver. In Prester John's country there is a distinctive language and letters that you can see here. And you should know that they name their letters like ours" (1426). This alphabet is found only in L.

32/173: "*the Land of Faith. Through it flows a large river that has the name Thebe.*" "Ogier the Dane besieged these people when he conquered this country of India, but he left right away when he had learned of their good habits. For this is all in the midst of the Land of Prester John, the emperor of India" (lxxxv).

32/177: "*that kill and devour whatever they can catch.*" "Priests and others look after them [the Trees of the Sun and the Moon] carefully in Prester John's name, for they are in his land. They live four or five hundred years thanks to the fruit that they eat from these trees, for these trees bear a good deal of authentic balm. It is found nowhere else in the world except there and in Cairo, as I told you. Ogier the Dane, about whom I have spoken, was at these trees and tasted some balm, as the people of the country say and as it is in their history where it says that by virtue of the balm he lived for a long time and is possibly still alive. You should know that we would very willingly have gone there, if it had been possible, but I believe that even one hundred armed men could not now make it, for there are so many snakes, dragons, and other animals there that eat all those who reach there" (lxxxv; supplemented from 1428).

32/177: *"why this emperor is called Prester John."* This story is told differently in L: "And since no one knows why the emperor of India Major is
called Prester John, I would like to explain it as they tell it and as it is
contained in their histories. First I tell you that when I was still in my
own country I often heard it said that there was once in India a worthy
emperor who was very handsome and a good emperor who was taken by
the desire to see the service of Holy Church, for Christianity at that time
extended. . . . So that the king took the name Prester John. But when
I was in India, I found that this was not so, for I found it in a very fine
chronicle that is in the Church of Our Lady, in the city of Nyze in India:
and it says that in the year 816 from Our Lord's birth, Ogier the Dane
crossed the sea with a large army where he conquered all India and
Cathay, and many other countries to the number of fifteen important
kingdoms at this time. He gave them to his cousins who had crossed the
sea with him. Amongst the others was the son of his uncle Gondebaud
of Frisia, who was named John in baptism, who in his youth frequented
the church and knelt every day before the church altars. So much so
that his father, king Gondebaud, said he would make a priest of him in
order to divert him from frequenting the churches outside the required
times. And to shame him he had him called Prester John by everyone in
such a way that he could never escape it in his entire life. He crossed the
sea with Ogier, and there Ogier gave him the kingdom of Pentexoire:
that is, of India. And inasmuch as he was the first king of India who was
Christian, all the other kings after him have been and will be named
Prester John, which is their name, just as the great emperor of Cathay
is named Can [Khan]" (lxxxi– lxxxii).

33/178: *"under Prester John's authority."* "is subject to Prester John, and
holds his land from him. And it is one of the kingdoms that Ogier the
Dane conquered" (lxxxvi).

33/179: *"that I have previously spoken to you about."* "and as I will tell you
about more fully in a book that I have made on the form of the earth
and its contents, right after this first book" (1431).

33/179: *"not so far forward, because I was not worthy."* "I would not know
how to speak properly about the Earthly Paradise beyond what was told
to me by the people of Prester John's court, for I did not go there and it
grieves me not to have been worthy to go there and enter it" (1431).

33/180: *"a king . . . in India who had the name Gangares."* The "king of
India when Ogier conquered it. He was thrown into this river because
he refused baptism and was drowned" (lxxxvi).

34/181: *"From these islands about which I spoke to you before in Prester John's
Land."* This passage seems to be located closer to the book's end in L,
but Deluz's translation does not cite folio numbers. The differences are
notable: "From this island one goes to other islands through the land of
Great Chan of Cathay about whom I told you above, so it is unnecessary
to start over again, for one returns by way of the route that I described
for you to come [here]. But, as I told you, someone who would not want

to return through where he has already passed and would like to launch out on the great sea beyond India and go by chance where God leads him, could return home while always going forward, for the earth is round. But it would be hard to keep to the right way, for the sea is so large, there are so many bad crossings, rocks, and other dangers, that one could easily die; and someone who departed from the route by the thickness of a finger, before having gone a league ahead, would go astray by more than three leagues. It is thus very difficult to keep to the right way. It would be better for us then to retrace our steps than to confront these dangers, although I would have attempted the adventure if my companions had wanted to, but they refused. And this can be both good and bad for me" (1434–35).

34/182: "*smaller islands, of which he has many.*" "The king of this island is very rich and very powerful, and he has three quarters of his land from Prester John and the rest from the Great Chan, and he is their subject. It is one of the kingdoms that Ogier the Dane conquered over there" (lxxxvi).

34/182: "*abundant in wheat, wine, and other goods.*" "And it is another of the kingdoms that Ogier the Dane conquered over there" (lxxxvi–lxxxvii).

34/183: "*in his father's memory.*" "Thus all men are holy, according to what they say, through this great ceremony against nature" (1433).

34/183: "*for men to have long nails*": "especially for the old lords who no longer fight" (1434).

34/183: "*they encircle the whole hand, and it is a very noble thing*": "fire cannot burn them [the long nails], and this is a very noble thing. But this noble thing is full of filth and they have stinking hands" (1434).

34/183: "*in comfort like a pig that is being fattened.*" "His finest deeds in arms will be drinking, eating, and living in comfort like a pig that is being fattened. I saw him in fact three times while [he was] eating at his table with a friend, an important man who often came to visit him. He is a person without honor, and I have seen such fine pigs that I do not want to compare them to him. He dresses in rich velvet and gold clothes adorned with precious stones" (1434).

34/183: "*for his pleasure alone.*" "This man is called Meleroth; he is the richest in the world according to his rank. He has the income of a duke or a count. His ancestors amassed great possessions and held the same rank as him. Thus was a great fortune accumulated. Just as pigs amass stinking and vile dung, he spends everything on drink and food without seeking to win honor or serve God" (1434).

34/185: "*And I John Mandeville abovesaid.*" L rewrites this testimonial (further elaborated in the Vulgate Latin: see Sec. 5 below): "And I, John of Mandeville, knight, although I am not worthy of it [the title], born in England in the town of St Albans—who left my country and took to the sea in the year of grace from the Nativity of Our Lord Jesus Christ 1322, on the day of Saint Michael the Archangel, who have visited and passed through many different countries as I have told you above, and have been in good company, thanks to God, and have often been at fine deeds of arms, although I never did any fair deed, nor any fine adventure, nor other good deed, and now have come to rest despite myself, because of arthritic gouts, which constrain me, [and] with which I have been very ill—while consoling myself in my wretched rest in recalling and recording the time past, have finished and put into writing this treatise such as I can remember, which was made and finished and arranged by me in the year of grace abovesaid 1357, thirty-five years since I left my country, in the noble city of Liège, in la Basse Sauvenière, in the house of Hannequin called le Volt,[12] at the request and bidding of the honorable and discreet Master John of Bourgogne, called 'with the beard,' a doctor who visited me in my illness, and while visiting me recognized me and recalled having seen me at the court of the Sultan of Egypt with whom he was dwelling when I was there" (translated from the text edited in de Poerck 1961, 39).

34/185: "*all the readers.*" "all those who read me with goodwill" (1435).

3. Three English Versions

Recently, the most widely read English *Mandeville* has been Moseley's,[13] a translation of one of three independent but related Middle English renderings (Cotton, Defective, and Egerton) from around 1400. Their exact relations remain uncertain. E derives partly from D (so named because of its many textual gaps), but neither the relation of D to C nor their relative priority has been resolved. D was the most widely circulated English text until the mid-eighteenth century. C, the fullest Middle English translation, survives in one copy (British Library MS Cotton Titus C xvi.); not printed until 1725, it has since then been in constant circulation, often lightly modernized.[14] The closest of the three to the French, it is sometimes so close as to be almost unreadable, and it contains some curious misrenderings: the zodiac ("*le sercle des signes du cel*": "the circle of the signs of the sky," Ch. 11) becomes "the Cercle of Swannes of hevene," presumably because the translator took *signes* for *cygnes,* or "swans." The third principal Middle English translation, E, also survives in a single copy (British Library MS Egerton 1982), and

---

12. On these and other historical details associated with the Liège tradition, see Lejeune 1964.

13. 1983; 2005 (with revised Introduction, new notes, and Bibliography).

14. See Higgins 2004 for more details. There is a fourth, abbreviated prose version (Bodley), probably from the early fifteenth century, in two manuscripts, plus a metrical redaction, probably also of the same date, in one copy (see Seymour 1973). For the English printings to the 1980s, see Seymour 1993, 50–52.

was not printed until 1889; a lightly modernized edition was published in 1953,[15] then Moseley's translation in 1983. Good as E is, though (and its distinctive northern Middle English is pithier than Moseley's elegant translation reveals), it handles the text freely, recasting the prose to improve its clarity, logic, and literary qualities. Even the phrase that C mangles, it clarifies: "a cercle *with the twelve* signez of the firmament."[16] The E maker rearranged, omitted, and added material for coherence, concision, and clarity, revealing him as not only an alert reader, but also pious, intelligent, well read, and something of an English nationalist. E is a translator's *Mandeville*, not the author's, as Moseley's rendering inadvertently suggests. Samples of E come from WBJM. D varies more textually, but not as significantly; samples come from Seymour 2002. C, in contrast, varies least; its variants are from HMT vol. 1. The Middle English has been lightly modernized.

Prol/3: "*called king.*" E: "called all anely [sole] king of that land, as the prophete says, '*Noli timere, filia Sion: ecce, rex tuus venit tibi mansuetus,*'[17] that es to say, 'thou doghter of Sion, drede thou not [fear not]; for, lo, thy king comes to thee, dulye [fittingly] mylde and meke'" (1).

Prol/5: "*I should have put this writing into Latin.*" C: "And yee schull undirstonde that I have put this boke out of Latin into Frensch and translated it agen out of Frensch into Englyssch [so] that every man of my nacioun may understonde it" (4). See Introduction (p. xv); D and E lack any reference to the original language, allowing them to be read as authorial.

7/29: "*heat of the sun.*" E: "Bot thay er black of colour; and that thay hald a grete beautee, and ay the blacker thay er the fairer tham think tham[selves]. And thay say that, if thay schuld paynt ane aungell and a fende, thay wald paynt the aungell black and the fende white. And, if thay think tham[selves] not black enough when thay er borne, thay use certayne medecynes for to make tham[selves] black withall. That cuntree es wonder hot, and that makes the folk thereof so black" (24).

10/46: "*this writing in Greek.*" E offers *two* versions of the Greek (39).

15/89: "*the names that they call them.*" E adds a second alphabet: "Here will I sett thaire letters on another maner, as I hafe sene tham made in sum other bukes; and this maner payes [pleases] me better than the tother" (71).

16/94: "*meat* Dabago *and wine* Vapa." Warner thinks that "and sum callez it [the city] Cardabago, and sum Vapa" translates the original (1889, 195, n. to 75, l. 10; cf. Seymour 2002, 67). In his view, "*la char Dabago et le vin Vapa*" represented *Chardabago,* from *Char bagh,* Persian

---

15. LMT vol. 1.

16. Warner 1889, 42; emphasis added. This variant is not recorded in DLMM 203.

17. John 12:15.

for "four gardens," meaning "palace," but a scribe, mistaking *Vapa* for *vappa* (Latin for "flat wine"), also misread the first name as containing the word "meat" (*char*).

17/99: *"powers of the diamond."* E: "And, if ye will knawe the vertuz of the dyamaund, I sall tell yow as Ysidre *libro* 16 *Ethicorum, capitulo de cristallo,* and Bertilmew *De Proprietatibus Rerum,* libro 16, *capitulo de adamante,* says" (79).[18]

18/106: *"feel better."* E: "I, John Maundevill, sawe this well and drank therof thrice and all my felawes, and evermare since that time I fele me the better and the haler [healthier] and supposez for to do till the time that Godd of His grace will make me to passe oute of this dedly [mortal] lyf" (84).

24/134: *"his sleeping father's uncovered back."* Both C (145) and E (109) render *dos* ("back") as "privy members" (genitals), hewing closer to the biblical account.

24/134: *"Cham because of his cruelty."* "Corrected" in E, but not necessarily by the translator ("Seem" and "Cham" are over erasures), making nonsense of the *Mandeville* author's explanation: "Seem . . . chose . . . Asy. Cham tuke Affryk, and Japhet tuke Europe . . ." (109).

25/143: *"This emperor can spend."* E seems familiar with paper money: ". . . for he makez na monee bot owther [except either] of lether, or of papire, or of barkez of treesse. And, when this monee es waxen alde [has grown old], and the prynte therof defaced by cause of using, it es broght to the kynges tresoury, and his tresourer giffez new for alde. This monee es prynted on bathe the sydes, as monee es of other cuntreez, and it gase [circulates] thurgh all the Grete Caan['s] landes. For thay make na monee thare of gold ne silver . . ." (117).

25/146: *"Under the firmament."* E moves this passage (except the last two sentences about marital customs) to Chapter 23. Warner (1889, 120), Letts (1953, 1.169, n. 4), and Moseley (1983, 156 n.) note its absence but fail to recognize that it was displaced not omitted.

28/155: *"no enemy could last against us."* E (correctly) separates and reattributes the second and third scriptural citations, and omits the last composite quotation (128–29).

28/155: *"many who take communion every day."* E simplifies this and again omits the miscited scripture: "And sum of tham are schryven [confessed] and howseld [given communion] ilke a day [every day]. And in this thay schewe mare devocioun than we do, that er unnethez anez [scarcely once] in a yere schryfen and howseld" (129).

30/162: *"and delicious to eat."* E adds: "and thay er right savoury in the mouth, bot thay er of other schappe than fischez er of other waters. I John Maundevill ete of tham, and tharfore trowez it for sikerly it es soth [believe it, for certainly it is true]" (134).

---

18. Isidore of Seville, *Ethics* 16, chapter on crystal; Bartholomew the Englishman, *On the Properties of Things* 16, chapter on adamant.

30/164: "*all the islands under [the] earth that we call under.*" E omits this gloss, adding instead an echo of the authenticating comment at the Chan's court: "Trowez [believe] all this, for sikerly [certainly] I sawe it with myne eghen [eyes] and mykill mare [much more] than I hafe talde yow. For my felaws and I ware dwelland with him in his courte a lang time and saw all this that I hafe talde yow and mykill mare [much more] than I hafe layser [leisure] for to tell" (137).

33/178: "*not allow human beings.*" E here inserts a long interpolation that Warner moved to his commentary (220, n. to 149, l. 20) and Moseley omitted because of "only slight interest" (1983, 183). Letts alone kept it in place (1953, 1.212–14). Too long to include here, it is well worth reading. Set "[b]eyond these isles [of Prester John] toward the east [in] yit another isle [. . .] called Tisle [Ultima Thule . . .] the ferrest [farthest] isle of the werld inhabited with men," it relates "a myracle" performed by "saint Thomas of Caunterbyry" that links the ends of the world and comments allegorically on relations between ecclesiastical and royal powers.

34/185: "*enough to say. And I John Mandeville . . .*" Between these sentences C adds:[19] "And yee schull undirstonde if it like you [if it please you] that at myn hom comynge I cam to Rome & schewed my life [confessed] to oure holy fadir the Pope & was assoylled [absolved] of all that lay in my conscience of many a diverse grievous point, as men must needs that ben [as required of those who are] in company dwellyng among so many a diverse folk of diverse secte & of beleeve as I have ben. And amonges all I schewed him this tretys that I had made after informacioun of men that knewen of thinges that I had not seen myself, and also of merveyles and customes that I had seen myself, as fer as God wolde geve me grace, And besoughte his holy fadirhode, that my boke mighte ben examined and corrected by avys [advice] of his wise & discreet conseill. And oure holy fader of his special grace remitted my boke to ben examyned & preved [tested] be the avys [advice] of his said conseill, be the whiche my boke was preeved for trewe in so moche that they schewed me a boke that my boke was examynde by, that comprehended full moche more be an hundred part, be the whiche the *Mappa Mundi* was made after. And so my boke, all be it that many men ne list not [do not wish] to geve credence to no thing but to that that they seen with hire [their] eye, ne be the auctour ne the persone never so trewe, is affermed & preved be oure holy fader in maner & forme as I have said" (209–10).

34/185: "*the thirty-fourth year since I left our countries.*" D and E add here: "And for als mykill [as much] as many men trowez [believe] not bot that that thay see with thaire eghen [eyes], or that thay may consayve with thaire awen kyndely wittes [that they can think of with their own natural intelligence], therfore I made my way in my commyng hamward

19. On the papal approbation, sometimes mistakenly read as authorial, see Higgins 1997a, 254–60.

unto Rome to schew my buke till oure haly fader the Pape. And I tald him the mervailes whilk I had sene in diverse cuntreez, so that he with his wise counsaile wald examine it with diverse folke that er in Rome, for thare er evermare dwelland men of all naciouns of the werld. And a lytill after when he and his wise counsaile had examinde it all thurgh, he said to me for certayne that all was soth [true] that was therin. For he said that he had a buke of Latyn that conteyned all that and mykill mare [much more], after whilk buke the *Mappa Mundi* es made; and that buke he schewed me. And therfore oure haly fader the Pape hase ratified and confermed my buke in all poyntes" (156; "Pape" was erased and rewritten in the manuscript. Cf. Seymour 2002, 136).

4. Two German Versions

A. Michel Velser's Version

Probably made in the 1390s in northern Italy,[20] Michel Velser's Version was the most successful of three Dutch/German translations from Continental. Velser came from south-Tyrolean landed nobility, but brought his French source into German via urban Italian courts (in particular, those of the Milanese Visconti). Some forty manuscripts survive, four of which seem to represent a first translation, the rest a second (some of Velser's interpolations appear in two different forms in two different places). The German text (from Morrall 1974) somewhat abridges the French.

10/47: "*he conquered all his enemies.*" "This very bit is in Milan in Lombardy high up in the church, and anyone who has been to Milan may see it; and the church is called Tega.[21] What I have told you about Milan, Sir Hans does not say in his book" (53).

18/104: "*rats of this island are as big as dogs here.*" "Also, you should know that I Michel Velser, who have brought his book into German, have seen a rat in the menagerie of Milan that was brought there from over the sea: it was like a bird dog" (106).

21/122: "*not on this side of the sea.*" "Also, you should know that I, Michel Velser, who have brought this book into German, have seen in the city of Pavia a dog that was born from an egg, and the Duke of Lancaster's son brought it with him over the sea.[22] And it was as large as a greyhound.

---

20. The evidence comes from the interpolations translated here, but see also *TBJM* Prologue, n. 14.

21. Probably the church of Saints Thecla and Pelagia.

22. Henry Bolingbroke (1366–1413, crowned Henry IV of England in 1399) tried in 1392 to join the Teutonic Knights on a *reyse*, or crusade, into pagan Lithuania, but finding there would be none that year made a pilgrimage to Jerusalem.

Afterwards I saw the bird from which the dog came. It was sent overseas
to the Lord of Milan, and he had it in his menagerie. And it is a little
bigger than a goose and has short legs and is very beautiful to look at. It
has a yellow star near the eyes and a red ring and beautiful plumage, and
the beak is bigger than a goshawk's and bent and on both sides black
feathers hang below; if it is seen from afar it seems to one that it has a
beard. It is called frakkales [francolin]. And whatever bone it is given,
it eats the whole thing and also digests it. It lays three eggs: two become
birds and the one, a dog, as I told you before. And this is certainly true"
(123–24; cf. second redaction 34, n. to l. 4, Ch. 7 of *TBJM*).

25/144: *"the number is always maintained."* 2nd redaction: "Know too
that I Michel Velser, who brought this book into German, spoke with a
Genoese man who spent eighteen years beyond the sea and is lord of
Serrafall[23] who told me that he saw the Great Cham on a hunt and there
were two hundred thousand men with him" (142, n. to l. 5).

31/167: *"entered, [all] fourteen [of us]."* This *earlier version* of the interpolation, comes *later:* "Also, before I proceed further, I Michel Velser,
who put this book into German, want to say a little, and let no one be
displeased. Everything I have read in this book is true, although I have
not read [anything else] that in my opinion would be as unbelievable as
this material. Therefore I shall make it known to you that it is true. For
when I first saw this book and when I was first learning French, that was
in a[nother] country and it was called Pemunt [Piedmont] and lay in
Lamparten [Lombardy]. At that time I was in charge of an entire castle
and jurisdiction, and the castle was called Bardarzan [Bardassano], and
there I had many books, and at that time I was reading in this book,
and that was in Lent. Then a Franciscan came to me, since I wanted
to confess, and he saw me reading in this book. Then he asked me
what it said. Then I told him. Then he said, 'If you come to the city of
Kier [Chieri], I shall bring you in our library a book that our guardian
had made on his deathbed. Then see [a] marvel and ask what he saw,
because he traveled through many countries beyond the sea.' I soon
saw the book, and it lay chained in the Franciscan Cloister in the city of
Chieri. For the monk was from Chieri from a family called Raschier.[24]
Then I found in the book that he was the one who had gone through
the valley with Sir Hans de Mandavilla. He did not refer to him by name,
though, [saying] only that he spoke with an English knight, and that
there were thirteen of them, and when they came through there, then
there were now nine of them; and he had brought a mark with him out

---

Returning, he passed through northern Italy in March and April 1393 and was
entertained in Milan by Duke Giangaleazzo Visconti (1351–1402), referred to
here as "Lord."

23. Possibly Jean de Serraval, lord of the castle of Faverges in the Rhône-Alpes
region (Morrall 1974, clxi).

24. A local noble family.

of the valley, like Sir Hans. And only then did I believe that it was true, because one confirmed the other, since the monks took him for a holy man. Therefore I shall let this lie and come to the first subject" (161–62; cf. 161, n. to l. 9).

B. Otto von Diemeringen's Version

As noted, L gave rise to two widely known versions, von Diemeringen's and the Vulgate Latin. In the Prologue, the translator refers to a Latin source, but recent scholarship suggests that while he may have known the Vulgate Latin he worked almost exclusively from the French, translating quite faithfully, if not literally.[25] His most radical change is a reordering of the whole into five books, the last two for all *TBJM*'s accounts of other religions, including Islam. He also added an introductory justification and a description of his text. Some forty-five manuscripts survive representing about six different redactions. No critical edition exists; the most easily accessible text is a facsimile of the first printing in 1480/1481: Bremer and Ridder 1991. Von Diemeringen seems to have come from the Metz-Strasbourg region; he probably studied in Paris, and in about 1367 or 1368 entered the chapter of Metz Cathedral as a canon.[26]

Otto's Prologue.[27] Since I have always been inclined to look at and hear about foreign lands and marvels . . . I Otto von Diemeringen, Canon of Metz (in Lotharingia), have thus turned this book from Latin and French into German to the delight of Germans who especially want to read about foreign things (so that the Germans too can read in it about many wonderful things that are written in it: about many wonderful countries and about many foreign animals and foreign peoples and their life and character and about clothing and many other wonders . . .).

(The first book speaks about the way to travel out of Netherland towards Jerusalem, and also about (to) Saint Catherine's grave, and about (to) Mount Sinai, and the countries and the wonders that are found en route, and also about the Sultan, his power, his lordship, and

25. Ridder 1991, 187; 1996, 234.

26. See the brief summary in Bremer and Ridder 1991, vii–ix. For details, see Ridder 1991, 191–211.

27. Quoted from Berlin, Staatsbibliothek Preussischer Kulturbesitz, mgf 205, fol. 1ra, as transcribed in Ridder 1991, 37, 225, 226, 227. This copy, Ridder claims, best represents the translator's original. Parenthetical words, a few of which are needed to make sense of Ridder's transcribed text and others that are simply variants, are from Crosby 1965, 1–3, 30–31 (quoting University of Kansas, Watson Library Summerfield MS. C 18, which here is fuller than Crosby's other text, Summerfield MS. E 16; Martinsson 1918, 13, also contains the words needed to make sense of the passage's final paragraph).

wives (character).[28] The second book tells anyone who at the same time wants to go around the world what wonders he might find in many countries, places, and islands to which he comes, and also tells the ways and countries right to the Great king (Chan) of Cathay's country. . . . The third book also tells us about the Great Caan. . . . The fourth book tells us about various overseas Christian beliefs . . . and also various Jewish beliefs. . . . The fifth book tells about Machomet. . . .)

[A]nd among all those who have traveled through those countries, one reads little by anyone who has seen as much of foreign lands as a knight who wrote this book in Latin and French about many lands. And so it seems to me not unuseful (to testify and publish it after his death, since it is) regarded as true at Paris, at Bruges, in England, and elsewhere by (many) noble (kings, princes, counts, lords,) knights and squires and (traveled) businessmen. And merchants (many people) from twenty-eight kingdoms come to Bruges, and each gladly hears this book. Thus I have taken it from Latin and French into German (in praise of the well-known knight,) who made the book for his eternal good fame after his death. And this book is new, and since some parts are probably unbelievable I thus have as witnesses some foreign scholars of natural history written in Latin that anyone may read who wants to hear what the scholar priests of nature should well understand. [. . .]

5. The Vulgate Latin Version

Unlike the four Latin translations from Insular, the Latin redaction made on the Continent from L had an international circulation and survives in some forty manuscripts. Almost nothing is known about its origins, except that it had to be made after L (therefore after c. 1390). In it a closed-minded translator meets an open text: cutting and rearranging material to emphasize the pilgrimage, he also dogmatically hardens *TBJM*'s religious attitudes and even deliberately reverses some of the author's claims, especially the speculative geographical ones.[29] There is no modern or scholarly edition; the excerpts are translated from Hakluyt 1589 and given according to its chapter divisions. Hakluyt is the work's first scholarly editor, and his concluding note to the reader (given here first) foreshadows the work's nineteenth-century reception.

Richard Hakluyt's Short Notice to the Reader. What I have accomplished in purifying our countryman John Mandeville (a learned and distinguished

---

28. The difference between these two words is smaller in the German: *wyben* and *wesen*.

29. For more on this version, see Higgins 1997a (index under "Vulgate Latin"); Ridder 1991, 169–78; Tzanaki 2003 (see index); and Tzanaki in Bremer and Röhl 2007, 79–82.

author, as witness Bale, Mercator, Ortelius, and others),[30] of the countless defects of scribes and printers through the collation of many copies,
and the best of those, let it be for educated men to judge, and especially
those well versed in geography and antiquity. As for the things he has
to say about monstrous human forms in Chapters 30, 31, [and] 33 of
his preceding itinerary, and here and there in the following [chapters],
although I do not deny that some of them have possibly been seen somewhere by him, they nevertheless seem to have been mostly taken from
Gaius Pliny the Elder, as will be evident to anyone ready to compare
them with these Plinian items I have placed here for that purpose [. . .].
Farewell, and either provide better or use these with me.[31]

Chapter 1. *A Brief Praise of the Land of Jerusalem.*[32] Since the Land of
Jerusalem, the Promised Land of God's children, is for many reasons
worthier to be possessed than all the world's lands together—and
especially for this [reason]: that God the maker of Heaven and earth
considered it to have been worthy of so much that in it He would show
to the human race His own son, Christ, Savior of the world, through
Incarnation in an undefiled Virgin, and through His most humble way
of life in the same place, and through the painful Consummation of
His death there, and after that through His wonderful Resurrection
and Ascension into Heaven, and finally because it is believed that He
will return there at the end of time, and judge everyone—it is certain
that it ought to be loved by all who are called Christian after Christ as
His own heirs and honored according to both its power and its measure.
By princes certainly and potentates, so that an attempt may be made
to recover it from the hands of the infidel, who some time ago now
took it from us, demanding our rewards, and have alas held it for many
years. Also by the common people and the strong, so that on devout
pilgrimage, chiefly in remission of sins, they may visit places so pious
and, through the traces of Christ and His disciples, so holy. Indeed, by
the weak and the burdened, insofar as they either urge on those mentioned above or help in some way, or at least utter faithful prayers. But
because it can now in our times be said more truly than in the past that
Virtue is gone, the Church trod under, the Clergy in error, the Devil in
power, and Simony dominant, see how through just God's judgment the
land so glorious and sacrosanct has been entrusted to the hands of the
impious Saracens, something which by pious minds is not to be heard
and reflected on without pain.

---

30. John Bale (1495–1563): English author of two important Latin catalogues of
English writers. Gerardus Mercator: Latinized name of Gerhard Kremer (1512–
94), Flemish mapmaker. Abraham Ortelius (1527–98): Flemish mapmaker and
Mercator's friend.

31. Hakluyt here appends excerpts from Pliny's *Natural History* 6.30 [35] and 7.2.

32. The Latin Chapter 1 corresponds to the French Prologue.

I John Mandevill [*sic*], bearing at least the name of the order of knights, born and raised in England, in the town of St Albans, was in my youth led by such a desire to regain the above-named land for its heirs that, although I could not do so, either by force or by my own men, I still went there for a certain time as a pilgrim and paid my small respects from nearby. That is why in the year 1322 since the Lord's Incarnation I sailed from Marseilles and until this time, the year 1355 (in other words, for 33 years), had remained overseas. I went as a pilgrim, traveled, and went around many and different countries, regions, provinces, and islands [. . .] where there live various peoples of diverse appearances, customs, laws, and rites. Nevertheless because through the greatest desire I was in the Promised Land, I took pains to go more carefully through the sites with the Son of God's traces, and remained longer in those. Therefore in this first part [. . .] I describe the way [. . .] from [. . .] England to that land, and briefly and carefully recall the especially holy places that are there, to the extent that this description might be effective in serving pilgrims in some way [. . .].

from **Chapter 3**. *About the City of Constantinople and the Relics Contained There.*[33] Constantinople is a beautiful city, and noble, triangular in shape, and securely walled; two sides are enclosed by the Hellespont, which most people now call Saint George's Arm, and others Buke, old Troy. Towards the place where the arm comes out of the sea there is a broad plain of land on which long ago stood Troy, the city about which wonderful things are read in the poets, but now very few traces of the city are evident. There are many wonders in Constantinople, and also many holy relics worthy of veneration, and above all the most precious Cross of Christ, or the greater part of it, as well as the seamless tunic, with the sponge and the reed, and one of the nails, and half of the Crown of Thorns, whose other half was taken to the King of France's Chapel in Paris. For I too, unworthy, have many times viewed both of them carefully; and a spine of the Paris crown was actually given to me, which I have preciously kept till now, and this stiff and piercing thorn is not made of wood, but as if of sea reeds.

The Church in Constantinople is said to be dedicated in honor of Sancta Sophia (that is, God's ineffable wisdom) and the noblest of all the world's churches, as much for the building's skillful design as for preserving holy Relics; for it also contains the body of Saint Anne, Our Lord's mother, translated there from Jerusalem by Queen Helen; and the body of Saint Luke the Evangelist translated from Bethany in Judea; and the body of Saint John Chrysostom, Bishop of the city, along with many other precious relics. For there is there, along with relics of this sort, a large vessel, *Enhydros,* as if of marble from Petra, continuously exuding water from itself; once a year it is found full of its exuded liquid.

---

33. Cf. Chapters 1–3 of *TBJM*.

In front of this church, on a marble column, there is a large statue, cast in gilded bronze, of the former Emperor Justinian sitting on a horse; there was moreover originally a round, forged sphere in the statue's hand that long ago now fell out of its hand, as a sign that the emperor had lost the lordship of many lands. For he used to be Lord of the Romans, the Greeks, Asia, Syria, Judea, Egypt, Arabia, and Persia, and now he retains only Crete, along with certain neighboring Greek lands [. . .] and the whole of Macedonia; and under him are the Caypolians, and the lofty Pyntenards [Pechenegs], and the majority of the Commans [Cumans]. Nevertheless, the statue holds a hand raised and extended out towards the east, as if a signal threatening the eastern infidel.

In the land of Thrace mentioned above, the philosopher Aristotle was born in the city of Stagira, and his tomb is there in place like an altar where on a certain day every year the people hold a celebration for him, as if he were a saint. [. . .][34]

All the people of the lands, regions, and islands who obey this Greek emperor are Christians and baptized; nevertheless, they each vary their faith in some article from our true Catholic faith and differ in many of their rites from the rites of the Roman Church, because they long since ceased to obey the Roman Pope, saying that the Apostle Saint Peter had had his seat in Antioch, although he was allowed in Rome. The Patriarch of Antioch therefore has in those eastern regions the same power as the Roman Pope in these western ones. The emperor of Constantinople moreover appoints their Patriarch and establishes, according to his will, the Archbishops and Bishops, and confers the offices and benefices, just as on fabricated pretexts he abandons, deposes, and deprives.

from **Chapter 7.** *About the Sultan's Palace, and the Number and the Names of Past Sultans.* [. . .][35] While staying at court, moreover, I saw around the Sultan a worthy and experienced physician originally from our parts. [. . .] We rarely met for conversation, however, because my service hardly corresponded to his. A long time after, though, and far from that place (namely, in the city of Liège) through the advice and assistance of the same worthy man, I put together this treatise, as I will explain at the end of the whole work. [. . .][36]

from **Chapter 14.** *About the Church of the Lord's Glorious Sepulcher in the City of Jerusalem.*[37] [. . .] The pilgrim coming into Jerusalem should first

---

34. The stories of Olympus, Athos, and the body of Hermes are told much as in *TBJM*, Chapter 3.
35. This passage follows the remarks about approaching the Sultan, as in *TBJM*, Chapter 6.
36. See Chapter 50 below. The account of the incubators in Cairo follows here, as in *TBJM*, Chapter 7.
37. Cf. *TBJM*, Chapter 10.

fulfill his pilgrimage at the venerated and sacrosanct Sepulcher of Our Lord Jesus Christ [. . . whose] entrance is lit for the approaching pilgrims by many lamps, at least one of which is always burning before the Sepulcher. [. . .] It is commonly said there too that the [. . .] lamp in front of the Sepulcher goes out every year on Good Friday at the ninth hour and is rekindled without human effort in the middle of the night on Easter, which (if it is so) is a clear miracle of divine favor. Although many Christians innocently believe it is a great reward of piety, it is nevertheless mistrusted by a good many. Perhaps the inventive Saracen keepers of the Sepulcher let such things be known so as to increase the profits of the tribute that may have resulted therefrom or those of the offerings that are given. Every year, however, on the day of the Last Supper, on Good Friday, and on Easter Eve, this Shrine remains open for these three days continuously and access is granted to all Christian peoples, but at other times in the year not without payment of a tribute.

Inside the church, beside the right wall, is the place of Calvary where Christ the Lord was hung crucified. One climbs by steps to this place, and it is a seemingly white-colored rock intermingled with some reddish rock in spots; it has a cleft that they call Golgotha, in which the greater part of Christ's precious blood is said to have flowed. An altar was also built there in front of which stand the tombs of Geoffrey of Bouillon and other Christian kings who around the year 1100 of the Lord's Incarnation conquered and took the holy city along with the whole country out of the hands of the Saracens, and through this acquired a great name for themselves that will last until the world's end. [. . .][38]

Not very far from this mount of Calvary there is also another altar where the column of the Lord's flagellation lies, close to which also stand four other marble columns continuously exuding water and, according to the opinion of the simple-minded, weeping for Christ's innocent suffering. [. . .] In the middle of the choir of this church is a place marvelously and beautifully covered with tiles in the complete figure of a circle where Joseph of Arimathea with his helpers washed Christ's body, which had been taken down from the cross, and preserved it with aromatic spices and herbs. Also, beneath this church to the north side is displayed the place where Christ appeared to [Mary] Magdalene after His Resurrection, when she believed him to be a gardener.

From the right side to the entrance of the church there are eighteen steps, under which is the Chapel of the Indians where only pilgrims from India through their priests sing masses according to their rite and celebrate what pertains to God. Indeed, they have a very short mass; in the beginning they perform with the necessary words the sacrament of Christ's body and blood with bread and wine, and afterwards with few added prayers they finish the whole service with the Lord's Prayer. This

---

38. The same Greek and Latin texts that are quoted in *TBJM*, Chapter 10 are quoted here.

is genuine, however, because they conduct themselves with the utmost attention, reverence, humility, and devotion, and they maintain what pertains to God.

On the other hand, what some have made known or supposed, that Judea or Jerusalem or this church stands in the middle of the whole world, according to the above-mentioned Scripture ("*in medio terrae*")— this cannot be understood spatially about the measure of the earth's body.[39] For if we consider the earth's breadth, which they estimate between the two poles, it is certain that Judea is not in the middle, because then it would be below the circle of the Equator and it would always be equinox there and it would remain at the horizon of both pole stars. Which is certainly not the case, because the Arctic Pole Star is raised very high to those in Judea.

Conversely, if we look at the earth's length, which can be estimated from the Earthly Paradise (that is, from the earth's worthier and more elevated place) towards its Nadir (that is, towards its opposite place on the earth's sphere), then Judea would be at the Antipodes of Paradise, which clearly is not so, because then the distance of the route going from Judea to Paradise would be the same for a traveler, whether it went towards the East or towards the West. But this neither appears true nor is true, as we know has been proved by the experience of many. To me, though, it seems that the above-mentioned Scripture of the Prophet can be explained: "*in medio terrae*," that is, around the middle of our habitable region, as evidently Judea may be about the midpoint between Paradise and the Antipodes of Paradise, being only ninety-six degrees from Paradise in the East, as I myself have tested by the eastern route— although about this it seems that complete certainty is not easy to be had, because in the sky's length no stars remain immobile, the way the Poles always remained fixed in breadth. Or it can be explained in this way: that David, who was King of Judea, said "*in medio terrae*": that is, in the main city of his land, Jerusalem, which was the royal or priestly city of the land of Judea. Or perhaps the Holy Spirit, which spoke through the Prophet's mouth in this phrase, does not want something bodily or spatial to be understood, but a spiritual whole, about which nothing should be written at present.

Chapter 21. *About the Hateful Sect of the Saracens, and their Faith.*[40] It now remains for me to write something about the sect of the Saracens, if briefly, according to what I have heard in often speaking with them and [what] Mahomet's book, which they call *Alcaron*, or *Mesahaf*, or *Harme*, teaches them, as I have often examined and diligently read through it. The Saracens believe in God, creator of Heaven and earth, who made

---

39. The rest of this chapter contradicts the *Mandeville* author's arguments in *TBJM*, Chapter 20.

40. Cf. *TBJM*, Chapter 15.

all things contained in them, and without whom nothing is made; and they await the final Day of Judgment on which the wicked will be sent body and soul down into Hell to be tormented forever and the good certainly will enter in body and soul into the Paradise of eternal happiness. Indeed, this belief in retribution belongs to the nations of all mortals who use language and reason, yet even so there is great diversity amongst believers about the nature of Paradise. For both the Saracens and the pagans, and all sects but the Jews and the baptized Christians, understand that there will be this Earthly Paradise of the good (out of which first-created Adam was cast for disobedience) which, as they suppose, flows, or will then flow, with many streams of milk and honey, and where, in houses and mansions nobly built, according to the merits of each person, of gold, silver, and precious stones, they will have full enjoyment of all bodily pleasures in delighting the soul eternally without end. Those therefore who are without the faith of the Holy Trinity and do not know Christ, who is the true light, walk in darkness. But the Jews and all the baptized rightly understand the Heavenly and spiritual Paradise, where each according to his merits will be united with the Divinity through thought and love. Nevertheless, the Jews, because they speak against their Scriptures of the Holy Trinity and impugn Christ, who is the true way, do not know where they are going. As for the baptized, however, who have steadfastly preserved the Catholic faith in the heart's humility under the Church's instruction, they alone are the children of the light, and will take the path to the Heavenly Paradise that Christ proclaimed with His Word, and to which in body and soul, being seen by His disciples, He in fact ascended.

The Saracens also believe to be true everything that God has spoken through the mouths of the prophets, but differently, because they do not know how they are to be distinguished, or rather they would contradict or readily deny the distinction. Amongst the prophets they consider four to be especially excellent. Of these they acknowledge Jesus, son of the Virgin Mary, as the highest and most excellent; they also call Him God's word, or utterance, or spirit, and the proclamation of God's intentions in a universal judgment to come, and God's messenger to the Christians to be taught. As for second place, they say that Abraham was God's true worshiper and friend. Third place they give to Moses as God's spokesman [and] messenger sent especially to instruct the Jews. They want the fourth to be Mahomet, God's holy and true envoy sent to them with the divine law fully contained in the said book. Thus they hold as beyond doubt that Saint Mary bore Jesus, and conceived while remaining an intact virgin, and they willingly hear talk about the Incarnation in her brought about through the Annunciation by the Archangel Gabriel. For their Alcaron also says that the Virgin was frightened at the Angel's greeting, because at that time there was in the regions of Galilee a sorcerer named Turquis who, having himself taken on the Angel's shape, had deflowered many virgins; and the blessed Virgin addressed the Angel, asking whether he might not be Turquis. It also records that she gave birth under a palm tree where there was an oxen's and ass's manger, and that there in the confusion of having given birth, as well as out of shame and anguish, she was almost without hope, and the little infant said to her in consolation, "Mother, do not be afraid: God has secreted in you his mysteries for the world's salvation."[41] This and many fictions similar to it are written there, and in recounting this they put many more amongst them that are not to be aired in this place.

The book says that Jesus—mild, pious, just, and utterly contrary to all vice—was the holiest of all the prophets conveying the truth in words and deeds; and likewise after the prophets mentioned above, Saint John the Evangelist was holier than the others. His Gospel too, they admit, is to be received as full in true teaching, and Saint John himself gave sight to the blind, purified lepers, raised the dead, and ascended alive into Heaven. He was indeed, as it says, more than a prophet, and without any sin, denying the same thing about himself: "if we say that we have no sin, the truth is not in us."[42] This is why when the Saracens hold Saint John the Evangelist's text, or that of Saint Luke ("the Angel Gabriel was sent"), they raise it above their head with both hands, out of reverence, both holding it before their eyes and kissing it very often with the highest devotion. A few of them indeed have become literate in Greek or Latin so as to read it often with a devout heart.

Also, the book says that the Jews were faithless because they refused to believe in Jesus, who was sent first to them by God and performed many miracles, and that through Him the whole people of the Jews was fittingly deceived and deservedly mocked in this way. At the moment when Judas kissed him as a sign of surrender, Jesus through metamorphosis placed his image in Judas himself, and thus the Jews, in the doubtful nighttime light, taking Judas for Jesus, binding, drawing, [and] mocking him, in the end crucified him, thinking to themselves that they did all this to Jesus, who, as soon as Judas had been taken and bound, ascended alive into Heaven—and will descend again alive at the Judgment on the last day. It adds that the most lying Jews to this very day deceive us Christians with their fraud, when they say that Jesus, whom they did not defend, crucified Himself. The stubborn Saracens maintain this error, and they attempt to make a certain case for it: if God, they assert, had allowed the innocent and just Jesus to be so wretchedly killed, He would have diminished the force of His highest justice. But since, as mentioned above, they walk in darkness, ignorant therefore of God's justice, they wish to establish justice, or rather they fashion injustice in

---

41. There is here a play on (or misunderstanding of) the words "secret" and "secretion": see (Pseudo-)William, *Tractatus* 34 (and n. 70), in Appendix B.2. "Infant" literally means "incapable of speech."

42. Cf. 1 John 1:8. The next quotation comes from Luke 1:26.

His heart, because we know the text about Christ's cross: "blessed is the wood through which justice comes."[43] Nevertheless, because in some things they approach the true faith, many of them at one or another time have been found to have converted, and many would be converted, if they had preachers to explain the Word correctly to them, since in fact they admit that Mahomet's law will at some point fail, just as the Jews' law has perished, and that the Christians' law will last until the end of the world.

Chapter 24. *The Case against Those Not Believing the Diversities of Lands throughout the Earth's Circle.*[44] Wonderful God created wonders through Himself alone so that He would be understood by His understanding creatures and through this be loved, and in this the Creator Himself and His Creatures would delight in each other. God therefore is especially wonderful in that He alone is sufficient unto Himself and wonderful Lord on high: that is, in Heaven and in Heavenly things, but also on earth and in earthly things. Nevertheless, if we were to judge truly, nothing is wonderful, because it should not be seen as a wonder, if He who is all-powerful has done what He pleased in Heaven and on earth. But consider that when we happen to see a thing that we have not seen before, our soul is amazed, not simply because it is wonderful, but because it is wonderful and new to us. The one God is indeed one only, even if Heavenly creatures, who are thus closer to God, prove to be simpler than He is.[45] Earthly creatures, however, because they are in a location farther away, are therefore more diverse amongst themselves, more opposite.

Anyone who is wise is therefore not astounded in his soul when he sees various and diverse things in earthly places, or when diverse things occur or are found in different parts of the earth. But those who do not raise the mind above the senses and who believe with the bodily eye more than with the spiritual and have never left their birthplace, scarcely want to believe or can believe true things told by others about the world's diversities. Nevertheless, such persons, if they wish, could easily see their errors. Because anyone who is born in one city, or country, if he would only move to the next city, will beyond doubt find there some difference or diversity in linguistic idiom, or in the manner of speech, in people's behavior, in occupations, in laws, in customs, or even in the crops of the fields, in the fruit of the trees, or in those things that arise on earth, in the air, and in the waters.

---

43. Wisd. of Sol. 14:7.

44. This chapter, which begins the Vulgate Latin's second part, has no counterpart in any French version.

45. There is here an untranslatable play on *simplex* ("single, simple, uncompounded"), rendered as "one only," and its comparative *simpliciores* ("simpler").

If difference therefore might in some way be found nearby, then the greater the distance is, the greater the difference is to be judged in a place far away, or farther away, or farthest away. Which is why—since in the preceding part of the treatise I began to relate some things that I saw in those places and on my pilgrimage to the Holy Promised Land that can be confirmed by many in our regions who have preceded me on the same pilgrimage, and will be by those who are to follow—I will proceed to describe some of the things that I saw and learned in my wandering,[46] in which for many years right down to the present time I traveled through many other lands and scanned many seas. And I will not be silent because of fools and disbelievers, but neither will I be sufficiently moved because of the believers or the wise. Yet I write for this reason: so that those who cannot look on God's diverse works with their own eyes can at least read or hear them. I have certainly seen few of those that do exist, but I will relate the few that I have seen.

from **Chapter 29**. *About Java and Certain Other Southern Islands, and About the Flour, Honey, and Fish of Ogier, Leader of the Danes.*[47] Proceeding farther south from there [Calamia] through many and wonderful lands for fifty-two days, one finds the large island of Lamory. Everyone there goes about naked, and almost everything is common to everyone. Nor do they use private keys and locks: on the contrary, all the women are also common to each and every man, provided that no force be used. But even worse than these things is their custom of willingly eating tender human flesh, which is why merchants bring them fat children for sale; but if they are not brought fat enough, they fatten them as we do a calf or a pig. The Antarctic Pole [Star] is seen here at a good height, and it begins to appear only in upper Libya, such that in upper Ethiopia it is eighteen degrees high, as I have myself tested with the astrolabe.[48] To the south of the land of Lamory is a good island, Sumebor, whose people consider themselves nobler than others, marking themselves in the face with a firm brand; they are always waging war against the above-mentioned naked people of Lamory. [. . .] Going south many other regions and islands follow about which much could have been recounted.

And there is a very large region, Java, which is 2,000 leagues in circumference. Its king is very powerful, and rules over the kings of seven nearby islands. [. . .] There is gold and silver there in immense quantities, as can be seen in the king of Java's palace, whose excellence is not easily described. All the steps ascending to the palace halls and

---

46. In contrast to the *Mandeville* author's presentation of his travels as unified, the redactor here contrasts *peregrinatio* ("pilgrimage") with *deambulatio* ("wandering"): religious travel with secular.

47. Cf. *TBJM,* Chapters 20–21.

48. The translator here omits the rest of the *Mandeville* author's discussion of geography in Chapter 20.

the royal rooms and the bedchambers are of solid gold or silver, but the entire breadth of the floors in the other rooms is also paved like a chessboard, one square of silver, the other of gold, with very thick tiles, and in these pavements diverse deeds and histories have been carved. In the main hall in fact the complete history of the Danish leader Ogier is displayed,[49] from his birth until the time he is said, fictitiously, to have returned to France, after this Ogier, in the time of Charlemagne, king of France, had with an armed band conquered for Christendom almost all the overseas regions from Jerusalem to the Trees of the Sun and the Moon, not far from the Earthly Paradise. To subjugate this kingdom of Java, which touches on the limits of the Empire of Tartary, the Emperor Grand Can has many times gone to war, but he has never been strong enough to prevail.

One can travel from here by sea to the kingdom of Thalamassa [. . .]. On this island are four kinds of tree, from one of which comes flour for bread, from the second honey, from the third wine, and from the fourth the worst poison. The flour is extracted from its trees in this manner. [. . .] In a similar way honey is drawn and wine flows from these trees, except that unlike the wine they are not dried first. It is also related there that the extraction of this flour, honey, and wine was originally shown to the foresaid leader of the Danes by an angel, when he and his army were troubled there by hunger. Against the poison that drips from the fourth kind of tree there is only one remedy for the person afflicted: to drink one's own dung dissolved in pure water. [. . .]

On the seashore there, miraculously, once a year for three days running, almost every kind of sea fish comes in great abundance, and they offer themselves freely to be taken by hand. Indeed, I too have taken many myself. Which is why it is to be noted that at the same time of year when the flour, honey, and wine mentioned above are extracted, these fish gather in this place. God once produced both miracles at the same time for His Ogier, and they are renewed every year in his memory until now. And in this territory are tortoises of a frightening size [. . .].

from **Chapter 35**. *About the Four Ceremonies That the Great Can Celebrates in the Year.* [. . .] [T]hey say that all earthly creatures should worship the Emperor Grand Can, the son of highest God[. . . .][50] Let us therefore observe in this place, I urge, how the pagans truly walk in darkness. Their devilish mind darkened by involution does not see how, although the emperor is a mortal human recently born, and likewise just as enveloped by this weakness, and going to die with them in a short time. They

---

49. On Ogier, see Sec. 3 above, and cf. the excerpts from Chapter 21 of Liège above.

50. This interpolation follows the description, given in Chapter 25 of *TBJM,* of the Chan's entertainments and the presentations made to him, both human and animal. The whole account is much altered.

do not doubt him, moreover, proclaiming him not God, but God's son, when they do not even know that he should not be praised or worshiped; but they pay no attention to Him, the other Son, the uncreated and co-natural[51] Son, who created both Himself and him [the emperor], alone in the world supremely praiseworthy. And contemplating this deep in our hearts, let us praise, worship, glorify, and supremely exalt God to all men—who wants us to be the sons of light and salvation, born, baptized, brought up, [and] educated in the purity of the Christian faith, schism and error having been shut out, and under the guidance of the most holy Mother Church, in which alone, out of almost the whole circumference of the earth's circle, the faith that saves and is served through love has now remained. And let us pray urgently for the pagans themselves, that through the acknowledged light of truth they will be able to see how they walk, that they reach Jesus Christ, God's co-equal Son, and in Him and through Him praise and worship the sole one true God.

from **Chapter 36**. *About the Entertainments and Illusions at the Feast, and About His [the Can's] Soldiers.* [. . .][52] It is certain that the people there are skillful in certain human arts, and clever in deceits above all regions of the new world,[53] which is why amongst themselves they have a saying that they alone see with two eyes and the Christians with one, all other peoples being blind; but they tell themselves wicked lies, because they see with a single eye earthly and passing things, and we Christians see with two, because with earthly eyes we see spiritual and lasting things. For Nahash (that is, the enemy of humankind) struck a treaty with them that they should have to pluck out their right eyes (that is, their spiritual eyes).[54] [. . .]

Chapter 50. *About the Composition of This Treatise in the Noble City of Liège.* In returning then from this island [of the rich man] one goes through the great provinces of the Empire of the Tartars in which a traveler can see, learn, and hear things always new, always marvelous, sometimes indeed unbelievable. And you know, as I said before, that I saw a few of the wonders that exist in these lands, but I have not written here a hundredth part of those that I saw, because I could not commit them all to memory,[55] and I have been largely silent about many of those that I did commit to memory, on account of modesty, which it is fitting to

---

51. I.e., sharing the same nature, a theologically orthodox definition.

52. Cf. the *Mandeville* author's comments in Chapter 23 on Cathayan ingenuity.

53. Note this expression for Cathay, which, ancient as it was, was indeed new to Latin Christians.

54. The Cathayans are here likened to those conquered by Nahash the Ammonite, who would have the right eyes of his enemies gouged out (1 Sam. 10:27–11:2).

55. Cf. the interpolated remarks on the author's "abridged records" in Chapter 34 of the French variants above (Appendix A.1).

attach to all actions. So that others therefore who either were in those regions before me or will go there might have room left to tell or write [something], I am limiting this treatise, shortening rather than fulfilling it, because it should not constrain the speaking of other things, nor fill up a listener's ears.

Thus in the year 1355 from Our Lord Jesus Christ's birth, in returning to my homeland, after I had reached the noble city of Liège and, because of my great age and arthritic gouts, had taken to bed in a street that is called Bassessanemi,[56] I consulted some doctors of the city on the subject of recovering my health. And it happened, by God's will, that there came one physician who was to be respected above the others for his age as well as his grey hair, and [was] clearly experienced in his art. In that place he was generally called Master John with the beard. While we were speaking together he said something in passing through which in the end we mutually renewed our old acquaintance that we had once had in Cairo of Egypt at the Sultan Melech Mandibron's, just as I touched on in Chapter 7 of the book.[57] While excellently demonstrating on me his experience in his art,[58] he strongly encouraged and entreated me to arrange in writing something that should usefully be read and heard about the things I saw during my pilgrimage and my journey through the world. And thus at last through his advice and assistance this treatise was composed, none of which certainly I had meant to write until I had at least reached my own territories in England. And I believe that the foregoing things happened around me through God's foresight and grace, because since the time I left, our two kings of England and France did not cease to inflict mutual destruction, pillaging, ambushes, and killings, through which, unless guarded by the Lord, I would not have passed without death, or risk of death, and without a great many offenses. And behold now in the thirty-third year of my going away, having stopped over in the city of Liège, which by sea is only two days from England, I hear that through God's grace the said hostilities of the Lords have been settled.[59] Which is why I also hope and intend in the remainder of my ripe age to be able to attain my body's rest and my soul's salvation in my own place. Here then is the end of this writing, in the name of the Father, the Son, and the Holy Spirit. Amen.

Here ends the itinerary from England to the Jerusalem territories overseas and those beyond, first set down in French by lord John Mandeville, knight, its author, in the year of the Lord's Incarnation 1355 in the city of Liège, and translated shortly afterwards in the same city into the said Latin form.

---

56. Basse Sauvenière. See Liège variants, Chapter 34 above (Appendix A.2).

57. *TBJM,* Chapter 6. See also Appendix C.4 "A Note on the Account of the Sultans."

58. That is, while improving my health.

59. During the Hundred Years' War, the year 1355 saw hostilities, not peace.

Appendix B:

The Sources of The Book of John Mandeville

The most thorough recent source study suggests that the *Mandeville* author drew largely on some twenty-five texts, consulting about another ten.[1] Some belong to more than one genre, but a rough sorting might look like this:

Accounts of the Near (Biblical) East

Burchard of Mount Sion, *Descriptio Terrae Sanctae* (*Description of the Holy Land,* c. 1283)

Eugesippus, *Tractatus de distanciis locorum Terrae Sanctae* (*Treatise on the Distances of the Places of the Holy Land,* twelfth century)

John of Würzburg, *Descriptio Terrae Sanctae* (*Description of the Holy Land,* mid-twelfth century)

Pseudo-Odoric, *Liber de Terra Sancta* (*Book of the Holy Land,* mid-thirteenth to early fourteenth centuries)

Thietmar, *Peregrinatio* (*Pilgrimage,* 1217)

William of Boldensele, *Liber de quibusdam ultramarinis partibus* (*Book of Certain Regions beyond the Mediterranean,* 1336) [main source: Chs. 1–14]

Accounts of the Far (Marvelous) East

Iter Alexandri Magni ad Paradisum (*Alexander the Great's Voyage to Paradise,* various dates)

Littera Presbyteris Johannis (*Letter of Prester John,* c. 1160s)

Odoric of Pordenone, *Relatio* (*Account,* 1330) [main source: Chs. 16–34]

Scripture and Its Supplements

The Bible (Vulgate)

Caesarius of Heisterbach, *Dialogus miraculorum* (*Dialogue of Miracles,* c. 1219–1223)

Defensor de Ligugé, *Liber Scintillarum* (*Book of Sparks,* late seventh to early eighth centuries)

---

1. Deluz 1988, 39–72, 428–91. My list is modified from Deluz 1988, 57–58. Sources with an asterisk were used less frequently. On works not described here, see Kohanski and Benson 2007, 135–42.

*Honorius Augustodunensis, *Elucidarium* (*Explanation,* early twelfth century)

Jacobus de Voragine, *Legenda Aurea* (*Golden Legend,* completed by the 1260s)

Peter Comestor, *Historia Scholastica* (*Scholastic History,* c. 1170)

(Pseudo-)William of Tripoli, *Tractatus de statu Sarracenorum* (*Treatise on the State of the Saracens,* after 1273) [main source: Ch. 15]

*"Sydrach," *La Fontaine de toute science* (*The Source of All Knowledge,* thirteenth century)

Histories

Albert of Aachen (also known as Albert of Aix), *Historia Hierosolomitanae Expeditionis* (*History of the Expedition to Jerusalem,* early twelfth century)

Alexander Romances (various dates)

Continuator of William of Tyre, a continuation of William's *Historia rerum in partibus transmarinis gestarum* (*History of Deeds Done beyond the Sea,* thirteenth century)

Hayton of Armenia, *Flor des estoires de la terre d'Orient* (*Flower of the Histories of the Land of the East,* 1307) [main source: Chs. 24 and 25 (part)]

Jacques de Vitry, *Historia Orientalis* (*Eastern History,* early thirteenth century)

*Flavius Josephus, *De belle judaico* (*The Jewish War,* late first century), *Antiquitates judaicae* (*Jewish Antiquities,* late first century) [both originally in Greek]

*Martinus Polonus (Martinus Oppaviensis or Martin von Trappau), *Chronicon pontificum et imperatorum* (*Chronicle of Popes and Emperors,* c. 1277)

*Orosius, *Historiarum adversum Paganos libri VII* (*Seven Books of Histories against the Pagans,* early fifth century)

Encyclopedias

Brunetto Latini, *Li Livres dou Tresor* (*Book of the Treasure,* early 1260s)

Gervase of Tilbury, *Otia Imperiala* (*Imperial Entertainments,* early twelfth century)

Honorius Augustodunensis (?), *Imago Mundi* (*Depiction of the World,* early twelfth century)

*Isidore of Seville, *Etymologiae* (*Etymologies,* early seventh century)

Vincent of Beauvais, *Speculum Historiale* and *Speculum Naturale* (*Mirror of History* and *Mirror of Nature,* 1240s–1250s)

Scientific Treatises

*Bede, *De temporibus* (*On Systems of Time,* early eighth century)

Johannes de Sacrobosco, *Tracratus de Sphera* (*Treatise on the Sphere,* early thirteenth century)

*Macrobius, *Commentarii in somnium Scipio* (*Notes on Scipio's Dream,* early fifth century)

1. William of Boldensele, *Book of Certain Regions beyond the Mediterranean*

Little is known about this German Dominican, whose real name was Otto von Nyenhusen (Neuhaus). In 1330 he left the cloister of Saint Paul in Minden without permission and, after sailing from Genoa to Constantinople, went to Egypt and Palestine, then to Avignon, where the papal curia resided, to seek absolution for his unauthorized departure from Saint Paul. In 1336, he composed a Latin memoir at the request of Cardinal Elie Talleyrand of Périgord (1301–1364).[2] Pious, tidy, and occasionally chatty, the memoir offers an informative, intelligent, and sometimes self-promoting account of what its author saw and felt, including not only holy places, but also curiosities. Less popular than Odoric's *Relatio,* this "little book on the state of the Holy Land," as William calls it, survives in some thirty manuscripts, of which six represent the French translation made in 1351 by Long John, monk of Saint Bertin in Saint Omer. The *Mandeville* author consulted both versions, but worked mostly from the French, as he radically remade William's book: following its route from start to finish, he turned its narrative into a general itinerary and added about fifty percent more material (while also making some cuts). Sometimes he disagrees with William, as about "Joseph's Granaries" (the pyramids). Most excerpts given here are from Long John's French; differences from the Latin are noted as needed. Both are translated from Deluz 1972, the Latin occasionally modified from Grotefend 1855. No other English translations exist.

The letter of lord William of Boldensele, most illustrious man and noble knight, to lord Peter, Abbot of Aula Regia, about the description of the Holy Land.[3] To his most loving father and lord, lord Peter, Abbot of Aula Regia of the Cistercian order in the diocese of Prague, [from] William of Boldensele, knight, [. . .]. Not wanting to forget the accepted kindness, I call to mind the sincere acts of goodwill and courtesy that last year in [. . .] Aula Regia you joyfully and with tender feeling showed me and my retinue for more than two months. The Lord willing, I will [. . .]

---

2. On Talleyrand, see Zacour 1956, esp. 683–84.

3. Nine Latin manuscripts contain this dedicatory letter; it is not found in Long John's French. Aula Regia, mentioned below, is Zbraslav (German: Königsaal), now part of Prague, where Wenceslas II founded a Cistercian monastery on the Vltava (Moldau) River.

freely and most zealously respond with the same display. Now however it is necessary for me to delay longer than I had thought at the court in Avignon[4] with my lord, lord Talleyrand of Périgord, cardinal priest of the Church of Saint Peter in Chains, since this same lord of mine was very pleased by my arrival at his pleasure, and I am now arranging and ordering towards the desired end all of my affairs that I told you about when I was with you. This business finished, I will [. . .] return to you at Aula Regia, staying permanently, the Lord willing. [. . .] Nothing will be able to draw me away but death alone. Nonetheless, as you requested and I promised, I am sending you through my servant Francis Cristani[5] of Prague, as a token of my great desire and love, my little book on the state of the Holy Land (which I put together[6] at the urging of my lord cardinal mentioned above) [. . .], and after my return I will explain more clearly in words where needed. May Christ protect you forever. Given at Avignon, A.D. 1337, Michaelmas.[7]

Here begins the prologue to the book about certain regions beyond the sea[8] and especially about the Holy Land. "As we have heard, so have we seen, in the city of the Lord of hosts, in the city of our God: God hath founded it for ever."[9] Although the land and its fullness belong to the Lord, as do the circle of lands[10] and all that live in them, nevertheless Jerusalem especially is said to be God's city, and its limits in particular are called the Lord's inheritance, because these regions belong to Israel's sons through God's fore-chosen gift[11] of the Savior's grace: [a gift] promised by Him to His adopted heirs since the beginning and given finally as a paternal inheritance freely possessed. For "the Lord chose Sion; He chose it as His dwelling place," insofar as He expressly added, "This is my rest for ever and ever: here will I dwell, for I have chosen it."[12] Because although spiritual substances may not be circumscribed in place nor God above limited in place, they are still chiefly said to be such and their

4. From 1309 to 1377 the papacy resided in Avignon, not Rome.

5. "Crista" in Grotefend (1855, 237).

6. *compilavi:* "compiled," the same verb used by the *Mandeville* author to describe his activities.

7. September 29, the Feast of Saint Michael: the day on which the *Mandeville* author claims to have set out.

8. The Mediterranean. *TBJM*'s Prologue was more likely inspired by Long John's French version (below).

9. Ps. 48[47]:9.

10. The whole planet: on the *orbis terrarum,* see Appendix C.1.

11. "gift": literally "privilege," which also has a relevant legal sense; "fore-chosen" (*preelecte*) makes Christians the Israelites' heirs rather than their displacers (Muslim occupation being overlooked).

12. Ps. 132[131]:14. The previous sentence quotes the psalm's preceding verse (13).

regions are mostly defined as such, where and in which the workings and effects of their power will have happened to appear to a greater extent. Consequently, because the works of divinity beneficial to human salvation beyond Nature's course have been freely shown by God in the previously mentioned regions as much in the era of natural law as of Mosaic law and the Gospels' grace, therefore, in order that they be, by a not-undeserved choice, the name of God's inheritance, we profess both that God has inhabited them uniquely and also that He will do so wonderfully at the world's end. [. . .]

Here begins a treatise about the state of the Holy Land *and also partly about the land of Egypt. [. . .] made [. . .] by the noble lord William of Boldensele, in the year of grace 1336; and [. . .] translated from Latin into French by friar John called Long [. . . in] 1351.*[13] "*Sicut audivimus sic vidimus in civitate dei nostri.*"[14] These words are written in the Psalter, and our author, who was himself in Jerusalem, sets them down while speaking in his own person; in our French they mean "as we have heard, so we have seen in the city of Our Lord God," as if he wished to say, I have heard many wonders recounted about the Holy Land, but indeed I can speak about them who now have seen them in Jerusalem, which is rightfully called the city of Our Lord God. For although the whole world is His, the city of Jerusalem especially should be called God's city and His territory God's inheritance. For as in special love He chose it from the beginning of the world, [a city] promised and given to his faithful friends, patriarchs, and prophets and his very beloved people of Israel, highly ennobled by His graces and His miracles, richly endowed by His bodily presence, and very dearly bought by His very precious blood. Thus because we are so much more perfect when we follow and strive after Our Lord God's words and deeds, and since it is said that He chose this city and country so very specially above all others in which He deigned to be born a man and dwell amongst the people, so we too, with Him, with all our heart and above all other lands, should choose it with very singular devotion and love it with very special affection, and turning to Him with a pure heart say with the prophet David, "*Adorabimus in loco ubi steterunt pedes eius.*"[15] This means in our French, "We will worship God in the same place where his feet walked."

This place truly is the said Holy Land where God deigned, as it is said, to dwell amongst the nations. This Holy Land and these holy places were chosen with very special devotion for dwelling in by many pagans before Our Lord's coming and after, without their knowing anything

---

13. Although he considerably simplifies the Latin argument in the Prologue, paraphrasing as much as translating, John's French is very Latinate syntactically.

14. Shortened from Ps. 48[47]:9 in William's Latin, translated in the next sentence in the text.

15. Ps. 132[131]:7.

either through Scripture or through renown, except that they dreamt by who knows what natural inclination that the mystery of our salvation would be fulfilled. Nevertheless, just as everyone should naturally love their own country, the origin of their lineage, so firmly that to defend it they should expose themselves to the risk of death in battle, so I dare say indeed that every good Christian should be incomparably much more attached to this Holy Land with very special love. For in our own country we were born only into our existence in Nature, but in this Holy land through God's glorious death we were born into our existence in Grace and Salvation. And the first birth would be worth nothing to us if we were not helped by this rebirth. Let us Christians together then all love this Holy Land as the common inheritance of Christians. For Jesus Christ dying on the cross gave it to us as a testament, and in rising to Heaven He left it to the children of Abraham's faith and we are those Christians.

I have desired since the time of my childhood to see this Holy Land as my own inheritance given to me as well as to every good Christian by the right of Jesus Christ's faith whereby my eyes could see the testimonies of those things that had often been offered to the eye and to the ears and with the prophet David I could truly say the first words set down, "*Sicut audivimus etc. . . .*" Thus all the things that I saw there, and the order of the places as I saw them in making my pilgrimage, through God's grace, I will faithfully explain to you very reverend father, according as your worthy fatherhood affectionately devoted to God and to the Holy Land mentioned above has required.

The first chapter *is about my voyage in Syria, where it speaks about many seas, the city of Constantinople, Troy the great, and many others.*[16] First I left Germany, my own country where I was born, passed through Lombardy, and came to a seaport in the boundaries of Genoa. There I entered a well-armed galley to make our journey by sailing through the sea [. . .] called the sea of the middle of the world,[17] for it is right in the middle of the three main parts of the world, Asia, Africa, and Europe, such that by itself and with its constituent parts it divides the three regions from one another. With one arm it joins Spain; this arm has the name Strait of Morocco, and it falls into the Ocean Sea, which is the sea that goes around the whole world. This sea of the middle of the earth has another arm that has the name Hellespont and Saint George's Arm, through which it is joined to the Black Sea; this sea has no islands. And because this sea of the middle of the earth is so long it is called the Great Sea.[18] This Arm of Saint George is in that country generally called the Mouth

---

16. From John's French. Cf. Chapters 1–5 in *TBJM*.

17. The literal meaning of Mediterranean.

18. John's text departs from William's Latin, where the Black Sea is the Great Sea, perhaps correcting it.

of Constantinople, because that noble city is situated above this arm. This arm divides Asia Minor from Constantinople and Greece.[19]

Another sea is in the east beyond the city of Sara,[20] which the Tartars of Cumania hold, and it is named the Caspian Sea. This Caspian Sea is not joined to the Ocean Sea, nor to the Great Sea, nor also to the Black Sea, by any visible arm that can be seen; some nevertheless say that through an underground stream it is joined to the Black Sea, which is the closest to it; and thus it is joined to the other seas, as they say.

This noble city of Constantinople [. . .] is situated on Saint George's Arm, and some call it lesser Rome. This city is built in the shape of a triangular shield well girdled by strong walls; two sides look out onto the sea, the third towards the land, and there is also a very fine and very large gate. In this city there is a great abundance of churches; most are very beautiful beyond measure, made of marble and of a wonderfully singular manner of construction; and there are also many very beautiful palaces. The main church is the Church of Saint Sophia: that is, holy wisdom, which is God Jesus Christ. The noble Emperor Justinian founded it, and proudly gave it fine privileges and very great splendors. I believe that under Heaven no one has ever made a great work that can or ought to be compared to his in nobility. In this church[21] is the statue of the Emperor Justinian who founded it, and he is on a horse cast in metal and has a gold crown on his head; in his left hand he holds a round apple that signifies and represents the world, of which he is the ruler; the right hand he holds up and extended towards the east as if threatening rebels; and this statue is set high on a masoned base of large stones very firmly cemented together. In this noble city by the emperor's order I saw a large part of the true cross, and Our Lord's coat that has no seams, the sponge with which He was given drink on the cross, and the reed on top of which it was fixed, and one of the nails, Saint John Chrysostom's body, and many other holy relics.

At the other end of Saint George's Arm on the seashore in Asia Minor that looks out on the sea was once situated that ancient and well-known city of Troy; it was situated in a most beautiful place on a favorable broad plain and [had a] beautifully favorable view of the sea. It seems not to have had a good port, but a river that once flowed there and could receive and shelter ships. Hardly any traces are visible of this so great and so very noble city. By God's grace I went without hindrance all the way to these Trojan regions, passing by all of the shores of Lombardy, Tuscany,

---

19. This passage occurs after the account of the Caspian Sea in William's Latin text.

20. Sarai Batu, or Sarai Berke, founded in the thirteenth century as the capital of the Golden Horde (the Khanate of Qipchaq), situated on the Volga.

21. Three Latin copies have *in* rather than *coram* ("in front of"), and John was working from one of these or a (lost) related copy; the *Mandeville* author consulted the Latin here.

Campania, Apulia, Calabria, and the renowned Italian islands Corsica, Sardinia, [and] Sicily, and the Gulf of Venice that separates Italy from Greece, [and] by the shores of Greece (Morea, Athens, Macedonia), and the other regions of Greece that are called Romania. Passing by all these countries I sailed by sea all the way to the Trojan regions.

I sought out and visited some Greek islands. Amongst others I was on Sio [Chios], where mastic grows and nowhere else, it is said. This mastic is a gum that flows from small shrubs through certain cuts that are made there with a kind of tool appropriate to it used to open the bark in the right season. From there I went to the island of Pathmos on which Saint John the Evangelist, sent into exile, wrote the Apocalypse. From there I went to the city of Ephesus where the above-mentioned Saint John placed himself in his tomb entirely alive.[22] On this tomb was built a very beautiful church, all covered with lead, in the form of a cross. This city of Ephesus is situated in a very beautiful and fertile place not too far from the sea. The Turks hold it and also all of Asia Minor, and they have driven away all the Christians or killed them or made them slaves. The churches that Saint John mentions in the Apocalypse are all destroyed except the above-mentioned church in Ephesus where I saw Saint John's tomb, and it is behind the great altar. This Asia Minor has lost its name since the Turks conquered it and it is now named Turkey.[23]

From there I went through many islands, for there is an abundance of them that were once very rich but are now all deserted through the Turks, and I came to a city on the sea in Asia Minor that has the name Pathera [Patara], in which lord Saint Nicholas was born; next I reached the city of Mirre [Myra] where he was then made bishop at God's command. Next is the very favorable island of Crete and the island of Rhodes, which the Hospitallers won from the emperor of Constantinople by force of arms; they hold their main assembly there and the head of their order. The place is quite healthy and delightful, not far from Turkey on an arm of the sea.

From there I went to Cyprus. On this island is found the very fine wine of Engaddy that Solomon mentioned in his Song of Songs.[24] These vines are on Cyprus near the city of Minos [Nicosia?], and those of the country call them *engadda*. The Cyprus grapes grow red but after a year they turn white, and the older they are the whiter and clearer they

---

22. Latin: "where . . . John died and was buried." The translator follows a variant (Grotefend 1855, 240).

23. John's French is sometime less negative than William's Latin: "This [church] they have adapted to their profane cult according to Machumet's law. After Asia Minor was taken by the Turks, it lost its former name and is commonly called Turkey by its unjust inhabitants."

24. Song of Sol. 1:13: "A cluster of cypress [*cypri,* "henna blossoms"] my love is to me, in the vineyards of Engaddi." As Deluz notes (1972, 209, n. 24), medieval travel books regularly make this error, which derives from linking the island's Latin name with the henna shrub's (both *cyprus*).

become. They are very healthy and fragrant and very grievously strong, such that no one can drink them without adding plenty of water. On Cyprus in an abbey of the order of Saint Benedict on a mountain is the good thief's cross, a part of Our Lord's nail, and many other noble relics. On this island of Cyprus is lord Saint Hilarius' body under the king's protection in the castle that has the name Dedamors.[25] There is on Cyprus another greatly revered saint who has the name Saint Zazomo;[26] his head is in the king's chapel. On Cyprus lord Saint Barnabus was born in the city of Salanna [Salamis], which was the city of Constance that is all destroyed near Famagusta.[27] In the mountains of Cyprus there are wild sheep similar to stags and they are very hard to see. I saw many taken on the hunt by dogs and especially by great lords' leopards. And they are found nowhere but on Cyprus.

From Cyprus I had a good wind and went to Syria in one day and one night.[28]

[*from* **Chapter 3**] *About the country of Egypt and about the desert that separates Egypt from Syria and about the city of Babylon and others.*[29] From the castle Darium I went to Egypt in seven days through the sandy desert. No water is found there. Thus I carried my food and other necessities with me. Nevertheless there are along the way certain hostels and inns run by the Saracens where necessities can be conveniently found. The desert crossed, I came to Egypt, where one finds countless very beautiful villages full of all worldly goods, except wine, which the Saracens do not drink at all. And therefore they do not cultivate vines as well; nor do they raise pigs, for they do not eat them, for this is strictly forbidden to them in their law. Through Egypt I went first to Babylon by way of the large famous city that is called Belleiz [Bilbeis]. I left to the right on the seashore the very noble cities of Alexandria and Damietta, and I went to Cairo and Babylon, the capital of Egypt, where the Sultan's sovereign seat is. [*W briefly describes the castle and the Sultan's staff and army.*]

Cairo and Babylon are two very large cities. [*W briefly describes them.*] It should be known that this Babylon is not that one where Nebuchadnezzar

---

25. *Dieu d'amour:* God of love.

26. The spelling varies much in the Latin manuscripts, making it unclear which saint is meant. Deluz (1972, 210, n. 27) thinks Saint Sozomen likelier than Saint Zosimus.

27. Deluz's punctuation (1972, 302) makes "near Famagusta" part of the next sentence in the French, but in the Latin it clearly belongs to this sentence.

28. Deluz (1972, 210) and Grotefend (1855, 242) read *in die natali* ("on Christmas day"), but several copies read *in die naturali* ("in a natural day," meaning perhaps "in a single day," or "in twenty-four hours"). Deluz wonders (302, textual note) whether the Latin should have read *die nocteque* ("in a day and a night," as in the French).

29. Cf. *TBJM*, Chapter 5 (end) to Chapter 7.

ruled and where the children of Israel were led into prison, but is the
new Babylon following that old one in name and works; for just as the
old city was once hostile to the children of Israel, who then were God's
chosen people, so this new Babylon, with its head the Sultan and its
members the Saracens, is more opposed to us Christians, the true
Israelites and God's true people, than any other misbelieving people.

For[30] this Sultan is the principal champion of Mahomet's false law. This false Mahomet got his start in country subject to the Sultan, and gave his law to the bestial people in the desert of Arabia subject to the Sultan. And this wicked Mahomet lies in the city of Mecca[31] twenty-five days' travel from this Babylon in very great reverence like a relic under the Sultan's most diligent care. No one believes that he hangs in the air by virtue of adamant, as some have reported. That is not true; rather, he lies in an expensive tomb that is raised up in one of their churches that they call mosques in their language. Saracens come there from every part of the world on pilgrimage to their prophet, as we do in Jerusalem to Our Lord's grave. And for that reason the Sultan of Babylon is the sovereign defender of Mahomet's law and more hostile than any one else to the Christian faith.

[The Sultan] is the principal champion and disseminator of Machomet's impious perfidy, since that wicked liar originated with the Sultan's rule. It was in that very place (that is, in the Arabian desert) that he first preached to bestial and ignorant men and imposed his diabolical law, and with a serpent's cunning duped them with false miracles and gathered them up for the father of falsehood and lies. And the body of this most depraved fraud is kept under the Sultan's most diligent care in the city that is called Mecca (situated in the Arabian desert about twenty-five days' travel from Babylon) in front of the great shrine in a beautiful church of theirs that is commonly called a mosque. Not that it hangs in the air by the power of those stones which attract iron, as has been falsely reported; rather, to the greater eternal damnation of the dead man himself he was placed in a raised and expensive tomb, to which the Saracens flock from every part of the world, these

30. John's French is set here beside William's Latin (in the right hand column) to show how much he has toned it down.
31. A common Christian pilgrim's error for Medina.

wretches believing themselves
to be there on a most devout
and religious pilgrimage to
their prophet. And on that
account the Sultan of this
new Babylon is taken by the
Saracens to be the great advocate and defender of their
perfidy—and perfidy more
than any error is most hostile
to the Christian faith.

[*W briefly describes Chaldea and the ancient Babylon, which some believe to be the Tower of Babel; having distinguished the two Babylons, W returns to the new and gives an account of the Nile, the churches in Cairo and Babylon, and the land of Egypt.*]

I saw in Cairo three entirely live elephants. It is a very large animal. Its skin is hard like fish scales. This is a highly intelligent and talented and teachable animal; it dances and jumps to the sound of musical instruments. It has great teeth judged by their size coming out of its mouth like a boar's teeth. Above its mouth it has a long tube like a round bag pointed in front. This bag is not a straight tube, for it is entirely cartilaginous, harder than flesh, softer than bone, and flexible everywhere. It uses this instead of a hand and picks up its food. When it has taken its food at the tip of this tube, it bends this tube under and thus puts the food in its mouth, and then eats like any other animal. Some say that an elephant cannot get up again when it has fallen down. This is not true, for it bathes and plays, lies down and gets up like any other animal. At its master's command, it celebrates visitors; it lowers its head, kneels, and kisses the ground, for such is the practice of honoring lords in this country. I saw in Cairo an animal called a Jarafan [giraffe]. In front it is very high and so tall and with a neck so long that from the ground it can indeed take its food from above a house of ordinary height; but behind it is so low that a man could reach its back with his hand. It is not fierce or cruel at all, but as peaceful as a horse or a mule. Its skin is very beautiful, and colored white and red in a very regular pattern. I saw many baboons, cat monkeys,[32] and parrots so well trained that with their behavior they gave people great pleasure and delight. One can find parrots there that will not be sold for one hundred gold coins, because the people of the country excessively seek out pleasure and bodily enjoyments.

In the highest parts of Egypt there is an emerald mine such that more emeralds are found there and at a better price than in any other part of

---

32. Latin *cattos mammones; gati maymones* are also mentioned by Odoric in China (1929, 466). It is not clear what they might be.

the world. In Egypt and Syria are found a kind of long apples that are called apples of paradise, and they are soft and excellent tasting, melting very easily in the mouth. When they are cut through the middle or in any other way a crucifix is found there: so perfectly made indeed that one can see and perceive the face and all the other forms of the body. They do not last long, which is why they cannot be brought by sea to our regions without rotting. [*Next comes an account of sugar cane and other plants in Egypt, poultry incubators, the market in non-Muslim slaves, and the fertile biblical land of Goshen.*]

Near Cairo on the side towards the Syrian desert is the yard where the very unique and very special balm grows. The yard is not very big or fenced in or walled. I was most amazed that so noble a place was not better enclosed. Balsam shrubs are not very tall or large, but are mid-sized, full of branches like a grapevine. This yard is watered by a small spring that is within the yard, and the Christians of the country say that Our Lady often washed and bathed her glorious son there, and washed His clothes there, and they agree that this yard should be watered from this spring to produce balm, for it received this power from Jesus Christ's body, as they say.

Beyond Babylon and the river of Paradise [the Nile] towards the desert that is between Egypt and Africa are many tombs and memorials of the ancients of former times, and these tombs and these memorials are built very high and very pointed like a very pointed bell tower with large, well-polished stones, amongst which there are two marvelously tall and large on which I found writings in various languages cut into the rock. And on one I found these verses in Latin:[33]

> *Vidi pyramidas sine te dulcissime frater*
> *Et tibi quod potui lacrimas hic mesta profudi*
> *Et nostri memorem luctus hanc sculpo querelam*
> *Sit nomen decimi centi anni pyramide alta*
> [Si<c> nomen Decimi <G>entia<n>i pyramide alta]
> *Pontificis comitisque tuis trayane triumphis*
> *Lustra sex intra censoris consulis esse*
> [lustra<que> sex intra censoris, consulis, e<x>s<t>e<t>].

I saw the pyramids without you, sweetest brother, and, in my sadness,[34] I here poured out what tears I could for you; and I carve this lament memorializing our grief; may the name of Decimus

---

33. The emendations (marked <>) follow John T. Quinn: www.stoa.org/diotima/anthology/terentia.shtml. See E. A. Hemelrijk, *Matrona Docta: Educated Women in the Roman Elite* (New York: Routledge, 1999), 171–72.

34. *mesta*: "sad," is grammatically feminine, making the speaker female.

Centiannius [Decimus Gentianus],[35] priest and companion in your victory parades, Trajan, censor and consul before age thirty, thus remain on the high pyramid.

These verses are very obscure in meaning, and I mused there for a long time, but nevertheless they testify that these columns, these structures, are tombs and memorials of the ancients. And anyone who looks carefully can see this also through many other signs. Nevertheless, the simple people of the country say that these were Pharaoh's barns and granaries in which Joseph had the wheat kept in the time of the great famine mentioned in the Bible,[36] and the people of the country call them Pharaoh's granaries. But this cannot be true at all, for no place for putting in the wheat can be found there, and there is inside these columns no empty space where anything can be placed. For from top to bottom they are closed and made entirely of huge stones well joined to one another—except that there is a very small door quite high above the ground and a very narrow and very dark little passage through which one descends there for a certain distance, but it is not all wide enough to put grain in, as those of the country say and believe.

[*from* **Chapter 4**] *About the way to Mount Sinai, and about Arabia and the holy places in it right to the start of the Promised Land.*[37] Leaving Cairo then and Babylon and the regions of Egypt, I hastened into Arabia and reached Mount Sinai on horseback in ten days. The way in between is all desert. The aged and honest monks of Mount Sinai asserted that they had never seen a Christian pilgrim come there on horseback before me, because other pilgrims were in the habit of coming on camels. For a camel eats thorn bushes and spiny plants that it finds in the desert, enduring for two whole days and the start of a third without a single drink. And the camel-drivers carry dried beans through the desert, and when they want to refresh their camels they give them a few of these beans, and they thus continue on their way working heavily laden for the whole day. A horse would have faltered with such work and provisions, which is why I had skins full of suitable feed and water for my horses borne on camels along with everything that I and my retinue needed. For the Sultan of Babylon did me a unique favor, mediated by God's kindness, giving me letters

---

35. Quinn thinks the "garbled" name to be "Decimus Terentius Gentianus, consul suffectus under the Emperor Trajan in 116," allowing the author to be one Terentia. Ferdinand Deycks, however, thinks it is likely Decimus Annius, already at thirty made *pontifex* ("high priest"), Trajan's companion in war, and consul (Deycks, ed., Ludolph of Suchem, *De Itinere Terrae Sanctae Liber* [Stuttgart, 1851], 55, n. 11).

36. Gen. 41.

37. William's Latin text is translated here, since the *Mandeville* author adapts it (not the French text) in Chapters 8 and 11.

with which he recommended me to all his subjects; and they allowed me to go freely to holy places throughout his entire realm without paying any tribute or customs fee, and they saved and honored me, my retinue, and my things, and protected us from any misdeeds and harms whatsoever. Because of this I went safely through the Sultan's entire land with my retinue; and with many shield-bearers wearing matching clothes and military dress with swords, spurs, [and] daggers, I proceeded as if in a land of Christians.

While en route I slept every night outside under a tent that I brought with me, and Saracens assigned by the official of the place to which I had come kept watch, carefully and attentively protecting me and my retinue from nocturnal dangers. Many men great and common, noble and unknown, have crossed the sea, but no one in our time in this way: which I consider a unique grace and freely bestowed gift from our Savior. I went everywhere and showed the Sultan's letters to those in charge of the road; they would immediately get up, kiss the letters, place them on their head, honor me, offer occasional gifts of food, and present themselves to me as gracious well-wishers. Thus leaving Cairo then I came first to the Red Sea [. . .].

[*from* **Chapter 6**] *About the city of Jerusalem and the holy places that are there, about Our Lord's Temple and the others.* [. . .] On this mountain [Mount Sion] Saint James the Greater[38] was beheaded, and there is a beautiful church there that is the church and the school of the Catholic Christians, for it alone is obedient to the Holy Father, the Pope of Rome, whereas all the others are churches of misbelieving and schismatic Christians and not obedient to the Holy Church. There are many kinds of these schismatics, and the sects are variously named according to the different errors that they follow, for there are Greeks, Arians, Nestorians, Jacobites, treacherous Turks, Nubians, Ethiopians, Indians, Georgians, Johannines, and other heretics who are called Christians. It would take too long to list all the errors of each sect, but the *Decretum* makes special reference to them.[39]

Our intention is not to write down everything that can be found in the Holy Land, but only the notable things that I have seen and that can further the reader's devotion. Whoever especially wants to know the greatness of the works and the miracles that God has performed there should look at Holy Scripture, which clearly contains them.

---

38. One of the Apostles, distinguished from Saint James the Less. This excerpt is from the end of Chapter 6, capping William's account of Mount Sion; the *Mandeville* author displaces his rewritten version to the end of Chapter 13, where his description of the Holy Land finishes.

39. *Gratian's Decretum* (twelfth century), a concordance of discordant canon (church) laws.

[*from* **Chapter 8**] *About the holy places that are around the city of Jerusalem and the River Jordan.* The holy city of Jerusalem well visited, I headed west towards the mountains of Judea, which are five miles from Jerusalem, there where Our Lady went to greet Saint Elizabeth, John the Baptist's mother, and there where Saint John rejoiced in his mother's womb, in the presence of the pregnant mother of God, [he] who only six months after his conception recognized his Savior, Jesus Christ; and the two holy mothers greeted each other and reinforced each other's praise of God who ordered His miracles shown in her [Mary]. In that place there is quite a beautiful church in which rest John the Baptist's father Zachary and mother Elizabeth. Quite close to there is the place where the tree grew from which Our Lord's Cross was made, as they say.[40] There is a fine church there and it is a cloister, an abbey of Georgian monks who are schismatic and misbelieving Christians. From there I returned quite close to Jerusalem to the graves of several prophets, and a well-educated German Jew accompanied me who had come there on pilgrimage, for the Jews commonly come there.[41] [. . .] [*William now proceeds past Jerusalem to the Valley of Josaphat, then to the Mount of Olives, Bethany, and through the desert to Jericho.*]

Near that place [Jericho], three miles away, is the Dead Sea, a lake, a foul and stinking pool openly showing God's vengeance on the sinners of Sodom and Gomorrah. Onto these cities God rained fire and sulfur and destroyed them, the above-mentioned cities, along with three others like them in that sin. And thus a long time ago they used to be under this above-mentioned punishment, in this place where now there is this stinking lake, this dead sea, which is still very ugly in witnessing against that sin.[42] And in memory of the vengeance that God took on it [the sin], I wanted to go to that place, but a Saracen, our interpreter, prevented me and said to me, you have come to visit the holy places, those that God has blessed, so you should not at all go to the place where through their wickedness they have met with His curse. The words of this Saracen edified me enough that I did not go at all to this dead sea, but I completed my journey [by going] straight to the Jordan River.

Around the Dead Sea, to the right, Lot's wife was miraculously turned into a salt rock, because she looked behind her against God's commandment when He destroyed Sodom and Gomorrah, but I could never actually find out whether any of it still remained. Quite close is the little city of Segor that was saved by Lot's prayer. Above the city is the mountain where this Lot was made drunk by his two daughters and

---

40. The preceding material is used in *TBJM*, Chapter 11, and that about the Dead Sea and Lot's family in Chapter 12.

41. Cf. the *Mandeville* author's quite different presentation of the Jews.

42. This sentence is the translator's addition to William's Latin text.

begot on them two sons, Ammon and Moab.⁴³ Beyond the Dead Sea to the east outside the Promised Land is a very strong castle on a mountain that has the name Mount Royal. In Arabic it has the name *Crach* [Krak]. Long ago it used to belong to the Christians, but now it belongs to the Sultan, and the Sultan stays there and retreats [to it] in times of great danger, and he has his treasure and his children kept there, for it is the most fortified site in Syria that the Sultan has in these regions. Beneath this above-mentioned castle in the town of Sobab and inside its border-lands there are said to be dwelling a good forty thousand schismatic Christians born in this same country.

[*from* **Chapter 10**] *About the city of Damascus and its boundaries, about Mount Lebanon and the end of our pilgrimage.* Having fully visited the Holy Promised Land in all its length and breadth, I crossed the River Jordan between the Sea of Galilee, from which it flows, and the Dead Sea into which it falls. And I came in three days to the very noble, famous city, and ancient city of Damascus. [*W describes the region and its city at some length in the Latin, which John shortens and simplifies, especially as regards the religious associations.*]

From Damascus I made a pilgrimage to the image of Our Lady in Sardany [Saidnaya].⁴⁴ It is a place situated on a rock in the form of a well-walled castle. In this place there is a very beautiful church. On the wall behind the great altar is a wooden panel, all black and always moist, on which the image of Our Lady is said to have been painted in former times, but because of its age, nothing can be seen of the image's form, except that in some places it seemed to me that I saw there a bit of the color red. This panel is of average size, set into the wall above a marble vessel, [and] enclosed by iron bars. This panel continuously and visibly drips with a kind of oil, and it falls into that marble vessel, and out of it the monks give some of it quite freely to pilgrims. It is said with certainty that out of this image real oil used to flow by God's miracle, but many believe that this liquid that now drips from it is not oil at all and they are of that opinion, but it nevertheless quite resembles olive oil. The monks and nuns from there dwell below the mountain in a very fine village. They are quite comfortable and have enough to plenty of wine, but they are schismatic Christians. This place is a day's travel from Damascus.

I returned from there and left to the right the noble city of Antioch and the famous city of Tripoli, both of which once belonged to the Christians but now have been destroyed by the Saracens. I crossed the Bokar Valley⁴⁵ [*the region and its geography are quickly described*], and I

---

43. Latin: "Lot committed incest with his daughters, who, getting pregnant by the father they got drunk, gave birth to sons. . . ."

44. Thirty kilometers from Damascus and still a site of pilgrimage to the Virgin. Cf. *TBJM*, Chapter 14.

45. The Beqaa Valley in east Lebanon.

reached Beirut in three days, and I crossed the pleasant mountains of Lebanon. [*Further brief geographical description follows.*] In the part of Mount Lebanon to the side near Tripoli that is generally called Black Mountain some twenty thousand Christians dwell, good archers and a bold people who very much desire a passage of the Latins,[46] such that we Christians of the West would come beyond the sea to reconquer the Holy Land, for they desire above all to be freed from the Sultan's lordship, more than other Christians of the country.

When I had crossed the mountains of Lebanon, I reached the good city of Beirut, very nobly situated on the sea, quite well fortified, and provided with plenty of beautiful fountains, beautiful gardens, beautiful trees, and noble fruits. [. . . *W now briefly describes another fortified town, Byblos.*] When I was in Beirut, which now belongs to the Saracens, my pilgrimage made through God's help, I put to sea to return to my country, to a Christian port, to rest after the labor of so great a journey. Spiritually speaking, the Christian port is God, Jesus Christ, to whom, after the miseries of this wretched life, all Christians should desire to come and take the trouble [to do so] not only with the body's limbs, but also to desire [this] with a pure heart. May God grant us to come to this port. *Here ends a treatise on the Holy Land* [. . .].

2. (Pseudo-)William of Tripoli,
Treatise on the State of the Saracens

The *Tractatus de statu Sarracenorum,* compiled after 1273, probably in Latin Christendom, has traditionally been attributed to William of Tripoli, a Dominican friar in Acre and author in 1271 of a *Notitia de Machometo* (*Information about Machomet*). The *Notitia* (a serious and reasonably accurate account of Muhammad's life, the rise of Islam, the Qur'an and its teachings, and Islamic rituals, plus a defense of Christianity by means of the Qur'an) was the main source of the longer, more detailed *Tractatus,* whose authorship is unknown. Not the anti-crusading tract that some have read it as, the *Tractatus,* more than the *Notitia,* does argue against armed force in evangelization and emphasizes Islam's closeness to Christianity, the consequent likelihood of Muslims being peacefully converted, and the supposed Muslim prophecies of Islam's demise. The work was twice translated into French. The *Mandeville* author drew heavily on the *Tractatus* in Chapter 15, freely rearranging it. The excerpts here, the first English translation of this text, are from William of Tripoli 1992, a Latin edition (with a parallel German translation).

46. A crusade. John glosses this in the rest of the sentence, his own addition as translator.

About the State of the Saracens *and about their False Prophet Machomet and about the People Themselves and their Law. To the venerable father and lord, Theald, archdeacon of the Church of Liège [and] worthy and holy pilgrim to the Holy Land, brother William of Tripoli, of the Monastery of the Order of Friars Preacher in Acre, [wishes] that he attain in Christ the vows of his pious pilgrimage.* Since I learned that your enlightened faith desired to know what the Saracen people and their book understand about the Christian faith, I have striven in the Lord to serve the wishes of your pious devotion and to offer what is desired by bringing forward and showing three things: first, who Machomet (the leader of the said people, guide and false prophet) was, where he came from, and when he took that honor; second, how the said people so forcefully and vigorously grew and expanded; third, their law or their book, which is called Alcoran, and what is contained in it about the faith of the Christians.

1. Who Machomet was and where he came from and when. In the year of the Savior Our Lord Jesus Christ 601 [. . .] there lived a certain religious man, a simple Christian, but of a strict life, named Bahayra, secluded in a certain monastery in the Arabian desert on the way from Meccan Arabia [. . .].[47] At this monastery where Bahayra lived enclosed, traveling merchants from Syria, Arabia, and Egypt, Christians and Saracens, used to gather [. . .]. Amongst them there was supposed to come to the monastery someone who would be part of a great and most powerful people through whom Christ's Church was to be greatly afflicted. These things were revealed to Bahayra the hermit, on account of which he very much wished to see the person to come, and he waited every day for his coming.

2. How Machomet came to be known to men. So the day came and a crowd or caravan of merchants, which the Arabs call *cafele*, arrived at the monastery.[48] The merchants were asked to come to the hermit, but amongst them the person sought was simply not found. Afterwards the merchants' servants came, and all those who look after the camels, and by divine revelation the person sought was discovered: a boy, clearly an orphan, sickly, poor and worthless, a camel-groom of Arab birth[49] of the generation of Ishmael, about whom it is said in Genesis 16: "He shall be a wild man: his hand will be against all men, and all men's hands against him: and he shall pitch his tents over against all his brethren."[50]

---

47. The date 601 is unusual, influenced perhaps by the Noah story in Gen. 8:13 (William 1992, 402, n. 188). Bahayra: Bahira, a Christian monk who, according to an Islamic tradition that exists in two main forms, revealed to the young Muhammad his prophetic destiny.

48. *cafele: qafila,* Arabic for "caravan." I have not always followed the text's typical medieval shifts between past and present tenses.

49. This account corresponds to what is known about Muhammad's origins.

50. Gen. 16:19. The connection with Ishmael was a commonplace of medieval Christian commentary.

Whoever reads this may understand whether this prophecy was fulfilled in this Machomet, since, as it seems, in none of his sons is Ishmael found so wild and powerful in pitching his tents against everyone as in this one [. . .]. Here the Saracens locate the first miracle that God performed, as they say, for his servant, who was still a boy, explaining that when the child wanted to enter the small gate of the monastery's court through which all pass, it grew wide and rose up bow-shaped through divine command, like the entry to an imperial court or the entrance to the home of a royal majesty.[51] The boy was finally received by the monk Bahayra, treated, fed, and clothed like a dear son, embraced by all, and named the hermit's adopted son. He was instructed and taught to flee the cult of idols, to worship the one God in Heaven, and to call frequently upon Jesus, the Virgin Mary's son, with all his heart. Nevertheless, the brothers of the monastery who did all those things just mentioned were unable keep the boy there. They let him depart, having received from him a promise that he would return to them. The boy was attached to a certain rich merchant who considered him his and called him his protégé.[52] And so the boy grew in time to be of sound judgment, hard working, and likewise handsome in body. Indeed, after he became a young man he faithfully carried and increased his lord's goods as a merchant, and he would go devout and often to his teacher, the hermit mentioned above.

3. *About Machomet's success and how it grew.* Eventually the young man's lord died rich [. . .] as a result of the young man's hard work and honesty. Seeing his handsome form and good fortune, the merchant's widow married him.[53] [. . .] Presents were offered and services promised, friends multiplied and his household grew, the first of whom was his maternal uncle named Ali, who eventually married Machomet's daughter named Fatima, his blood relative.[54] Thus he came to be honored by all his people and called their chief[55] and adored as lord and teacher. He

---

51. Not a miracle traditionally ascribed to Muhammad; its source is unknown. Medieval Christians used a lack of miracles to bolster their claim that Muhammad was a false prophet.

52. After his parents' death Muhammad was looked after by his uncle Abu Talib (d. c. 619), who was not especially wealthy but was head of the Hashim clan of the Quraysh, the powerful Meccan tribe.

53. Khadija bint Khuwaylid, who hired Muhammad to help with her business dealings, was his first and only wife until her death in about 619, and the first person to believe in his prophetic vocation. She was about forty and he about twenty-five when they married; their children included Fatima (mentioned here).

54. Typically called an uncle in medieval Christian writings, Ali ibn Abi Talib was Muhammad's cousin and son-in-law (he married Fatima), possibly the second convert to Islam and certainly the fourth Sunni caliph (656–661) and the first imam of Shi'a Muslims (who believe that Muhammad appointed him as successor). He was assassinated in 661.

55. *primus:* "first," but also "chief" or "leader."

chose ten companions, the first of whom was Ebobex[56] (the names of the others cannot be given in Latin script, however). He gathered around him the clans of Arabs living in the deserts of southern Arabia.[57] [. . .] Thus Machomet grew and so did his circle, his troops, and his might. The regions and the kings of the regions and all the people's leaders and all the judges in the world came to fear him.

He often went to his teacher [. . .] Bahayra, and in going and spending time with him upset his companions. Yet Machomet gladly listened to him and did many things for him. For this reason Machomet's companions considered killing Bahayra, but they were afraid of their chief. It then happened that, while annoyed one night by the long conversation the hermit was having with their leader, they realized their leader was drunk, and with Machomet's sword they cut the holy man's throat on that very night, intending to tell their leader that he had killed his teacher and patron while he was so drunk as to be out of his mind. When morning came and Machomet looked for the holy man to take his leave and say farewell, he found him dead. Terribly afflicted, he set out to look for the murderers. But because his companions alleged that he was the drunken agent of the evil deed, he believed what they said to be true, aware that he was drunk that night; and seeing his own blood-spattered sword, [he turned] against drunkenness and its cause, wine, cursing all wine-bearers as well as wine-drinkers, -sellers, and -buyers. For this reason devout Saracens, like the Rechabites,[58] do not drink wine. With Bahayra the Christian thus dead, Machomet's band dropped their military discipline, as if the reins had been released. They roamed like thieves. These robbers plundered, slaughtered, and laid waste, throwing the regions and kingdoms into confusion until Machomet died.

8. *About the rise of the Arabs and the humiliation of the Christians.* After the capture of Damascus [. . .] the capital of Syria, the Emperor Heraclius returned to Constantinople in pain and grief. The military might of the Christian name and empire had been overthrown with a huge slaughter and the Arabs' horn raised and roused in great pride. [. . .] Machomet's name and reputation and glory were also increased, and he was said and believed to be the messenger of God on high. This is why his first successor Bobecre was also called heir and successor to God's messenger, and why his successor Gomar was called heir to the heir to God's messenger.[59] For this reason it was established as the Heavenly God's divine

56. Abu Bakr, the first Sunni Caliph (632–634).

57. In 627–630 Muhammad took control of Medina and Mecca and was making alliances with many of the Bedouin tribes. In 631 envoys from all over Arabia surrendered to him.

58. Israelites known for a simple, austere way of life, including abstinence from wine: see Jer. 35.

59. Heraclius returned to Constantinople in 636, giving up Palestine and Syria after losing Damascus and being defeated at Yarmuk. Engels (William 1997, 409,

decree and command that everyone for their salvation believe in their hearts and profess with their mouths that there is one God, and that there is no God but God, and Machomet is God's messenger; and whoever refused to profess and say this was dead. This is why, just as we have a verbal formula with which we are baptized and made Christians ("*In nomine Patris et Filii et Spiritus Sanctis*"), they too have a verbal formula with which they are made Saracens: "*La eleh ella Alla, Mahomad rosol Alla,*" that is, "There is no God but God and Machomet is His messenger."[60] Consequently many people, misled by error, are made Saracens: and not only Jews, but also great and ordinary Christians.

22. *About the Sultan's death.* In the same year [1273], as the learned Saracen astrologers and mathematicians say, the Sultan will die and after his death another Turk will arise who will die within the years of his rule. And after this Christ's lordship ought to arise and the banner of the Cross will be raised and carried through all Syria right to Caesaria in Cappadocia; and then there will be great excitement of the peoples on earth. The true God knows when.[61]

23. *About the end of the Saracens.* There is amongst them certain knowledge of and firm faith in the Saracens' end, as they all say without any contradiction from Machomet's testimony. Indeed, Machomet said this: "The Saracens conquered as wanderers [and once again they will begin to be and will become wanderers as they were]."[62] Their learned interpret the statement like this, saying that the Saracens will cease to exist when they are divided into three parts: one part will fall under the sword, another part will seek to flee to the desert and perish, and the third part will cross over to the faith of the Christians. Also, one of the articles of the creeds amongst them says this: "The faith of the Saracens arose through Machomet's sword and will fall by a sword that will be

---

n. 226) notes that "the Arabs' horn" (*cornu Arabum*) is of uncertain meaning: an allusion to the horned beast in Dan. 7:8, an image of force (as in a bull's horn), or a metaphor for pride? Gomar: Umar ibn a-Khattab ("Hatrab's son"), the second Sunni Caliph (634–644). Bobecre: Abu Bakr (see n. 56 above). Caliph: "successor." Abu Bakr called himself "Khalifat Rasul Allah," correctly rendered here.

60. The *Shahada*, or Muslim profession of faith in a single God. It is translated correctly. A current transcription might read, "*La ilah illâ Allâh wa Muhammad rasûl Illâh.*" The *Tractatus* is the only Latin Christian text to compare it to the baptismal formula ("In the name of the Father and the Son and the Holy Spirit") like this (William 1997, 410, n. 22).

61. These prophecies go back to the astrological calculations of the ninth-century scholar al-Kindi, known in twelfth-century Latin Christendom through his pupil Abu Masar (William 1997, 432–33, n. 332).

62. The square brackets mark a later interpolation. As for the interpretation given next, a *hadith* (a saying traditionally and authoritatively attributed to Muhammad) states that the Muslim community will be divided in three (William 1997, 402, n. 185).

God's," as if it said: "By the sword he began, by the sword he will end."[63] Also, another article says: "The Jews had their time and their place and they fell; thus the place and reign of the Saracens will be ruined, but the faith and the place of the Christians will last until Christ descends again from Heaven, where he now lives, and razes and rights all things and kills Antichrist." Also, another article [. . .] in Alcoran: "The Romans were conquered" (the Latins are meant, but others understand the Greeks, who lost the Holy Land, as stated above, in Emperor Heraclius' time) "but those who were conquered will yet conquer and be victors."[64]

Also, another article, which no one denies, says that when Machomet's descendants and lineage fall [. . .] the faith and people of the Saracens will fall. But this house collapsed when the Tartar leader named Hulaon took Baghdad and killed its caliph, as is said, in the year of the Lord 1253.[65] They say therefore that their end is at the gates and nearby. Also, there is another article that no more than fifty-two caliphs will descend from the line of the first caliph of Baghdad named Hebbas.[66] This number was reached before Hulaon killed the fifty-third caliph. Also, another piece of evidence confirming what has been said is that the kingdom and lordship of the Saracens passed from Arab hands into Turkish; and now the Saracens are without a true Sultan descended from the Arabs who took the land from Greek Christian hands; and they are likewise without a caliph, whom they cannot in future expect from the Arabs, in accordance with Machomet's statement that when the lordship of the caliphs ends, the Arab kingdom will end.

24. How the book Alcoran was put together. After what has been said about the emergence, progress, and end of Machomet and those associated with him, it remains to see what should be thought about their law or book, which is called Alcoran, *Meshaf,* or *Hatine.*[67] [. . .]

30. How the Blessed Mary was taught.[68] Also, in another place [Alcoran] says that she was taught by angels [. . .].

31. How the Conception was revealed to her. Also, in another place [Alcoran] says how the Annunciation was made to her by angels before [the Conception] had happened [. . .]: "They said to Mary, 'Oh Mary,

---

63. Cf. Matt. 26:52.

64. Cf. Qur'an 30.2–4.

65. The Mongols under Hülegü (r. 1256–1265) conquered Baghdad in 1258, ending the Abbasid caliphate. Cf. *TBJM,* Chapter 24, n. 465.

66. Abu al-Abbas al-Saffa, first Abbasid caliph (750–754).

67. *Meshaf:* "book," especially the official Qur'an. For *Hatine* Engels suggests: *hikma,* "wisdom"; *hatam,* "seal"; *haram,* "holy"; or *hatim,* part of the Kaaba, ultimate goal of Meccan pilgrimage (William 1997, 434, n. 342).

68. The only woman named in the Qur'an, Mary is also its most prominent female figure. Her story is told in suras 3, 4, 5, 19, 21, 23, and 66. Much of this material can be found in suras 3.33–50 and 19.16–35. Cf. *TBJM,* Chapter 15, n. 294.

know that God will preach the Word to you out of Himself: its name is
Jesus Christ, son of Mary. He will be a distinguished leader in this time
and in the future; and He will belong to those who draw near to God,
and He will speak as a little baby[69] in the cradle and become a man and
belong to the holy and the just.'"

32. *How she spoke with God.* Also, in another place [Alcoran] shows how
Mary spoke to God and God answered her [. . .]: "Mary said, 'Oh God,
will I indeed have a son, even though I have not been touched by a man?'
And God said, 'God will make what He wants, and when He decrees
that it will be done and says "let it be done!" it is done right away. And
we shall teach him, our messenger to the sons of Israel, the Book and
wisdom and the law and our Gospel, and He will say: "I came to you as
God's sign, because out of clay I will create for you the forms of birds,
and I will breathe into them and they will be brought to life with God's
authority; and I will heal the mute and the leprous and raise the dead to
life with God's authority, and I will teach you what you must eat and what
you must save, because this will be a sign to you, if you show yourselves
faithful, since I am the truth in those things pertaining to the law and
in those that I will allow you from the [previously] prohibited and forbidden; and I came as a sign from your God. Believe in God therefore and
obey Him, for my God is also your God. Obey Him therefore, since this
is the straight (that is, the right) way."'"

33. *About the praise of the Virgin Mary and how she conceived.* Also, in
another place [in Alcoran] is shown the Annunciation made to her
about her son's conception [. . .]: "Remember Mary, who took herself
away from her family and stayed in place towards the east and concealed
herself from them; and we sent her our Spirit and appeared to her in
a man's shape. And Mary said, 'I call on God's mercy against you, if
you are Taquia' (*the Saracen gloss:* Taquia was a certain magician who
suddenly came upon virgins and, bright and beautiful as an angel, over-
whelmed them). And he said, 'I am a messenger from your God. A son,
guiltless and pure, will be given to you.' But Mary said, 'Am I to have a
son? No man will touch me and yet I will conceive?' He said, 'If God has
decreed this for you, it will happen easily. And we shall make him a sign
to men and mercy from us, and it was ordained.'"

34. *How she gave birth and her baby comforted her.* Also, in another place
[Alcoran] shows how she bore the son that she had conceived and how
the son born of her comforted his mother [. . .]: "Mary conceived a son
and went off with him to a place far away and remote; and when the
moment of birth came, she bore him under a palm, and then said, 'Oh,
if only I had died before this happened to me and I had been forgotten.'
And then her newborn said, 'Don't be sad,' he said, 'God has placed his

69. *infantulus,* diminutive of *infans* (whence "infant"), literally "not speaking."

secret under you.[70] Get yourself a palm branch with fruit and choice, ripe fruit will fall upon you. Eat some and drink and be glad. And if someone appears to you and says "Eat!" say, "I have vowed a fast to merciful God," and speak to no one as if you were keeping a secret.'"

35. *How she was rebuked and her son excuses her.* Also, in another place [in Alcoran] it is shown how Mary, having borne her son, returned with him to her family and he excused his mother, who was rebuked [. . .]: "Mary came to her family carrying her newborn and they said to her, 'Oh Mary, you have done something great. Oh daughter of Aaron, your begetter was not a bad man and your mother did not show herself off.' But she silently pointed out the boy and they said, 'How is an infant in a cradle to speak?' And the child himself said, 'I am God's servant and God gave me the Book and made me a blessed prophet wherever I will be. And He taught me to pray and serve the innocent while my life lasts, forgiving my mother. Health and peace upon me on the day I was born, on the day I will die, and the day I rise alive again.'"

36. *About the Blessed Mary's chastity.* Also, in another place [in Alcoran] Mary is praised in these words: "Mary made her womb as a castle and we breathed into it with our Spirit and established her and her son as a model and a sign to everyone."

41. *That Christ is superior to all of God's envoys and messengers.* Also, Christ is praised and is said to excel all prophets and be above everyone, and it says this: "Our messengers are many and we have preferred one to the others, and they belong to those to whom God has spoken, and by degrees he preferred one of them. We have however given to Jesus, Mary's son, clear signs, miracles, and portents, and we have strengthened him through the Holy Spirit. And if God had wanted it, wars would not have happened after miracles were seen. But people are contrary: there are those who believe, and others who disbelieve. God however does what he wants."

42. *Christ and his Gospel are praised.* Also, the Lord Jesus is praised and His Holy Gospel, and [Alcoran] says this: "In the steps of the earlier prophets we have guided Jesus, Mary's son, our faithful messenger, in those things pertaining to the law of Moses; and we gave Him the Gospel, in which is guidance and light and the truth of those things pertaining to the law; and it is a guide and a proclamation to the God-fearing that He will judge the believers by the Gospel, which came down upon Him, and by those things that are in it; but those who do not believe in the things that God has made come down from Heaven, they are indeed wicked."

43. *About the wickedness of the Jews to Christ and about His Ascension.* And about the wickedness of the Jews against Christ and His Blessed Virgin Mother, [Alcoran] says this: "Of the Jews only a few believed, and in their

---

70. Citing Qur'an 19.22–24, Engels notes that the translator has mistakenly rendered "secretion" (God's stream) as "secret," with consequences for the rest of the passage.

unbelief and talkativeness they told a great lie about Mary and about Christ, saying, 'We killed Christ, Mary's son.' But they neither crucified nor killed him, but rather his likeness. Moreover, those who disagree with Jesus without exception know nothing about Him, because the Jews did not kill Him, but God raised Him and took Him up to Him and exalted Him. And God is dear and wise."

44. *About the false opinion of Christ's death.* The interpreters of Alcoran say this: that the Jews did not crucify Christ but the traitor Judas, who was taken while he was seeking his teacher in a cave; he changed his appearance to Jesus', and the accomplices who took him crucified him. And they therefore say that Christians know nothing about Him, because they say that Christ was crucified by the wicked Judas: Christ who was not crucified or dead, but ascended alive to Heaven and will come down again.[71] Also, they say that God would have acted against His divine justice, had He allowed the innocent Christ to be killed.

48. *It is shown that educated and wise Saracens are close to the Christian faith.* Having shown the preceding things—which the Saracens believe in their hearts to be true and declare in speech to be God's words written in their Alcoran about the praises and proclamations of Jesus Christ, about His teaching and His Holy Gospel, about Blessed Mary His mother and His followers who believe in Him, granted that they are enfolded in many lies and adorned with fictions—it should be quite clear that, nevertheless because these things are pious, the Saracens are neighbors to the Christian faith and close to the way of salvation.

49. *What draws the Saracens to Christ's faith.* A disposition to believe attracts them to the true faith, and a certain universal notion located in everyone's heart as foreknowledge that Machomet's teaching and faith will soon end, as did the cult of the Mosaic Law, and only Christ's faith, along with the Christian people, will be stable and enduring for as long as the world lasts. Also, they are attracted by the contemplative or speculative faculty of reason, through which they discern that their prophet Machomet taught no faith whereby the way to God can be distinguished, nor any way of conduct or discipline whereby one comes to God, nor any reward for good faith or good works except a secular one.

50. *About the faith of the Saracens.* If anyone should ask them what then their faith is, they do not know what to say but this: "We believe God to be the creator of all things, [we believe in] Judgment Day, on which the services of human beings will be recompensed, and [that] it is true that God has spoken through the mouths of all his holy prophets."

51. *About their instruction or teaching.* Also, if someone should ask about their instruction and the way of life that Machomet taught them to keep, they say: "You may have two and three and four wives and thus nine, and [as many] concubines as your right hand can acquire. And if your

---

71. This story draws loosely on Qur'an 4.157–59, elaborated by the addition of Judas. See *TBJM,* Chapter 15, n. 298.

wife displease [you] in your eyes, then give her a notice of divorce and you may let her go; and you are permitted to use, not to misuse, what your hand has acquired, just as it is permitted to use an ass or a horse." Also, if you should ask about the ultimate reward that God will render on Judgment Day to those who observe Machomet's law, they all say, as it is written in their book, that God will render Paradise.

52. *About their hope and the Paradise that they hope for.* If you happen to have asked, "What is the Paradise that you hope for?" they say that it is a place of delights in which every man will have ninety-nine delightful virgins, all of whom he can enjoy every day and he will always find them intact and untouched. At the will of desire moreover tree branches will extend the best fruit to the eater's mouth. Rivers of milk and honey, of pure wine and the clearest water will flow down; smaller and larger dwellings built of precious stones, of costly gold from Ophir, will be assigned to each according to each person's merits; and what is even more wonderful, the site of this glory is said to be greater than the space of Heaven and earth, and therefore this paradise will certainly not be in Heaven or on earth.[72] On account therefore of this sort of thought about Machomet their false prophet, not without reason they despise and condemn him and his teaching, if it is his, and the learned move on to examine the divine spectacle, the Heavenly secret, Jesus, Mary's son, and His Holy Gospel, the teaching of the salvation of everyone.

53. *About the divine Trinity.* They are amazed when they hear about the mystery of the divine [. . .] Trinity, without knowledge of which no one on earth can be acquainted with the true God.[73] For if they hear that God, whom they worship, as they affirm, is the creator of Heaven and earth and of all creatures (God who created everything from nothing with His to-Him-coeternal Word), they rejoice to acknowledge that God has the Word[74] through which everything together was created and without which nothing is made. Also, if they hear that God, who consists

---

72. Qur'anic accounts of Paradise and its pleasures: suras 2.25, 13.35, 55.54–56, 56.1–40, 76.12–22. No mention is made of the number of *houris* (virgins of Paradise), but seventy-two wives are mentioned in the *hadith*. Ophir: a distant land of gold in 1 Kings 9:28. Qur'an 3.133 and 57.21 refer to Paradise as the same size as Heaven and earth. The *Encyclopedia of Islam* notes that Paradise is most commonly located under the throne of God, above the highest heaven (entry for *Djanna,* "Garden," the name substituted for Paradise in the Qur'an). Other Latin Christian texts make similar claims to those here.

73. The Christian notion of a triune God is at odds with the Islamic insistence on God's absolute oneness, as the three Qur'anic mentions of the Trinity show (4.171, 5.73, 116).

74. "*Deus habeat verbum.*" *Habeat* could also mean "possesses" or "knows." *Verbum* could mean "a word" or "the Word." Another rendering might thus be "God is capable of speech." This passage depends on Gen. 1 and John 1:1–5, where God's creative work and being are represented as speech and the Word.

of the Word (that is, is possessed of the Word)[75] lives and is the Life of Lives, granting life to all the living, Life living in itself, the unfailing source of life, from which fleshly and spiritual creatures draw their life, they acknowledge that God has life or a Spirit that we call Holy. And if they grasp that God's Word is God's through divine and eternal generation, and that the Holy Spirit comes from God, eternally begotten by God and the begotten Word, they understand that the Father and the Son and the Holy Ghost are three things or persons existing by themselves, in which there is one godhead, one greatness, one divine essence, one power, one potentiality, and one God. For if this God, who is worshiped by all, lacked the Word, they would certainly say that God is mute. Also, if he did not have the Spirit, could one not then say that God is not living but dead, which it is wicked to believe about God.

54. *About the Sacrament of the Incarnation.* Also, when they hear that every creature was created through God's word and every prophecy brought by God's word and all wisdom and knowledge were revealed to human beings through God's word and the resurrection of the dead, the examination of merits, [and] the distribution of rewards are to be accomplished through God's word, they call out, "Father, this word is God's great power!" and they draw this conclusion, "Whoever knows nothing of God's word likewise also knows nothing of God Himself." And again if they hear the testimony of their own law, which was set out above, where through the angels is said, "Oh Mary, God will announce or preach the Word to you from His own mouth and its name will be called Jesus Christ, son of Mary," they have no choice but to say (and they all do say), "Jesus Christ truly is God's Word," with Saint John, "In the beginning was the Word, and the Word was with God, and the Word was God; all things were made by Him, and without Him nothing was made."[76] This is why there is amongst the said Saracens, amongst those who believe, a very great statement: "Abraham is God's friend, but Moses is God's spokesman, Jesus the son of Mary God's Word and Spirit, and Machomet is God's messenger."[77] Amongst these four, Jesus, God's Word, is the greatest, the praises and proclamations of whose greatness were shown above. And so they accept that the Lord Jesus is God's word made flesh in the Virgin's womb and Himself the Word made flesh, born of the Virgin, named Jesus, son of Mary.[78]

55. *About Christ's teaching.* Also, when they hear that in Christ's teaching is contained the perfect and complete faith [. . .] and that the reward of believers is the holy life to come with the angels in Heaven: that is, the hoped-for eternal state of blessedness, they indeed grasp the

---

75. "*Deus, qui est verbalis, hoc est habens verbum.*"

76. John 1:1, 3.

77. Abraham: cf. Qur'an 4.125; Moses: cf. Qur'an 4.164.

78. Jesus as God's Word: cf. Qur'an 3.39, 45. Nowhere does the Qur'an express the Christian belief in the Incarnation, nor do Muslims accept it.

powers commemorated [here]. And thus through ordinary conversation about God without philosophical arguments or military force, they like ordinary sheep ask for Christ's baptism and cross over into God's sheepfold. He who said and wrote this has already baptized more than one thousand in God's authority.[79] May God be praised forever and ever. Amen.

3. Odoric of Pordenone, *Account*

The Franciscan friar Odoric, born probably in the 1260s, spent three decades from about 1300 in missionary work in Russia and the East, both Near and Far, as part of the extensive Franciscan mission of his day. In 1322 he left Venice, passed through Trebizond, and sailed from Hormuz to India, where he gathered the remains of four Franciscans martyred there in 1320; he then made his way by sea to China, spent three years in Khanbaliq (Beijing), and returned overland in 1329. In Padua in May 1330, eight months before his death, he dictated a Latin memoir of his Asian missionary journey. Although in close contact with other Franciscans on his travels, Odoric says less about his and their activities than about wonders. His somewhat breathless and untidy account of eastern *mirabilia* is inferior in intelligence and style not only to William of Boldensele's memoir, but also to the records of his Franciscan predecessors in Asia, John of Plano Carpini and William of Rubruck, yet it proved popular enough that in 1340 a second Latin version was made; in addition, translations were made into French, German, and Italian. Some 140 manuscripts survive. The 1351 French translation by Long John, monk of Saint Bertin in Saint Omer, served (sometimes with the Latin text) as the template for the latter part of *TBJM*. Omitting Odoric's long report of the Franciscan martyrs in India, the *Mandeville* author handles this account even more freely than William of Boldensele's. Doubling the length of his source, he again turns a personal memoir into a general itinerary, rearranging it (especially in its later sections) to suit his own purposes and sometimes even writing himself into the friar's own deeds. Except as noted, the excerpts below are from John's French (Odoric 1891), their first translation into English. A somewhat archaic English translation (Odoric 1913) of the Latin (Odoric 1929) is still available, and only a few excerpts from it (newly translated) are given here.

Here begins the route of the pilgrimage and the voyage *that was made by a good man of the order of Friars Minor named brother Odoric of Friuli, born in a land called port of Venice, who through the pope's order went beyond the sea to preach God's faith to the misbelievers.* And contained in this book are the marvels

---

79. Engels thinks these claims are exaggerated (William 1998, 35–40).

that the said friar saw while there and also many others he heard told in those above-mentioned regions from trustworthy people. But those that he heard told and that he did not see, he does not recount as the truth but as hearsay and he says it in his own language when he comes to this. This book was made in Latin by the above-named friar in the year of grace 1330, completed the 14th day of January, and [. . .] translated from Latin into French by brother John called Long [. . . in] 1351.

[**Chapter 1**] *About Trebizond.*[80] Although many things are told about the circumstances and the state of this world, I do not want to put anything here in this book as the truth but what I have seen. If I set anything down that I heard told by trustworthy people born in the country that these wonders are told about, it will be little, and I will set down the wonders as hearsay and witness them as heard only. For I friar Odoric of Friuli have been overseas in the misbelievers' regions and countries at the command of the holy father the pope so as to produce a crop and harvest some souls for Our Lord God. I daresay I saw many wonders there that I can truly recount.

When I first crossed the sea, I went to the land of Trebizond [. . .]. From this city I went to a mountain called Sabissa Colloasseis. Near it is Mount Ararat on which is Noah's Ark. I would most willingly have climbed this mountain, if my company would have waited for me, even though the people of this country told us that no one could climb it. For it seems that it would not please the most-high God, as the people of that country say.

[*from* **Chapter 10**] *How Pepper Grows and Comes into Being.*[81] The province where pepper grows has the name Minibar, and pepper grows nowhere in the world but in this country. [. . .] The people of this country worship an ox for god. They raise this ox for six years and they make it work and pull the plow, and in the seventh year they lead it out in public to worship. They worship it in this way when it is brought out of the stable in the morning. His master collects his urine in a silver basin and his dung in a gold one as well, and they present them to the country's ruler. From these the ruler washes his face and hands with the urine, and then his brow and his chest with the dung, most reverently. All those of the country who in any way can get some of this filth take it and are very pleased and wash themselves in the way just mentioned, and through washing like this they think themselves to be good and holy.

The people of this country worship another idol that they depict as half man and the other half ox. This idol gives a response, however, when it is sprinkled and anointed with the blood of forty virgins. In

---

80. Cf. *TBJM,* Chapter 16. Chapters 1–2 in Latin (Odoric 1929). Chapter divisions differ yet again in Odoric 1913.
81. Cf. *TBJM,* Chapter 18. Chapters 9–10 in the Latin (Odoric 1929).

front of this idol the people of the country are moved by devotion just as we Christians are by our saints, and in this way these unfortunate people kill their sons and their daughters to anoint this idol with their blood so as to receive an answer to what they have asked for. As a result it happens that a great many of them die a bad death. These people do many other things that one would scarcely believe.

The idolators of this country have yet another custom. When anyone dies they burn him, for they say that he has departed to another realm. And if this dead man has a wife, they burn her with her husband, so that she will keep him company in the other realm. But if this wife has young children by her husband, according to the country's law, if she pleases, she can remain with her children to feed and raise them. But if she chooses to remain with her children, she will never have any honor. Thus she will always live in great shame and in great ill-repute. But if the wife dies before her husband, her husband will go with her, if he pleases, but he is not bound by the country's law. Thus as soon as she is dead he can remarry another wife, if he pleases.

There is another custom in this country, for the women drink wine, not the men. Also, the women have their beards shaved and not the men. And so [there are] many other bestial things and wonders that they do that it would not be good to recount in front of any good Christian.

[*from* **Chapter 11**] *The Kingdom of Mobarum.*[82] From this city of Polumbum I went in ten days [. . .] to a kingdom called Mobarum. [. . .] In this kingdom is the body of my lord Saint Thomas the Apostle, but the Church of Saint Thomas the Apostle is entirely full of countless idols. In this church is an idol made very luxuriously of gold and precious stones [. . .] as big as or bigger than Saint Christopher in this country.[83] [. . .] This idol and everything that belongs to it are of such great value that no one knows how to judge the worth of the gold and the stones and the craft that are there. The false Christians of this renegade country had this idol made, and all the misbelievers of this place worship it above all other idols, and they come there on pilgrimage, as we Christians here go to Saint James in Galicia, or to Saint Peter or Saint Paul in Rome.

This is the way that this idol is worshiped. All of them variously afflict their body in their own way. Some strike their head against the ground and hold it there for a long while and consider themselves unworthy to look at the sky in this idol's presence. Others wound themselves in the hands and in many other parts of their bodies with knives and swords. Many others incomparably more stupid who also believe themselves to be more devout than the others sacrifice their sons and their daughters

---

82. Cf. *TBJM*, Chapter 19; also Chapter 11 in the Latin (Odoric 1929).

83. A popular medieval saint, he was traditionally a giant some twelve feet tall; his name (Greek *Christophoros*, or Christ-bearer) commemorates his good deed of carrying the boy Jesus across a river.

to this idol as if to their own sovereign god; and when they have thus murdered their children in front of this idol, they sprinkle it with the blood just as Christians make their blessing with holy water.

The local citizens and those who live nearby stay there. If they want to begin their pilgrimage as soon as they leave their houses, they kneel in the middle of the road and then prostrate their whole body and stretch it along the ground, and from that spot they make their journey all the way to the idol. That is to say, they place themselves flat on the ground in the way just mentioned; they do this every three steps, and when they reach the idol they take fire and incense and cense it very devoutly. And when these idolaters reach the idol they gather in a certain location where they place their offerings. Some offer gold, others silver, and others precious stones, each according to their devotion and their wealth. And these offerings are kept so as to care for this idol and maintain it. And when something is needed to repair this idol or its shrine, they take all that they need from these offerings, for the treasury there is very great.[84]

This idol has a feast day every year, and it is the general day of its institution. On this day they hold a very great celebration, these idolaters. They take this idol and they place it on a throne richly decorated with gold and precious stones, and they lead it through the country. Ahead of the throne the young virgin women go in twos, [and] behind [it walk] the pilgrims who have come there from far countries. After them come those who are ill with various illnesses. After them come a great many minstrels. And then many of these idolaters out of great devotion lay themselves down in the middle of the road where the idol has to pass so that the throne passes over them, and thus wickedly they lose their lives, their souls, and their bodies. More than two hundred people die every time they hold this wicked celebration. And when they are dead, the people take up their bodies with great reverence and say that they are holy, for they peacefully allowed themselves to die out of love of god.

These idolaters do something else that is even more horrible. When anyone wishes to die for his god and cannot make it to the celebration just mentioned, he gathers his friends and his relatives and tells them his wish. And then his friends have messengers come who spread the news, and then they take this wicked person right to the idol and as they go the friends and these messengers walk along striking this wretched person with five very sharp knives all the way until they come to this idol. And when they have arrived there, these wretched people take one of these knives that slice well and cut off a piece of his own flesh, and they throw this piece in their god's face. And then with the other four knives he stabs himself again and again all over his body, and thus he kills himself. When he is dead his friends light a great fire and burn this

---

84. The *Mandeville* author follows the Latin: this "certain location" is "a lake made by hand."

whole body to ashes. And then everyone takes some of the ash with very great devotion and takes it away with them, and they say that whoever thus willingly dies for his god is holy.

I saw many other wonders in this country that I do not set down in writing, for no one would believe them, and I myself would not have dared believe them if I had not witnessed them. The king of this country is very rich in gold and precious stones.

[**Chapter 12**] *About the Island of Lamory, also known as Samory.* From this country I went south through the Ocean Sea. In fifty days I came to an island that has the name Lamory. There I lost sight of the Tramontane,[85] for the earth took away our view of it. On that island it is so hot that everyone goes about naked, men and women, without having any covering. They made fun of me and said, "God made Adam completely naked and you through your ill will want to wear clothes." In this country all the wives are common, such that no one can say, "this is my wife."[86] But when a woman has given birth to a child, she gives it to the man she wants from those she has her fun with, and this man is named that child's father. The entire country is common, such that no one can say, "this land or this house is mine." They have very few things individually. This land is very good, for there is a great abundance of meat, wheat, rice, gold, cloves of gillyflower, and of all other goods. The people there are very wicked and very cruel. They eat human flesh. The merchants from foreign countries bring children there for sale; and when these people here buy them, they kill them and eat them. Many other things are found on this island that I am not writing down here.

[*from* **Chapter 22**] *About the City of Casay the Great, or Catusie.*[87] I went to a city that had the name Catusaye, which in English means City of Heaven. [. . .] It is the royal city in which the king of the province of Mangy [Manzi] [. . .] used to have his throne. In this city there was a powerful man who had become Christian through the preaching of three friars. I lodged at his house. He always called me "*Acha*": that is to say, "father." On one occasion he took me to see the city and we came to an abbey. He called one of the monks from in there and said to him, "See this Frankish Rabban[88] with me," he said, "that is to say, this monk: he is

---

85. Pole star. Cf. *TBJM*, Chapter 20. This is Chapter 12 in the Latin also (Odoric 1929).

86. "[Or] this is my husband" in the Latin, as in *TBJM*.

87. The Mongol Kinsay (Hangchow/Hangzhou), the Sung capital from 1132. Cf. *TBJM*, Chapter 22.

88. "Frank" (from the name of a Germanic nation that conquered Gaul in the sixth century) came to be used in the East for any Latin Christian. "Rabban" is related to the Hebrew *rabbi*, "master" or "teacher."

from the bottom and the end of the world[89] where the sun sets [and] has come to this country for the life and salvation of our Kaan, so I ask you therefore to show him some wonders in here."[90] This monk led me to a place and showed me two large containers full of leftovers that were at the table. Then he opened the door to a garden for me and led me right to a small hill that is in the midst of the garden. Next he rang a small bell and as soon as it rang almost a good three thousand animals came down from the mountain that all had faces like people's, just as monkeys do. These animals came down together in a very orderly and peaceful manner. The said monk put some leftovers in front of these animals in a silver vessel, and when they had eaten he rang the small bell again and each one went back to its place. I thought this a great wonder, and I asked him what it was. He answered that they were the souls of noble men whom they feed there out of the love of God. I very much rebuked him for this belief, while also saying that they were in no way the souls of people, for they were animals lacking reason; but regardless of anything I could say, he would never believe me that they were not the souls of noble men; and he said that the souls of the noble entered noble animals—the more noble the man, the more noble the animal— and the souls of the peasants and the poor entered filthy animals and wicked vermin. He would believe nothing else. [. . .]

[**Chapter 27**] *About the Kingdom of Cadili, or Caloy.*[91] I heard trustworthy people relate and confirm a great wonder, but I never saw it. In the kingdom of Cadili, also known as Caloy, there are some mountains that are named Crispean. They say that in these mountains grow marvelously big melons. When they are ripe, they are opened and there is found a small creature of living flesh that is just like a little lamb, and these melons and these little creatures are eaten. Many people do not want to believe it: nevertheless it is just as possible and believable as those geese that in Ireland grow from trees.

[*from* **Chapter 28**] *About Penthexoire, Prester John's Land.* From this kingdom of Caloy [Catha] I went for many days towards the west. I went through many lands and cities, and I came to Prester John's Land and it is named the island of Penthexoire, but it is not the hundredth part

---

89. John's addition of this phrase suggests that he was thinking of the T-O maps. See Appendix C.1.

90. The request differs in Latin (Ch. 23): "Please show him something therefore so that he may see how full of wonders it is here, so that if he should return to his countries he can also say, 'I saw such a novelty in Camsay.'" Novelty (we would call it unfamiliarity) was clearly part of the marvelous. Since curiosity was still held to be a vice, especially amongst the religious orders, Odoric may be attributing to his host what we take to be a "normal" desire to go sightseeing.

91. Cf. *TBJM*, Chapter 29; Chapter 31 in the Latin (Odoric 1929). The "Crispean" mountains may be near the Caspian Sea.

of what is said about how it is a rich land and a noble country.[92] The main and capital city has the name Cosan. It is better and bigger than Vincensie [Vicenza], but it has many cities under it. Between him and the Great Caan of Cathay are such agreements and alliances that Prester John always has as his wife the Great Caan's daughter and so too their predecessors and forever more.

From this province I went to another that has the name Cossam.[93] [. . .]

[**Chapter 29**] *About the Kingdom of Riboth.*[94] From this province [of Cossam] I went all the way to another very large province that has the name Riboth [Tibet] and borders on India. This kingdom is under the Great Caan, and bread and wine are found there in greater abundance than anywhere else in the world. The people of this country dwell in felt tents. Their capital city is very beautiful, made entirely of white stone, and the streets are well paved. It is called Gota. In this city no one dares spill human blood, nor that of any animal as well, out of reverence for an idol that is worshiped there. In this city dwells their *l'obassy,* which is to say "pope" in their language. He is head of all the idolaters and gives the benefices of the country in his fashion.

In this country the custom is that the women there wear more than one or two hundred large boars' teeth. There is another custom there. When anyone dies there, the son wants to honor his dead father. He summons the priests and the monks of his law, the minstrels and all his neighbors and friends, and when they have gathered, they take the dead body into the fields and right on a dresser[95] the priests cut off the head and give it to his son. Next this son and all his companions begin to sing, and make a great noise and a large celebration and say many prayers for the dead man. Then these priests come and cut the body all into pieces, and then those eagles and those vultures come, and each is thrown its piece and the birds carry them away. Next the priests call out in a loud voice, "See," they say, "how he was worthy and holy, for God's angels are carrying him to Paradise." The son considers himself very honored when he believes that the angels have taken his father to Paradise. Then everyone departs and returns. When the son has arrived at the inn with his friends, he cooks his father's head and eats it, and with the skull makes a goblet from which he drinks, and all his company and all his kin, very devoutly in the dead father's memory, and they believe that they have done the dead man a great honor.

When I was in the province of Mangy [Manzi] that I spoke about above, I came to the palace of an ordinary man who was not a prince or

---

92. Cf. *TBJM,* Chapter 30; Chapter 32 in the Latin (Odoric 1929).

93. The *Mandeville* author returns to this passage in Chapter 34.

94. Cf. *TBJM,* Chapter 34; Chapters 33–34 in the Latin (Odoric 1929).

95. A table on which an animal is dressed, or prepared as meat.

a landed lord. He was thus a commoner, that is to say, from the common people. This was the life that he led. He had fifty virgin maidens who serve him at table and bring him all his courses in pairs of four or five. These virgins bring him these dishes while singing and playing different kinds of musical instruments and remain in front of him continuously singing right until all his food is eaten and then just like this they bring him the other dishes until the end of the meal. These virgins feed him as if he were a young sparrow and put the pieces in his mouth. This man leads his life just like this until he dies. Each year he has the profit of thirty tuman *togas*[96] of rice. His palace is a good two miles around. The palace's paving is one gold tile, then one silver. And in these tiles are engraved castles, small monasteries, and bell towers and other things that are made for his pleasure.[97] The king of Mancy has in his kingdom four men just like this one.

To have long nails seems very beautiful to them, and they let their nails grow so much that they cover all their hands. For the women beauty is having small feet, so that the mothers, when they have daughters, bind their feet so that they cannot grow afterwards.

[**Chapter 30**] *About the Old Man of the Mountain.*[98] When I left Prester John's Land, I made my way to a very rich mountain that has the name Mellestoire. The lord of the country is called the Old Man of the Mountain. This Old Man had a mountain enclosed with a very strong wall. At the foot of this mountain were the best and most beautiful fountains in the world, and there he put the most beautiful maidens that he could find and everything that gives pleasure to the human body, and they call this place Paradise. When he found any fine and strong man, he placed him in this Paradise amongst these delightful things and showed it to him such that the young man believed himself to be in Paradise, for by certain subtle machines and pipes, he made wine[99] come and flow there, and prepared for these young men all the pleasures that the human body can ask for. When this old man wanted a certain man to be killed, he had some of these young men given a beverage to drink that made them fall deeply asleep, and while they slept he had him [*sic*] carried out of the Paradise, and when they woke up he called them before him and told them that they would never enter Paradise if they did not kill such a man, such a lord, and if they killed them he would put him [*sic*] back into Paradise and let him stay there where they

---

96. A "tuman . . . makes ten thousand. A *tagar* (given here as *toga*) is the weight of a large ass-load" (Latin Ch. 34).

97. Latin (also used by the *Mandeville* author): "In the court of this palace is a hill made of gold and silver, on which monasteries and bell towers were built, as people have made for their pleasure."

98. Cf. *TBJM*, Chapter 30; Chapter 35 in the Latin (Odoric 1929).

99. Latin: "wine and milk."

would have pleasures incomparably better than at first. These young men, open and strong as was said about them, truly believed that this was the Paradise of Heaven where they would have eternal life, and they offered their bodies and lives to the Old Man so as to please him, [and offered] to kill at his command not only the intended man but a thousand more, if he wished, and so they gave themselves to the danger of death to kill that man. In this way this Old Man avenged himself on his enemies, such that everyone feared him and all his neighbors paid him tribute, and if they owed him any tribute he would thus have them killed. Tartars heard this news, and they came upon him with a large army and conquered him and had him put to a very cruel death and destroyed all his buildings.

[**Chapter 32**] *A Great Marvel.*[100] I saw a most hideous thing as I made my way along one of the rivers of Paradise. I was coming towards a valley that was quite close to this river. As I approached it, I heard different kinds of musical instruments, and especially harps. The closer I came the louder the noise I heard. Finally I heard a noise so loud that I was very afraid and horrified. This valley is a good seven or eight miles long, and the people of that country say that anyone who enters it can never come out, and nevertheless I went in there in order to know what it was. I found so many dead bodies lying there that no one could believe it. When I went farther in I saw a very horrible and very hideous human face to one side of the mountain in a rock. It was so horrible that I thought I would die of fear and I said these words: "*Verbum caro factum est,*"[101] etc. I never dared go closer than eight paces, as I climbed up a sandy hill on the other side. I looked all around me, but I neither saw nor heard anyone there, but I found a large amount of silver. I took some of it into my lap, but I carried none away, and so I went out of there.[102] All the Saracens who saw me coming and who knew that I had been in there greatly revered me and said that I was a baptized and holy man but those who remained were devils of hell. *Explicit.*[103]

[*from* (Latin) **Chapter 38**] *About the reverence that the Great Canis pays to the most holy sign of the cross.*[104] I will record one thing about the Great Canis that I saw. The custom in these regions is that when the foresaid lord travels through this country people light fires in front of their houses and put aromatics in them and make smoke to send to their lord as he

---

100. Cf. *TBJM*, Chapter 31. This is the last chapter in John's French, the second-to-last (Ch. 37) in the Latin.

101. "And the word was made flesh" (John 1:14).

102. Latin: "So by God's gift, I came out of there unharmed."

103. *Explicit:* "here ends [the account]."

104. Cf. *TBJM*, Chapter 25. This account appears (with less detail) in Chapter 26 of Long John's French.

travels past, and many people rush towards him. Once when he came to Cambalec and his arrival was announced with certainty, a Bishop of ours and other Friars Minor of ours and I went towards him for a good two days, and as we approached him, we placed the cross on top of a staff so that it could be publicly seen. I was holding in my hand the censer that I had brought with me, and we started singing in a loud voice, saying "*Veni Creator Spiritus,*"[105] etc. As we sang, he heard our voices, and he had us called and ordered to come to him. Although his highness had laid down that no one except his guards dare approach his chariot within a stone's throw unless summoned, seeing that we had come to him with the raised cross, he immediately removed his *gallerium* or hat of almost incalculable worth, and revered the cross. Right away I placed the incense that I had in the censer, and our Bishop took the censer from my hand and censed him. Those who approach this lord always carry some gift with them, observing the ancient law: "*Non apparebis in conspectus meo vacuus.*"[106] We therefore carried with us some fruit, and he ate a little from one of them, and thus our above-mentioned Bishop gave him his blessing. When this was done, he ordered us to withdraw so that the horses and crowd coming after him would not harm us. We left immediately and went out by separate ways, and went to some of his lords [who had been] converted to the faith by our brothers of the Order [and] who were in the army and presented them with the apples just mentioned. They received them with great joy, seeming to be as delighted as if in a friendly way we had given them a great gift. [. . .][107]

4. *How to Mount a Crusade Overseas* (Excerpt)

The *Directorium ad Faciendum Passagium Transmarinum* is not one of the *Mandeville* author's sources, but the excerpted passage may have inspired Chapter 20. Completed in 1330 and addressed to Philip VI of France by an unnamed Dominican who spent twenty-five years overseas as a missionary, the *Directorium* is of interest here less for its religious hostility or crusading propaganda, than for its geographical ideas, especially about the southern hemisphere.[108]

About the second reason to mount a crusade. The second reason is longing and eagerness to spread the Christian faith. [. . .] If in fact, as I have claimed and shown elsewhere, the part of the world inhabited by human

---

105. "Come, Creator Spirit."

106. "You shall not appear before me empty-handed" (Exod. 23:15).

107. The Latin text closes here, ending variously in different copies (Odoric 1913, 270–77).

108. Translated from Beazley 1907, 819–22; see 810–13 and 66–79 for a detailed discussion of this work.

beings is divided into ten parts, then we who are true Christians and are called true believers, who were used to being the whole, are not the tenth part. This can be deduced and shown as follows. The ancients divided into three parts the quarter suited to human and animal habitation, such that Asia occupied one entire half, and Europe and Africa divided the other half into two parts. Now in Africa, however, where Christ's worship had flourished gloriously, there is no Christian people, while in Asia, although there are many peoples and countless Christians, they do not have the true faith and the Gospel teaching is not kept. In Europe, which is our region, there are many peoples who are pagans and near the Germans and the Poles. There are Saracens in a certain part of Spain. There are moreover in Europe also many Christians of different languages who do not walk with us in faith or teaching. [. . .][109]

It can also be shown in another way that we occupy the smallest part or particle of the inhabited world, such that with the Psalmist we can lament, "*Ad nihilum redactus sum, et nescivi.*"[110] For Asia [. . .] extends farther than is indicated in the description of the climates.[111] How was the entire Asian continent not indicated? I believe it was for this reason: that is, either it was not inhabited in those days, or if it was inhabited, it did not come to the attention of those making the descriptions, just as we have found many inhabited places and provinces towards the Arctic Pole that are known to be beyond the broad latitude of the last climate, because in those places the Arctic Pole [Star] is at a height of more than 52 degrees, which is, as one goes forward [north], the greatest extent of the climates. Therefore to support my claim I will also add what I myself have seen and experienced. After I had departed to preach the faith amongst [other] peoples, heading unfailingly below and beyond the summer tropic, I found myself below the equinoctial.[112] This is proved by three facts [. . .]. First, it was evident in that place that the hours or even the minutes of day and night did not perceptibly differ at any time of the year.[113] Second, when the sun was in the first degree of Aries and Libra, the shadow there at noon was to the right. Third, at all hours of the night I saw th[e] pole stars [. . .] both at the same height above the circle of the horizon. To be brief I will omit many other reasons [. . .]. I went farther south to a place where I did not see our Arctic Pole and I saw the Antarctic Pole at a height of about 24 degrees. From this place I did not go any farther. But merchants and men worthy of faith every-

---

109. Slavic and Balkan peoples, most of whom would have been Greek (or Orthodox) Christians.

110. "I am brought to nothing, and knew not" (Ps. 72[73]:22).

111. Beyond the fiftieth parallel. On the medieval theory of climates, see *TBJM*, Chapter 18, n. 349.

112. "summer tropic": Tropic of Cancer, the northern latitude at which the sun lies directly overhead on the June solstice (about 23.5°); "equinoctial": the equator.

113. They are of equal length, whatever the season.

where went farther south to places where they claimed that the Antarctic Pole was at a height of 54 degrees.[114]

If the smallest width of the climates, which is twenty-two degrees [. . .], is joined with those fifty-four degrees to which the Antarctic Pole was elevated in the place to which the above-mentioned merchants had reached, it is evident that four conclusions are open to careful consideration. First, outside the climates towards the inhabited east and south there is more than the whole space that is allotted between the smallest and the largest of the climates.[115] Second, the region of Asia is larger than is usually allowed. Third, it is not silly or false to allow the Antipodes. Fourth, to approach our purpose more closely, we who are the true Christians are not, I would say the tenth, but we are not even the twentieth part [of the earth]. Yet although we are so small and, as mentioned, squeezed as if in a very tight corner, I think (I state this from experience) that if this tiny little part of ours were placed on one pan of a scale and all the rest of the great world on the other pan, it would be found to be like gold in a mine, heavier through its men and its virtues, not only in the truth of teaching and purity of faith [. . .].[116]

5. Hayton of Armenia, *Flower of the Histories of the Land of the East*

The *Flor des estoires de la terre d'Orient* is a pro-crusading treatise dictated in French in 1307 while its author, a Premonstratensian monk related to the Armenian royal family, was in France at Clement V's papal court. Hayton's scribe, Nicholas Falcon, also translated the work into Latin. Eighteen French and twenty-nine Latin manuscripts survive. The first two books outline the historical geography of Asia from Syria to India and Cathay, focusing especially on the Islamic world; the third book offers an account of the Mongols; the fourth, a plea for another crusade. The *Mandeville* author uses Hayton to supplement Odoric.

[*from* **Book 3**] *Here begins the third part* [. . .] *which speaks about the nation of the Tartars.*

Chapter 1. *How the Tartars first came to their lordship.* The land and the country where the Tartars first existed is beyond the large mountain of Belgian [Baljuna]. The histories of Alexander speak about this mountain where he mentions the wild men that he found. In this country

---

114. No such star exists: see *TBJM,* Chapter 20, n. 380.

115. What lies outside the traditional climates is greater than what lies inside them.

116. This extravagant self-praise of Latin Christendom continues for several more clauses.

the Tartars first dwelt like bestial men who had no faith or law; they went from place to place like wandering animals and were considered worthless by the other peoples that they served. Many clans of Tartars who were called Mogols [*sic*] gathered together and appointed leaders and rulers amongst themselves. They very much believed that they were divided into seven nations, and until now those belonging to one of these clans are considered nobler than the others. The first of these seven clans is called Tartars, the second Tangot, the third Eurach, the fourth Jalair, the fifth Sonit, the sixth Mengli, the seventh Tebet.[117] While these seven clans were subject to their neighbors, as mentioned above, it happened that an old man, a poor blacksmith with the name Canguis,[118] saw a vision in a dream; for he saw an armed knight on a white horse[119] who called him by his name and said to him, "Canguis, the immortal God's will is such that you[120] must be ruler and lord of the seven clans of Tartars that are called Mogols [*sic*] and that through you they will be freed from slavery, where they have long been; and they will have lordship over their neighbors." Canguis arose very joyful, understanding God's word, and told everyone the vision that he had seen. The nobles and the elders did not want to believe it, so they mocked the old man, but it happened that on the following night, the chiefs of the seven clans saw the white knight and the vision, just as Canguis told it, and he ordered on behalf of the immortal God that they all obey Canguis and act so that everyone should follow his orders. At this point it happened that the seven chiefs named above gathered their people of the Tartars together, and had them show obedience and reverence to Canguis, and they did the same, as to their natural lord.

Chapter 2. *How the Tartars first made and chose their lord and named him Can.* After this, the Tartars set up a throne in the midst of waters and spread a black felt cloth on the ground and made Canguis sit on it. The chiefs of the seven clans lifted him with the felt and placed him on the throne and named him Can, and while kneeling to him showed him all honor and reverence, as to their lord. No one should marvel at this ceremony that the Tartars made to their lord at that time, for perhaps they did not know better or they did not have a finer cloth on which to have their lord sit. But one might well marvel at the fact that those who have conquered so many lands and kingdoms have not wanted to change the original custom and still hold to their first ceremony. When they want to choose their lord—and I have twice been at the election of the emperor

117. See *TBJM*, Chapter 24, n. 458 for the clans' modern names.

118. His original name was Temüchin, Mongolian for "[black]smith." See *TBJM*, Chapter 24, n. 459.

119. In the Latin as in *TBJM*, Chapter 24, the knight's arms are also white.

120. Canguis is here addressed familiarly as *tu*, not *vous*. Some copies have "Jesus Christ" for "God."

of the Tartars and have seen how the Tartars gather together in a large field and the one who is to be their lord is made to sit on a black felt cloth and placed on a rich throne in the midst of waters; and the great men and those of Changuis Can's line come and lift him up and place him on the throne, and then they show him all reverence and honor, as to their cherished and natural lord. Not for lordship or for riches that they have conquered will they change their original custom.

Appendix C:

Contexts and Commentary

1. A Note on Geography and Cosmology

In contrast to the heliocentric universe elaborated by Copernicus, Galileo, and Kepler, the medieval cosmos was geocentric; in contrast to the infinite and expanding universe bequeathed by Newton and Einstein, respectively, it was finite and spherical.[1] This cosmos (adapting an image articulated by the Greek astronomer Ptolemy [mid-second century CE] adapting Aristotle [384–322 BCE]) was explained mathematically by one of the *Mandeville* author's sources, Johannes de Sacrobosco in *On the Sphere* (c. 1230), an elementary Latin treatise used for nearly four hundred years.[2] In this medieval Ptolemaic cosmology, the earth, the heaviest object in the universe, lay motionless at the center and bottom, while around it rotated nine other spheres: the Moon, Mercury, Venus, the Sun, Mars, Jupiter, Saturn, the fixed stars, and the *Primum Mobile* (First Moveable). The *Primum Mobile,* whose motions set the other spheres moving, itself required a *Primum Movens* (First Mover): God in Heaven, the "place" beyond the First Moveable.[3]

This concentric universe was divided by the lunar sphere: above it the heavenly spheres moved in the indivisible, unchangeable ether; beneath it lay a region where everything changed and decayed like the four elements (earth, water, air, fire) from which they were made. This Aristotelian view of the sublunary realm was Christianized, being associated with a fallen Nature, whose corruptible state resulted from Original Sin in Eden: the only place, says *TBJM* (Ch. 33), to escape Noah's Flood, because located so high as almost to touch the moon's sphere. If human beings were at the center of the universe, then, they were also at its bottom (only Hell was farther from God: see Chs. 8 and 31), inhabitants of "a mere point"[4] full of demons, evil spirits, and death: all of which Sir John and company meet in the Perilous Valley (Ch. 31).

The corruptible sublunary region was not completely independent, however, since the moving superlunary spheres were thought to have earthly effects. Latin Christians since the Venerable Bede's time (early

---

1. Lewis (1964, Chs. 5, 7) remains a lively introduction to the medieval cosmos, but see also Grant 1994.

2. Pedersen 1985.

3. For more detail, see Grant 1994, Chapter 13.

4. *quasi punctus:* Thorndike 1949, 84 (Latin), 122 (English).

eighth century) knew that the moon's movements affected the tides and that the sun's (apparent) movements affected the seasons, so they had little trouble accepting other heavenly influences. Some early Christian thinkers (notably Augustine, 354–430) were critical of astrology, but most medieval writers accepted it in at least a limited form, so long as celestial movements did not deprive human beings of free will. Astrological influence came not only from the twelve signs of the Zodiac, but also from the other heavenly bodies, the influence of each varying with its character, which was largely determined by its place, size, and motion. Thus the distant Saturn, taking thirty years to pass through the twelve signs, was cruel and cold, influencing persons or even events characterized by slowness, gloominess, or violence.

Related to this astrological understanding was the theory of the climates, also adapted from Ptolemy and quite different from the modern notion (a characteristic weather pattern). From the Greek *klima* ("inclination"), a climate was originally an east-west band around the earth's habitable surface defined by its longest day. Seven (occasionally eight) parallel bands were recognized, the first starting about fifteen degrees north of the equator, the seventh ending about fifty degrees north.[5] The climates were often associated with the seven planets (moving northwards on earth and inwards from Saturn). Drawing on Islamic astrologers, Latin Christian thinkers from the twelfth century used this association of climate and planet to explain national or regional characteristics, as the *Mandeville* author does in Chapter 18. The thirteenth-century Franciscan Roger Bacon, for example, states that "according to the diversity of each climate and even of the parts of a climate do the manners of the inhabitants differ . . . due to the complexions of their bodies innate from the nature of the heavens, under the different parallels and stars of which they are situated."[6] Bacon is a learned scholar, but similar ideas about cosmology and geography are found in the much-translated encyclopedia of another thirteenth-century Franciscan: *De proprietatibus rerum* (*On the natures of things*) by Bartholomaeus Anglicus (Bartholomew the Englishman). His views are even closer to the *Mandeville* author's than Bacon's, in that both present climatic diversity as balancing contraries on earth.[7]

As for basic geography, medieval thinkers, working from their Roman inheritance, generally believed that there were three continents (Asia, Africa, Europe) encircled by the Ocean Sea, and divided from each other by the Mediterranean and two large rivers (the Tanais, or Don; the Nile). Sometimes called the *orbis terrae* or *terrarum* (circle of land[s]), this schema could take the form of a T-O map, the Ocean Sea forming

---

5. Mathematically described by Sacrobosco (Thorndike 1949, 110–12 [Latin], 138–40 [English]).

6. Bacon 1964, 1.272.

7. See *TBJM*, Chapters 18 and 20, and Akbari 2004, 160–63.

the O, the other bodies of water the T.[8] Literally oriented (with east at the top), this map depicted Asia as a semicircle in the O's upper half, and Africa and Europe as quadrants to the lower right and left, respectively. The Tanais divided Asia from Europe on the left (north), and the Nile divided it from Africa on the right (south), the two rivers forming the T's crossbar. Between Europe and Africa rose the T's vertical, the Mediterranean.

Some thinkers believed in a fourth continent, and it was added to a small number of T-O maps, placed on the right (south) and separated from Asia and Africa by a vertical band of the Ocean Sea. Nothing was known about this southern land, often called the Antipodes (Greek, "opposite-footed," because those who lived there dwelt opposite those in the known lands), but it was generally believed to be uninhabited.[9] Both geographical theory and Christian history offered reasons for the Antipodes to be uninhabited. Medieval thinkers typically divided the earth into five zones, shown on so-called zonal maps, usually oriented to the north: two frigid (at the poles), one torrid (around the equator), and two temperate (between the frigid and the torrid). The frigid and torrid zones were often considered uninhabitable, even impassable, preventing human traffic between the two temperate zones. The northern temperate zone (where most of Ptolemy's seven climates lay) was peopled through descent from Adam via Noah and his three sons (see Gen. 9:19 and 10:32). But since everyone had to be thus descended, and since the torrid zone might be impassable, it was considered unlikely that the southern land was inhabited, for belief in a non-Adamic human race would have been heretical.

Such speculation, however, had largely been discouraged since the fifth century, when Augustine's infuential *City of God* (16.9) argued against conjectures about the world's other side based on its assumed spherical shape. Discussing Noah's sons, the Flood, and human diversity, Augustine argued that a spherical earth need not have southern lands, nor would they have to be peopled, should such lands exist. Still, Augustinian-inspired doubts were waning by the fourteenth century, partly due to increased Asian and African travel. By then, as shown by the *Directorium* (Appendix B.4) and the *Mandeville* author's arguments in Chapter 20 (inspired by the very extrapolation that Augustine had warned against), some people were ready to entertain the notions of a passable torrid zone and an inhabited Antipodes.

8. Maps did not come into widespread use until the fifteenth century: see Woodward 1985; for more detail, see Akbari 2004 and 2009 (Ch. 1); Edson 1997; Harley and Woodward 1987 (Chs. 17–20); and Harvey 1991. On the *Mandeville* author's geographical views, see Deluz 1998, 147–265; Ridder 1996; Taylor in LMT 1.li–lix; and Edson 2007, 104–9; Edson 2006 is disappointingly general.
9. See McCready 1996 for a helpful summary.

Whatever the beliefs about a fourth continent, the T-O schema was diagrammatic, not "realistic," showing relations and proportions rather than topography. As noted, it was often assimilated to Christian history (one scholar suggests that it should be called a "Cross and Orb Icon"),[10] fusing space and time, as through the Noah story, for instance. In a common reading of Genesis 9:19 and 10:32, the three continents were re-peopled after the Flood by Noah's sons, Shem taking Asia, Ham Africa, and Japheth Europe.[11] In Chapter 24, though, the *Mandeville* author gives this geo-genealogy a twist, linking Ham (Cham) with the Great Khan (Chan) to accommodate the new Mongol world. The T-O schema was further Christianized through the placement of the Earthly Paradise at the top and, on some thirteenth-century and later maps, of Jerusalem at the exact center. Three famous maps (Ebstorf, Hereford, and Psalter) are Jerusalem-centered, but this mode of geo-Christianization was not very common, and the *Mandeville* author makes more of it than most.[12] The three maps go still further, assimilating the whole earth to Christ: Ebstorf depicts it as Christ's crucified body, while the other two place it under His risen body. Supplementing (and absorbed into) this vision of the earth as the theater of Christian history is a plethora of other images and lore from classical and biblical sources, including Noah's ark, monstrous races, and the Trees of the Sun and the Moon reached by Alexander.

Geography in these three Christianized world maps, then, is used to organize an encyclopedic and theological presentation of history and exotica, and this system of organizing space ideologically and temporally is analogous to the *Mandeville* author's scheme. A glance at any thirteenth-century *mappamundi* reveals many correspondences with *TBJM,* starting with the locations of Paradise and Jerusalem and extending to the classical lore. In this respect, the maps and *TBJM* share Roger Bacon's view of place: "The things of the world," Bacon says, "cannot be known except through a knowledge of the places in which they are contained . . . and not only is this true in the things of nature, but in those of morals and the sciences."[13]

The principal differences between the encyclopedic *mappaemundi* and *TBJM* are that the maps take no interest in the Antipodes and were probably made too early to include Cathay. For that, we have to turn to another pictorial, conceptual, and informational analogue: the *Catalan Atlas* (c. 1375). What makes this unique work a helpful analogue is less the cosmology of the first two of its six folding boards than the cartography of the subsequent four panels. The geographical images

10. Braude 1997, 114–15.

11. As in Peter Comestor's *Historia Scholastica,* Gen. 36. On Noachid traditions, see Braude 1997. See the Isidoran T-O map on page 1 above.

12. See Prologue, n. 6.

13. Bacon 1964, 1.320.

there move from east to west, shifting visually from the circular *map-pamundi* to the *portolan* chart: that is, from a schematic representation to a "realistic" one that in principle could be used for practical navigation. This shift from diagrammatic to "realistic" (although it occurs in the opposite direction in *TBJM*) represents an analogous attempt to fuse different genres and older and newer modes of thought. The circular *mappamundi* and the practical (typically north-oriented) *portolan*[14] seem contrary to modern eyes, but the *Catalan Atlas* blends them. Similarly, *TBJM*'s detailed, retraceable pilgrim itineraries (*portolan*-like in their "port-to-port" movement) are simply extended into the vaguer far-eastern routes traced by Odoric, whose accounts of Asia, India, and Cathay are assimilated to the older Asian/Indian lore. Like *TBJM*, the *Catalan Atlas* synthesizes different representational modes, and it updates the *mappamundi*'s Asia to include Cathay as well as India, drawing on Marco Polo and depicting not only Taprobane, Gog and Magog, and Amazonia, but also "Chambaleth," the Great Khan's capital. Also like *TBJM*, the *Atlas* offers its information in the vernacular, presenting the scholar's world to a wider public (texts on world maps before the fifteenth century were almost always in Latin). Unlike *TBJM*, however, and unlike the famous *mappaemundi* noted above, the *Catalan Atlas* does not place its world under the sign of Christian history; in particular, it neither depicts the Earthly Paradise nor maintains the recent central placement of Jerusalem. The relationship between *TBJM* and the *Atlas*, then, does not extend to the ideological.

One question that the T-O maps raise concerns the earth's shape. Ignoring the fact that such maps are diagrammatic (rather than mathematical planar projections of a spherical image),[15] modern observers have frequently inferred that medieval people believed the earth to be flat. Nothing could be further from the truth. The earth's schematic representation as a circular disc tells us almost nothing about medieval conceptions of the earth's shape, which, as in mainstream ancient thought, was considered spherical. Certainly, the historian Bede (c. 673–735) and almost everyone after him take the idea for granted,[16] since in the Ptolemaic cosmology a disc at the center of a spherical cosmos would have made little sense. In any case, it was also possible to argue empirically as well as logically for a spherical earth, as Sacrobosco does.[17]

---

14. It is unclear whether the typical northern orientation of the *portolan* has to do with the magnetic compass, used in the Mediterranean from the thirteenth century (Harley and Woodward 1987, 384–85).

15. Cartographic mathematics reemerges after the fifteenth-century rediscovery of Ptolemy's *Geography*.

16. See Harley and Woodward 1987, 318–23, and McCready 1996.

17. Thorndike 1949, 80–83 (Latin); 120–22 (English).

2. A Note on the Astrolabe

The astrolabe, a late-antique Greek invention that reached Latin Christendom through Arab-Islamic intermediaries and was widely used by the twelfth century, served "to find time, direction, and latitude, to observe stars and planets, to know risings and settings, to cast horoscopes and teach astronomy, to perform mathematical calculations, and to conduct surveys."[18] Four kinds are known.[19] The commonest, and likely the kind referred to in Chapter 20, was planispheric, projecting the heavens onto a planar surface. It had nested discs for observation or calculation,[20] calibrated to a given latitude (a climate). The tympan (climate plate) had thus to be changed with any movement of more than one degree of latitude (seventy miles north or south). The "Chaucer astrolabe," for example, the earliest dated European astrolabe (1326), has climates for Oxford, Paris, Montpellier, Rome, Jerusalem, and "Babilonie."[21] A pilgrim could thus have used it, but such a pilgrimage was likely to have been virtual: astrolabes were typically used by stay-at-home astronomers. Was the *Mandeville* author one?

He could have measured the North Star's height, as in Chapter 20 he claims to have done, even without traveling, but how plausible are his measurements? The 53 degrees for Brabant (now central Belgium and the Netherlands) is roughly plausible. Brabant lies between about 51° 50' and 52° 50' north, and "the latitude of any place in a region," says Chaucer's *Treatise on the Astrolabe,* is "the space between the zenith of them that dwellen there and the [equator]. . . . And the same space is as much as the Pole Artike is high in that same place from the horizon."[22] It is unclear whether the *Mandeville* author knew that "finding the latitude was not a simple matter of taking the altitude of the pole star, for that is not at the pole itself,"[23] something that Chaucer explains. Nevertheless, the measurement is roughly correct, according with Chaucer's for Oxford (at the roughly same latitude).[24] Germany and Bohemia lying *north* of Brabant at 58 degrees presents a problem, however (one scholar concludes that for the *Mandeville* author an astrolabe is merely a *sign* of scientific competence),[25] yet this erroneous claim could have resulted from the author's having approximated the second and

---

18. Schechner 2008, 208.

19. North 1974, 97.

20. For technical details, see North 1974 and Schechner 2008.

21. For more information go to http://www.britishmuseum.org/explore /highlights/highlight_objects/pe_mla/t/the_chaucer_astrolabe.aspx.

22. See *Treatise* II.25 (Chaucer 1987, 676; lightly modernized); and see North 1988, 61 and Fig. 12.

23. North 1988, 73.

24. See *Treatise* II.22 (Chaucer 1987, 675).

25. Ridder 1996, 239, n. 23.

third measurements with a T-O map. The Hereford map, for example, places the three named sites in the south-to-north order they have in Chapter 20.[26]

Still, the *Mandeville* author could not have measured the Antarctic Star's height. Since it does not exist, no tympans would have been made for it. His readers would not necessarily have known this, however,[27] and it is possible that the other star is Canopus (Alpha Carinae), second brightest in the night sky and circumpolar when viewed from latitudes south of 37°18' S. Vincent of Beauvais knew that Canopus could be seen in Egypt, but not in France.[28] Again, then, one can ask, how plausible are these (fictitious) measurements? The answer is similar: more or less, especially on the assumption of spherical symmetry. The highest that the Antarctic Star appears is some 33 degrees above the horizon, half as high as the North Star in its largest measurement: a modest claim, even more so when compared to that made in the *Directorium*, whose author says that he heard from merchants that they saw it at 54 degrees.[29] If one roughly equates the polar star's height with latitude and imagines the southern hemisphere mirroring the northern, as the *Mandeville* author appears to do, it hardly seems too much to ask readers to believe that he made it *only half as far south* as he did north. This would have taken him only to the third of the seven southern climates, mirroring the "clime of Alexandria" centered in northern Egypt.[30] Fictional though the *Mandeville* author's astrolabe measurements are, then, they are plausible, and important as ostensibly empirical evidence alongside the anecdotal, scriptural, and inferential.

3. A Note on the Alphabets

Although the alphabets in *TBJM* changed much in copying, three main groups have been identified: manuscripts with six alphabets, eight, or none.[31] Copies in the first two groups can lack one or more alphabets, presumably because the scribes found them too hard to copy, but some

---

26. See map Section 9 and legends 592 (Brabant), 538 and 534 (upper and lower Germany), and 551b (Bohemia) in Westrem 2001. The same order would obtain on the Ebstorf world map.

27. A fifteenth-century manuscript includes a schematic T-O map showing the two pole stars (Berlin, Staatsbibliothek MS mgf 204, fol. 88r): see Ridder 1996, 248.

28. *Speculum Naturale* 1.9; cited in HMT 2.102–3, n. to 119, l. 27.

29. See Appendix B.4.

30. Sacrobosco 1949, 111 (Latin); 139 (English).

31. Przybilski 2002, 301. Their classification remains tentative, requiring further study.

added more accurate alphabets.[32] Six alphabets (Greek, Egyptian, Hebrew, Saracen, Persian, Chaldean) are the norm in Continental and Insular and their descendants; they derive from alphabet collections found as early as the late eighth century. The exact sources remain unidentified, but as always the *Mandeville* author draws on culturally accepted knowledge. Eight alphabets (the usual six plus those of Cathay and Prester John's Land) are found in Liège and its offshoots. As well, two Dutch manuscripts contain *fifteen* alphabets, including Russian, Georgian, and Armenian.[33]

TBJM's alphabets signal the author's abiding interest in language.[34] Non-Latin and graphically exotic, they "prove" that he traveled; but they also may have a structural function as visual punctuation marks, since each comes at the end of an account of difference in similarity, iconically revealing how "over here" (*deçà*) and "over there" (*delà*) are at once similar and different. Both Letts and Moseley note that it was "not unusual" for fourteenth-century and later travelers to include alphabets in their memoirs,[35] yet this is to make a founder into a follower: such alphabets are *not* in *TBJM*'s predecessors. Rather, one sometimes finds foreign words for particular purposes. The twelfth-century pilgrim's guide to Santiago de Compostela, for instance, lists some Basque words (God, bread, priest, water, etc.) to show that the "language is . . . completely barbarous,"[36] while Pegolotti's fourteenth-century merchants' handbook (*Pratica della mercatura*) gives local names of weights, measures, and goods essential to trade there.

Like much else in *TBJM*, the alphabets mix the genuine and the fake. The Greek and Hebrew, Seebold argues, come from real alphabets, while the Egyptian derives from an eighth-century invention in the Isidoran catalogue tradition (negating Letts' claim that it is "genuine Coptic"). The Saracen, Persian, and Chaldean alphabets likewise derive from that tradition, the Saracen invented from runes. Cathayan and Pentoxoirean are not authorial, of course; the former draws on "pseudo-Gothic" alphabets, while the Pentoxoirean repeats the Saracen or the Cathayan, depending on the manuscript.[37]

---

32. See the table of alphabets in or missing from Insular (DLMM 59). E adds a "better" Saracen alphabet (LMT 1.101), while the 1371 Continental copy (Paris, Bibliothèque Nationale, MS nouv. acq. fr. 4515) contains a genuinely corrected Hebrew alphabet at the end (see LMT 2.413, and n. 12).

33. Seebold 1998, 439 (six), 435 (eight), 435 (fifteen; not seventeen, as Bennett claims [1954, 325]).

34. In Chapter 22, for example, he notes that a speechless race uses sign language.

35. LMT 1.xl; Moseley 1983, 191.

36. Melczer 1993, 94.

37. Seebold 1998, 440 (Greek, Hebrew), 441–42 (Saracen, Persian, Chaldean), 442–43 (Cathayan, Pentoxoirean); LMT 1.xli.

The most important thing about the alphabets, however, is not their authenticity (even Letts admits that they are "inventions"), or that "their usefulness is [therefore] extremely limited,"[38] but that they have been extracted from their original encyclopedic record and replaced in culturally contextualized, geographical settings. Consider a mid-twelfth-century Benedictine manuscript (Pierpont Morgan Library MS M.832) with a list of alphabets (one folio) followed by an illustrated bestiary (nine folios): alphabets, antelopes, and ants are all free-floating wonders. In contrast, the Mandevillean alphabets have been rehumanized, and belong to peoples who resemble Latin Christians even as they differ. Like national borders today, they connect as they divide. Thomas More, who gave his Utopians an alphabet, would have understood this gesture.

Noting that the six alphabets are mainly found in the pilgrimage section, two scholars have emphasized their divisive role. One suggests that the alphabets themselves distinguish a known world whose inhabitants have writing in common from a less-well-known, marvelous world whose inhabitants lack writing and sometimes even make only animal noises. The biblical East is thus separated from the marvelous East by a linguistic "distinction between human beings and monsters or beasts."[39] Similarly, another scholar claims that the "alphabet-lore reinstall[s] a hard line between West and East," since the text "leaves alphabets behind on the Indian archipelago and enters a world governed by stars."[40] Both of these claims rightly prevent any idealizing of the *Mandeville* author's new use of the alphabets, but they also oversimplify matters: the marvelous East also contains the civilizations of Cathay and Prester John's Land and the morally superior society of Bragmey, all of which are said to use writing, while in *TBJM*'s own geography the alphabets are not Western but Eastern. More persuasive is the claim that Hebrew, in its alphabetic form and as the universal Jewish language in Chapter 29, can be read as marking the Jews as permanent outsiders and eternal enemies:[41] A recent study of a French manuscript with an additional Hebrew alphabet proves that at least one scribe read the text this way, for he copied its corrected alphabet into Chapter 29 rather than leaving it at the end or moving it back to its original place in Chapter 12.[42]

Clearly, the *Mandeville* author's interest in alphabets is part of his larger interest in the linking and dividing roles of linguistic capacity and can be related to his habit of giving the local names of things, translating foreign words, explaining etymologies, and noticing whether or not any given people "lacks" language. One scholar rightly calls this interest

38. "inventions": LMT 1.xl.; "usefulness": Moseley 1983, 191.

39. Rodríguez Temperley 2002, 562.

40. Biddick 2003, 30–31.

41. Biddick 2003, 31–32; Rodríguez Temperley 2002, 564.

42. Kupfer 2008, 73.

"systematic" and suggests nine motives for the alphabets' appearance, including (besides those mentioned above): to complete the sources; to add to a collection; due to their relation to the fourteenth-century papal and Franciscan interest in languages necessary for the eastern mission; and delight in writing.[43] More than "mere" local color, the alphabets reveal the *Mandeville* author's own "take" on the world.

The "Jewish" alphabet in a fifteenth-century copy of Otto von Diemeringen's German translation of *TBJM*. Lawrence: University of Kansas, Kenneth Spencer Research Library MS C18 (fol. 72r). By Permission.

---

43. Rodríguez Temperley 2002, 558, 564–68.

4. A Note on the Account of the Sultans in Chapter 6

Chapter 6 draws on the late thirteenth-century *Treatise on the State of the Saracens* attributed to William of Tripoli (see Appendix B.2) and Jacques de Vitry's *Eastern History* for the Sultan's power, possessions, and title (DLMM 146, n. 7). It confuses Sultan ("ruler") and Caliph ("successor" to Muhammad, thus leader of the Muslim religious community, as the text explains). The names of the Sultans of Egypt, except the last two, are from Hayton of Armenia's 1307 *Flor des estoires* (*Flower of the Histories;* DLMM 146, n. 10). On the Egyptian Ayyubid and Mamluk dynasties, see the genealogical chart in DLMM (487), which reveals the defects of *TBJM*'s account.

The Kurdish **Xaracon** (Shirkuh): penultimate vizier of the Shi'ite Fatimid Caliph of Egypt in 1169; conquered Cairo with the help of his nephew **Sahaladin** (Salah al-Din, or Saladin), himself Sultan of Egypt and Syria from 1171 to his death in 1193 and founder of the Sunni Ayyubid dynasty (1171–1252). **Boradin** (al-Afdal Nur al-Din): governor of Damascus (1186–1196). **Melechsala** (As-Salih Ayyub, aka al-Malik al-Salih): Sultan of Egypt from 1240 to his death in 1249, followed briefly by **Timpieman** (al-Muazzam Turan Shah; 1249–1250, assassinated). After the Ayyubids in Egypt came the Bahri Mamluk Sultans (1250–1382). **Cachas** (Saif al-Din Qutuz, or Kutuz) had a short reign (1259–1260, assassinated); **Melechimees** may come from his epithet, al-Malik al-Muzafar. **Bendochdar / Melechdar** (al-Dahir Baibars al-Bunduqdari, often known as Baibars I): Sultan from 1260 to his death in 1277; hero of the *Sirat Baibars,* a popular Arabic folktale based on historical events. Baibars' son, **Melechsach** (al-Said Barakah) reigned in 1277–1278. **Elphi** (Saif al-Din Kalawun al-Sahali, known as Qala'un or Kalawun; his epithet included al-Alfi): Sultan from 1279 to his death in 1290; **Mellechassera** (al-Ashraf Khalil) from 1290 to 1293 (assassinated). **Melechnasser** (al-Nasir Muhammad) reigned as Sultan three times, starting as a nine-year-old (1293–1294, 1299–1309, 1310–1341); **Guytoga** (Kitbuqa, or Kitbugha): an Amir (or governor), briefly usurped power from the young al-Nasir and reigned as Sultan **Melechadel** (al-Adil Zein) (1294–1296, deposed). **Melechmanser** (al-Mansùr al-Din Lajin) followed him equally briefly (1296–1299, murdered). **Melechmader**, if he was Melechnasser's son, would likely have been al-Salih Imad al-Din, Sultan (1342–1345, deposed). **Melechmadabron** is uncertain, since it remains unknown whether the *Mandeville* author was ever in Egypt, and if so when; the genealogy reaches the 1340s, when some seven Sultans reigned, the likeliest of whom would be al-Muzaffar Hadji (1346–1347) or al-Nasir Badr al-Din, known as Hasan (1347–1351).

5. A Note on the Mongol Emperors and Their Early Empire

Chingiz (Genghis) Khan's Empire was divided on his death amongst his four sons (Ch. 24, n. 459). Through his grandson Batu (d. 1255), son of his eldest son Jochi (who died in 1227 before his father), arose the western **Qipchaq Khanate** (also known as the **Golden Horde**) that extended into Russia. Through his second son Chagatai (d. 1242) arose the Central-Asian **Chagatai Khanate**. Through his third son Ögedai (d. 1241) arose the **Great Khanate** of Mongolia and China. Through his grandson Hülegü (d. 1265), third son of his own fourth son Tolui (d. 1233) and younger brother of the Great Khans Möngke and Qubilai [Kubilai], arose the Persian **Ilkhanate**. The three other khans were nominally subject to the Great Khan, also known as the Khakhan (ruler of rulers), but their relations were not always easy. The Great Khanate and the Ilkhanate (in ancient sedentary cultures quite different from the Mongols' nomadic origins) were the first to collapse. The Great Khans (and early Yüan emperors) were as follows:[44] (1) **Chan Guys**: Chingiz Khan (d. 1227); (2) **Ettocha**: Ögedai (1229–1241), Chingiz Khan's third son; (3) **Guyo**: Güyük (1246–1248), Ögedai's son; (4) **Mango**: Möngke (1251–1259), Güyük's cousin; the Khan known to William of Rubruck; (5) **Cobila**: Qubilai (1260–1294), Möngke's younger brother, first Yüan emperor of China, the Khan known to Marco Polo; (6) Temür Öljeitü (1294–1307), Qubilai's grandson and second Yüan emperor.

---

44. Dates indicate period of rule. See the dynastic tables in Morgan 1986, 222–25. For a concise overview, see Gregory G. Guzman, "Mongols (Thirteenth and Fourteenth Century)" in Friedman and Figg 2000, 408–15.

WORKS CITED AND SELECT BIBLIOGRAPHY

1. Editions and Translations of *The Book of John Mandeville* and Other Primary Sources

Adamnan. 1958. *Adamnan's* De Locis Sanctis. Ed. Dennis Meehan. Dublin: Dublin Institute for Advanced Studies.

Bacon, Roger. 1962. *Opus Maius.* Trans. Robert Belle Burke. 2 vols. New York: Russell and Russell.

Bartholomaeus Anglicus. 1975. *On the Properties of Things: John Trevisa's Translation of* Bartholomaeus Anglicus De Proprietatibus Rerum. 3 vols. Oxford: Clarendon Press. [Vol. 3 is dated 1988.]

Beazley, C. Raymond, ed. 1907. "*Directorium ad Faciendum Passagium Transmarinum.*" *American Historical Review* 12.4: 810–57; 13.1: 66–115.

Bremer, Ernst, and Klaus Ridder, eds. 1991. Jean de Mandeville. *Reisen: Reprint der Erstdrucke der deutschen Übersetzungen des Michel Velser (Augsburg, bei Anton Sorg, 1480) und Otto von Diemeringen (Basel, bei Bernhard Richel, 1480/81).* Deutsche Volksbücher in Faksimiledrucken, Reihe A, vol. 21. Hildesheim: Georg Olms.

Brunetto Latini. 1993. *The Book of the Treasure (Li Livres dou Tresor).* Trans. Paul Barette and Spurgeon Baldwin. New York: Garland.

————. 2003. *Li Livres dou Tresor: Edition and Study.* Eds. Spurgeon Baldwin and Paul Barette. Tempe: Arizona Center for Medieval and Renaissance Studies.

Caesarius of Heisterbach. 1851. *Dialogus miraculorum,* vol. 1.185–88. 2 vols. Ed. Joseph Strange. Cologne.

Chaucer, Geoffrey. 1987. *The Riverside Chaucer.* 3rd ed. Gen. ed. Larry D. Benson. Boston: Houghton Mifflin.

Columbus, Christopher. 1492–93. *The* Diario *of Christopher Columbus's First Voyage to America 1492–1493 Abstracted by Fray Bartolomé de las Casas.* Ed. and trans. Oliver Dunn and James E. Kelley, Jr. Norman: University of Oklahoma Press, 1989.

Crosby, Edward W., ed. 1965. *Otto von Diemeringen: A German Version of Sir John Mandeville's 'Travels.'* Ph.D. dissertation. University of Kansas.

Dawson, Christopher, ed. 1980. *Mission to Asia.* London: Sheed and Ward. Rpt. Medieval Academy Reprints for Teaching. Toronto: University of Toronto Press. Orig. publ. 1955 as *The Mongol Mission.*

Defensor de Ligugé. 1957. *Liber Scintillarum.* Ed. H. M. Rochais. *Corpus Christianorum. Series Latina,* vol. 117. Turnhout, Belgium: Brepols. xxxiii–xxxv; 2–234.

Deluz, Christiane, ed. 1972. *Liber de quibusdam ultramarinis partibus et prae-cipue de Terra Sancta de Guillaume de Boldensele (1336) suivi de la traduction de Frère Jean le Long (1351): Edition critique.* Thèse de doctorat de troisième cycle. Paris: Sorbonne.

————, trans. 1997. "Le Livre de messire Jean de Mandeville." [Liège Version, excerpts.] In *Croisades et pèlerinages: Récits, chroniques et voyages en Terre Sainte XIIe–XVIe siècle,* 1393–1435. Ed. D. Régnier–Bohler. Paris: Editions Robert Laffont.

————. 2000. *Le Livre des Merveilles du Monde.* [Insular Version.] Paris: CNRS Editions.

Gerald of Wales. 1978. *The Journey through Wales. The Description of Wales.* Trans. Lewis Thorpe. Harmondsworth, UK: Penguin.

————. 1982. *The History and Topography of Ireland.* Trans. John J. O'Meara. Harmondsworth, UK: Penguin.

Gervase of Tilbury. 2002. *Otia Imperialia: Recreation for an Emperor.* Ed. and trans. S. E. Banks and J. W. Binns. Oxford: Clarendon Press.

Grotefend, C. L., ed. 1855. "Des Edelherrn Wilhelm von Boldensele Reise nach dem gelobten Lande." *Zeitschrift des historischen Vereins für Niedersachsen,* 1852, 209–86 (text 236–86). Hannover.

Guillaume Le Clerc. 1852. *Le Bestiaire divin du Guillaume, Clerc du Normandie.* Ed. M. C. Hippeau. Caen: A. Hardel.

————. 1892. *Le Bestiaire: Das Thierbuch des normannischen Dichters Guillaume Le Clerc.* Ed. Robert Reinsch. Leipzig: Reisland.

Gunderson, Lloyd L., trans. 1980. *Alexander's Letter to Aristotle about India.* Meisenheim am Glan: Anton Hain.

Hakluyt, Richard, ed. 1589. *Liber Ioannis Mandevil.* [Vulgate Latin Version.] In *The Principall Navigations, Voiages and Discoveries of the English Nation (London, 1589): A Photo-Lithographic Facsimile,* vol. 1.23–79. Hakluyt Society, extra series 39. 2 vols. Cambridge: Cambridge University Press, 1965.

Hamelius, P., ed. 1919–1923. *Mandeville's Travels, translated from the French of Jean d'Outremeuse: Edited from MS. Cotton Titus C. XVI, in the British Museum.* Early English Text Society, original series 153–54. 2 vols., issued for 1916. London: K. Paul, Trench, Trübner & Co. Rpt. London, 1960–1961.

Hayton. 1906. *La Flor des estoires de la terre d'Orient.* In *Recueil des historiens des croisades: Documents Arméniens.* Vol. 2.111–253. Paris: Imprimerie Nationale.

————. 1906. *Flos historiarum terre Orientis.* In *Recueil des historiens des crois-ades: Documents Arméniens.* Vol. 2.255–363. Paris: Imprimerie Nationale.

Hilka, Alfons, ed. 1920. *Der Altfranzösische Prosa-Alexanderroman nach der Berliner Bilderhandschrift nebst dem lateinischen Original der Historia de Preliis (Rezension J^2).* Halle, 1920. Rpt. Geneva: Slatkine, 1974.

Isidore of Seville. 2006. *Etymologies.* Trans. Stephen A. Barney et al. Cambridge: Cambridge University Press.

Jacques de Vitry. 1611. *Historia Hierosolimitana abbreviata.* In *Gesta Dei per francos,* 1047–1172. 2 vols in 1. Ed. Jacques Bongars. Hannover.

————. 2008. *Histoire Orientale / Historia Orientalis.* Ed. and trans. Jean Donnadieu. Turnhout, Belgium: Brepols.

John of Plano Carpini. 1980. *History of the Mongols.* In Dawson 1980, 3–72.

————. 1929. *Ystoria Mongalorum.* In Wyngaert 1929, 27–130.

Kempe, Margery. 1996. *The Book of Margery Kempe.* Ed. Lynn Staley. Kalamazoo, MI: Medieval Institute Publications.

Kohanski, Tamarah, ed. 2001. *The Book of John Mandeville: An Edition of the Pynson Text with Commentary on the Defective Version.* Medieval and Renaissance Texts and Studies, 231. Tempe: Arizona Center for Medieval and Renaissance Studies.

Kohanski, Tamarah, and C. David Benson, eds. 2007. *The Book of John Mandeville.* [Defective Version.] TEAMS Middle English Text Series. Kalamazoo, MI: Medieval Institute Publications.

Kratz, Dennis M., trans. 1991. *The Romances of Alexander.* New York: Garland.

Laurent, J. C. M., ed. 1864. *Peregrinatores medii aevi quatuor* [Burchard of Mount Sion, Ricold of Monte Croce, Pseudo-Odoric, Willibrand of Oldenburg]. Leipzig.

Letter of Prester John. 2005. "Appendix: Translation of the Original Latin *Letter of Prester John.*" In Uebel 2005, 155–60.

————. 1879. [Latin text.] Ed. in Zarncke 1879, 909–24.

Letts, Malcolm, ed. and trans. 1953. *Mandeville's Travels: Texts and Translations.* [Egerton, Continental, Bodley Versions.] Hakluyt Society, 2nd ser. 101–2. 2 vols., issued for 1950. London: Hakluyt Society.

Martinsson, Sve, ed. 1918. *Itinerarium Orientale: Mandeville's Reisebeschreibung in Mittelniederdeutscher Übersetzung.* Lund: Gleerupska Universitets-Bokhandeln. [Middle-Low-German text of von Diemeringen Version]

Montaigne, Michel de. 1967. *Oeuvres Complètes.* Ed. Robert Barral and Pierre Michel. Paris: Seuil.

Morrall, Eric John, ed. 1974. *Sir John Mandevilles Reisebeschreibung in deutscher Übersetzung von Michel Velser nach der Stuttgarter Papierhandschrift Cod. HB V 86.* Deutsche Texte des Mittelalters, 66. Berlin: Akademie-Verlag.

Morris, Richard, ed. 1863. *The Pricke of Conscience (Stimulus conscientiae).* Berlin: A. Asher.

Moseley, C. W. R. D., trans. 1983. *The Travels of Sir John Mandeville.* Harmondsworth, UK: Penguin. Reprinted with a revised Introduction, new Notes and Bibliography, 2005.

Mourin, Louis. 1955. "Les lapidaires attribués à Jean de Mandeville et à Jean à la Barbe." *Romanica Gandensia* 4: 159–91.

Odoric of Pordenone. 1891. *Les Voyages en Asie au XIVe siècle du bienheureux Frère Odoric de Pordenone.* Ed. Henri Cordier. Paris: Ernest Leroux.

————. 1913. *The Eastern Parts of the World Described.* In Yule 1913, vol. 2.

————. 1929. *Relatio.* In Wyngaert 1929, 381–495.

Polo, Marco. 1928. *Il Milione.* Ed. Luigi Foscolo Benedetto. Florence: Leo S. Olschki.

————. 1958. *The Travels*. Trans. Ronald Latham. Harmondsworth, UK: Penguin.

Ralegh, Sir Walter. 1848. *The Discovery of the Large, Rich, and Beautiful Empire of Guiana*. Ed. Robert H. Schomburgk. Hakluyt Society, 1st series, 3. London: Hakluyt Society.

Régnier-Bohler, Danielle, gen. ed. 1997. *Croisades et pèlerinages: Récits, chroniques et voyages en Terre Sainte XIIe–XVIe siècle*. Paris: Editions Robert Laffont.

Seymour, M. C., ed. 1967. *Mandeville's Travels*. [Cotton Version.] Oxford: Oxford University Press.

————. 1973. *The Metrical Version of* Mandeville's Travels. Early English Text Society, original series 269. London: Oxford University Press.

————. 2002. *The Defective Version of* Mandeville's Travels. Early English Text Society, original series 319. Oxford: Oxford University Press.

Simon of Saint-Quentin. 1965. *Histoire des Tartares*. Ed. Jean Richard. Paris: Librairie Orientaliste Paul Geuthner.

Sterne, Laurence. 1967. *The Life and Opinions of Tristram Shandy, Gentleman*. Ed. Graham Petrie. Harmondsworth, UK: Penguin.

Thorndike, Lynn, ed. and trans. 1949. *The* Sphere *of Sacrobosco and Its Commentators*. Chicago: University of Chicago Press.

Vincent of Beauvais. 1624. *Bibliotheca mundi seu Speculi maioris Vincentii Burgundi*. Douai.

Warner, George F., ed. 1889. *The Buke of John Maundeuill Being the Travels of Sir John Mandeville, Knight 1322–56: A Hitherto Unpublished English Version from the Unique Copy (Egerton MS. 1982) in the British Museum Edited Together with the French Text, Notes, and an Introduction*. Westminster: Nicholas and Sons.

Westrem, Scott D. 2001. *The Hereford Map: A Transcription and Translation of the Legends with Commentary*. Turnhout, Belgium: Brepols.

William of Boldensele. See Deluz 1972 and Grotefend 1885.

William of Rubruck. 1929. *Itinerarium*. In Wyngaert 1929, 164–332.

————. 1980. *Journey*. In Dawson 1980, 89–220.

William of Tripoli. 1992. *Notitia de Machometo. De statu Sarracenorum*. Corpus Islamo-Christianum. Series Latina 4. Ed. and trans. Peter Engels. Würzburg: Echter.

Wyngaert, Anastasius van den, ed. 1929. *Itinera et Relationes Fratrum Minorum Saeculi XIII et XIV. Sinica Franciscana*, vol. 1. Florence: Collegium S. Bonaventurae.

Yule, Henry, ed. 1913–1916. *Cathay and the Way Thither, Being a Collection of Medieval Notices of China*. New ed. Rev. by Henri Cordier. 4 vols. Hakluyt Society, 2nd series 33, 37–38, 41. 2 vols. Cambridge: Cambridge University Press.

Zarncke, Friedrich. 1879. *Der Priester Johannes*. In *Abhandlungen der philologisch-historischen Classe der Königlich-Sächsischen Gesellschaft der Wissenschaften* 7. 826–1030. Leipzig.

2. Other Works

Akbari, Suzanne Conklin. 2004. "The Diversity of Mankind in *The Book of John Mandeville.*" 156–76. In Allen, ed., 2004.

————. 2009. *Idols in the East: European Representations of Islam and the Orient, 1100–1450.* Ithaca, NY: Cornell University Press.

Akbari, Suzanne Conklin, and Amilcare Iannucci, eds. 2008. *Marco Polo and the Encounter of East and West.* Toronto: University of Toronto Press.

Allen, Rosamund, ed. 2004. *Eastward Bound: Travel and Travelers, 1050–1550.* Manchester: Manchester University Press.

Appleby, John H. 1997. "The Royal Society and the Tartar Lamb." *Notes and Records of the Royal Society of London* 51.1: 23–34.

Bennett, Josephine Waters. 1954. *The Rediscovery of Sir John Mandeville.* New York: Modern Language Association of America.

Bennett, Michael J. 2006. "*Mandeville's Travels* and the Anglo-French Moment." *Medium Aevum* 75.2: 273–92.

Benson, C. David. 2004. *Public* Piers Plowman*: Modern Scholarship and Late Medieval English Culture.* University Park: Pennsylvania State University Press.

Biddick, Kathleen. 2003. *The Typological Imaginary: Circumcision, Technology, History.* Philadelphia: University of Pennsylvania Press.

Bork, Robert, and Andrea Kann, eds. 2008. *The Art, Science, and Technology of Medieval Travel.* Burlington, VT: Ashgate.

Bovenschen, Albert. 1888. "Untersuchungen über Johann von Mandeville und die Quellen seiner Reisebeschreibung." *Zeitschrift der Gesellschaft für Erdkunde zu Berlin* 23: 177–306.

Braude, Benjamin. 1995. "*Mandeville's* Jews among Others." In *Pilgrims and Travelers.* Ed. Bryan F. Le Beau and Menachem Mor. Omaha, NB: Creighton University Press, 141–68.

————. 1997. "The Sons of Noah and the Construction of Ethnic and Geographical Identities in the Medieval and Early Modern Periods." *William and Mary Quarterly* 54.1: 103–42.

Bremer, Ernst, and Susanne Röhl, eds. 2007. *Jean de Mandeville in Europa: Neue Perspektiven in der Reiseliteratureforschung.* Munich: Wilhelm Fink Verlag.

Burnett, C. S. F. 1984. "An Apocryphal Letter from the Arabic Philosopher Al-Kindi to Theodore, Frederick II's Astrologer, Concerning Gog and Magog, the Enclosed Nations, and the Scourge of the Mongols." *Viator* 15: 151–67.

Burnett, Charles, and Patrick Gautier Dalché. 1991. "Attitudes towards the Mongols in Medieval Literature: The Twenty-Two Kings of Gog and Magog from the Court of Frederick II to Jean de Mandeville." *Viator* 22: 153–67.

Campbell, Mary B. 1988. *The Witness and the Other World: Exotic European Travel Writing, 400–1600.* Ithaca, NY: Cornell University Press.

Carey, George. 1956. *The Medieval Alexander.* Ed. D. J. A. Ross. Cambridge: Cambridge University Press.

Crombie, A. C. 1959. *Augustine to Galileo.* 2nd ed. 2 vols. Rpt. Harmondsworth, UK: Penguin, 1969.

de Kock, Josse. 1965. "Quelques copies aberrantes des 'Voyages' de Jean de Mandeville." *Moyen Age* 71: 521–37.

de Poerck, Guy. 1955. "La tradition manuscrite des 'Voyages' de Jean de Mandeville: à propos d'un livre recent." *Romanica Gandensia* 4: 125–58.

————. 1961. "Le corpus mandevillien du ms Chantilly 699." In *Fin du Moyen Age et Renaissance: mélanges de philologie française offerts à Robert Guiette,* 31–48. Ed. Guy de Poerck et al. Antwerp: De Nederlandsche Boekhandel.

Deluz, Christiane. 1988. *Le Livre de Jehan de Mandeville: une "géographie" au XIVe siècle.* Louvain-la-Neuve: Université Catholique de Louvain.

————. 1995. "Jérusalem 'coeur et milieu de toute la terre du monde.'" In *Le Mythe de Jérusalem du Moyen Age à la Renaissance,* 91–100. Ed. Evelyne Barriot-Salvadore. Saint-Etienne: Publications de l'Université de Saint-Etienne.

————. 2007. "L'originalité du *Livre* de Jean de Mandeville." In Bremer and Röhl, eds., 2007, 11–18.

DiMarco, Vincent. 1991. "The Amazons and the End of the World." In Westrem, ed., 1991, 69–90.

Dunn, Ross E. 1986. *The Adventures of Ibn Battuta: A Muslim Traveler of the Fourteenth Century.* Berkeley: University of California Press.

Edson, Evelyn. 1997. *Mapping Time and Space: How Medieval Mapmakers Viewed Their World.* London: British Library.

————. 2006. "Traveling on the Mappamundi: The World of John Mandeville." In *The Hereford World Map: Medieval World Maps and Their Context.* Ed. P. D. A. Harvey. London: British Library, 389–403.

————. 2007. *The World Map 1300–1492: The Persistence of Tradition and Transformation.* Baltimore: Johns Hopkins University Press.

Emmerson, Richard Kenneth. 1981. *Antichrist in the Middle Ages: A Study of Medieval Apocalypticism, Art, and Literature.* Seattle: University of Washington Press.

Friederich, W. P. 1949. "Dante through the Centuries." *Comparative Literature* 1.1: 44–54.

Friedman, John Block. 1981. *The Monstrous Races in Medieval Art and Thought.* Cambridge, MA: Harvard University Press. Rpt. Syracuse, NY: Syracuse University Press, 2000.

Friedman, John Block, and Kristen Mossler Figg, eds. 2000. *Trade, Travel, and Exploration in the Middle Ages: An Encyclopedia.* New York: Garland.

Ginzburg, Carlo. 1980. *The Cheese and the Worms: The Cosmos of a Sixteenth-Century Miller.* Trans. John and Anne C. Tedeschi. Rpt. Baltimore: Johns Hopkins University Press, 1992.

Goosse, A. 1960. "Les lapidaires attribués à Mandeville." *Les dialectes belgo-romans* 27: 63–112.

Gow, Andrew. 1995. *The Red Jews: Antisemitism in an Apocalyptic Age, 1200–1600.* Leiden: Brill.

Grant, Edward. 1994. *Planets, Stars, and Orbs: The Medieval Cosmos, 1200–1687.* Cambridge: Cambridge University Press.

Greenblatt, Stephen. 1991. *Marvelous Possessions: The Wonder of the New World.* Chicago: University of Chicago Press.

Hahn, Thomas. 1978. "The Indian Tradition in Western Medieval Intellectual History." *Viator* 9: 213–34.

Harley, J. B., and David Woodward, eds. 1987. *Cartography in Prehistoric, Ancient, and Medieval Europe and the Mediterranean. The History of Cartography,* vol. 1. Chicago: University of Chicago Press.

Harvey, P. D. A. 1991. *Medieval Maps.* Toronto: University of Toronto Press.

Heng, Geraldine. 2003. *Empire of Magic: Medieval Romance and the Politics of Cultural Fantasy.* New York: Columbia University Press.

Higgins, Iain Macleod. 1997a. *Writing East: The "Travels" of Sir John Mandeville.* Philadelphia: University of Pennsylvania Press.

———. 1997b. "Defining the Earth's Center in a Medieval 'Multi-Text': Jerusalem in *The Book of John Mandeville.*" In *Text and Territory: Geographical Imagination in the European Middle Ages,* 29–53. Ed. Sylvia Tomasch and Sealy Gilles. Philadelphia: University of Pennsylvania Press.

———. 2004. "Mandeville." In *A Companion to Middle English Prose,* 99–116. Ed. A. S. G. Edwards. Cambridge; Rochester, NY: D. S. Brewer.

Hodgen, Margaret T. 1964. *Early Anthropology in the Sixteenth and Seventeenth Centuries.* Rpt. Philadelphia: University of Pennsylvania Press, 1971.

Howard, Donald R. 1971. "The World of Mandeville's Travels." *Yearbook of English Studies* 1: 1–17.

———. 1980. *Writers and Pilgrims: Medieval Pilgrimage Narratives and Their Posterity.* Berkeley: University of California Press.

Kieckhefer, Richard. 1989. *Magic in the Middle Ages.* Cambridge: Cambridge University Press.

Kittay, Jeffrey, and Wlad Godzich. 1987. *The Emergence of Prose: An Essay in Prosaics.* Minneapolis: University of Minnesota Press.

Kupfer, Marcia. 2008. "'. . . lectres . . . plus vrayes': Hebrew Script and Jewish Witness in the *Mandeville* Manuscript of Charles V." *Speculum* 83: 58–111.

Larner, John. 1999. *Marco Polo and the Discovery of the World.* New Haven, CT: Yale University Press.

Lejeune, Rita. 1964. "Jean de Mandeville et les Liégeois." In *Mélanges de linguistique romane et de philologie médiévale offerts à Maurice Delbouille,* vol. 2.409–37. Ed. Jean Renson. 2 vols. Gembloux: Duculot.

Lengeler, Rainer. 1992. "Reisender in Sachen Universalismus: Das Zeugnis von Mandevilles Bibelzitate." In *Diesseits- und Jenseitsreisen im Mittelalter*

/ *Voyages dans l'ici-bas et l'au-delà au Moyen Age.* Ed. Wolf-Dieter Lange. Bonn: Bouvier, 91–100.

Lewis, C. S. 1964. *The Discarded Image: An Introduction to Medieval and Renaissance Literature.* Cambridge: Cambridge University Press.

Marcus, Jacob, ed. 1938. *The Jew in the Medieval World: A Sourcebook: 315–1791.* Cincinnati: Union of American Hebrew Congregations. Rpt. New York: Atheneum, 1969.

McCready, William. 1996. "Isidore, the Antipodeans, and the Shape of the Earth." *Isis* 87: 108–27.

Melczer, William, trans. 1993. *The Pilgrim's Guide to Santiago de Compostela.* New York: Italica Press.

Morrall, Eric John, ed. 1968. "The Text of Michel Velser's 'Mandeville' Translation." In *Probleme mittelalterlicher Überlieferung und Textkritik: Oxforder Colloquium 1966.* Ed. Peter F. Ganz and Werner Schröder. Berlin: Erich Schmidt, 183–96.

Morgan, David. 1986. *The Mongols.* Oxford: Blackwell.

Moseley, C. W. R. D. 1974. "The Metamorphoses of Sir John Mandeville." *Yearbook of English Studies* 4: 5–25.

———. 1975. "The Availability of *Mandeville's Travels* in England, 1356–1750." *Library,* 5th ser., 30: 125–33.

North, J. D. 1974. "The Astrolabe." *Scientific American* 230.1 (Jan.): 96–106.

———. 1988. *Chaucer's Universe.* Oxford: Clarendon Press.

Olschki, Leonardo. 1943. *Marco Polo's Precursors.* Rpt. New York: Octagon, 1972.

Paselk, Richard A. 2008. "Medieval Tools of Navigation: An Overview." In Bork and Kann, 169–80.

Pearsall, Derek. 1992. *The Life of Geoffrey Chaucer.* Oxford: Blackwell.

Pedersen, Olaf. 1985. "In Search of Sacrobosco." *Journal of the History of Astronomy* 16: 175–221.

Phillips, J. R. S. 1988. *The Medieval Expansion of Europe.* Oxford: Oxford University Press.

———. 1993. "The Quest for Sir John Mandeville." In *The Culture of Christendom: Essays in Medieval History in Commemoration of Denis L. T. Bethell,* 243–55. Ed. Marc Anthony Meyer. London: Hambledon Press.

Przybilski, Martin. 2002. "Die Zeichen des Anderen: Die Fremdsprachenalphabete in den 'Voyages' des Jean de Mandeville am Beispiel der deutschen Übersetzung Ottos von Diemeringen." *Mittellateinisches Jahrbuch* 37.2: 295–320.

Richard, Jean. 1981. *Les récits de voyages et de pèlerinages.* Typologie des sources du moyen âge occidental, fasc. 38. Turnhout, Belgium: Brepols.

Ridder, Klaus. 1991. *Jean de Mandevilles "Reisen": Studien zur Überlieferungsgeschichte der deutschen Übersetzung des Otto von Diemeringen.* Müchener Texte und Untersuchungen zur deutschen Literatur des Mittelalters 99. Munich: Artemis.

————. 1996. "Übersetzung und Fremderfahrung: Jean de Mandevilles literarische Inszenierung eines Weltbildes und die Lesarten seiner Übersetzer." In *Übersetzung im Mittelalter: Cambridger Colloquium.* Ed. Joachim Heinzle et al. Berlin: Schmidt, 231–64.

Riquer, Martí de. 1988. "El 'Voyage' de Sir John Mandeville en català." In *Miscellània d'homenatge a Enric Moreu-Rey, I–III.* Ed. Albert Manent et al. Monserrat: Abadia de Monserrat, 3.151–62.

Rodríguez Temperley, María Mercedes. 2001. "Alfabetos, lenguas y gruñidos (o sobre el lenguaje en Juan de Mandevilla)." In *Studia in honoren Germán Orduna*, 557–70. Ed. Leonardo Funes and Jose Luis Moure. Alcalá de Henares: Universidad de Alcalá de Henares.

Röhl, Susanne. 2004. *Der* Livre de Mandeville *im 14. und 15. Jahrhundert: Untersuchungen zur handschriftlichen Überlieferung der kontinentalfranzösischen Version.* Munich: Wilhelm Fink Verlag.

Ross, David J. A. 1988. *Alexander Historiatus: A Guide to Medieval Illustrated Alexander Literature.* Frankfurt am Main: Athenäum.

Salih, Sarah. 2003. "Idols and Simulacra: Paganity, Hybridity and Representation in *Mandeville's Travels.*" In *The Monstrous Middle Ages.* Eds. Bettina Bildhauer and Robert Mills. Cardiff: University of Wales, 113–33.

Schechner, Sara. 2008. "Astrolabes and Medieval Travel." In Bork and Kann, 181–210.

Seebold, Elmar. 1998. "Mandevilles Alphabete und die mittelalterlichen Alphabetsammlungen." *Beiträge zur Geschichte der deutschen Sprache und Literatur* 120: 435–49.

Seymour, M. C. 1993. *Sir John Mandeville. Authors of the Middle Ages.* Vol. 1. Aldershot, UK: Variorum.

————. 2007. "More Thoughts on Mandeville." In Bremer and Röhl, 19–30.

Stoneman, Richard. 2008. *Alexander the Great: A Life in Legend.* New Haven, CT: Yale University Press.

Sumption, Jonathan. 1975. *Pilgrimage: An Image of Mediaeval Religion.* London: Faber.

Taylor, E. G. R. 1935. "Some Notes on Early Ideas of the Form and Size of the Earth." *Geographical Journal* 85.1: 65–68.

Tomasch, Sylvia, and Sealy Gilles, eds. 1998. *Text and Territory: Geographical Imagination in the European Middle Ages.* Philadelphia: University of Pennsylvania Press.

Toynbee, Paget. 1892. "Christine de Pisan and Sir John Maundeville." *Romania* 21: 228–39.

Tyssens, Madeleine. 2005. "La version liégeoise du *Livre* de Jean de Mandeville." *Bulletin de la Classe des Lettres et des Sciences Morales et Politiques,* 6th ser. 16.1–6, 59–78.

Tzanaki, Rosemary. 2003. *Mandeville's Medieval Audiences: A Study on the Reception of the Book of Sir John Mandeville (1371–1550).* Aldershot, UK: Ashgate.

Uebel, Michael. 2005. *Ecstatic Transformation: On the Uses of Alterity in the Middle Ages.* New York: Palgrave Macmillan.

Vogels, J. 1886. "Die Ungedruckten Lateinischen Versions Mandeville's," *Programm des Gymnasiums zu Crefeld,* Schuljahr 9: 3–23.

Westrem, Scott D., ed. 1991. *Discovering New Worlds: Essays on Medieval Exploration and Imagination.* New York: Garland.

————. 1998. "Against Gog and Magog." In Tomasch and Gilles, 54–75.

Wittkower, Rudolf. 1942. "Marvels of the East: A Study in the History of Monsters." *Journal of the Warburg and Courtauld Institutes* 5, 159–97. Rpt. in his *Allegory and the Migration of Symbols.* London: Thames and Hudson, 1977, 45–74, 196–205.

Woodward, David. 1985. "Reality, Symbolism, Time, and Space in Medieval World Maps." *Annals of the Association of American Geographers* 75.4: 510–21.

Yeager, Suzanne M. 2008. *Jerusalem in Medieval Narrative.* Cambridge: Cambridge University Press.

Zacher, Christian K. 1976. *Curiosity and Pilgrimage: The Literature of Discovery in Fourteenth-Century England.* Baltimore: Johns Hopkins University Press.

Zacour, Norman P. 1956. "Petrarch and Talleyrand." *Speculum* 31.4: 683–703.

INDEX OF SCRIPTURAL AND RELATED CITATIONS IN LATIN[1]

Liturgical

Benedicite ("Bless [the Lord]"), also known as "The Canticle [Song] of the Three Holy Children," derived from a sixty-eight-verse passage in Daniel (at Dan. 3:23) (p. 23)

Gen. 18:2 (adapted) (p. 40)

Office of the Dead (Ps. 129[130]:1) (p. 175)

Officium Marianum Ordinis Sancte Birgitte per hebdomadam or *De Trinitate* (under *in tercio nocturno*) (p. 175)

Ordo commendationis animae (*Service for the Commendation of a Soul* [*to God*]) (p. 182)

New Testament

Acts 10:11–15 (p. 175)

Colossians (title only given in Latin; p. 18)

2 Cor. 3:6 (p. 86)

John 1:29 (p. 65); 5:8 (p. 54); 10:16 (p. 175); 19:21 (p. 3); [19:26–27, in French only (p. 49)]; 20:19, 21, 26, 28 (p. 55); 20:27 (p. 108)

Luke 1:26 (p. 83); 1:28 (p. 69); 4:30 (p. 69); 10:13–15 (p. 68); 11:27–28 (p. 20); 22:42 (p. 58); 24:35 (p. 72)

Matt. 4:3 (p. 60); 3:17 (p. 63); 5:3–11 (p. 58); 10:41 (p. 59); 11:21–23 (p. 68); 17:4 (p. 70); 17:5 (p. 70); 20:30–31 (p. 60); 27:29 (p. 11)

Old Testament

Deut. 32:30 (p. 155, cited as Psalter verses)

Esther 13:2 (paraphrase, p. 175)

---

1. Names alone given in Latin in *TBJM* from scriptural sources (e.g., *Probatica Piscina*, Pool of Bethsaida) are not noted here. In Chapter 15 the *Mandeville* author claims to know the Qur'an, but his references to it are all secondhand.

Other

SELECT INDEX OF PROPER NAMES

For reasons of space, only the most important names in *TBJM* or names of particular interest to modern readers are indexed here. Modern place names, when known, are given in parentheses; page and note numbers given in **boldface** type denote a name defined elsewhere.